Handbook of Behavioral Assessment *edited by Anthony R. Ciminero, Karen S. Calhoun, and Henry E. Adams*

Counseling and Psychotherapy: A Behavioral Approach *by E. Lakin Phillips*

Dimensions of Personality *edited by Harvey London and John E. Exner, Jr.*

The Mental Health Industry: A Cultural Phenomenon *by Peter A. Magaro, Robert Gripp, David McDowell, and Ivan W. Miller III*

Nonverbal Communication: The State of the Art *by Robert G. Harper, Arthur N. Weins, and Joseph D. Matarazzo*

Alcoholism and Treatment *by David J. Armor, J. Michael Polich, and Harriet B. Stambul*

A Biodevelopmental Approach to Clinical Child Psychology: Cognitive Controls and Cognitive Control Theory *by Sebastiano Santostefano*

Handbook of Infant Development *edited by Joy D. Osofsky*

Understanding the Rape Victim: A Synthesis of Research Findings *by Sedelle Katz and Mary Ann Mazur*

Childhood Pathology and Later Adjustment: The Question of Prediction *by Loretta K. Cass and Carolyn B. Thomas*

Intelligent Testing with the WISC-R *by Alan S. Kaufman*

Adaptation in Schizophrenia: The Theory of Segmental Set *by David Shakow*

Psychotherapy: An Eclectic Approach *by Sol L. Garfield*

Handbook of Minimal Brain Dysfunctions *edited by Herbert E. Rie and Ellen D. Rie*

Handbook of Behavioral Interventions: A Clinical Guide *edited by Alan Goldstein and Edna B. Foa*

Art Psychotherapy *by Harriet Wadeson*

Handbook of Adolescent Psychology *edited by Joseph Adelson*

Psychotherapy Supervision: Theory, Research and Practice *edited by Allen K. Hess*

Psychology and Psychiatry in Courts and Corrections: Controversy and Change *by Ellsworth A. Fersch, Jr.*

Restricted Environmental Stimulation: Research and Clinical Applications *by Peter Suedfeld*

Personal Construct Psychology: Psychotherapy and Personality *edited by Alvin W. Landfield and Larry M. Leitner*

Mothers, Grandmothers, and Daughters: Personality and Child Care in Three-Generation Families *by Bertram J. Cohler and Henry U. Grunebaum*

Further Explorations in Personality *edited by A.I. Rabin, Joel Aronoff, Andrew M. Barclay, and Robert A. Zucker*

Hypnosis and Relaxation: Modern Verification of an Old Equation *by William E. Edmonston, Jr.*

Handbook of Clinical Behavior Therapy *edited by Samuel M. Turner, Karen S. Calhoun, and Henry E. Adams*

Handbook of Clinical Neuropsychology *edited by Susan B. Filskov and Thomas J. Boll*

The Course of Alcoholism: Four Years After Treatment *by J. Michael Polich, David J. Armor, and Harriet B. Braiker*

Handbook of Innovative Psychotherapies *edited by Raymond J. Corsini*

The Role of the Father in Child Development (Second Edition) *edited by Michael E. Lamb*

Behavioral Medicine: Clinical Applications *by Susan S. Pinkerton, Howard Hughes, and W.W. Wenrich*

Handbook for the Practice of Pediatric Psychology *edited by June M. Tuma*

Change Through Interaction: Social Psychological Processes of Counseling and Psychotherapy *by Stanley R. Strong and Charles D. Claiborn*

Drugs and Behavior (Second Edition) *by Fred Leavitt*

(*continued on back*)

27-1791 HQ767.9 88-18704 CIP
Children's social networks and social supports, ed. by Deborah Belle. Wiley-Interscience, 1989. 373p indexes **ISBN 0-471-62879-4, $39.95**

The study of various aspects of social development has been a popular pastime of developmental psychologists for many years. Mother-infant attachment, parenting styles, the advantages and disadvantages of preschooling, children's friendships, and peer-group influences are topics that each would easily fill several library shelves. The novelty of this book is not its topic, but the method it uses to investigate the subject. Conceptualizing the social world of the child as a social network does not seem to produce new or startlingly different outcomes from those of previous methods, but it may allow more systematic examination of the relevant data. Unfortunately, an undergraduate reader is unlikely to understand the fine points of the method and would more easily grasp the fundamentals of social development from standard texts. Several articles might be of general interest, however—e.g., Hareven's description of historical changes in the family, Parke and Bhavnagri's report on how parents manage their child's peer contacts, and Hirsch and Dubois's discussion of how the transition to junior high school affects adolescent friendships and adjustment. Remaining chapters would be of interest primarily to those engaged in social network research. Upper-division and graduate collections.—*K. L. Hartlep, California State University, Bakersfield*

About the editor

DEBORAH BELLE is an assistant professor in the department of psychology at Boston University. She is the editor of *Lives in Stress: Women and Depression* and coeditor of *The Mental Health of Women*. Dr. Belle, who received her EdD in Human Development from the Harvard Graduate School of Education, is a William T. Grant Foundation Faculty Scholar in the mental health of children.

Children's Social Networks and Social Supports

Edited by

DEBORAH BELLE

A WILEY-INTERSCIENCE PUBLICATION

JOHN WILEY & SONS

New York • Chichester • Brisbane • Toronto • Singapore

To the memory of Cynthia Longfellow Lincoln

Library of Congress Cataloging-in-Publication Data:

Children's social networks and social supports / edited by Deborah Belle.

p. cm.—(Wiley series on personality processes)

Bibliography: p.

ISBN 0-471-62879-4

1. Children—Social networks. I. Belle, Deborah.

HQ767.9.C456 1988

305.2'3—dc19

88-18704

CIP

Printed in the United States of America

10 9 8 7 6 5 4 3 2 1

Contributors

JANETTE BEALS, Ph.D., Faculty Research Associate, Department of Psychology, Program for Prevention Research, Arizona State University, Tempe, Arizona

DEBORAH BELLE, Ed.D., Assistant Professor, Department of Psychology, Boston University, Boston, Massachusetts

THOMAS J. BERNDT, Ph.D., Professor, Department of Psychological Sciences, Purdue University, West Lafayette, Indiana

NAVAZ P. BHAVNAGRI, Ph.D., Assistant Professor of Early Childhood Education, School of Education, University of Houston—Clear Lake, Houston, Texas

BRENDA K. BRYANT, Ph.D., Professor, Department of Applied Behavioral Science, University of California at Davis, Davis, California

DAVID L. DUBOIS, Doctoral Candidate, Department of Psychology, University of Illinois at Urbana-Champaign, Champaign, Illinois

CANDICE FEIRING, Ph.D., Associate Professor, Institute for the Study of Child Development, University of Medicine and Dentistry of New Jersey, Robert Wood Johnson Medical School, New Brunswick, New Jersey

WYNDOL FURMAN, Ph.D., Associate Professor, Department of Psychology, University of Denver, Denver, Colorado

TAMARA K. HAREVEN, Ph.D., Unidel Professor of Family Studies, University of Delaware, and Member, Center for Population Studies, Harvard University, Cambridge, Massachusetts

BARTON J. HIRSCH, Ph.D., Associate Professor, School of Education and Social Policy, Northwestern University, Evanston, Illinois

MICHAEL LEWIS, Ph.D., Professor of Pediatrics, Chief, Institute for the Study of Child Development, University of Medicine and Dentistry of New Jersey, Robert Wood Johnson Medical School, New Brunswick, New Jersey

PAUL MILLER, Ph.D., Assistant Professor of Psychology, Department of Arts and Sciences, Arizona State University—West Campus, Phoenix, Arizona

ROSS D. PARKE, Ph.D., Professor, Department of Psychology, University of Illinois at Urbana-Champaign, Champaign, Illinois

IRWIN N. SANDLER, Ph.D., Professor, Department of Psychology, Program for Prevention Research, Arizona State University, Tempe, Arizona

JEROME SHORT, Doctoral Candidate, Department of Psychology, Arizona State University, Tempe, Arizona

ANNE MARIE TIETJEN, Ph.D., Acting Assistant Professor, Department of Psychiatry and Behavioral Sciences, University of Washington, Seattle, Washington

THOMAS S. WEISNER, Ph.D., Professor of Anthropology, Departments of Psychiatry and Anthropology, University of California, Los Angeles, Los Angeles, California

MARTHA WENGER, Ed.D., Associate Director, Carolina Policy Studies Program, Frank Porter Graham Child Development Center, University of North Carolina at Chapel Hill, Chapel Hill, North Carolina

SHARLENE A. WOLCHIK, Ph.D., Associate Professor, Department of Psychology, Program for Prevention Research, Arizona State University, Tempe, Arizona

PHYLLIS ZELKOWITZ, Ed.D., Research Associate, Center for Research in Human Development, Concordia University, Montreal, Quebec, Canada

Preface

This volume grows out of an interdisciplinary study group on the social support needs of school-age children, which was sponsored by the Society for Research on Child Development with funding from the Foundation for Child Development. The study group was convened at a propitious time to integrate emerging ideas about social networks and supports with child development theory and research. Social network analysis and the study of social support had recently developed a higher level of conceptual clarity and methodological sophistication. Developmental psychologists were increasingly interested in the larger ecology of children's lives and in children's relationships with fathers, siblings, other relatives, peers, and friends, as well as with mothers. The study group meeting demonstrated the richness of current theorizing and research on children's networks and sources of support, while making clear many crucial directions for future research.

The book attempts to synthesize this new knowledge, to suggest implications from this research for supportive interventions for children, and to raise new questions and provide new tools for further study. The volume takes an inclusive view of childhood, with some chapters focusing on a particular developmental period and others spanning the entire age range from infancy to adolescence. The book also takes an inclusive view of social networks, including under this heading individuals both inside and outside the child's household, institutional connections, and even pets. The book is meant for researchers, clinicians, and those with public-policy concerns about the well-being of children, as well as for students of these topics.

DEBORAH BELLE

Cambridge, Massachusetts
February 1989

Acknowledgments

This book was made possible by the generosity of two private foundations. The Foundation for Child Development funded the study group on children's social support needs that sparked the idea for this volume. We shared insights, arguments, and manuscripts, learned a great deal from each other, and continue to do so. The William T. Grant Foundation, through its faculty scholars program, supported me in editing the volume and introduced me to other researchers whose work has both enriched this book and contributed to my own understanding of children's social networks and social supports. Both foundations have provided more than financial support to their grantees. They have also created supportive social networks for scholars studying the social needs of children. For all of this I am deeply grateful.

D.B.

Contents

INTRODUCTION

Studying Children's Social Networks and Social Supports

DEBORAH BELLE

Humans are a social species, and it has long been recognized that the social environment is critical in human adaptation. While this realization goes back at least to Aristotle, it has not been easy to conceptualize and measure the relevant attributes of the social environment, nor to specify the processes by which these factors foster or inhibit adaptation.

In recent years, the concepts of social network and social support have focused attention on aspects of the social environment that appear to be critical to well-being. The social network construct orients us to the cast of characters in an individual's social world, to the interrelationships among these people, and to the connections between differently structured social networks and larger social systems. The social network of interest in this volume is the personal social network that is centered on a particular child. Definitions of social network draw attention to the ties or linkages that connect individuals (and sometimes groups or institutions)—linkages that can be conduits for diverse resources. Social support, defined as resources that are provided by other people and that arise in the context of interpersonal relationships, reaches individuals through their social network connections. Supportive resources can include information, material assistance, affection, physical comforting, empathic listening, assistance in problem solving, and reassurance of worth.

Social support research has evolved over the last 15 years from an enthusiastic but conceptually and methodologically muddled research area into a sophisticated field of study with reliable multidimensional research instruments. Social network analysis has also evolved "from a sensitizing metaphor into a comprehensive paradigm" (Wellman, 1981, p. 171). A sizable body of research demonstrates the impact of social network characteristics and social support resources on coping, adaptation, and health (e.g., Cohen & Syme, 1985; Gottlieb, 1981; Sarason & Sarason, 1985).

Since children have a great need for instrumental and emotional resources from others, it is ironic that the impact of social networks and social support has been studied far more frequently among adults than among children. In part, this may reflect methodological limitations, as social network and social support research has relied on questionnaire and interview methods that are most easily suited to the capacities of adults. It may also be that children's social networks have been viewed implicitly as derivative from their parents' networks and of limited importance in their own right.

While developmental psychologists have been acutely aware of the social needs of children, they have directed most of their attention to the relationships most central to the child, and have tended to neglect more distal connections. Much of developmental psychology has focused on the mother–child relationship, although in recent years fathers and siblings have been "discovered," and peer relations have attracted renewed interest (e.g., Dunn & Kendrick, 1982; Lamb, 1976; Lewis & Rosenblum, 1975; Parke, 1981). This research on fathers, siblings, peers, and friends has helped to pave the way for a comprehensive study of children's social networks and support providers.

Within developmental psychology, several theorists and researchers have long been calling for a more comprehensive and contextual view of children's social relationships. Urie Bronfenbrenner has argued eloquently for attention to the larger social context or ecology in which children develop (Bronfenbrenner, 1977, 1979), and Beatrice and John Whiting and their colleagues have investigated children's social companions in diverse cultural contexts (Whiting & Edwards, 1988; Whiting & Whiting, 1975). It is not coincidental that many of those who currently study children's social networks and systems of social support have worked with either Bronfenbrenner or the Whitings.

When developmental psychologists have studied social networks they have most often examined the social networks of mothers, as these might affect maternal morale and child-rearing competence, and thus affect the child indirectly. In their influential article, Cochran and Brassard (1979) argued that social networks could influence children's development both directly and indirectly, through impacts on parents. They detailed the specific mechanisms through which each type of effect might operate. Social networks were thought to affect parenting through the provision of emotional and material assistance, controls on parenting style, and role models. Networks could also influence children directly, through providing cognitive and social stimulation, direct care and support, observational models, and opportunities for the development of network-building skills and the incorporation of members of the parents' network into the child's own, emerging network. While the authors provided this explicit direction to guide future research, their own primary focus and that of most researchers influenced by their article was on the parental social network, most typically that of the mother. Studies in this tradition demonstrated that appropriate support to mothers was reflected in enhanced maternal morale and sensitivity and in positive outcomes for children (Belle, 1982;

Colletta, 1979; Crnic, Greenberg, Ragozin, Robinson, & Basham, 1983; Crockenberg, 1981).

Another factor that may have contributed to the scarcity of research on children's own social networks and social supports is the emphasis developmental psychologists have placed on the early years of life. While developmentalists have recognized the lifelong importance of social connections, their interest in children's social needs has tended to focus on those of the first few years. Attachment researchers, for instance, have just recently begun to chronicle the vicissitudes of attachment beyond infancy and toddlerhood (Cassidy, 1988; Kobak & Sceery, 1988; Main, Kaplan, & Cassidy, 1985). The exclusive focus on maternal networks rather than the child's own networks is probably more appropriate for very young children than for older ones (Cochran & Brassard, 1979).

Much research demonstrates the value of particular supportive relationships for children. Parents, of course, are very important sources of social support for children. Mothers are primary sources of nurturance and intimacy throughout the school years and well into adolescence (Belle & Longfellow, 1983; Kon & Losenkov, 1978; Youniss & Smollar, 1985). Children who report positive relationships with their mothers have been found to have high academic achievement and personality adjustment (Woods, 1972), while children who frequently confide in their mothers report high levels of self-esteem and internal locus of control (Belle & Longfellow, 1984). Positive father–child relationships are also associated with high self-esteem, internal locus of control, intellectual development, and satisfactory peer relations (Biller, 1976; Parke, 1981). A good relationship with at least one parent has been identified as a protective factor that buffers children from the potentially adverse effects of marital discord, parental mental illness, and social disadvantage (Rutter, 1979).

Parental support to children may decline when parents are themselves highly stressed, depressed, or demoralized (Longfellow, Zelkowitz, & Saunders, 1982; Weissman & Paykel, 1974; Zelkowitz, 1982). The tribulations of unpleasant or demanding work (Piotrkowski, 1978), the difficulties of single-parent life-styles (Weiss, 1979), and the oppression of racism and poverty (Silverstein & Krate, 1975) can lead parents to withdraw emotional support from children. Parents whose children must become responsible and independent at a young age may also try to discourage the children's emotional dependency on adults, believing that such support "spoils" children and leaves them dangerously vulnerable in a world where others will not be so supportive or nurturant (Jeffers, 1967; Silverstein & Krate, 1975).

Nonparental adults often support parents in caring for children, and such assistance has been shown to protect the mental health and thus the supportive capacity of parents, indirectly providing great benefits to children, as has been discussed. It is sometimes difficult to distinguish between direct and indirect effects on children, however. Wahler (1980) observed, for instance, that on days marked by visits from supportive nonhousehold adults, both mothers and children exhibited improved, positive social behavior to each other.

While adults appear to be the major providers of support to children, there is evidence that other children can provide stress-buffering support to children under stress. In many cultures children are cared for more by siblings than by parents (Weisner & Gallimore, 1977), as was also true of American children during earlier periods of history (Hareven, 1981). Freud and Dann (1951) found that peers could provide emotional security to children experiencing extreme stress including the loss of both parents. Sandler (1980) has presented evidence that children with older siblings were protected from the negative impact of stressful life events. Long and Long (1982) reported that "latchkey" children without adult supervision were less likely to develop high levels of fear and sleep disturbance if they spent their unsupervised time at home with siblings rather than alone.

Only in recent years have attempts been made to map children's complete social networks and to understand the flow of resources directly to children from members of these social networks. Among the earliest studies was that of Garbarino, Burston, Raber, Russell, and Crouter (1978), who studied the social "maps" of preadolescents in relation to maturational, demographic, and socioeconomic factors. The results of this exploratory study suggested that neighborhood ecology (urban vs. suburban vs. rural setting) and maturational level were related to differences in subjective mappings of the social network of significant others. Children's perceptions of their network's size and of the role of adults in their lives, as well as the extent of agreement between the children and their mothers, were associated with neighborhood type, stage of physical development, or both.

Tietjen carried out a conceptually related analysis of social networks among preadolescent children in Sweden. She documented provocative age, gender, household structure, and neighborhood differences in children's networks (1982) and was also able to show that children's networks bore significant relationships to those of their mothers, and that a variety of disparate processes probably mediate these relationships (Tietjen, 1985).

Zelkowitz (1978, 1982) studied the networks of younger children (ages 5 to 7) in low-income urban families and relied on maternal report to determine which individuals other than the mother provided the child with physical care, nurturance, and discipline. She tested the crucial hypothesis that under stressful life circumstances supportive resources provided by others would facilitate social adjustment. Her analysis demonstrated that support from adults was associated with lower levels of observed aggressive behavior in children and that physical care by fathers was particularly important for children whose mothers experienced high levels of depressive symptoms or were minimally nurturant to the children themselves.

Bryant's (1985) important monograph demonstrated the value of questioning school-age children about the sources of support in their own lives and also offered a particularly rich vision of the components of children's social networks. Bryant inquired about supportive relationships with persons in the peer, parent, and grandparent generation, as well as with the child's own pets. Bryant also offered a provocative methodological innovation with her research technique of interviewing the child in the course of a walk around familiar places in the neighborhood. She argued that this technique could facilitate recall of network members. Bryant's findings demonstrated the connections between supportive network involvements and social–emotional functioning as well as the significance of age, gender, and family size in moderating these associations.

While investigators repeatedly call for longitudinal research on children's networks, virtually all of the research that has been done is cross-sectional. One important exception is the research of Lewis, Feiring, and their colleagues (see Feiring & Lewis, this volume). These authors have followed the evolution of children's networks from age 3 to 9. When the children were 3 years old, only maternal reports on the network were sought, but when the children were seen again at ages 6 and 9, both maternal reports and information from the child were solicited.

In recent years interest in the child as the anchor of his or her own social network and as a recipient of social support resources from others has increased dramatically, as the richness of conceptual and empirical work in this volume demonstrates. While the study of children's social networks and social supports may be out of its infancy, it is still a fledgling field with much important theoretical and empirical work to do. This book attempts to synthesize what is known and to stimulate and guide future research. The volume takes an inclusive view of the child's social network, considering under that rubric individuals both inside and outside the child's household, institutional connections, and even pets. The book also takes an inclusive view of childhood, with some chapters considering the entire developmental range from infancy to adolescence, and other chapters focusing on only one or two specific developmental periods.

ORGANIZATION OF THE BOOK

Children's social worlds differ vastly from culture to culture and across historical time, and attending to these differences illuminates the distinctive characteristics of our own time and place as it reveals the underlying principles that govern successful human adaptations. Part 1 of this book provides such a perspective by considering the ways in which children's social networks and experiences of social support have varied in other times and in different cultures. Each chapter goes beyond mere description to consider the sources of such variation and the implications of diverse social experiences for children's development.

Hareven reviews the striking demographic, social, and cultural changes in our American past that have affected the cast of characters with whom children live, work, and play. In the process she explodes several nostalgic myths about the past, and forces us to view our own contemporary situation in new ways. Some of the historical trends Hareven discusses have added new elements to children's networks, as increased longevity, for instance, has allowed more children to know their grandparents. In other cases historical change has reduced the cast of characters typically available to children. From a historical perspective the networks of contemporary American children are rich in same-age peers and in institutional connections, but barren in siblings and in nonrelatives who share the household. Recent trends, such as the increase in "blended families," have begun to restore some of the complexity and age diversity that had been lost to children's networks. Hareven considers the significance of contemporary network styles for children's development and calls for more collaboration between historians and developmentalists to illuminate these questions.

Tietjen argues that one cannot understand what types of social networks will be supportive or what constitutes support without an appreciation for the particular ecology in which the child lives. Turning to her own diverse field research, she contrasts the networks of children in contemporary urban Sweden with those of children in a remote village in Papua New Guinea. The contrasts she finds in some ways parallel those chronicled in American history by Hareven: the New Guinea village networks are dense and rich in kin, while the urban Swedish children have more same-age peers and ties to institutions. Tietjen discovers supportive networks in both settings, although they look strikingly different and provide very different types of support. Tietjen explicates a conceptual model relating ecological factors to the development of appropriate social support systems for children, and she reviews empirical research on the links between ecological factors and children's social support systems. She concludes her chapter by considering research and policy implications of the ecological model she has created.

Weisner raises the question of what constitutes support, noting that, while some behaviors are perceived and experienced as supportive in all cultures, other behaviors require culturally specific interpretation. His examination of episodes of social interaction observed in a Kenyan community demonstrates that certain forms of supportive behavior that are commonplace in contemporary American culture, such as empathic questioning about a child's emotions, are so rare as to be almost nonexistent among the Abaluyia he studied. On the other hand, native informants classified other behaviors as highly supportive when these same behaviors would have no supportive significance in the American context. Weisner argues that in order properly to understand supportive behaviors in diverse cultures we must appreciate the social organization and values of those cultures and must recognize that culturally appropriate styles of support provision are those that prepare children for success as adults within the culture. Reflecting back on our own western styles of support provision illuminates many unstated but crucial dimensions of our own society and many of our expectations for appropriate child development.

Wenger examines the impact of cultural arrangements for children, particularly the age- and gender-linked assignment of tasks, on children's daily experiences and daily companions. She argues that in nonindustrialized societies children have meaningful work roles at an early age, and these roles typically help to prepare children for their responsibilities as adult men and women. In the Kenyan community she studied, as in many other nonwestern societies, girls' task assignments place them in proximity to adult women and to infants, while boys are given more opportunities for peer play and for unsupervised time. These gender differences in daily companions and activities then give rise to differences in the skills and social proclivities of male and female children and help to prepare them for their adult roles.

Together, the chapters in this section of the book challenge many of our assumptions about what constitutes social support and who can effectively provide it. They force us to ask, "Support for what purpose?" and to acknowledge that some of our most deep-seated notions about the nature of social support are not universal, but are derived from our particular cultural traditions. The skills required of adults are vastly different in nonindustrialized societies than in contemporary America, and the social relationships that ensure success in adult tasks are quite different as well. These chapters make it clear that the forms of support that are provided to children function not only to alleviate the distress of the moment, but also to teach skills and values that will be crucial in adulthood. Examining the forms of social networks and social support that appear to function well in settings so different from our own illuminates many facets of our own social life that we might otherwise take for granted.

Part 2 of the book considers developmental characteristics of children's networks, examining both age-related trends and gender differences. Feiring and Lewis explore the importance of social networks in the process of development, focusing specifically on the changes children's networks undergo as children move from a home-centered environment in the preschool years to a more school-oriented environment in middle childhood. They draw on their unique longitudinal study of 75 children and utilize both mothers and the children themselves as informants. Their analyses suggest that development is accompanied by shifts in both the size and the structure of social networks. While some shifts seem to accompany school entry, other changes in children's networks take place during the early school years.

Furman's chapter complements Feiring and Lewis's structural approach by considering the ways in which children's needs for other people and the social provisions they receive from other people change over the course of development. He examines evidence for developmental change on several different levels: at the level of face-to-face interaction; at the level of dyadic relationships; at the level of group experiences; and at a global level. On a global level, for instance, a child may register satisfaction with the amount of support she receives from her network as a whole, while this satisfaction may not extend to her one-to-one relationships with specific network members or with specific social groups, or to the interactions she has with particular network members. Each level of analysis contributes a different perspective to our understanding of children's developing social networks. Furman discusses the major theories of developmental change in supportive relationships and reviews the limited empirical research in this area. His own program of research provides some support for the major theoretical formulations, but also challenges them at several points. Furman calls for more conceptual and methodological innovation in this area, to test the provocative theories we already have and to expand our understanding of developmental shifts in children's multifaceted social networks.

Belle next examines the importance of gender as a factor that shapes children's social networks and their ways of relating to network members. Boys' and girls' networks are compared on size, structure, sex cleavage, modes of interaction, specific support figures, and support giving. The differences that are found are compared to those previously reported for adult men and women, and the implications of these differences are also explored. In reviewing empirical research in this area Belle finds many striking gender differences, more in the area of network functioning than in the area of network structure. She discusses the implications of these differences for children's well-being and for their development into adulthood.

Part 3 of the volume addresses methodological issues in assessing children's social networks and supports. Wolchik, Beals, and Sandler first discuss conceptual issues critical to defining and assessing social support for children. They next offer an encyclopedic survey of the instruments currently in use to study children's support networks, providing published and unpublished data on the internal consistency and reliability of these measures. Throughout the chapter the authors utilize a typology of social support measures: those that assess social embeddedness, those that assess the perceived quality of support, and those that reflect the occurrence of supportive transactions. The authors argue that each of these ways of conceptualizing and operationalizing social support provides different information about an individual's social network, and that researchers should therefore be encouraged to collect information using more than one method of operationalizing social support. The final section of the chapter demonstrates the use of structural equation modeling to explore the relationships between different dimensions of social support and between social support and adjustment.

One of the crucial methodological decisions facing researchers is the choice of an informant concerning a child's social network. While maternal reports are generally used in studying the networks of preschool children, during middle childhood and adolescence the children themselves are generally queried. Very little research has compared the reports of mothers and children concerning the child's network or has examined the potentially distinct perspectives that children and parents bring to the enterprise of mapping the child's network. Zelkowitz reviews the limited research in this area and then turns to her own study of 60 young children and their mothers to compare these different types of informants. Her analysis suggests that there is substantial agreement between mothers and children about the social network and the support it provides, but that children and mothers also have distinct perspectives on children's networks. Zelkowitz explores the meaning of these differing viewpoints and offers several provocative questions for future research.

How do supportive relationships and supportive networks come into being? This question is rarely addressed in the social support field, and yet it is critical if we wish to understand how to foster supportive relationships for children. In Part 4, Parke and Bhavnagri examine the role of parents as active facilitators of their children's peer relationships, both as arrangers of opportunities for peer interaction and as monitors and supervisors of their children's interaction with peers. The authors argue that such parental facilitation of peer bonds, when carried out with understanding of the child's developmentally appropriate needs, can result not only in richer social networks for children but also in improvements in children's social skills.

Hirsch and DuBois next consider how early adolescent friendships are begun and maintained in both school and nonschool settings. They first look at the vicissitudes of peer friendships across the transition to junior high school, evaluating the evidence to determine whether junior high schools deserve their reputation as obstacle courses for peer friendships. Recognizing that the school is only one setting in which early adolescent friendships are developed, they next examine the linkages between school and outside-school ties, paying particular attention to the obstacles that make it difficult for young people to deepen school friendships in nonschool contexts.

Part 5 considers the impact of supportive involvements on children's well-being. Sandler, Miller, Short, and Wolchik note that most research on social support makes predictions about the effects of support on adjustment without direct examination of the intervening processes through which support has its effect. In this chapter the authors look inside the "black box" of stress buffering to consider the mechanisms through which support operates. They offer a developmentally sensitive examination of this topic, one that takes into account the evolving capacities of the child.

Berndt integrates research on social support done primarily with adults with research on children's friendships to consider how children's peer friendships might function as supportive relationships. He first examines whether children's friendships have the attributes that social support researchers have identified as supportive in research with adults, next, whether the friendships children view as supportive actually promote social adjustment in periods of stress, and, finally, the role of both environmental and personal factors in creating variations in the support that children draw from their friends.

In the final chapter of the volume, Bryant addresses the tension throughout development between a child's need for support and his or her need for autonomy. She first reviews theory and empirical research on the dual need for support and autonomy across the life span. She next focuses on middle childhood and discusses the child's needs for support and autonomy in that period of life. Using data from her own unique study of children's support resources, Bryant demonstrates that a balance of supportive and autonomous experiences is necessary for healthy social–emotional functioning in middle childhood.

REFERENCES

Belle, D. (1982). *Lives in stress: Women and depression.* Beverly Hills: Sage.

Belle, D., & Longfellow, C. (1983). *Emotional support and children's well-being: An exploratory study of children's confidants.* Paper presented at the biennial meeting of the Society for Research in Child Development, Detroit.

Belle, D., & Longfellow, C. (1984). Turning to others: Children's use of confidants. Paper presented at the meetings of the American Psychological Association, Toronto.

Biller, H. B. (1976). The father and personality development: Paternal deprivation and sex-role development. In M. E. Lamb (Ed.), *The role of the father in child development.* New York: Wiley.

Bronfenbrenner, U. (1977). Toward an experimental ecology of human development. *American Psychologist, 32,* 513–531.

Bronfenbrenner, U. (1979). *The ecology of human development: Experiments by nature and design.* Cambridge, MA: Harvard University Press.

Bryant, B. (1985). The Neighborhood Walk: Sources of support in middle childhood. *Monographs of the Society for Research in Child Development, 50*(3, Serial No. 210).

Cassidy, J. (1988). Child–mother attachment and the self in six-year-olds. *Child Development, 59* (1), 121–134.

Cochran, M., & Brassard, J. (1979). Child development and personal social networks. *Child Development, 50,* 609–616.

Cohen, S., & Syme, S. L. (Eds.). (1985). *Social support and health.* Orlando, FL: Academic.

Colletta, N. (1979). Support systems after divorce: Incidence and impact. *Journal of Marriage & the Family, 41,* 837–846.

Crnic, K., Greenberg, M., Ragozin, A., Robinson, N., & Basham, R. (1983). Effects of stress and social support on mothers and premature and full-term infants. *Child Development, 54,* 209–217.

Crockenberg, S. (1981). Infant irritability, mother responsiveness, and social support influences on the security of infant–mother attachment. *Child Development, 52,* 857–865.

Dunn, J. & Kendrick, C. (1982). *Siblings: Love, envy, and understanding.* Cambridge, MA: Harvard University Press.

Freud, A., & Dann, S. (1951). An experiment in group upbringing. In *The psychoanalytic study of the child* (Vol. VI). New York: International Universities Press.

Garbarino, J., Burston, N., Raber, S., Russell, R., & Crouter, A. (1978). The social maps of children approaching adolescence: Studying the ecology of youth development. *Journal of Youth & Adolescence, 7* (4), 417–428.

Gottlieb, B. (Ed.). (1981). *Social networks and social support.* Beverly Hills: Sage.

Hareven, T. (1981). American families in transition: Historical perspectives on change. In F. Walsh (Ed.), *Normal families in social cultural context.* New York: Guilford.

Jeffers, C. (1967). *Living poor.* Ann Arbor: Ann Arbor Publishers.

Kobak, R. R., & Sceery, A. (1988). Attachment in late adolescence: Working models, affect regulation, and representations of self and others. *Child Development, 59* (1), 135–146.

Kon, I. S., & Losenkov, V. A. (1978). Friendship in adolescence: Values and behavior. *Journal of Marriage & the Family, 40,* 143–155.

Lamb, M. E. (Ed.). (1976). *The role of the father in child development.* New York: Wiley.

Lewis, M. & Rosenblum, L. (1975). *Friendship and peer relations.* New York: Wiley.

Long, T., & Long, L. (1982). Latchkey children: The child's view of self care. (ERIC Document Reproduction Service No. ED 211 229)

Longfellow, C., Zelkowitz, P., & Saunders, E. (1982). The quality of mother–child relations. In D. Belle (Ed.), *Lives in stress: Women and depression.* Beverly Hills: Sage.

Main, M., Kaplan, N., & Cassidy, J. (1985). Security in infancy, childhood, and adulthood: A move to the level of representation. In I. Bretherton & E. Waters (Eds.), Growing points of attachment theory and research. *Monographs of the Society for Research in Child Development, 50*(1–2, Serial No. 209).

Parke, R. (1981). *Fathers.* Cambridge, MA: Harvard University Press.

Piotrkowski, C. (1978). *Work and the family system.* New York: Free Press.

Rutter, M. (1979). Protective factors in children's response to stress and disadvantage. In M. W. Kent & J. E. Rolf (Eds.), *Primary prevention of psychopathology: Vol. III. Social competence in children.* Hanover, NH: University Press of New England.

Sandler, I. (1980). Social support resources, stress, and maladjustment of poor children. *American Journal of Community Psychology, 8* (1), 41–52.

Sarason, I. G., & Sarason, B. R. (Eds.). (1985). *Social support: Theory, research and applications.* Dordrecht: Martinus Nijhoff.

Silverstein, B., & Krate, R. (1975). *Children of the dark ghetto.* New York: Praeger.

Tietjen, A. M. (1982). The social networks of preadolescent children in Sweden. *International Journal of Behavioral Development, 5,* 111–130.

Tietjen, A. M. (1985). Relationships between the social networks of Swedish mothers and their children. *International Journal of Behavioral Development, 8,* 195–216.

Wahler, R. (1980). The insular mother: Her problems in parent–child treatment. *Journal of Applied Behavior Analysis, 13,* 207–219.

Weisner, T., & Gallimore, R. (1977). My brother's keeper: Child and sibling caretaking. *Current Anthropology, 18*(2), 169–190.

Weiss, R. (1979). Growing up a little faster: The experience of growing up in a single-parent household. *Journal of Social Issues, 35,* 97–111.

Weissman, M., & Paykel, E. (1974). *The depressed woman.* Chicago: University of Chicago Press.

Wellman, B. (1981). Applying network analysis to the study of support. In B. Gottlieb (Ed.), *Social networks and social support* (pp. 171–200). Beverly Hills: Sage.

Whiting, B., & Edwards, C. (1988). *Children of different worlds: The formation of social behavior.* Cambridge, MA: Harvard University Press.

Whiting, B., & Whiting, J. (1975). *Children of six cultures: A psycho-cultural analysis.* Cambridge, MA: Harvard University Press.

Woods, M. (1972). The unsupervised child of the working mother. *Developmental Psychology, 6*(1), 14–25.

Youniss, J., & Smollar, J. (1985). *Adolescent relations with mothers, fathers and friends.* Chicago: University of Chicago Press.

Zelkowitz, P. (1978). *Children's support networks: An exploratory analysis.* Special qualifying paper, Harvard Graduate School of Education.

Zelkowitz, P. (1982). *Children's support networks: Their role in families under stress.* Unpublished doctoral dissertation, Harvard Graduate School of Education.

PART 1

Children's Social Networks and Supports in Context

CHAPTER 1

Historical Changes in Children's Networks in the Family and Community

TAMARA K. HAREVEN

INTRODUCTION

Children have interacted with those who nurtured them, played with them, educated them, disciplined them, and employed them. Such activities have taken place in networks which include family members, other kin, friends, peers, caretakers, employers, within the family and in educational, correctional, and welfare institutions.

This chapter examines historical changes in children's social networks in American Society. Its main argument is that children's networks have changed over time from complex and age-diverse patterns to simpler and age-standardized ones; that on the one hand, age and functions have become streamlined and homogenized within the family; and on the other hand, institutions and peer groups have come to play an important role in children's networks, often at the expense of familial ties. These two developments have occurred along parallel tracks since about the middle of the nineteenth century. This chapter examines these changes and their impact on children's lives and raises some questions about their implications for child development.

Over the past two centuries, demographic factors combined with social and cultural ones have affected the status of children in the family and in the larger society. These factors have shaped children's interactions with various family members and with the larger community. They have had a significant impact on the changing configurations and functions of networks accessible to children: Demographic changes have affected both the number of surviving relatives available to children and the length of their temporal overlap. Urbanization has led to a higher concentration of people in cities, and therefore to a greater exposure of children to larger numbers of age peers outside the family. Urbanization and industrialization have also led to the emergence of institutions of education, welfare, and social control specifically aimed at children and youth. Children have, therefore, been placed in larger peer groups.

Industrialization rendered children (initially even young children) desirable as workers and established them as an important commodity in the labor market as well as in their family's economy. Local migration and immigration from abroad have frequently brought children into new social environments, thus providing them with new networks outside the family, and challenged them to form new networks.

DEMOGRAPHIC CHANGES AFFECTING THE POSITION OF CHILDREN IN THE FAMILY

Over the past century and a half the configurations of family members with whom children travel through life have changed considerably, as a result of the decline in mortality and fertility rates and changes in the age of marriage. These changes have affected both the composition of the networks available to children and the character of their interaction.

Life and Death

Declining mortality and fertility rates since the late nineteenth century, combined with changes in the timing of the transition to parenthood, have affected the age configurations and the position of children in the family. The decline in mortality in American society over the nineteenth century, most prominently since the 1870s, has increased the chances for children's survival to adulthood, especially for those who survived the hazards of infancy. The decline in mortality also enabled children to grow up with their siblings and to overlap with them over an extended period (Vinovskis, 1972). Before the late nineteenth century, the birth rate had not declined sufficiently to deprive children of large numbers of siblings. Moreover, the decline in fertility among the native born was counteracted by the higher fertility of the immigrants (Vinovskis, 1981). Even though mortality began to decline in the 1850s, the most dramatic decline has occurred since the 1870s (Smith, 1978). Peter Uhlenberg calculated that in 1870 only about 70% of children survived to age 10: "Nevertheless, a child born in 1870 to a mother who gave birth to seven children (the mean number of siblings for a person in this cohort was over six) would be expected to have at least four siblings survive past age 15" (1978, p. 77).

Changing Age Configurations of Children in the Family

The decline in mortality since the 1870s along with the decline in fertility has also affected the size and the configurations of membership in the family. One of the major historical changes in this respect has been a transition from a large family size to a smaller one, and from a broad age spectrum of children within the family to the compressed, closely spaced 2.3-child family in contemporary American society. Prior to the 1870s a larger number of children in the family of orientation meant not only the presence of a larger number of siblings but also a diversity in their age configurations.

Children were exposed to a greater age spread within their own families. Thus, for example, in families where children were spaced 2 or 3 years apart, and where the family had five children, the oldest child would be 15 while the youngest child would be 5, or in families with five or six children, the oldest child would be ready to leave home or get married, while the youngest child would still be in primary school. As Uhlenberg put it:

> Consider, for example, children in a family in which eight children are born, compared with those in a two-child family. In the larger family, the first born enters a family with 3 members, but as he ages it keeps expanding up to a maximum of 10. The youngest child in the family enters a very large unit, which then contracts in size as he ages until finally he or she is the only remaining child. Furthermore, the ages of parents and ages and numbers of siblings present at different childhood stages will vary considerably for the various children in the large family, depending upon their birth order. In the small family, in contrast, the two siblings may be born a few years apart, and throughout their childhood no additional changes occur. (1978, p. 77)

Such varied age configurations among siblings had significant implications for their relationships to one another, and especially for their interaction over their life course. Children growing up in families with age diversity were exposed to a variety of roles and responsibilities among their own siblings. Teenagers or young adults often acted as surrogate parents—they took care of their younger siblings, played with them, tutored them, and at times, disciplined them. Child care by older siblings was especially needed when mothers worked in factories. In many working-class immigrant families 8- or 10-year-olds took care of infants 4 or 5 years old (Hareven, 1978, 1982).

This type of interaction among siblings of various age groups was disrupted, however, in immigrant families where the older children migrated first in order to prepare the way for the rest of the family. Although the parents and the younger children eventually followed, there were many cases where young siblings met up with older ones only in adulthood, or were never reunited.

In families with a wider age spread among children, the youngest children had greater contact with the older siblings than with their own parents. Given the later age at marriage, parents would have already been in middle age when their youngest child was growing up. Under such circumstances, older siblings (especially sisters) often functioned as caretakers for their younger siblings. When one or both parents were dead, older siblings acted as surrogate parents.

In working-class families, older brothers or sisters initiated younger siblings into jobs and provided them with role models. Children of mill workers' families, for example, envied their siblings for starting to work in the factory and for earning money. Many former textile workers whom Hareven interviewed reminisced about their desire to follow their siblings. After seeing their brothers or sisters go to work, they could barely wait to start work themselves. The example of their older siblings stimulated many children's aspirations to embark on factory work, even when their parents were not pushing them out of school and into the workplace. Older siblings also provided younger siblings with access to jobs and with skills and training if they worked in the same place (Hareven, 1982).

Another major demographic change since the 1870s has been the increasing survival of parents beyond the child-rearing stage, and their opportunity to see their children reach adulthood. Uhlenberg has calculated that, of 1000 infants born around 1870, only 515 survived to age 15 and had both parents still alive, while of those born in 1950, 925 had this experience. Thus, there has been an 80% decline in the number of children who die during childhood, and an 85% decline in orphanhood among those who do survive. Uhlenberg concludes that "the necessity of coping with the economic, social, and psychological problems associated with orphanhood moved from a fairly common childhood experience to a rare one" (1978, p. 78).

In the demographic regime of late marriage, high fertility, and lower life expectancy, the overlap in age between children and their parents also differed significantly before the turn of this century. The oldest child in a family was the one most likely to overlap with his or her father in adulthood; the youngest child was the least likely to do so. The oldest children were most likely to embark on an independent career before the parents reached old-age dependency; the youngest children were most likely to be left with the responsibilities for parental support, and to overlap in adulthood with a widowed mother. The oldest child had the greatest chance to know his or her grandparents, at least in childhood; the youngest child had the least. Late-marrying children were most likely to be responsible for the support of a widowed mother, while early-marrying children depended on their parents' household space after marriage.

Thus, in the larger families of the past, age differences among siblings and birth order were much more powerful factors affecting children's lives than they are today. Since 1870, however, the continuous decline in fertility (except for the "baby boom" cohort) has led to a shrinking of the family of orientation to three or fewer children. This has resulted in much greater age uniformity within the family.

Configurations of Other Family Members and Nonrelatives in the Household

Contrary to the prevailing myths, it is now a commonly accepted historical reality that children did not grow up in extended families with kin other than their parents and siblings in the household. Even in the colonial period the basic household unit was that of a nuclear family, consisting of parents and children. (There were, however, unrelated individuals living in the household. Their role will be discussed later in the chapter.) Grandparents, aunts, uncles, and cousins did not share the same household (Demos, 1970; Greven, 1970).

Historical households differed, however, from contemporary ones in the composition of their membership and in the relations with extended kin. In the seventeenth and eighteenth centuries grandparents and other relatives resided in greater proximity to the nuclear family than in later time periods, even though they did not share the same household. Children may have experienced, therefore, greater contact with their grandparents on a daily basis, and may have had greater opportunities to interact with aunts, uncles, and cousins than they do in contemporary society. This situation varied considerably, of course, among ethnic groups, and also depended on the family's migration status. Among immigrant families grandparents often remained behind in the old country.

Proximity to extended kin was also counteracted by a briefer temporal overlap between children and their grandparents. Before the end of the nineteenth century, the average grandfather lived to see only his first grandchild. Grandparents rarely survived to see their grandchildren into adulthood. By contrast, grandparents today overlap with all of their grandchildren into adulthood, and they also experience great-grandparenthood as a new demographic luxury of our times.

Ironically, in recent decades, the opportunities for the temporal overlap of grandparents with their grandchildren as a result of the longer lifespan have been counteracted by increasing geographical dispersion. Erosion of values of interdependence of extended kin especially in the middle class among second-, third-, and fourth-generation ethnics has further weakened the chances for grandchildren's interaction with their grandparents on a regular basis. Consequently, even though there is the opportunity for grandchildren to overlap with grandparents over a longer period of their lives, grandparents' communication with their grandchildren is often limited only to family reunions, because of geographical distance or lack of familial involvement.

Nonrelatives in the Household

The presence of nonrelatives in the household has been another area of change which has affected the networks available to children. In contrast to the private, isolated family today, the family in past centuries customarily admitted various unrelated individuals into its abode. In the colonial period, households typically included apprentices, servants, and dependent members of the community, who were placed with the family by the local authorities (Demos, 1970). The presence of such nonrelatives reflected the household's important functions as the main place of production, as an institution of welfare and social control, and as a refuge designated by the local authorities for members of disrupted families.

The live-in presence during the colonial period, of orphans, dependent elderly or sick people, delinquents, servants, and apprentices meant that children growing up in the cramped quarters of such households were exposed to a variety of nonrelatives, many of whom were in their teens. Servants or boarders often took care of children, along with performing other tasks. In the colonial period especially, servants were "life cycle" servants—young people who had been sent out by their own parents to live and serve in other people's homes. The exchange of children across households was customary, since parents (especially Puritans) did not trust themselves to discipline their own children (Demos, 1972).

By the nineteenth century, the custom of sending children out into other people's households had disappeared almost completely, except where children of very poor or broken families were concerned. Following the first stage of industrialization, apprenticeship almost completely disappeared as a household-based practice. The employment of servants had become more strictly a practice of middle- and upper-class families, rather than a form of a life course exchange. The social origins of servants changed as well. The majority of servants were immigrant women, especially Irish women. They replaced the native-born young farm women, who had formerly worked as servants. Despite the decline in live-in apprenticeship and in the number of servants, children continued to be exposed to nonrelatives in the household, since all through the nineteenth century working-class as well as middle-class families were taking in boarders and lodgers.

The practice of boarding and lodging was widespread in families of all classes, in urban as well as rural society, throughout the nineteenth century. Boarding and lodging served as a kind of social equalization of the family—a practice whereby young boarders replaced the head of the household's own children who may have left home. Boarders and lodgers were young adults within the age range of 14 to 21 who had left their parents' households to migrate into new areas where they could find employment opportunities. They often served as surrogate children of the families with whom they boarded (Hareven, 1982; Modell & Hareven, 1973). The economic exchange relationship between boarders or lodgers and their host families varied considerably across classes and occupational and ethnic groups. In urban working-class families where the mother held a job outside the home, boarders often fulfilled child-care functions in exchange for room and board. Whether they were involved directly with child care or whether they only attended meals and some household activities, boarders and lodgers formed an important component to children's networks in the household.

As the practice of boarding and lodging became widespread, especially in urban areas, social reformers began to worry about the potentially corrupting impact that the presence of strangers in the household might have on their age peers as well as on younger children in the household. These moralists lacked an understanding of the constructive, cohesive impact of boarding and lodging in facilitating the absorption of young migrants into chaotic urban areas. In reality, boarding and lodging provided stability and sociability for young people during periods of frequent migration (Modell & Hareven, 1973).

The presence of boarders and lodgers in nineteenth century households, similar to that of servants in earlier periods, provided other role models for children in addition to those coming from their own relatives and siblings. Until about the 1920s, when the practice of boarding and lodging died out due to the increasing commitment to familial privacy and to the increasing availability of separate housing for young individuals, a considerable number of American urban children were growing up in households containing some unrelated individuals.

In summary, children prior to 1900 grew up in households that were considerably more diverse in membership and age than households in contemporary society. The implications this diversity in households and kinship networks had for the development and socialization of children is an important question to which we shall return (Hareven, 1985).

IMPACT OF THE DOMESTIC CHILD-CENTERED FAMILY ON CHILDREN'S NETWORKS

A major development affecting children's networks was the emergence of the child-centered domestic family, characterized by increasing specialization of child-rearing as a distinct family function. This change was intricately connected to the emergence of the child-centered domestic family in the urban middle class during the early nineteenth century and to the new views of childhood that became popular in that period.

The separation of the workplace from the home, following industrialization, led to the physical and temporal separation of the father from his family during the work day. This resulted in a separation of the sphere of women and the sphere of men. Consequently, children fell more exclusively into the women's sphere. The child-centered domestic family, which viewed the home as a retreat from the outside world, placed children at the center of the family, and redefined the role of the mother as the chief rearer of children and as the custodian of "Home, Sweet Home" (Degler, 1980; Welter, 1966).

A central feature of these developments was the concentration of child-rearing functions in the mother's hands. Prior to the early nineteenth century, child-rearing was not the exclusive domain of motherhood. In the colonial period, children were reared and educated by both parents, by their siblings, by other relatives, and by the various nonrelatives living in the household (described earlier), as well as by other members of the community. Except for instruction in reading, writing, and religion, actual child-rearing was carried out through the participation of older children along with other members of the family or household in various tasks and activities. As Philippe Ariés observed about children in European society:

> Generally speaking, transmission from one generation to the next was ensured by the everyday participation of children in adult life. Everyday life constantly brought together children and adults in trade and crafts. . . . In short, wherever people worked, and wherever they amused themselves, even in taverns of ill repute, children were mingled with adults. In this way they learned the art of living from everyday contact. (1962)

The same pattern was common in American society from the colonial period through the early nineteenth century.

The gradual segregation of children from interaction with adult society, the specialization of child-rearing, and the emergence of the mother as the main rearer of children were products of the cult of domesticity which emerged in the first half of the nineteenth century among urban middle class families, following the first stage of urbanization and industrialization.

The emergence of child-rearing as the family's central responsibility stimulated the production of advice manuals to parents as a major enterprise of the publishing industry (Wishy, 1968). A large body of domestic advice and child-rearing literature, which started to flood the market from the early nineteenth century on, glorified the role of the mother, and provided practical advice on child rearing. Urban, middle class mothers became avid readers of this literature (Sunley, 1955). The increase in mothers' consumption of child-rearing manuals represents an important shift from reliance on friends and kin for advice on child-rearing to reliance on formally printed guidance.

The cult of motherhood during the first half of the nineteenth century and the concentration on child-rearing as the mother's main responsibility laid the foundation for the typical pattern of parent-child relations that has characterized American society until the 1960s, and that still persists in some forms even today. Despite the resemblance of the mid-nineteenth century child-centered family patterns to those of our time, there were, however, significant differences. For example, children experienced a greater exposure to various role models, resulting as described earlier from the presence of larger numbers of siblings in the family and the presence of nonrelatives in the household.

The new domestic child-centered family was initially limited to the middle class. It took the better part of a century for this phenomenon to spread among working-class and rural families and various ethnic groups. In order to understand this phenomenon fully, it is important to remember that the specialization of child-rearing in the domestic family coincided with the emergence of external agencies such as the school and the reformatory, which began to take over the family's functions of education and social control.

EMERGENCE OF INSTITUTIONS AND PEER GROUPS OUTSIDE OF THE FAMILY

During the past century and a half, the family has gradually been divested of many functions that it had originally held. New institutions emerging since the middle of the nineteenth century have taken their respective functions over from the family: schools have become widespread and compulsory school attendance laws, passed first in Massachusetts and then in other states, set specific age requirements on school attendance (Kaestle & Vinovskis, 1980). Factories and other enterprises took over the household's production functions; reformatories, hospitals, and various agencies took over the household's functions of welfare and social control.

Most of the institutions which had sprung from the family's earlier functions modeled themselves on the family and used family metaphors to justify their new roles in society. Despite the fact that these agencies paid lip service to the family model, they led to the regimentation of children in distinct age groups and the partial segregation of children from their families. Parents did not let the transfer of educational functions to the schools go unchallenged (Lightfoot, 1978). In the occasional "school wars" of the nineteenth century parents tenaciously tried to retain control over their children's education, because they saw in the school and in the constant exposure to peer groups a potential threat to their children's character and to their own control over their children's education (Rawitch, 1974).

While middle-class parents opposed the school primarily because they were concerned with retaining moral control over their children, urban working-class and rural parents were concerned with retaining control over their children's time as workers and wage earners, which was being threatened by compulsory school attendance laws. Parents who viewed their children's labor as an essential contribution to the collective family economy resisted the requirements for school attendance and the age limits imposed by child labor legislation, which deprived them of income from their children's work (Hareven, 1982). Eventually, middle-class parents accepted the school, and began to control it, but working-class parents found means to circumvent the requirements for compulsory education, often sending their children to work with falsified birth certificates (Bremner, Barnard, Hareven & Mennell, 1970; Hareven, 1982).

During the nineteenth century, most of the children attending school were between the ages of 8 and 12. Only toward the end of the nineteenth century did 6 or 7 become the standardized, official school entry age. While reformers had little interest in lowering the school age for middle-class children, several reform movements did aim to start the schooling of the children of the poor in infancy.

This concern was expressed in the infant school movement, which, in spite of its short duration, set a precedent for kindergarten and for earlier commencement of schooling. In the 1820s a group of civic-minded educational reformers in Boston launched the infant schools for children of the poor in order to rescue them from what the reformers considered to be damaging and corrupting environments in their families, especially during a period of such rapid urbanization.

> Infants, taken from the most unfavorable situations in which they are ever placed, from the abodes of poverty and vice, are capable of learning at least a hundred times as much, a hundred times as well, and of being a hundred times as happy, by the system adopted in infant schools, as by that which prevails in the common schools throughout the country. The conclusion most interesting to every friend of education is, that the infant school system can be extended through every department of the *popular education.* (*Boston Recorder and Religious Transcript,* 1829, cited in Vinovskis & May, 1977)

The debates surrounding the infant schools reflect the attitudes of the time toward the age limits of childhood.

The infant school movement peaked by 1830, then began a slow decline in the 1840s, and became extinct by the 1850s. In 1840 at least 10% of children under 4 were attending schools in Massachusetts. The percentage was even higher in many specific localities. During the 1840s the practice of sending young children to school gradually died out in response to the formalization of the public school system, which eventually set lower limits on the age of school admission. A resurgence of interest in infant education was expressed in the establishment of kindergarten in the 1860s and 1870s. Like the infant schools, the kindergarten was directed at poor and immigrant children (Vinovskis & May 1977). Thus while middle class children started their exposure to peers and teachers in the schools at around age 6 or 7 the working class and immigrant children began to experience such exposure by age 3 or 4.

The spread of the public school system from the middle of the nineteenth century on led to the segregation of children from their families for a considerable part of the day. A slow but continuous development of age grading within the schools over the course of the nineteenth century led to the formation of more streamlined age groups among children within the schools. The number of private and public schools rapidly increased after the American Revolution. By the mid–nineteenth century most children in the United States received at least some schooling (Angus, Mirel, & Vinovskis, 1988).

Initially, schools accepted children of all ages and did not divide them into specific age groups. During the second half of the nineteenth century, however, the minimum school entry age was set at 7 or 8. With the establishment of public high schools during that period, the length of schooling was extended. Since students often entered high school at 12 or 13, and most did not stay long enough to graduate, nineteenth century children typically completed their formal education by their mid-teens. By the end of the nineteenth century, schooling had been expanded, and childhood education had become compressed to a more specific age span (between 7 and 13). The average minimum age of leaving school increased from 14 years and 5 months in 1900 to 16 years in 1930 in the states which had enacted a compulsory schooling law.

The proportion of children's time claimed by the school also changed over the nineteenth century. The average length of the elementary and secondary public school year has increased over the past century. School terms in urban areas have become shorter. Nearly year-round school attendance in the 1830s changed to a 40-week school year by the turn of the century, while rural terms expanded from 132 days in 1870 to 179 days in 1970 (Angus et al., 1988).

Along with the increase in school attendance over the nineteenth century, more systematic age grading began to emerge within the schools. While the typical pattern in rural schools continued to be that of the one-room schoolhouse, urban schools gradually developed a grading system over the course of the century. Initially, the grading was based on children's accomplishments in the curriculum, rather than on age per se. Age grading in the schools did not develop at a significant pace until the 1930s. The process spread unevenly across the nation, and varied considerably by region. The industrial Northeast and Midwest advanced that system over the first three decades of this century, while the South and West lagged behind. The emergence of schooling thus affected children's networks in two mutually re-enforcing directions. First, children were segregated from adult society during their schooling (except from teachers), and second, children were gradually, though unevenly, segregated into age peer groups in the schools (Angus et al., 1988).

The school and the peer groups within it thus became important competitors with the family for children's time and involvement. As the required age of school entry was lowered and the upper age requirements of compulsory school attendance were pushed up, children began to spend increasingly longer portions of their lives with peers outside the family. Initially, children were not rigidly separated into age groups. They were exposed to peers of a variety of ages. As the age-graded class system emerged as the norm, children began to spend most of their schooling time with their age peers and teachers. In many instances children also became their parents' educators, bringing home new ideas and information acquired in the schools. Especially in the case of immigrants, the school functioned as an agent of acculturation of parents through their children.

While school attendance in the 1800s was a privilege limited primarily to middle-class children, the proportion of immigrant children attending school began to increase toward the end of the century. Several factors combined to increase the proportion of immigrant children attending school: child labor laws were more rigidly enforced, children's employment declined due to new technology which made child labor obsolete, and attitudes toward education began to change among immigrant parents. The proportion of children attending school and the number of years spent there have increased continuously since the late nineteenth century. For recent cohorts, school attendance after the age of 15 has become almost universal, and with few exceptions, children attend classes with other children of the same age throughout most of their childhood.

The Workplace

For working-class children, the main peer groups outside of the family were their co-workers in factories, in street trades, and in various industries, such as food processing and canning. Child laborers were thus exposed to networks composed of mixed age groupings, ranging from their peers to adults, and varying according to their workplace and their age. Throughout the nineteenth century, workers transferred their family networks to the workplace. Parents, older relatives, and siblings or cousins often worked in the same place, instructed the younger workers, helped them, and at times protected them. Even nonrelatives with whom younger children worked assumed the roles of surrogate parents, protecting younger children and helping them adapt to the workplace and its various routines. This surrogate familial role was especially important when children started to work at a young age (10 or 11).

Within the mixed age groupings in the workplace, children formed peer networks among co-workers close in age. Despite the demanding pressures of the workplace, children played with their age peers during breaks (*Lowell Offering* 1840–45). Carrying some childhood mischief into the factory, they often played tricks and practical jokes on one another. The networks of the workplace were crucial for children's adaptation to difficult working conditions and taxing time schedules, and for diminishing the bewilderment they may have encountered upon first entering a new workplace. While older co-workers provided protection, the presence of their own-age peers meant that children could carry some of their childlike qualities into the workplace. In many cases children were not mere recipients of adult support, however. At times, experienced child workers shared their savvy and crucial information, especially about shortcuts on the job, with new adult workers, or with other children (Hareven, 1982).

The Street

One of the important networks competing with the family was the peer groups on the street. In urban society the streets had become an important arena for sociability, play, and peer activity for children seven and older. A more acceptable place for boys than for girls, the street became a magnet for young boys and teenagers in the middle classes as well as for the urban poor and immigrants. Moralists, educators, and clergy from the middle of the nineteenth century on denounced the corrupting dangers of the street. They viewed almost all peer group activities as threatening, degenerate, and seductive, leading in a straight line to crime and delinquency (Bremner, Barnard, Hareven, & Mennell, 1971).

The mounting anxiety expressed in the moralists' and educators' writings was especially dramatic with regard to children of immigrants and the poor. One of the most striking expressions of these anxieties was in the *Dangerous Classes of New York* written by Charles Loring Brace in 1854—a book that compared the "gangs" of immigrant children roaming around the alleys and wharves of New York City to the *proletaires* of Paris, whose revolutionary activities had led to the establishment of the Paris Commune in 1848. "There are no dangers to the value of property or the permanency of our institutions so great as those from the existence of . . . a class of vagabond, ignorant, ungoverned children." For Brace the dangerous classes were "the outcast, vicious, reckless multitude of New York boys, swarming . . . in every foul alley and low street" (1854, cited in Bremner, 1976).

This anxiety over the street gangs of New York and other major cities with a high concentration of immigrants led Brace to the establishment of the New York Children's Aid Society—which was then established in other cities. The society's major purpose was to rescue children from the streets and place them in the "wholesome" homes of farmers in the Midwest. The most frequent solution to the problems of urban "delinquents" and dependent poor children from the 1850s on was, however, to place them in the institutions of welfare and social control that had begun to emerge in midcentury.

The Reformatory

Institutions of welfare and social control designed specifically for children and teenagers developed as an alternative to the family. These institutions took over the family's earlier functions of welfare, education and social control. These institutions emerged as a result of urbanization and in response to the panic caused by the influx of large numbers of Irish immigrants to major eastern cities. The juvenile reformatories emerging in the 1850s, first in Massachusetts and subsequently in other states, introduced the principle of segregating young offenders by age and reforming them within an institution (Rothman, 1971).

These institutions congregated juvenile "offenders" in peer groups, thus unintentionally creating networks of homeless and "delinquent" children and youths (Bremner et al., 1971). As the case records of some of these institutions suggest, their young inmates displayed remarkable resourcefulness within the institutions as well as back on the streets. Inmates made new friends within the reformatory. These friendships formed the base for new networks which the young delinquents formed or joined following their release. These adolescent networks linked the streets and the reformatory, and facilitated the transmission of knowledge and skills among current and former inmates. The "repeaters," who were arrested again a short time after their release, were especially instrumental in fostering and utilizing such networks.

The juvenile reformatory represented the nineteenth century's answer to a larger question: What would be the most regenerating and redeeming place for a child, the family or an institution? In addressing this question, educators followed a double standard: among middle class families, the cult of domesticity and the child-centered family extolled the virtues of the home and opposed child labor. At the same time, the advocates of this familistic ideology believed that the way to keep poor and delinquent children out of trouble and "reformed" was either to put them to work or place them in other people's homes or in institutions. Prior to the 1850s, the "binding out" of children—their contractual placement by the authorities in other people's homes as servants—was the dominant practice. Following the introduction of the reformatory, the institution triumphed over the family (Bremner, 1976).

Thus while the middle class family and home became the central locus for child rearing, competing forces in schools and institutions of social control made increasing demands upon the portion of children's time that came under institutional control.

THE SEGREGATION OF CHILDHOOD AND CHILDREN

The overall trend since the nineteenth century has thus been one of increasing segregation of children as a distinct age group and a further segregation of children from adult society into specific age groups within the larger category of "children." This streamlining of children by age has been expressed in their increasing separation from adults in daily life, in their education, work, disciplining, and sociability, and in the introduction of age grading in the schools as well. Except for farm families and working-class families, children's activities have become gradually disengaged from adult activities and from interaction with mixed age groups. The portion of time that children spend with their age peers has increased progressively since the nineteenth century.

The identification of children as distinct from adults and the recognition of childhood as a separate developmental stage, with its own needs and potential underlie these developments from the early part of the nineteenth century on. As Philippe Ariès has shown, the discovery of childhood occurred in western Europe in the seventeenth and eighteenth centuries as part of the emergence of the "modern family" (Ariès, 1962).

In American society, childhood was "discovered" and identified as a distinct stage of life first in the private lives of middle-class urban families in the early part of the nineteenth century. The discovery itself was related to the family's retreat into domesticity discussed earlier, the separation of the workplace from the home, the redefinition of the wife's role as the custodian of the domestic sphere and as the main rearer of children, and the emergence of sentiment as the basis of familial relationships. An important consequence of these new attitudes toward children was children's increasing segregation from adult society and activities. By contrast, children in the seventeenth and eighteenth centuries mingled with adult society and participated in the various tasks and "sociability" of the household. They were not sheltered as "innocent" creatures. As Cott (1976) found in eighteenth century divorce testimonies, children even witnessed sexual activity in the household.

The new child centeredness of urban domestic families in the early nineteenth century was also a response to the decline in infant and child mortality and to the conscious practice of family limitation. Following this recognition of children as the central focus of middle-class family life, childhood became the subject of a voluminous body of the child rearing and family advice literature, described earlier. In addition, the moralists' and reformers' literature popularized the concept of childhood and the needs of children, prescribed the means to allow them to develop as children, and called for the regulation of child labor. Childhood became publicly recognized as a special stage through compulsory school attendance laws, child labor legislation, the establishment of juvenile reformatories, kindergartens, and age-graded schools. All these institutions were part of the effort to protect children and to enable them to realize their potential in their unique developmental stage (Hareven, 1976; Skolnick, 1973).

Over the nineteenth century, the period of childhood gradually become prolonged, extending its boundaries into adolescence. The recognition of adolescence in the late nineteenth century and its gradual institutionalization in the twentieth century provided children with a moratorium from adult responsibilities. By the time G. Stanley Hall published his first article on adolescence (1905), "adolescent" peer groups were already easily identifiable in urban society, high school age had been extended, and reformers were developing such organizations as the Boy Scouts and various other clubs for boys in order to keep urban teenagers out of trouble. Like kindergarten, these organizations, which were initially aimed at the children of the poor and immigrants, were eventually taken over by the middle class, who could afford leisure time for their children.

Over the course of the twentieth century, demographic and socioeconomic changes led to a further reduction in the age diversity of children within the family and their age grading in tight groups outside the family. The decline in fertility eventually resulted in a small compact family with its children closely spaced. Increasing privatization of the family led to the withdrawal of boarders and lodgers from the household. The diversity of role models previously provided by older siblings and boarders also disappeared, except among newly arrived ethnic groups and in the Black family.

Demographic factors affecting the life course have also led to a greater age uniformity within the family. Earlier marriage, earlier childbearing, and the bearing of fewer children have brought parents and children closer together in age. Most children now know their parents as young people, while in the past, only the oldest child knew the parents as young people, and the youngest child knew his or her parents in middle age only. (There now seems to be a partial return to this historical pattern, because many professional couples now have children in their thirties and early forties.) Contemporary families have been characterized by an increasing age uniformity.

On the other hand, children are now starting to cluster with their peers in institutions outside the family at much younger ages. School entry has been lowered to age six, and kindergarten and institutional child care have become more widespread. Thus children aged three or younger now spend a major portion of the day with peers if the mother is working outside the home.

Increase in mothers' labor force participation since World War II, especially the dramatic increase since the 1960s, has further affected the networks of children. While earlier a mother's gainful employment had been almost exclusively a working-class phenomenon, the absence of the mother from the home for a partial or an entire working day has become widespread in the middle class as well.

Even though the mother continues to be the main rearer of children within the family, children spend increasingly less time with their mothers because of mothers' more widespread participation in the work force. This was true, of course, for working-class mothers all along. The novelty of the phenomenon is the decline in the amount of time middle-class mothers spend with their children. Day-care centers have replaced the earlier patterns of child care by older siblings or by elderly relatives when the mother was employed. As a result, children of working mothers are now exposed to their peers in day-care centers even before kindergarten.

The increased participation of fathers in child rearing and child care, has been another important development since the 1960s, especially in middle-class families and among dual-career couples (Bronfenbrenner, 1969). Changing perceptions of parental roles in the wake of women's liberation and men's new consciousness along with the increasing sentimentalization of childhood have led to fathers' more active participation in child rearing and child care. The extent to which this pattern represents a radical departure is still a question open to historical research. Ross Parke and Peter Stearns (1987) have hypothesized that fathers' involvement with their children might have been even greater during the heyday of domesticity and mother-dominated child rearing than it is today. Fathers may have invested their time and emotions to a greater extent than the mid–nineteenth century child-rearing literature may have led us to believe. Since that type of "modern" domestic family emphasized the emotional closeness among fathers as well as mothers and children, the authors conclude that, "while systematic inquiry remains to be done, it is clear that fathers were more diverse and on balance probably more active than expert child-rearing literature allowed for" (Parke & Stearns, 1987, p. 13).

The authors consider the possibility of greater paternal involvement in shared leisure and play with their children. They date this development from the late nineteenth century, and believe that this type of shared leisure with children fulfilled the additional functions of instilling certain skills and values. If this hypothesis is borne out we might be able to identify several significant historical transitions in fathers' involvement with child rearing: From sharing work together in the preindustrial period (and in working-class and farming families as well, following industrialization), to sharing leisure time since the late nineteenth century, and to a greater sharing of child-care responsibilities over the past two decades. One could argue, therefore, that children are now more exposed to their fathers on a daily basis, and from a younger age, than they had been previously.

The more recent involvement of fathers in child rearing and child care varies considerably, of course, among various groups in the population. Data from a recent survey show that between 1975 and 1981, fathers increased their time invested in child care by 26% over this six-year span. Mothers were still responsible, however, for 66% of the child care, compared to fathers' 34% (Jessa, 1987, cited in Parke & Stearns, 1987). Fathers' greater involvement in child care is reflected in Dr. Spock's revision of his 1976 edition of *Baby and Child Care:*

> I always assumed that the parent taking the greater share of the care of young children (and of the home) would be the mother, whether or not she wanted an outside career. . . . Now I recognize that the father's responsibility is as great as the mother's. (p. xix)

By contrast, Dr. Spock's first edition (1946) devoted only nine pages to the father's role, advising fathers to play an occasional role in child care in order to give mothers a rest. The actual extent of fathers' present involvement in child care and the ways in which it differs from earlier patterns of paternal involvement await systematic study (Weiss, 1977).

THE RETURN OF DIVERSITY

The patterns of increasing paternal involvement in child rearing have been counteracted in recent years by the increasing numbers of American children growing up without fathers or with only occasional contact with their fathers. The increasing percentage of single-parent families (mostly headed by mothers) has led to a dramatic change in children's parental configurations. The demographic opportunities enabling fathers and mothers and their children to go through life together which were gained over the past century through the decline of mortality, have been counteracted by divorce and single parenthood (Cherlin, 1981).

The current pattern of a great number of fatherless children and blended families is actually not an entirely new phenomenon in American society. It resembles in some ways the patterns of the seventeenth and eighteenth centuries, when high mortality disrupted families and remarriage resulted in the formation of new families.

Over the last two decades, in American society, divorce has wreaked havoc in a way similar to the effect of death in earlier times. Thus there is some resemblance between the current and past one-parent families and blended families and their complicated kin networks, in terms of the complexity of networks available to children. There are also, however, several differences. When remarriage occurs after divorce (as opposed to after the death of one partner), the biological parent remains, and sometimes even lives in the same community. In the past, if the surviving parent began a new relationship, it usually resulted in marriage. In contemporary single-parent families, the mother or father does not always marry his or her new partner, and children are sometimes exposed to a sequence of partners of their biological parent living in the household. Nevertheless, complexity, age diversity, and variability in family and household membership have partly replaced the streamlined age-homogenization of the family that had emerged in the 1950s.

In another chapter of this volume Tietjen concludes from her survey of the literature on children of divorce that boys of school age have difficulties in peer interaction and experience disrupted relationships with both parents for up to 2 years. Remarriage of the noncustodial parent often results in decreased contact between the children and that parent, and contact between the child and his or her noncustodial grandparents is often decreased as well. In their study of children's contact with their "outside" parent following divorce, Furstenberg and Nord (1985) found that "marital disruption effectively destroys the ongoing relationship between children and the biological parents living outside the home" (p. 000). The residential parent usually carries the major responsibilities of child rearing. Activities with outside parents are generally confined to entertainment and recreation. There is, however, a difference between children's relationships to outside mothers and to outside fathers; children tend to maintain closer contact with outside mothers and express greater satisfaction with that relationship (Furstenberg & Nord, 1985).

Blended families resulting from remarriage after divorce have brought new family and kinship ties into the lives of an increasing number of American children. These blended families are, in fact, reintroducing some of the complexity and diversity that has been characteristic of the past. Blended families bring several sets of siblings together, thus increasing the variety of age configurations in the family. They also establish contact among stepfathers or stepmothers and unrelated children, thus reintroducing nonrelatives into the household, exposing children to new extended kin.

Remarriage following divorce has also led to the rearrangement of the kinship networks available to children outside the household. Some children have three to four sets of grandparents, and several new sets of aunts, uncles, and cousins. Precisely how children relate to these new and complicated networks has not been systematically studied. However, this area is one that definitely needs to be addressed.

IMPLICATIONS FOR CHILD DEVELOPMENT

The past century has brought a continuous stabilization and age-homogenization into the networks available to children in the family and kin group (Hareven, 1985). The decline in mortality and the younger age at marriage have provided children with the chance to survive to adulthood together with their siblings, to overlap with parents into their own adulthood, and to know their grandparents in adulthood. The decline in fertility, on the other hand, has reduced the number of siblings with whom they grow up. The development of age-graded schooling and the universal requirement for school attendance have extended children's opportunities for overlap with their age peers. Increasing affluence combined with more effective legislation and the obsolescence of child labor has enabled children to stay in school regularly and over a longer time period, and to extend their period of play and study before assuming work responsibilities. Child rearing itself has become a science, supported by various professional groups and manuals.

The question is, however, what children have actually gained from these historical developments. The answer still depends on collaborative research between historians and developmentalists. One of the key questions that links these historical developments with child psychology is the impact of diversity in age, membership, and roles in the household vis-à-vis greater uniformity. Talcott Parsons has argued that the specialized, private, and child-focused family is much more effective in rearing adults who function effectively in a complex, bureaucratic society. Parsons claims that the ego development which enables adults to function well in a complex world is best achieved in a private family that shelters the individual. On the other hand, Arieś has argued that the modern, private family serves as a retreat from the outside world and cuts children off from the rest of society. Children growing up in such families are deprived, therefore, of much of the experience of the adult world. As a result, such children are handicapped in their future adjustment to adult roles. Hence, according to Arieś, children who experience a greater diversity and variety of role models in their family of orientation and through the family's involvement with the larger society are more adaptable and able to function in a modern, complex society. While Arieś and Parsons never debated these issues directly, Richard Sennett (1971) has staged a theoretical debate between the two in order to discern the relationship between family structure and individuals' adaptability and mobility in complex, modern society.

These two conflicting points of view are linked, of course, to a larger question: What price have the family and children paid for the family's retreat into privacy and the resulting loss of its earlier "sociability" (its interaction with the community)? Has the family's retreat from the community and the withdrawal of nonrelatives from the household deprived children of greater exposure to a diversity of social roles? Even though parent–child relations have become much more informal and sentimental than in the past, has the actual process of child rearing become too specialized in the family and too professionalized in the institutions outside the family?

In addressing these questions it is important to remember that "historical" family configurations and child-rearing patterns still survive in varying degrees and in various forms among more newly arrived ethnic groups and among Black families. If the middle-class family discovers that its retreat from the community and its child centeredness have become excessive and counterproductive, some of the earlier historical models are still available for consideration of modes of adaptation.

Thus the historical examination of these issues provides a perspective on the contemporary issues, not only because it offers an understanding of patterns of change, but also because the historical experience offers models of adaptation that are still relevant in contemporary society.

REFERENCES

Angus, D. L., Mirel, J. R., & Vinovskis, M. A. (1988). *Historical development of age-stratification in schooling.* Unpublished manuscript.

Ariès, P. (1962). *Centuries of childhood: A social history of family life.* New York: Vintage.

Bremner, R. H. (1976). Other people's children. *Journal of Social History, 16* (3), 83–103.

Bremner, R. H., Barnard, C., Hareven, T. K., & Mennell, R. (Eds.). *Children and youths in America: A Documentary History,* vol. 1 (1600–1865) (1970), vol. 2 (1866–1932) (1971), vol. 3 (1933–1973) (1976). Cambridge, MA: Harvard University Press.

Bronfenbrenner, U. (1969). The changing American child—A speculative analysis. In John N. Edwards (Ed.), *The family and change.* New York: Knopf.

Cherlin, A. J. (1981). *Marriage, Divorce, Remarriage.* Cambridge, MA: Harvard University Press.

Cott, N. F. (1976). Eighteenth-century family and social life revealed in Massachusetts divorce records. *Journal of Social History,* 10(1):20–43.

Degler, C. N. (1980). *At odds: Women and the family in America from the Revolution to the present.* New York: Oxford University Press.

Demos, J. (1970). *A little commonwealth: Family life in Plymouth Colony.* New York: Oxford University Press.

Demos, J. (1972). Developmental perspectives on the history of childhood. *Journal of Interdisciplinary History, 2,* 315–327.

Furstenberg, F. F., Jr., & Nord, C. W. (1985). Parenting apart: Patterns of child rearing after marital disruption. *Journal of Marriage & the Family,* 47(4):893–904.

Greven, P. (1970). *Four generations: Population, land, and family in colonial Andover, Massachusetts.* Ithaca, NY: Cornell University Press.

Hall, G. S. (1904). *Adolescence: Its psychology and its relations to physiology, anthropology, sociology, sex, crime, religion and education.* New York: D. Appleton & Co.

Hareven, T. K. (1976). The last stage: Historical adulthood and old age. *Daedalus,* 105(4):13–27.

Hareven, T. K. (Ed.). (1978). *Transitions: The family and the life course in historical perspective.* New York: Academic.

Hareven, T. K. (1982). *Family time and industrial time.* Cambridge, England and NY: Cambridge University Press.

Hareven, T. K. (1985). Historical change in the family and the life course: Implications for child development. In A. B. Smuts & J. W. Hagen (Eds.), *History and research in child development* (pp. 8–23). Chicago: University of Chicago Press.

Hareven, T. K., & Modell, J. (1980). Family patterns. In S. Thernstrom (Ed.), *Harvard encyclopedia of American ethnic groups* (pp. 345–354). Cambridge, MA: Harvard University Press.

Kaestle, C., & Vinovskis, M. (1980). *Education and social change in nineteenth century Massachusetts.* Cambridge, England & NY: Cambridge University Press.

Lightfoot, S. L. (1978). *Worlds apart: Relationships between families and schools.* New York: Basic.

The Lowell Offering (1840–1845) Repository of Original Articles Written by Factory Operatives v. 1–5. Lowell, MA.

Miller, D. & Swanson, G. (1969). The changing American parent. In J. N. Edwards (Ed.), *The family and change.* New York: Knopf.

Modell, J., & Hareven, T. K. (1973). Urbanization and the malleable household: Boarding and lodging in nineteenth century American families. *Journal of Marriage & the Family,* 35(3):467–479.

Parke, R. & Stearns, P. (1987). *Changing patterns of fatherhood.* Manuscript prepared for 1987 meeting of Historians and Developmentalists, Belmont, MD.

Ravitch, D. (1974). *The great school wars: New York City, 1805–1973.* New York: Basic.

Rothman, D. (1971). *The discovery of the asylum.* Boston: Little, Brown.

Sennett, R. (1971). *Families against the city: Middle class homes of industrial Chicago, 1872–1890.* Cambridge, MA: Harvard University Press.

Shore, M. F. (1976). The child and historiography. *Journal of Interdisciplinary History, 6* (3), 495–505.

Skolnick, A. (1973). The limits of childhood: Conceptions of child development and social context. *Law & Contemporary Problems,* 39(3):38–77.

Smith, D. B. (1978). Mortality and family in the colonial Chesapeake. *Journal of Interdisciplinary History, 8* (3), 403–427.

Spock, B. (1946). *The commonsense book of baby and child care.* New York: Duell, Sloane & Pearce.

Spock, B. (1976). *Baby and child care.* New York: Hawthorn.

Sunley, R. (1955). Early nineteenth century American literature on child rearing. In M. Wolfenstein & M. Mead (Eds.), *Child rearing in contemporary American culture.* Chicago: University of Chicago Press.

Uhlenberg, P. (1978). Changing Configurations of the Life Course. In T. K. Hareven (Ed.), *Transitions: The Family and the Life Course in Historical Perspective.*

Vinovskis, M. A. (1981). *Fertility in Massachusetts from the Revolution to the Civil War.* New York: Academic Press.

Vinovskis, M.A. (1972). Mortality rates and trends in Massachusetts before 1860, *Journal of Economic History,* 32:184–213.

Vinovskis, M. A., & May, D. (1977). A ray of millennial light: Early education and social reform in the infant school movement in Massachusetts, 1826–1840. In T. K. Hareven (Ed.), *Family and kin in American urban communities.* New York: Franklin & Watts.

Weiss, N. P. (1977). Mother, the invention of necessity: Dr. Benjamin Spock's *Baby and child care. American Quarterly,* 29(5), 519–546.

Wells, R. V. (1971). Demographic change and the life cycle of American families. *Journal of Interdisciplinary History, 2* (2), 273–298.

Welter, B. (1966). The cult of true womanhood, 1820–1860. *American Quarterly, 18,* 151–174.

CHAPTER 2

The Ecology of Children's Social Support Networks

ANNE MARIE TIETJEN

Several of the chapters in this volume and a growing body of research literature have shown that the various functions of social support play important roles in children's social and emotional adjustment and in their ability to cope with stress. From a broader perspective the abilities to cope with stress and to make a good social and emotional adjustment may be seen as aspects of competence, defined as a set of functional or instrumental skills, including intellectual, social–emotional, and practical abilities (Ogbu, 1981). In this chapter my goal is to place the issue of the role of social support systems in the development of children's competence into ecological perspective. The thesis of this chapter is that, just as the components of human competence vary with cultural and ecological circumstances (Ogbu, 1981), the form and function of children's social support systems vary in ways that make them adaptive for preparing children to become competent persons within the particular ecological context, or niche, in which they live.

From an ecological viewpoint the form and function of children's social support systems are influenced by environmental as well as personal factors as part of a culturally organized ecological system. Different ecological circumstances result in support systems with different forms and functions. Since societies consistently produce individuals who are able to function competently according to the requirements of the culture, societies must also develop the means for producing these individuals. It is proposed here that children's social support systems are an important means by which children learn the competencies relevant to their ecological circumstances, and that these support systems develop in ways that are congruent with the

---

Support for data collection was provided by the Spencer Foundation, the American-Scandinavian Foundation, Cornell University, and the Social Sciences and Humanities Research Council of Canada. Many thanks to Moncrieff Cochran and members of the SRCD Study Group, who provided helpful comments on earlier drafts of this chapter.

ecological contexts in which they live. In turn, the nature of children's social relationships also influences the kinds of opportunities and experiences they will have, and hence the competencies they will develop. When congruence between the function of the child's network and the demands of the ecological context does not exist, support is inadequate, and vulnerability results.

Consider the lives of two 8-year-old girls. One, Erica, lives in a 20-year-old suburb of a large city in Sweden. The other, Iris, lives in a village on a beach between the sea and the jungle in Papua New Guinea.

> Erica lives in an apartment with her parents and younger brother in a suburb of a city of more than one million people. Her family moved to this apartment 2 years ago from a different city. Erica visits her mother's parents about once a month, and sees her father's parents about twice a year. Erica's mornings are spent eating a quick breakfast with her parents and brother, and then being driven to a day-care center attached to her school, where she plays with other children until school begins. Erica is one of 90 second graders in her school. After school Erica sometimes goes to her dance class, her soccer practice, or to visit her best friend, whom she has known for about a year. She usually eats dinner with her parents and brother, and in the evenings she watches television, or reads, or does her homework. She often talks with her mother about the work she is doing at school, and her mother meets with Erica's teacher at least three times a year. Erica's usual chores are to keep her room neat and to set the table for dinner. On weekends Erica sometimes goes shopping with her mother in the city or plays with friends or with children she doesn't know in a nearby playground.
>
> Iris lives in a village of 250 people. She and her parents and five siblings live in a two-room house made of sago palm stalks. The most used part of the house is the large veranda in front, where most household activities, including cooking, craft making, socializing, and even sleeping, take place. Her father's parents live in a house about 10 feet away from Iris's, and her paternal uncles and their wives and children also live within a few yards. Iris participates in daily exchanges of cooked food with their households. She sees both sets of grandparents nearly every day, as well as numerous cousins, aunts, and uncles. There are several villages like Iris's within a few hours' walk or canoe trip, but the nearest town, with a population of 2000, is more than 100 miles away and accessible only by airplane or motorboat. Iris has never been there. She has lived in her village all

her life and knows that when she marries she will probably move to a hamlet within a few miles of where she is growing up.

In the morning Iris looks after her two younger siblings while her mother prepares breakfast. After breakfast she goes to the river behind her house to wash the breakfast dishes and herself, in preparation for school. At the river she meets other people of various ages engaged in the same activities. Iris is one of 17 second graders in her school. When not in school she spends her time caring for her younger siblings, helping with household tasks, or playing with other girls, all of whom are related to her. She already has learned to do most of the work she will do as an adult. Iris rarely has schoolwork to do at home, and her parents cannot help her with it when she does. Iris's Saturdays are spent working in the family's subsistence garden or visiting and helping her grandparents. Sunday afternoons are usually spent attending a community event, such as an intervillage soccer match, or a life cycle transition ceremony, such as a celebration of the end of a period of mourning, or food exchanges confirming social ties established through marriage.

The lives of these two children differ in many obvious ways. They live in very different physical surroundings and spend their time in different ways. The social support systems of the two girls also differ. They differ in the breadth of the girls' exposure and access to different kinds of people, in the amount and nature of the contact they have with parents, kin, and unfamiliar people, in the types of activities they participate in with children and adults, and in the obligations and privileges that accompany their various relationships. Along with these differences in network structure and relationship content they may be experiencing different types of social support (Berndt, this volume), such as esteem support, informational support, instrumental support, and companionship, in differing amounts or configurations.

In our desire to know how we can promote optimal social support for children, it is tempting to ask the question of whether one of these girls can be said to be receiving more social support or better social support than the other. From an ecological developmental perspective, however, this question is too simple to be answerable. It is pointless to try to assess the quality or quantity of social support experienced by children without considering the nature of the ecological contexts in which the children live, and the fit between the support and the context. The basis for judging the adequacy of support, then, should be whether or not the amount and type of support received is helping the child develop the skills, knowledge, attitudes, and social connections he or she will need to become a competent person within the society in which he or she will live.

For example, living in urban Sweden, Erica will benefit from a social support network that will expose her to a wide range of people, giving her a chance to develop the social skills needed for meeting and developing relationships with previously unfamiliar people. For Iris, social support that will enable her to learn the skills involved in maintaining high levels of instrumental support among her kin is more likely to be truly helpful. When social support is viewed in this way, the question of whether there are specific ecological factors associated with levels of social support becomes more complex. It becomes evident that the effects of any particular ecological factor must be considered in terms of multiple levels of the ecological context.

In the following section of this chapter a conceptual model is presented for understanding how ecological factors influence the development of appropriate social support systems for children in particular ecological contexts and how vulnerabilities can occur in the process. The third section of the chapter presents a review of existing research on ecological factors that have been found to influence the nature of children's social support systems. The fourth section offers an illustration of contrasting social support systems based on data from Sweden and Papua New Guinea. In the final section implications of the model and the data for research and policy are considered.

AN ECOLOGICAL FRAMEWORK

Anthropologists and cross-cultural psychologists have shown that the particular skills that define competence vary widely among cultures (Cole, Gay, Glick, & Sharp, 1971; Greenfield, 1966) and that they do so in accordance with the economic, political, and social roles required of adults in the culture (Inkeles, 1968). It is also established that cultures consistently produce individuals who are able to function competently within culture-specific definitions of competence.

The question of how this congruence between individuals' competence and the needs of the social system is achieved has usually been answered in terms of variations in child-rearing practices among cultural groups and the effects of different patterns of child rearing on child behaviors (Aberle, 1961; Barry, Child, & Bacon, 1959; Berry, 1977; Inkeles, 1966; Ogbu, 1981). In contrast, Whiting (1980) has proposed that in many nonwestern cultures parent–child interaction styles are less important influences on the development of competence in children than parents' placement of children in particular settings, defined to include place, task, and the company of other persons of a specific age and gender. In these settings children learn by trial and error and intrinsic reinforcement the appropriate skills and behaviors for their ecological context.

An ecological approach to the concept of social support systems allows us to recognize the contribution of factors beyond family and other immediate settings to the development of context-appropriate competence in children as they develop into adults. The model proposed here maintains that children develop context-appropriate competence through the experiences accorded to them by the specific characteristics of their social support networks. The form and function of these networks are influenced by events and circumstances in the environment, as well as by characteristics of the developing person. Relevant experiences for the development of context-appropriate competence include, but are not limited to, patterns of interaction with family members and other important people in various roles, and exposure to tasks and activities appropriate to the ecological context.

Dimensions of Social Support

A framework for understanding how ecological factors influence the development of social support systems that promote context-appropriate competence requires a broad definition of social support systems that includes structural features as well as dimensions of relationship content, and can accommodate cultural variations. It should be stressed that the list that follows is not considered to be universal. Just as competence takes culture-specific forms, it is likely that dimensions of social support also vary from one culture to another not only in degree but in kind. In order to understand what dimensions of social support are relevant within a given culture it would be necessary to address this question directly through research in the culture. However, several dimensions of social networks and support systems emerge from the literature on children's and adults' social networks and support systems that may be hypothesized to have an influence on the development of context-appropriate competence in many, if not most, cultures.

Among the relevant structural dimensions is the *number of different roles represented* in the child's support system, including parents, siblings, peers, relatives, teachers, and community members. Most studies of children's networks now include people in all or most of these various roles and have reported that people in different roles provide different kinds of support. People in various roles can also provide exposure to different modes of interpersonal interaction and to different kinds of activities and skills the child may need for developing competence. *The number of different people in each role* in the child's network may be a useful indicator of the child's breadth of exposure to different types of people. This dimension can indicate the presence of a concentration of people in one or a few roles and a lack of exposure to people in other roles. The *frequency and extent of contact* the child has with network members can indicate whether the child is learning intensive or superficial modes of relating to people, and whether the child's exposure to people in various roles is adequate for learning what the people have to offer. The *longevity* of the child's relationships can indicate whether the child has the opportunity to experience changes in relationships over time. It can indicate whether the emphasis is on meeting new people and maintaining short-term relationships or on learning to weather changes in long-term relationships. Ther *interconnectedness* of the child's support system members can indicate whether there is a high degree of social control and consistency of demands or greater opportunity for individual development (Bott, 1957).

Among the content dimensions potentially relevant to understanding the development of context-appropriate competence are four major types of social support experienced by American adults and children (see Berndt, this volume). *Esteem support* is defined as statements or actions that convince people of their own worth or value. *Informational support* is defined as advice or guidance helpful in coping with problems. *Instrumental support* is sharing, helping, and other forms of prosocial behavior, and *companionship support* involves a sense of belonging through shared activities. Each of these types of support can be said to provide the recipient with different experiences that could contribute to the development of different kinds of competence, not only in learning how to provide the same kind of support to others, but also in accomplishing tasks (informational and instrumental support) and in defining one's place in the social system (esteem and companionship support).

According to the ecological model proposed here, the relative importance of each of these dimensions, and possibly others specific to a given culture or type of culture, will vary from one culture to another in accordance with the nature of competence as defined within the culture as well as with the needs and abilities of children at various developmental stages. In order to begin to understand how this variation may occur it is helpful to consider ways of conceptualizing differences among cultures.

Social Competence and Social Support in Contrasting Cultures: Some Hypotheses

For the purposes of understanding the role of social support in the lives of people, one useful way of distinguishing among types of cultures is to look at societal concepts of the individual in relation to the group, or the degree to which processes of individuation and separation are emphasized, in contrast to processes of integration among individuals in society. Shweder and Bourne (1984) contrast cultures in which the individual is abstracted from the social role and is of worth simply because he or she is an individual with cultures in which the individual is not differentiated from his or her social role and receives no recognition independent of social context. These two types of cultures may also be referred to as individualistic and collectivistic, respectively. In more concrete terms, Weisner (1982) contrasts the values of individuation and separation salient in western societies with the values of being cared for and caring for others, which are prominent in many non-western societies. Although this dichotomy does not adequately capture the full diversity of human societies, it does provide a useful starting point for understanding differences in cultural definitions of appropriate competence and the role of ecological factors in influencing how children develop context-appropriate competence.

In a recent study of social networks and social competence in early adolescents in the United States, Cauce (1986) used a definition of social competence that included school competence as a measure of children's ability to meet societal expectations; the ability to interact effectively with peers; and self-esteem, or a sense of self-competence. These dimensions are insightfully chosen and appropriate for early adolescents in the individualistic United States, reflecting skills that will be necessary for competent functioning in adult roles in our society. They would not, however, constitute adequate functional skills for children in a collectivistically oriented culture. The important aspects of competence in such societies would seem likely to include the ability to perform tasks that contribute to the welfare of the community; the ability to interact effectively with people of all ages; a sensitivity to the needs of others; and the ability to subordinate one's own needs to those of the community.

Referring to the broad definition of social support given earlier, it could be hypothesized that, in societies emphasizing individuation, social support systems adaptive for developing appropriate competence would be characterized by having a large number of roles represented, a low level of interconnectedness among network members, and a percentage of relationships that are relatively short-term and limited in scope. In societies that stress integration with the group and a dominant ethic of caring and being cared for, support systems characterized by a relatively small number of roles represented among network members and by frequent, extensive, and long-term relationships would be most likely to facilitate the development of competence in maintaining integration with the group. Esteem support would be less important, while instrumental support and companionship support would be more important in such societies than in western individualistic ones.

Levels of the Ecological Context

The idea that children's social support systems are organized in ways that reflect influences from various aspects of their ecological context is based on Bronfenbrenner's ecological model for human development. In this model the environment is conceptualized in terms of four nested or hierarchical structures ranging from the immediate settings in which children are found (microsystems) through the ideological or cultural blueprints for society and its institutions (macrosystems) (Bronfenbrenner, 1977, 1979, 1986). Intermediate levels include linkages among the immediate settings containing the child (mesosystems) and settings in which the child does not participate directly but which are arenas in which events and decisions take place that impinge indirectly on the child's life (exosystems). This hierarchical model offers a way of understanding the processes by which environmental factors influence behavior by tracing them through the ecological levels from abstract and overarching values to concrete and immediate settings. Influences at each level are exerted on the developing person through structures in the intermediate levels.

The immediate settings in which children are universally found include families, schools, and neighborhoods or communities. Each of these settings has a characteristic structure, composition, and patterns of human interaction. Each of these features may vary widely, depending on the characteristics of the individuals within them, on the beliefs and assumptions of the culture, and on the social institutions that structure the settings. It is at this level that the child experiences social support. The fit between a child's experiences within these settings and the demands of the child's place in his or her ecological context determines the quality of social support. When the fit is close, social support contributes to the development of context-appropriate competence. When it is not, the model predicts, children run the risk of not being supported in the development of the abilities and attitudes they need to function competently in settings within their own ecological context.

At the level of links among the child's immediate settings, the model predicts that strong links providing consistency among settings will, in general, strengthen the child's experience of support. In circumstances where social change is especially salient and rapid, there may be some advantage to discrepancies among such settings as home and school, for example. This may be true if school, as an agent of change, provides experiences that will facilitate the development of adaptability by promoting a process of working through discrepancies to new solutions.

The role of exosystems in supporting the development of effective social support systems is to provide the kind of structures that will enable families, schools, peer groups, and neighborhoods to function in ways that will maximize the fit between the child's developing competence and the demands of the ecological context. The model predicts that, when parents' workplaces and social decision-making bodies set policies that are sensitive to the needs of children, they will be instrumental in promoting competence. When they do not, they can make it difficult for children to acquire appropriate competence.

The role of macrosystems in influencing the development of children's competence is to provide the "cultural blueprints" that define the social, political, and economic patterns of a society. These ideological underpinnings determine the nature of social institutions and the ways people will interact with each other in terms of such practical matters as distribution of resources, gender and ethnic relations, and the value of the individual in relation to the community. Cultural beliefs, which have evolved over time in accordance with geographical, historical, and economic circumstances, define what roles, activities, and skills will set the standard for competence in a particular ecological context.

It should be noted that Bronfenbrenner's four-level model was developed to describe complex western societies. In small-scale societies, however, in which all of the members of a cultural group know one another and interact on a face-to-face basis, the relationship between macrosystem and microsystem is usually much more direct, with few intermediate bodies such as planning boards, parental workplaces, and so on in which children do not participate directly. In addition, microsystems such as family and community may blend together in these societies until it is difficult to say where one ends and another begins. In such societies the concepts of mesosystems and exosystems may be less useful than in larger-scale societies.

An ecological perspective is in no sense antithetical to a developmental perspective. Development is viewed from an ecological perspective as a product of the reciprocal interaction of the individual and the environment over time (Bronfenbrenner, 1977, 1979). It is fully recognized that children's own characteristics influence the nature of the social support they experience, and that this influence is likely to increase as children grow older and become more active "niche builders" (Scarr & McCartney, 1983). It is also recognized that personal characteristics may be determined both by genes and by environmental influences, such as child-rearing practices, experienced at an earlier point in time. Because people at different developmental levels need and have the capacities to form and maintain different types of social support networks, different ecological factors may be associated with the kinds of social support networks that meet the developmental needs of children at different developmental levels.

Summary

An ecological model for understanding the role of social support systems in the development of context-appropriate competence in children has been proposed here. The model states that cultural and ideological beliefs, which have evolved over time in response to geographical and historical circumstances, shape the economic, social, and political roles of a particular ecological context and thereby determine what skills and abilities will define the nature of competence in that context. Policy-making bodies and other arenas in which decisions are made that affect children shape the families, schools, and communities (and the relationships among them) in which children experience social support. The adequacy of the social support for providing children with the experiences they need to develop context-appropriate competence depends on the congruence between the demands of the context and the characteristics of the social support the child receives within the settings of family, school, and community. Figure 2.1 provides an illustration of the model.

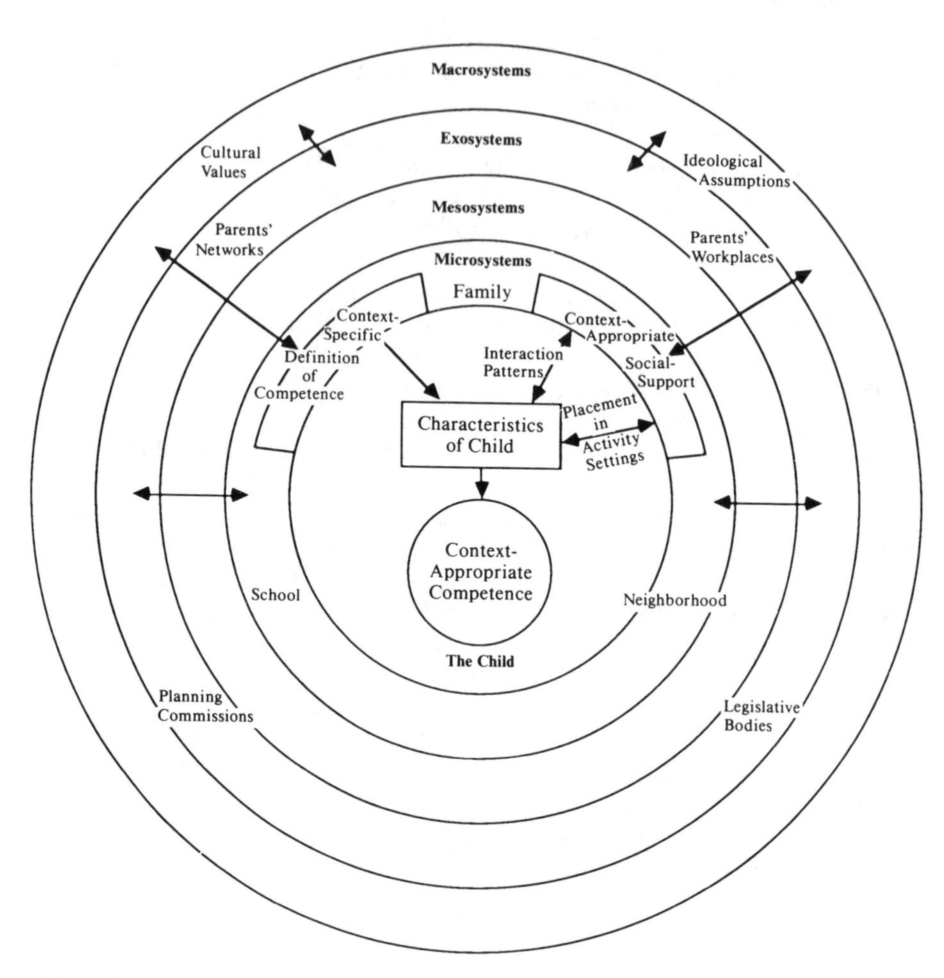

Figure 2.1. An ecological model for the development of context-appropriate competence in children through social support.

ENVIRONMENTAL INFLUENCES ON CHILDREN'S SOCIAL SUPPORT: A REVIEW OF THE LITERATURE

Elsewhere in this volume, other writers have presented data supporting the idea that social support enhances children's ability to cope with stress and make successful adaptations to new situations. In doing so they have addressed aspects of the link between social support and competence. In this section of the present chapter a review is presented of research on ecological factors that have been found to influence the nature of children's social support systems. The review primarily addresses the link between ecological context and social support, although links to the development of competence are made where possible. Although most of the studies cited were done in the

United States, studies from nonwestern societies are included wherever possible. Bronfenbrenner's four ecological levels provide the framework for organizing the review.

Microsystem Influences

A microsystem may be defined as an actual setting in which the individual experiences and creates day-to-day reality (Garbarino, 1982). Examples of children's microsystems that are universal (or nearly so) include the family, the school, and the neighborhood or community. Each of these settings is a potential source of supportive relationships, and the child's support system draws from each. The structure of the settings and the patterns of social interaction within them influence the nature of the child's experience of social support.

Although they are rarely referred to as such, microsystem influences on children's social support systems have been studied more than influences at any other ecological level. They are the most accessible, often among the easiest to operationalize, and also the most immediate and direct in their influence on the child. Microsystem variables can include structural factors, such as family size or neighborhood density. They may also include factors that are concerned with the dynamics of the system or with relationships among elements in the system, such as patterns of parent–child interaction, changes within the system such as divorce or the birth of a child, or transitions between systems, such as moving to a new school or neighborhood.

Families

Among American families several characteristics of family structure have been found to influence the form and content of children's social support networks. Family size affects networks, and the nature of the influence varies with the age of the child. Preschool children in large families have been found to have more siblings in their networks but no more peers or adults than children from smaller families (Zelkowitz & Jacobs, 1985). Among children 5 to 7 years old, those from larger families reportedly come into contact with fewer people outside the nuclear family than do children from small families. As children grow older, however, this situation changes. Bryant (1985) reported that school-age children from large families (three or more children) had more extensive contact with peers and more intimate contact with their grandparents than children from small families, who had more intimate contact with the parent generation. It appears that in households with many children parents must spread themselves more thinly among the children, and the siblings, in turn, may come to rely on each other and on peers more than on adults. In western societies, where adults other than parents are relatively inaccessible to children and where many of the primary activities of adults are not accessible to children, being a member of a large family might result in low levels of at least some kinds of social support. In nonwestern societies, in which many adults other than parents are available to children, and adult roles and activities are learned early, being one of many siblings in a large family would seem less likely to constitute a risk for social support.

A family structural factor with important implications for children's social support systems is the number of parents in the home. Following their parents' divorce, school-age boys in the United States have been found to have peer interaction problems and disrupted relationships with both parents for up to 2 years (Hetherington, Cox, & Cox, 1978). Remarriage of the noncustodial parent often results in decreased contact between the children and that parent (Hetherington et al., 1978; Warshak & Santrock, 1983), and contact between the child and the noncustodial grandparents is often decreased or lost (Ahrons & Bowman, 1981). Social support has been found to have a beneficial effect on the mental health of children of divorce (Wolchik, Ruehlman, Braver, & Sandler, 1985). It seems likely that the effects of divorce on children's support systems would be mitigated in ecological circumstances such as those typical of many small-scale societies in which children have close relationships with several adult relatives besides their parents, and in which family members remain within the same community after divorce.

Of course, even when patterns of family interaction do not lead to divorce they have a major role to play in the nature of social support experienced by children. The relationship between parents affects the relationship between each parent and the child (Belsky, 1979). A high level of conflict between the parents can be detrimental to the interaction between a child and his or her mother, who is, in many families, the child's most frequent confidant (Belle & Longfellow, 1984).

Baumrind's research (1979) on parenting styles suggests that, among U.S. parents, those who respect their children's point of view and who have and enforce clear standards for their children have children who are more socially competent in peer interactions. The attachment literature also indicates that the quality of relationships with parents is reflected in the quality of later relationships with peers. Children who are securely attached to their mothers during infancy are more well adjusted and popular with peers in preschool than children who were insecurely attached (Lieberman, 1977; Waters, Wippman, & Sroufe, 1979). Parents who are warm, nurturant, and empathic with their children are likely to be providing high levels of esteem support and possibly other types of support. They are also likely to be providing models for social relationships that may, in turn, increase the likelihood that their children will develop more adaptive support networks of their own.

Research done in the United States has emphasized the importance of parent–child relationships in the development of competence in children. Connolly and Bruner (1974) concluded, on the basis of their studies of competence, that the origins of human competence lie in intrafamilial relationships and parent–child interaction, and that general skills, both cognitive and emotional, depend on a "hidden curriculum in the home" (p. 5). It has generally been concluded that the middle-class American pattern of frequent close and democratic interaction is most conducive to producing socially competent people. However, observations from small, homogeneous, nonindustrialized societies reported by the Whitings (B. Whiting & J. Whiting, 1975; J. Whiting & B. Whiting, 1973) suggest that this pattern is not the one favored by parents in those ecological contexts for producing competent people. After spending an indulged infancy and toddlerhood in such societies children have relatively little interaction with their parents or other adults, and the interaction that does occur rarely involves negotiation of parental demands. Parents and other adults make relatively heavy demands on children in comparison with middle-class American parents, and assert power if they encounter resistance. This approach is effective in rearing children who grow up competent to take on adult roles in their own societies.

The American middle-class pattern of child rearing, with its emphasis on cooperative parent–child interaction, democratic decision making, and mutual affection, is well adapted to fostering self-regulation in children (Maccoby & Martin, 1983). The pattern is also well suited to encouraging self-differentiation and a sense of self-worth as an individual apart from one's social position. Of the types of social support described in the previous section of this chapter, it would seem that high levels of esteem support, as well as practice in making decisions, characterize the warm, democratic approach to parenting, encouraging in children a sense of their own power and importance to a much greater degree than in the more authoritarian pattern. In the child-rearing pattern that characterizes the Whitings' small, homogeneous, nonindustrialized societies children are likely to experience relatively low levels of esteem support, and relatively high levels of instrumental and companionship support, especially through relationships with siblings and other children. This pattern is more adaptive for the development of a sense of integration with the group. Contrasting patterns of parent–child relations, then, may result in different types of support provided to children, which in turn foster different kinds of social competencies, each suited to a particular kind of ecological niche.

Another aspect of the family setting that may influence the development of context-appropriate competence is the nature of support provided by siblings. Weisner (1984) has described cultural variations in sibling relationships. The number of siblings available to children, the spacing of the siblings, and the patterns of interaction that emerge as a function of the roles played by siblings all may have implications for the development of children's social support systems. Families in which siblings play a major role in caregiving are likely to foster in their children a sense of interdependence. Weisner suggests that particular interaction patterns among siblings, such as indulgence of younger children, may have implications for the kinds of social relationships children will be able to form with others outside their families. Such patterns provide direct experience in caring and being cared for, essential competencies in societies in which the person is valued primarily for his or her social role in relation to other members of the group.

Schools

Schools are the microsystems in which children spend most of their time when not at home, and are an important source of children's friendships. Yet we know little about the ways in which characteristics of these settings influence the development of children's social support networks. Cochran and Riley (1985) point out that such factors as nearness to the school and the ethnic mix of children in the school influence the degree to which school will be a source of supportive relationships, with children tending to develop friendships among those schoolmates who live near them and are of the same race. Hirsch and Rapkin (1987) found that peer social support increased during the transition to junior high school only for Black adolescents of high academic competence. The authors suggest that "the greater salience of academics in junior high may provide a valued social identity on which to elaborate their social network, particularly with new white classmates" (p. 1242). This interpretation suggests the hypothesis that schools emphasizing different values may foster different types of relationships among children. A study of contrasting preschools operated by Polynesian and European ethnic groups in New Zealand adds further weight to this hypothesis. Graves (1974) reported that Polynesians emphasized group interaction with little selectivity, whereas the Europeans placed a high value on privacy and independence. The two styles were evident in interactions between teachers and students in the preschools and were reflected in the peer interaction patterns of elementary-school-age children. Polynesian girls were found to be more cooperative than European girls, who showed higher levels of independence.

Barker and Gump's (1964) classic study of school size also suggests that characteristics of schools may influence children's social relationships, and in turn, different types of competence. Small schools tend to offer better opportunities for students to participate directly in school activities, to develop leadership skills, and to experience a sense of belonging. Larger schools, on the other hand, may provide more of a challenge to work out one's own style of forming and maintaining relationships. These two patterns seem well suited to the development of integration and individuation, respectively.

Neighborhoods

The neighborhood is another microsystem in which children spend a great deal of their time. Bryant (1985) describes the neighborhood as a primary social context for the development of specialized and differentiated relationships. Neighborhoods in western societies are potentially the source of both casual and intimate friendships with agemates, and of relationships with adults in roles ranging from parents of the child's friends to shopkeepers, librarians, and church workers. The same is true of neighborhoods in nonwestern societies, although in small-scale societies the neighborhood may actually be equivalent to the entire community. Many of the same characteristics of neighborhoods in western cities that influence children's development in those contexts are likely to influence children's development in small villages, although the nature of the influence would be mediated by cultural beliefs about interaction patterns and by the kinds of activities that take place in the settings.

Some of the characteristics of neighborhoods that have been found to be associated with larger networks for children in the United States are population density, including child density (van Vliet, 1981); accessibility of commercial and social services (Tietjen, 1982); and safety (Cochran & Riley, 1985). Bryant (1985) has also measured such neighborhood characteristics as the degree to which the child has access to places to get off by oneself, structured and unstructured activities provided by formally sponsored organizations, and informal, unsponsored meeting places. Defining these variables as sources of support, Bryant reported that they interacted with personal and family characteristics to predict several aspects of social–emotional development. The availability of informal meeting places was associated with greater acceptance of peers and decreased individualism for children from small families, although this variable predicted the opposite for children from large families. Availability of informal meeting places also predicted more competitive attitudes for 7-year-old boys but less competitive attitudes for 10-year-old boys and for girls of both ages. Involvement with formally sponsored organizations was associated with increased individualism for children in small families and decreased individualism for children in large families.

Bryant's work demonstrates that characteristics of neighborhoods can have an effect on factors that may be associated with competence by providing particular settings in which children can interact with others in various formal and informal activities. These findings support B. Whiting's proposition that the socialization of competence takes place in the context of participation in activity settings. They also suggest that certain kinds of relationships develop within these settings through which children learn skills and attitudes. A useful direction for research would be to explore the nature of these relationships in terms of social support variables, in order to clarify our understanding of the role of social support in the socialization of competence.

Summary

Characteristics of families, schools, and neighborhoods have been found to influence the nature of children's relationships as well as some aspects of competence. By analyzing the relationships and activities that take place in these settings in terms of social support variables we can gain insight into the processes by which children's experiences contribute to the development of particular types of competence.

Mesosystem Influences

Bronfenbrenner defines mesosystems as links between contexts (or microsystems). Examples of mesosystems include the relationship between a child's home and school, between home and day care, or home and neighborhood. In general, mesosystems serve to strengthen and enrich the influence of microsystems on the child's development. The stronger and more diverse the links between the microsystems, the more powerful the influence of the microsystems (Garbarino, 1982).

There are few studies in the child development literature in general that have examined mesosystem variables, and the topic of children's social support systems is no exception. Cochran and Riley's (1985) study provides the only findings to report at this ecological level. These researchers found that children whose mothers had higher levels of education were more likely to include their teacher as a member of their social network than were children of less well educated mothers. Cochran and Riley suggest that this may be because it is easier for well-educated mothers to form relationships with teachers than it is for poorly educated mothers. This link between home and school strengthens the child's sense of the teacher as a significant person with whom he or she has a personal relationship, and may also strengthen the child's sense of the mother as a person competent to function in settings beyond the home.

Other possible mesosystem effects not yet studied include the influence of the relationship between divorced parents in binuclear families on the child's support networks, relationships between the child's parents and grandparents and other relatives with whom the child spends time, relationships between home and community, and transitions between microsystems such as those involved in geographical moves. In studying mesosystems in rapidly changing small-scale, nonindustrialized societies the hypothesis that some degree of discrepancy between home and school promotes adaptability as a form of context-specific competence could easily be tested, and findings could have practical significance for children in those societies.

Mesosystem considerations are a potentially fruitful source of understanding about the role of ecological factors in children's social support systems. Knowing more about the kinds of links among those microsystems that are most effective in supporting the development of children's social support systems for people in various kinds of ecological contexts and at various ages could greatly improve our understanding of how context-appropriate competence develops and of how to foster more effective support systems for children.

Exosystem Influences

An exosystem is a setting in which the child does not participate but which has indirect effects on the child through the meso- or microsystems

(Bronfenbrenner, 1977, 1979; Garbarino, 1982). In the United States the exosystems most likely to influence children's social support systems include parents' workplaces, parents' own social support systems, and such bodies as school boards, planning commissions, and legislative bodies. Each of these may have profound indirect effects on children's relationships with their parents, relatives, friends, and neighbors. In the small-scale, nonindustrialized societies of the world exosystems may include legislative bodies and development agencies.

Parents' employment patterns have been found to affect their availability to their children in various ways in western industrialized societies. Evidence from two studies suggests that the more hours per week mothers are employed outside the home, the smaller their children's networks tend to be (Tietjen, 1985; Zelkowitz & Jacobs, 1985). Fathers' working hours, in contrast, were reported by Zelkowitz and Jacobs to be positively associated with their children having larger networks including more relatives. Perhaps when fathers are less available to assist in child care, mothers rely on the involvement of relatives. It is unclear whether mothers' reduced availability to their children results in reduced opportunities for the children to become involved in activities with other children or adults, or whether reduced maternal availability somehow affects the social skills of their children.

Several studies suggest that mothers' feelings about their work may mediate the effects of their absence from the home and affect the nature of the social support children receive from their parents. Employed mothers who are satisfied with their jobs are more effective as parents than those who are unhappy with their jobs (Gold & Andres, 1978; Hoffman, 1974). Unpleasant or demanding work can adversely affect parents' ability to provide their children with the nurturance they need (Piotrkowski, 1979). Another way in which employers affect children's support systems is that they are frequently the source of decisions that necessitate high rates of geographic mobility among families with children. Frequent moves reduce the possibility for maintaining enduring relationships with people outside the family.

Not only do fathers' and mothers' employment patterns have their own direct effects on children's networks, but they may have indirect effects as well. An Australian study (Cotterell, 1986) reported that mothers whose husbands were unavailable because of shift work or frequent long absences associated with work had lower mean scores on measures of play and cognitive stimulation of their children. The wives of these absentee husbands had smaller social support networks of their own and felt less integrated into their communities.

Parents' own networks may be considered to be exosystems that can help parents to deal with the stressors that may interfere with their parenting roles, or provide them with modeling or sanctions for parenting behavior (Cochran & Brassard, 1979). There is of course a large body of literature on the direct and indirect, or stress-buffering, effects of social support for adults. A few studies (Colletta, 1979; Cotterell, 1986; Crnic, Greenberg, Ragozin, Robinson, & Basham, 1983; Crockenberg, 1981) have demonstrated that parents' social support also has indirect effects on children, through the parent–child relationship. Parents with more supportive networks of their own are more responsive and supportive in their relationships with their children. Parents' social support networks may, as Cochran and Brassard (1979) suggest, provide parents with modeling or sanctions for the parenting role as well as buffering stress. Research on Swedish mothers and their children suggests that mothers' network involvement may influence their children's networks by the processes of modeling, teaching, sanctioning, providing opportunities, and providing a secure base (Tietjen, 1985). As Cochran and Brassard have pointed out, parents' network members often interact directly with children and in that sense may also function as members of the child's own network. The form and content of parents' relationships with their own network members would seem to be an especially important vehicle for the transmission of context-appropriate social competence in all types of societies.

Planning boards may affect children's social relationships through their decisions about separations between business and residential areas, which may decrease opportunities and incentives for contact between children and adults in a variety of roles (Bronfenbrenner, 1974), or they may increase children's opportunities for safe play with peers in their own neighborhoods. Decisions made by school boards can affect the opportunities and incentives children have for participation in support-promoting activities and for contact with other children of diverse backgrounds. In third world societies the plans of development agencies and corporations can result in mass social disruption and relocation, or they can facilitate a more gradual form of social change if they take into account the needs of the people their policies affect.

In understanding exosystem influences, one of the challenges is to recognize and identify those exosystems that are likely to affect children's social support systems. Although psychology traditionally has not concerned itself with variables at this level, recent studies of social policy and child development have made it clear that the conditions in which children live are often determined by decisions made at the level of exosystems. There is much room for exploration of the ways in which these decisions influence the social support experienced by children.

Macrosystem Influences

Macrosystems are the broad ideological and institutional patterns of a culture (Garbarino, 1982). They are the shared assumptions underlying the institutions of a society or culture. Examples of influences on development at the level of macrosystems could include values concerning the distribution of resources, assumptions about appropriate social roles for people of different genders and ethnic backgrounds, and cultural values concerning the role of the individual in relation to the community. These values and assumptions shape the actions of institutions such as the structure of employment, social service systems, and legislative bodies at the exosystem level.

In the United States, assumptions about the way resources should be distributed are based on the notion that every individual must make his or her own way in the world through hard work, which is rewarded financially. This assumption produces policies and institutions at the exosystem level that result in large variations in socioeconomic status, with many families living in poverty. The social support systems of families in poverty have been found to differ from those of middle-class families. Among low-income single-parent families, Belle (1982) and Stack (1974) both found that only the most economically hard-pressed women became heavily involved in exchange of goods and services because of the burdensome obligations that accompany such involvement when it is at the level of a "strategy for survival" (Stack, 1974). Colletta's (1979) sample of low-income divorced mothers were receiving more support than middle-income mothers, especially from relatives, but were less satisfied with their social support systems. The low-income divorced mothers were more satisfied than their moderate-income counterparts with their children's caregivers, who were often relatives. For women in both income groups, mothers' social support was positively related to more responsive, nurturant child-rearing practices. In the only study to consider the relationship between socioeconomic status and children's social support systems, Cochran and Riley (1985) reported that among White, married mothers there was no relationship between per capita income and the size, composition, or content of children's networks, although per capita income was associated with having larger numbers of nonkin in the networks of both mothers and fathers. The children of high-SES parents are receiving wider exposure to a variety of people in different roles than their lower-SES counterparts, which would be adaptive for making individual choices about career and for dealing with the diversity of our society. The research findings on the effects of SES illustrate how a societal belief about the distribution of resources influences the institutions of a society, such as the job market, employment practices, and the social welfare system. These institutions, in turn, influence family patterns and, through them, the nature of social support available to children.

Societal beliefs about the distribution of resources also affect the degree of access its members have to educational resources. Parents' education has been found to have a bearing on U.S. children's support systems. Zelkowitz and Jacobs (1985) found that preschool children whose parents had more education had larger networks, including family friends, peers, and substitute caregivers. Cochran and Riley (1985) found a similar pattern for elementary-school-age children, and explained the relationship in terms of the social opportunities provided by better-educated parents and the greater social skills of such parents. Other researchers (Bott, 1957; Campbell & Cochran, 1983;

Feiring & Lewis, 1978) have also reported that the networks of parents of higher social status are likely to include more friends (nonkin) than those of lower-SES parents.

Although in our society socioeconomic status is often closely linked to race and to gender, the values our society places on race and on gender and the policies it sets to ensure that these values are put into practice have effects of their own independent of socioeconomic status. The racial and ethnic minority groups in our society can be said to be influenced by both the values and beliefs of the dominant society and the values and beliefs of their own cultures or subcultures. Ogbu (1981) has shown that different forms of competence are appropriate for children growing up Black and White in the United States. The few studies of ethnic minority group children's networks suggest that different social experiences, including different patterns of social support, are vehicles for the development of these competencies.

Cochran and Riley (1985) reported that the networks of Black children contained far more Whites than the networks of White children contained Blacks, and a similar imbalance has been reported in the network patterns of Black and White parents (Cross, 1982). This may reflect disproportionate numbers of Blacks and Whites in many settings as well as in the population in general, or it may reflect differing perceptions of the importance of people of an ethnic background different from one's own. Cochran and Riley (1985) also found that the networks of Black children of single mothers contained more kin than did the networks of White children of single mothers. This finding more clearly reflects subcultural value differences. The parenting efforts of Black mothers are often supported by kin regardless of the mother's marital status (Stack, 1974), whereas this is less often the case among White families. In a study of the support systems of Black, White, and Hispanic adolescents, Cauce (1982) found that Blacks rated family members as significantly more helpful than did either Whites or Hispanics, and perceived a greater degree of support available to them than did Whites or Hispanics.

Western societies, particularly the United States, have come to take a great deal of pride in our emphasis on individualism as a philosophy and a way of life (Bellah, Madsen, Sullivan, Swidler, & Tipton, 1985; Hareven, 1976). In its most extreme form individualism would suggest that parents should raise their children to have a strong sense of their own power to affect the course of their lives and to improve their own conditions, and to reject passivity, dependence on others, and traditional sources of authority and support such as the church and the family. This extreme form of individualism is tempered to some extent in our society by other values, but there is no doubt that it has strongly influenced the ideas that people have about the way they should live their lives, and hence the way their lives are structured. One example of the influence of individualism is the American emphasis on the right to privacy. Garbarino and Stocking (1980) make a strong case that when families' right to privacy is too rigidly upheld, family stress or pathology can be allowed to develop to the point where child abuse and neglect occur. There are, of course, many societies in the world in which the value of the community takes precedence over the value of the individual, and where social ties are more important, even more acceptable as justifications for behavior, than individual choice and achievement.

Hareven (1976) has argued that the shift away from a collectivist view toward one of individualism and sentiment that has characterized the U.S. family's response to modernization has resulted in changes in relationships among family members and in relationships with people outside the family. She maintains that the removal of the economic function of the family has resulted in an erosion of the assumption that family members will be engaged in mutual obligations and reciprocal relationships with each other. At the same time, the removal of the family's economic function has produced an exaggerated emphasis on emotional nurturance, intimacy, and privacy as the major justification for family relations, eroding the resilience of the family and its ability to handle crises. Viewed in terms of differences in social support, Hareven's analysis suggests that in the shift from collectivism to individualism the prevalent mode of social support among family members has changed from instrumental and companionship support to esteem and informational support. This change recalls the hypothesized differences in social support between collectivistic and individualistic societies discussed at the beginning of this chapter.

NICHES AND SUPPORT SYSTEMS: ILLUSTRATIONS FROM SWEDEN AND PAPUA NEW GUINEA

With the impact of context at each of these ecological levels in mind we can return to the very disparate ecological niches occupied by Erica in Sweden and Iris in Papua New Guinea for an illustration of the relationship between characteristics of ecological niches and the social support systems of children who live in them. The observations and data presented in this section were collected as part of research projects I carried out during a year of field work in Sweden in 1976–1977 and a year of field work in Papua New Guinea in 1981–1983.

The Ecology of Children's Social Support Systems in Sweden

Among the macrosystem values of Swedish society the value of individualism is strong, although less so than in many other western industrialized societies. Despite large-scale social welfare programs, in interviewing Swedish families about their social support systems I often heard the proud statement, "We manage by ourselves," although this was always an exaggeration.

Success is achieved by individual effort rather than by family connections, social role, or other ascribed characteristics. At the same time, Swedes are egalitarian in outlook and highly value a sense of belonging for all members of their society. A closely related value is that economic resources should be distributed more or less equitably. Although Sweden has traditionally been a homogeneous society there is a strong commitment to ethnic and racial equality that is being tested as immigrant families from Finland, Turkey, Yugoslavia, and other countries settle in Sweden to better their economic situation. Another strong value underlying Swedish society is the high value placed on children and on the relationship between children and their parents.

All of these values are reflected in the arrangements by which Swedes live and work, which constitute exosystems, mesosystems, and microsystems in the lives of children. Sweden has a particularly well developed level of exosystems, through which societal values are expressed clearly. Egalitarian values are reflected in economic policy and planning, which produce a much narrower range of income levels than in the United States, relieving families from the burden of economic stress. Egalitarian values are also expressed in policy requiring that immigrant families are provided with many services in their own language. The value placed on families and children is manifested in a comprehensive family policy and extensive services to families and children including high-quality day care. Exosystems such as parents' workplaces reflect this value by offering maternity and paternity leaves that are generous by U.S. standards, enhancing the family microsystem by increasing the amount of time that parents are available to their children at a particularly important phase of the development of both the child and the family.

The high level of centralized policy-making and planning and the homogeneity of Swedish society facilitate strong links between such microsystems as school and day care, and home and school, and home and day care, resulting in the relatively consistent transmission of values to children in these settings. The provision of immigrant children with specialized services in their own languages within school and day-care settings is a way of strengthening links between home and the public agencies of the Swedish society for children whose sense of belonging is at risk.

Swedish families tend to be small. Swedish children tend to have few if any siblings and many, especially those in urban areas, have infrequent contact with relatives. The main functions of the Swedish nuclear family are to support the upbringing of children and to provide for the emotional needs of family members. Swedish families fit, in many ways, the description by Hareven (1976), discussed in the previous section, for American families, and child-rearing practices are generally warm and democratic. These family patterns are well suited for preparing children for life in a society in which they will probably have few close and enduring social ties, but many casual, relatively short-lived friendships and acquaintanceships.

Swedish suburban neighborhoods and schools also fit this pattern to some extent, although planners have tried to limit the scale of planned suburbs in order to minimize residents' feelings of anomie and to promote a sense of belonging. The planned suburban communities provide residents with access to localized social, medical, and commercial services and gathering places, and they incorporate many features that enhance the safety of children's play. Elementary schools are also neighborhood based, although they tend to be as large as most American suburban schools.

Given the ecological niche of the urban Swedish school-age child, an adaptive social support system for the development of context-appropriate competence would be one that would enable her to develop the attitudes and skills needed for meeting and getting along with people in a wide variety of roles, with whom she will have relatively weak ties based on personal preference and similarity. There would be little interconnectedness among her network members, to allow her to develop her individuality. The types of social support most adaptive to her would be esteem support, to provide her with the self-confidence to make her own way in the world; information or personal problem-solving support, to help her learn to deal with the many interpersonal issues that arise in relationships with diverse individuals; and companionship support, in order to give her a sense of belonging. Instrumental support would seem to be less important for Swedish urban children than other types of support, since relationships are built on similarity of interests rather than on concrete assistance.

The Ecology of Children's Social Support Systems in a Papua New Guinea Society

As citizens of a developing nation and members of a traditional tribal group, the Maisin people of Papua New Guinea can be said to be living within at least two macrosystems, which at times conflict with each other and at other times have produced cultural innovations. The Maisin are one of more than 700 different language or cultural groups within the country of Papua New Guinea, which has been an independent nation only since 1975. The Maisin live in small villages like the one described at the beginning of the chapter and make their living by subsistence gardening, gathering, hunting, and fishing. They are relatively isolated in an area without roads, a harbor, or much economic development.

On the traditional side of Maisin life, cultural beliefs and practices remain strong and cultural values are lived out with little mediation from exosystems or mesosystems. In traditional Maisin society there are few settings in which children do not participate directly. Clan elders meet to make decisions regarding social issues but in general, the roles of exosystems and mesosystems in traditional Maisin society are minimal. Instead, cultural values are enacted directly and concretely.

The orientation of the Maisin is strongly collectivistic, rather than individualistic (Barker, 1985a, 1985b; Tietjen, 1986; Tietjen & Walker, 1985). An overarching Maisin cultural value is *marawa wawe,* which translates as a state of amity among members of the community. *Marawa wawe* is said to exist when the community is in a state of balance, with no outstanding debts or grievances to be resolved. The value of a person is based on his or her connections with other people by birth and marriage. Individual achievement is valued only if it results in a greater contribution to the welfare of the group. Maisin mourning customs demonstrate dramatically that a person's life is important for the relationships the person has established and maintained with others through kinship and marriage (Barker, 1985b). When a married adult dies the surviving spouse is stripped of all possessions and must undergo a long and gradual process of being released from the obligations established by the old marriage before receiving permission to enter into new exchange relationships. On a daily basis, the value of social ties is demonstrated through sharing of labor and exchanges of cooked food.

The Maisin's strong egalitarian ethic is closely related to their collectivistic orientation. The Maisin believe that one must never place oneself or one's needs above others. This value is manifest in a physical sense in a rule that no one may stand on a raised surface such as a veranda or canoe platform when others are around. In a moral sense the ethic is demonstrated in a proscription against making personal gains at the expense of others. Placing oneself or one's needs above others is regarded as antisocial, and may be grounds for the use of sorcery against a person who violates this norm.

Cooperation and helpfulness are highly valued and indeed are necessary for physical and social survival. People who violate this norm by being greedy, selfish, or prideful risk sorcery or social ostracism. Maisin children are taught from an early age to be aware of others' needs and to respond to them. In a study of prosocial reasoning among Maisin children and adults (Tietjen, 1986) I found that the reasons Maisin children and adults give for prosocial behavior are based on a concern with the needs of others, in contrast to the reasons given by mature Americans, which are based on awareness of internal states (e.g., guilt, or living up to one's internal standards) or abstract notions of the functioning of large-scale society (Eisenberg-Berg, 1979). The proximity of houses as well as the fact that most of life is lived out of doors for the Maisin makes it easier to be aware of the needs and actions of others than in our own society.

Another important aspect of the traditional Maisin macrosystem is that it is rooted in kin relationships, which carry with them mutual obligations for support. The kinship system also ensures that nearly every child has several persons whom he or she calls "mother" and "father," and numerous other people are often referred to by kin terms. Kinship relations are an important vehicle for the provision of instrumental and companionship support and for the transmission of the values of caring and being cared for.

Maisin families tend to be large by modern western standards. Large family size decreases parents' availability to any particular child to some extent, but children observe and participate in their parents' work (food production and making of household items) from an early age. Following an indulged infancy, children are cared for largely by older siblings. Older children are expected to look after their younger siblings and the sibling group is to remain loyal and helpful to one another throughout life.

Another traditional microsystem in which Maisin children participate is the village. The village is a physically open place in which it is possible to see and know much about other people's lives and difficult to be alone. As indicated in the vignette about Iris at the beginning of this chapter, residence and clan membership are based on patrilineal descent, and houses of clan families are built within a few feet of each other. The nearby jungle and gardens afford some privacy, but the structure of the village is geared toward maximizing close relations among community members.

Because of the kinship system, the links between home and village are, in most cases, so strong that the distinction between the two is blurred. Only families in which there is social deviance, such as polygyny, experience any degree of social isolation, and even such cases the isolation is only to a mild degree.

The introduction of western influences in the form of a national government, national economy, national education system, and Christian missionaries has placed the Maisin in the position of living within a second, nationally based macrosystem as well as within their own traditional one. The Maisin have been fortunate in that western influences have entered their lives very gradually, beginning with their first contact at the turn of the century. They have adapted to western influences by developing innovative solutions to problems raised by conflicting values, thereby enabling their culture to survive, although in a rather rapidly evolving state. The areas where children encounter western influences most directly are their school and relations between home and school.

Village schools include grades one through six and are taught by Papuan teachers from tribal groups other than those among whom they teach. Students are taught English along with reading, writing, arithmetic, and science (in English). Along with this curriculum they also learn about interpersonal competition and individual achievement. My study of prosocial reasoning showed a significant increase in use of self-interested reasoning between grades one and two, and a decline thereafter, as children became more fully integrated into their own culture and resumed use of other-oriented reasoning (Tietjen, 1986). In previous decades many Maisin have left their villages for employment in towns, but current economic conditions make it unlikely that there will be opportunities for many Maisin youth beyond their villages. This situation affects the school and relations between home and school. Because of the economic uncertainties at the national level, the educational goals of the village school are ambiguous, and it becomes difficult to determine which values and experiences are supportive for children. Schoolteachers claim they are educating children for life in the village, while most parents hope that at least some of their children will be able to get jobs in the towns so that they can send remittances, villagers' primary source of income, home to the village. This, together with the fact that most parents are unable to help their children with schoolwork because of their own limited educational attainment, means that relations between home and school are somewhat weak and sometimes strained. This may dilute the impact of each, resulting in confusion and alienation for the children (Barker, 1986). At present, traditional values prevail, although, as noted, these are very much in transition. The introduction of western values through the school may be a vital step toward developing an ability to adapt to changing ecological circumstances.

Given the ecological niche of the Maisin child, it would seem that an adaptive social support system would be one involving strong, multistranded ties based on kinship bonds, and that these bonds would be maintained by high levels of instrumental support and companionship. Personal problem-solving support would be less important for Maisin children than for Swedes because of the relative homogeneity and clarity of expectations for Maisin children's behavior. Esteem support would be nonadaptive for Maisin children because of the cultural collectivistic orientation.

Children's Networks in Sweden and Papua New Guinea

Although I did not set out to test directly the hypotheses just presented, my data on the social networks of Swedish and Maisin children provide some support for them. The differing bases of social support are evident in data I collected on the social networks of 72 Swedish second- and third-grade children (Tietjen, 1982) and on the social networks of 25 Maisin second- and fourth-grade children. Maisin children named, on average, 3.2 children they usually play with at school, and 4.38 children they usually play with at home, for a total (subtracting friends named in both settings) of 5.87 children they consider themselves close to. Siblings were excluded from this count. These figures are comparable to those reported for Swedish children, who reported an average of 3.67 friends at school, 2.85 friends at home, and a total of 5.54 friends.

Maisin children's networks were more likely than Swedish children's networks to contain children of the opposite sex and children of different ages. Maisin children named, on average, 1.64 friends of the opposite sex, whereas Swedish children named only 0.25. All Maisin children named friends older and younger than themselves, whereas among Swedish children, 78% said that some of their friends were a year or more older, and 64% said they had some friends who were younger than themselves. These differences reflect not only the smaller number of agemates available to a Maisin child than to a Swedish urban child, but also the greater Maisin emphasis on kinship relations and clan solidarity.

Another reflection of the importance of kinship ties for Maisin children is evident in the striking difference between Swedish and Maisin children in the number of relatives children knew. Swedish children named, on average, 1.93 adult relatives and 0.81 child relatives. Maisin children named, on average, 10.93 adult relatives and 10.80 child relatives.

The importance of social connections for the Maisin is also reflected in children's answers to the questions of whether they played more often alone or with others, and whether they played more often with one friend at a time or with several. Among the Maisin, 24 of the 25 children interviewed said they played more often with others than alone, whereas 77% of the Swedish children gave this response. Twenty-three of the 25 Maisin children said they played more often with several friends at once than with one at a time, in contrast to the 61% of Swedish children who said they played more often with one friend at a time than with several at once. The collectivistic orientation of the Maisin and the more individualistic orientation of the Swedes are already evident in the social networks and interaction patterns of children.

Ecological Risk in Sweden and Papua New Guinea

In every society there are children at risk for receiving inadequate social support. In Sweden, as in other western countries, some of the ecological factors that contribute most to this risk are divorce, geographic mobility, and unavailability of parents due to circumstances of their employment. In the sample of Swedish children I interviewed, children of single mothers had more limited support systems than children from two-parent families. They had fewer friends in their neighborhood, they were less likely to belong to activity groups such as sports teams or scouts, and they were more likely to report that their evenings and weekends were spent with friends or alone, rather than with family members (Tietjen, 1982). These children were at risk for receiving less of all types of social support from both friends and family.

Among Maisin children the chances of social isolation are much lower than in western urban industrial niches, but the situation is not entirely free from risks. Those children in the Maisin sample who listed the fewest adult and child relatives, and who said they more often played alone than with others, or with one friend at a time rather than several, were adopted children. Adoption is a common practice throughout the South Pacific (Brady, 1976). Among the Maisin, children are given in adoption most often as part of bride price, if they are born out of wedlock and their mother subsequently marries, or if they are orphaned. Maisin adults claim that adopted children are usually not treated as well as children living with their biological parents. Adopted children are at greater risk than nonadopted children for an inadequate sense of belonging.

Another risk factor for Maisin children is the possibility of rapid and far-reaching social and economic change. The support they are receiving now will prepare them for life in their own villages, but changing social and economic circumstances could alter their ecological niche drastically and they are poorly prepared for life beyond their village. The highly interconnected networks that play so essential a part in maintaining Maisin society are, as Bott (1957) found for her London families, also very effective at maintaining high levels of conformity. The gradual introduction of western values through the school, church, and other sources over a period of 80 years has so far allowed the Maisin to work out their own resolutions to conflicting values in their own ways. More rapid and encompassing change through an intrusive influence such as a commercial logging project, a very real possibility for the Maisin, would likely present a serious challenge to their ability to cope with the consequences. Accustomed to a more or less direct expression of cultural values in behavior, they would have particular difficulty in coping with exosystems. For example, the Maisin were certain that they could simply ask a logging company to leave if they were unhappy with the proceedings after logging of their forests, the source of their livelihood, had begun, despite evidence that other tribal groups had been unable to do so. They were unaware of the structure of such institutions and lacked the experience to build competence in dealing effectively with them. This situation illustrates that children can be said to be at risk for not receiving adequate context-appropriate social support if their ecological context changes too rapidly.

CONCLUSIONS AND IMPLICATIONS

Building on the idea that the components of competence vary with ecological circumstances, I have developed a theoretical model and presented evidence supporting the following points. First, characteristics of children's social support systems vary with ecological circumstances, as well as with characteristics of individuals. Bronfenbrenner's ecological framework serves as a useful way of understanding how environmental factors from the level of cultural values to the level of immediate social and physical settings influence the nature of the social support that children experience. Second, the concept of social support, broadly defined, can be useful for understanding the processes by which children develop the forms of competence that are adaptive for the ecological niche in which they live. Social support can take many different forms depending on the ecological circumstances in which the child and the members of his or her social support system are living. The concept of social support can encompass a variety of processes, which may also vary with ecology, including patterns of interpersonal interaction and placement of children in settings in which they have the opportunity to gain context-appropriate competence through their own trial-and-error experiences. Third, context-appropriate competence develops when there is congruence between the demands of the ecological niche and the nature of the social support a child experiences. In other words, when the types of social support available to the child are well suited to the development of skills adaptive for functioning successfully in a given ecological context, context-appropriate competence will develop. And fourth, when congruence between context and type of support does not exist, vulnerability results.

There is clearly a need for much more research on competence and on social support systems in different ecological contexts. Psychologists have recognized increasingly in recent years that research in other cultures can teach us much about what is humanly possible and about what is and is not universal in human development. These insights are much needed in the study of children's social support systems and of competence. The model presented here suggests that researchers doing ecological studies need to pay attention to ecological issues in at least two ways. They need to develop definitions and measures of both competence and social support that reflect the ecological context in which the research is done. In addition they need to attend to ecological factors at all levels in order to understand the relationships between context and competence, context and support, and competence and support.

The model also suggests that an important research issue is the study of the processes by which social support builds context-appropriate competence. Microanalysis of interactions between children and members of their support systems could be one useful way to approach this issue; analysis of children's behavior in settings that have important socializing influences is another.

The model and supporting data have implications for intervention with children whose support systems are inadequate for developing context-appropriate competence. The importance of attending to environmental factors as well as personal characteristics in both the outcomes and the processes of social support is clear for those devising interventions for children with inadequate social support. Finally, awareness of the influence of environmental factors can be used to guide policy decisions in a wide variety of institutions, including many whose influences on the psychological and social development of children are not normally given enough recognition.

REFERENCES

Aberle, D. F. (1961). Culture and socialization. In F. Hsu (Ed.), *Psychological anthropology.* Evanston, IL: Dorsey.

Ahrons, C., & Bowman, M. E. (1981). Changes in family relations following divorce: Grandmothers' perceptions. *Journal of Divorce, 5,* 49–68.

Barker, J. H. (1985a). Missionaries and mourning: Continuity and change in the death ceremonies of a Melanesian people. In D. L. Whiteman (Ed.), *Missionaries, anthropologists, and cultural change. Studies in third world societies* (No. 25). Williamsburg, VA: College of William and Mary.

Barker, J. H. (1985b). *Maisin Christianity: An ethnography of the contemporary religion of a seaboard Melanesian people.* Unpublished doctoral dissertation, University of British Columbia, Vancouver.

Barker, J. H. (1986). From bachelor house to youth club: A case study of the youth movement in Uiaku and Ganjiga villages, Oro Province. In M. O'Collins (Ed.), *Youth and society: Perspectives from Papua New Guinea.* Political and Social Change Monograph 5. Canberra: Australian National University.

Barker, R. G., & Gump, P. V. (1964). *Big school, small school.* Stanford, CA: Stanford University Press.

Barry, H., Child, I. L., & Bacon, M. K. (1959). Relation of child training to subsistence economy. *American Anthropologist, 61,* 51–63.

Baumrind, D. (1979). Current patterns of parental authority. *Developmental Psychology Monographs, 41,* (1, Pt. 2).

Bellah, R. N., Madsen, R., Sullivan, W., Swidler, A., & Tipton, S. (1985). *Habits of the heart.* New York: Harper & Row.

Belle, D. (Ed.). (1982). *Lives in stress.* Beverly Hills: Sage.

Belle, D., & Longfellow, C. (1984). *Turning to others: Children's use of confidants.* Paper presented at the meetings of the American Psychological Association, Toronto.

Belsky, J. (1979). The interrelation of parental and spousal behavior during infancy in traditional nuclear families: An exploratory analysis. *Journal of Marriage & the Family, 41,* 62–68.

Berry, J. W. (1977). *Human ecology and cognitive style: Comparative studies in cultural and psychological adaptations.* New York: Halsted.

Bott, E. (1957). *Family and social network.* London: Tavistock.

Brady, I. (Ed.). (1976). *Transactions in kinship: Adoption and fosterage in Oceania.* ASAO Monograph No. 4. Honolulu: University of Hawaii Press.

Bronfenbrenner, U. (1974). Developmental research, public policy, and the ecology of childhood. *Child Development, 45,* 1–5.

Bronfenbrenner, U. (1977). Toward an experimental ecology of human development. *American Psychologist, 32,* 513–531.

Bronfenbrenner, U. (1979). *The ecology of human development.* Cambridge, MA: Harvard University Press.

Bronfenbrenner, U. (1986). Ecology of the family as a context for human development: Research perspectives. *Developmental Psychology, 22,* 723–742.

Bryant, B. K. (1985). The neighborhood walk: Sources of support in middle childhood. *Monographs of the Society for Research in Child Development, 50* (Serial No. 210).

Campbell, M., & Cochran, M. (1983, April). *Social ties and parental perceptions: The personal networks of single and married mothers.* Paper presented at the biennial meeting of the society for Research in Child Development, Detroit.

Cauce, A. M. (1982). Social support in high-risk adolescents: Structural components and adaptive impact. *American Journal of Community Psychology, 10,* 417–428.

Cauce, A. M. (1986). Social networks and social competence: Exploring the effects of early adolescent friendships. *American Journal of Community Psychology, 14,* 607–628.

Cochran, M. M., & Brassard, J. (1979). Child development and personal social networks. *Child Development, 50,* 609–616.

Cochran, M. M., & Riley, D. (1985). *Mother reports of children's personal networks: Antecedents, concomitants, and consequences.* Paper presented at the meetings of the Society for Research in Child Development, Toronto.

Cole, M., Gay, J., Glick, J. A., & Sharp, D. W. (1971). *The cultural context of learning and thinking: An exploration in experimental anthropology.* New York: Basic.

Colletta, N.D. (1979). Support systems after divorce: Incidence and impact. *Journal of Marriage & the Family, 41,* 837–846.

Connolly, K. J., & Bruner, J. S. (1974). Competence: Its nature and nurture. In K. J. Connolly & J. S. Bruner (Eds.), *The growth of competence.* London: Academic.

Cotterell, J. L. (1986). Work and community influences on the quality of child rearing. *Child Development, 57,* 362–374.

Crnic, K. A., Greenberg, M. T., Ragozin, A. S., Robinson, N. M., & Basham, R. B. (1983). Effects of stress and social support on mothers and premature and full-term infants. *Child Development, 54,* 209–217.

Crockenberg, S. B. (1981). Infant irritability, mother responsiveness, and social support influences on the security of infant–mother attachment. *Child Development, 52,* 857–865.

Cross, W. E. (1982, June). The ecology of human development of Black and White children: Implications for predicting racial preference patterns. Chapter in a report: *The ecology of urban family life—A summary report to the National Institute of Education.* Cornell University.

Eisenberg-Berg, N. (1979). Development of children's prosocial moral judgment. *Developmental Psychology, 15,* 128–137.

Feiring, C., & Lewis, M. (1978). The child as a member of the family system. *Behavioral Science, 23,* 225–233.

Garbarino, J. (1982). *Children and families in the social environment.* New York: Aldine.

Garbarino, J., & Stocking, S. H. (1980). *Protecting children from abuse and neglect.* San Francisco: Jossey-Bass.

Gold, D., & Andres, D. (1978). Developmental comparisons between ten-year-old children with employed and unemployed mothers. *Child Development, 49,* 75–84.

Graves, N. (1974, March). *Inclusive versus exclusive interaction styles in Polynesian and European classrooms: In search of an alternative to the cultural deficit model of learning.* Auckland, N.Z.: University of Auckland, Research Report No. 5.

Greenfield, P. M. (1966). On culture and conservation. In J. S. Bruner (Eds.), *Studies in cognitive growth.* New York: Wiley.

Hareven, T. (1976). Modernization and family history: Perspectives on social change. *Signs: Journal of Women in Culture and Society, 2,* 190–206.

Hetherington, E. M., Cox, M., & Cox, R. (1978). The aftermath of divorce. In J. H. Stevens, Jr., & M. Matthews (Eds.), *Mother–child, father–child relations.* Washington, DC: National Association for the Education of Young Children.

Hirsch, B. J., & Rapkin, B. D. (1987). The transition to junior high school: A longitudinal study of self-esteem, psychological symptomatology, school life, and social support. *Child Development, 58,* 1235–1243.

Hoffman, L. (1974). Effects of maternal employment on the child: A review of the research. *Developmental Psychology, 10,* 204–228.

Inkeles, A. (1966). Social structure and the socialization of competence. *Harvard Educational Review.*

Inkeles, A. (1968). Society, social structure and child socialization. In J. A. Clausen (Ed.), *Socialization and society.* Boston: Little, Brown.

Lieberman, A. F. (1977). Preschoolers' competence with a peer: Influence of attachment and social competence. *Child Development, 48,* 1277–1287.

Maccoby, E. E., & Martin, J. A. (1983). Socialization in the context of the family: Parent–child interaction. In P. Mussen (Ed.), *Handbook of child psychology.* New York: Wiley.

Ogbu, J. U. (1981). Origins of human competence: A cultural-ecological perspective. *Child Development, 52,* 413–429.

Piotrkowski, C. S. (1979). *Work and the family system: A naturalistic study of working-class and lower middle class families.* New York: Free Press.

Scarr, S., & McCartney, K. (1983). How people make their own environments: A theory of genotype–environment effects. *Child Development, 54,* 424–435.

Shweder, R., & Bourne, E. (1984). Does the concept of the person vary cross-culturally? In R. Shweder & R. LeVine (Eds.), *Culture theory: Essays on mind, self, and emotion.* Cambridge, England: Cambridge University Press.

Stack, C. B. (1974). *All our kin.* New York: Harper & Row.

Tietjen, A. M. (1982). The social networks of preadolescent children in Sweden. *International Journal of Behavioral Development, 5,* 111–130.

Tietjen, A. M. (1985). Relationships between the social networks of Swedish mothers and their children. *International Journal of Behavioral Development, 8,* 195–216.

Tietjen, A. M. (1986). Prosocial reasoning among children and adults in a Papua New Guinea society. *Developmental Psychology, 22,* 861–868.

Tietjen, A. M., & Walker, L.J. (1985). Moral reasoning and leadership among men in a Papua New Guinea society. *Developmental Psychology, 21,* 982–992.

van Vliet, W. C. (1981). The environmental context of children's friendships: An empirical and conceptual examination of the role of child density. In A. E. Osterberg, C. P. Tiernan, & R. A. Findlay (Eds.), *Proceedings from the Twelfth Annual Conference of the Environmental Design Research Association* (pp. 216–224).

Warshak, J., & Santrock, J. (1983). The impact of divorce in father-custody and mother-custody homes: The child's perspective. In L. Kurdek (Ed.), *Children and divorce.* New Directions for Child Development, No. 19. San Francisco: Jossey-Bass.

Waters, E., Wippman, J., & Sroufe, L. A. (1979). Attachment, positive affect, and competence in the peer group: Two studies in construct validation. *Child Development, 50,* 821–829.

Weisner, T. (1982). Sibling interdependence and child caretaking: A cross-cultural view. In M. E. Lamb & B. Sutton-Smith (Eds.), *Sibling relationships: Their nature and significance across the lifespan.* Hillsdale, NJ: Erlbaum.

Weisner, T. (1984). Ecocultural niches of middle childhood: A cross-cultural perspective. In W. A. Collins (Ed.), *Development during middle childhood.* Washington, DC: National Academy Press.

Whiting, B. B. (1980). Culture and social behavior: A model for the development of social behavior. *Ethos, 8,* 95–116.

Whiting, B. B., & Whiting, J. W. M. (1975). *Children of six cultures: A psychocultural analysis.* Cambridge, MA: Harvard University Press.

Whiting, J. W. M., & Whiting, B. B. (1973). Altruistic and egoistic behavior in six cultures. In L. Nader & T. W. Maretzki (Eds.), *Cultural illness and health: Essays in human adaptation.* Washington, DC: American Anthropological Association.

Wolchik, S. A., Ruehlman, L. S., Braver, S. L., & Sandler, I. N. (1985). *Social support of children of divorce: Direct and stress buffering effects.* Paper presented at the meetings of the American Psychological Association, Los Angeles.

Zelkowitz, P., & Jacobs, E. (1985). *The composition of the social networks of preschool-age children.* Paper presented at the meetings of the Society for Research in Child Development, Toronto.

CHAPTER 3

Cultural and Universal Aspects of Social Support for Children: Evidence from the Abaluyia of Kenya

THOMAS S. WEISNER

INTRODUCTION

Understanding social support for children requires a sense of the cultural context of support, and the cultural meaning of behaviors defined as help or support. Consider the following two vignettes, taken from naturalistic observations of children among the Abaluyia, a Bantu-speaking group from western Kenya. In the first, note how offers of support, help, and nurturance are accompanied by teasing, aggression, and responsible work. The mother in this household is away for the day visiting, and the children are responsible for the home:

A 2½-year-old boy, his two older sisters, their infant brother, and a neighbor girl are huddled around a small charcoal fire inside their house. The boy's sister, age 6, covers the boy with a towel because he appears cold. The older sister, age 9, then entertains the boy by talking and giving him objects to hold, while at the same time playing with her 6-year-old sister. The boy laughs with his older sisters, but they begin to play by themselves, ignoring him. The 9-year-old girl then takes a glowing stick from the fire and pretends to burn the boy, and he starts to cry. The two sisters laugh and play together, as the boy continues to cry. The 6-year-old then comforts the boy by putting him on her lap and offering him some food. She carries the

The Carnegie Corporation of New York, the Child Development Research Unit of Kenyatta University College, Nairobi, the Academic Senate research grant program of UCLA, and the Department of Psychiatry and Biobehavorial Sciences of UCLA all provided support for data collection and analysis. Debbie Summers assisted in the preparation of the observations for analysis. Ronald Gallimore, Sandra Kaufman, and participants in the SRCD symposium held at Boston University made helpful comments on the chapter.

boy over to the door and helps dress him to go outside; she talks affectionately to him while doing this. The 9-year-old sister has gone outside, and calls out to the boy to come outside, and he proceeds to run around the two sisters and neighbor girl, laughing. He picks up his infant brother and physically entertains the infant by joggling it up and down and laughing at it. This continues for several minutes. The boy cleans the baby's running nose, and talks to it.

In this second example, the mother is "teaching" aggression, and a teasing style of helpfulness, to her infant; to the participants, this is a common pattern for offering support to children.

Three sisters (a 4-year-old, a 3-year-old, and an infant under a year old and still crawling) are home together in their rural homestead with their mother. The mother wants to nurse the baby, who is several meters away crawling around on the earthen floor. So the mother tells the 3-year-old to come over to her and suck on her breasts in order to get the baby to come over to the mother and nurse. The 3-year-old comes over and nurses; the baby sees this going on—and does indeed start to crawl over to the mother in order to nurse.

(later in the observation) The 3- and 4-year-old sisters enter the house laughing together while the mother is in the house with the baby. The mother jokingly tells the baby to beat the sisters with a stick for teasing her so much. The girls hear this remark, but make no comment.

African observers of, and participants in, these interactions found the mixture of nurturance, help, support, and aggression in these young children to be unremarkable. They did not consider it unusual that the children in the first example were home alone caring for other children, cooking, and tending a fire inside their house, nor did they see in either example anything remarkable in the combination of threats, domestic tasks, and support given to and offered by children. Such behaviors frequently go together during interactions in Abaluyia families.

Social support and assistance for children in Euro-American families, and as defined in Western psychology, differs from the Abaluyia data. Support and assistance are associated with overt empathy and affection for the person assisted, and by gratitude or some kind of acknowledgment on the part of the person assisted. The provision of comfort and warmth for children is an expectable part of offers of help and assistance. Help is usually accompanied by efforts by parents or others to verbally frame the problem with the child, along with offering support: "What is the matter?" "Oh, are you feeling scared?" "I'm sorry. . . ." This negotiation over the nature of the problem and inquiries regarding the internal state and feelings of the person needing support, should include the person being assisted. The mutual questions regarding a problem and support needed for that problem or trouble are themselves a kind of giving and receipt of sensitive and appropriate assistance to others, as well as signalling support to come.

Most assistance and support of Alaluyia children did not have this verbally negotiated and framed, solicitously affectionate character. Rather, social support for these children is more sociocentric, requiring the children to seek and offer assistance in the context of a large, heirarchical network of siblings and adults, who are doing joint tasks. Much more assistance is provided by other children than by mothers and fathers, even when adults are present and available for support. Assistance is often indirect and delayed rather than immediate and focused on the individual child. This paper describes such patterns of support and assistance among Abaluyia children, and the shared management family system which provides the context for support.

CULTURAL AND UNIVERSAL ASPECTS OF SUPPORT

Although this paper focuses on cultural differences in provisions of help and support, there are universally recognized behaviors that signal that help and support are needed, or that they are going on. Here for example is another brief vignette.

A 3-year-old girl trips and falls down on a dirt path outside her homestead and starts to cry. Her older sister comes over and brushes her off and hands her some maize to eat. The 3-year-old stops crying and starts to eat the maize, while the older sister stands next to her.

Both African and American observers agreed that this was an instance of supportive behavior. The immediate circumstances—the child's crying after being hurt—and the subsequent helpful behavior of the sister are both clear. Some ways to comfort young children seem to be universal. The provision of help and support has a recognizable character around the world, particularly regarding children. It includes "affection, physical comforting, . . . assistance in problem solving" (Belle, Burr, & Cooney, in press; Sandler & Barrera, 1984), offering food or other material resources, and protective interventions to prevent aggression or harm. That these similarities exist may be due to a shared human capacity for recognizing signals of distress in others, and for responding to offers of help (cf. Edwards's [1985, p. 320] comments in discussing ethical discourse). Younger, smaller, cute-appearing children elicit similar kinds of protective and nurturant responses (B. Whiting & Edwards, 1988) everywhere.

Shared features in providing support may come not only from biosocial evolution but from common social and functional requirements as well.

Cohen and McKay (1984) cite four support functions likely to be found everywhere in the world: tangible help, positive appraisal, self-esteem enhancement, and a sense of belonging. Lin, Dean, and Ensel (1986) review definitions of social support from sociology, social psychology, and psychiatry and propose a synthetic definition:

> . . . the perceived or actual instrumental and/or expressive provisions supplied by the community, social networks, and confiding partners. (p. 18) . . . social support can be operationally defined as access to and use of strong and homophilous ties. (p.30) [Homophilous ties are those between people similar in nature—in social characteristics, attitudes, and life-styles.]

Other useful distinctions include the idea that provisions of support include actual as well as perceived ("subjective") benefits of interactions with others; that there are at least three levels of supportive relationships (community, network, and intimate); and that emotional, informational, and tangible (material) kinds of support frequently differ in their meaning and effects.

The existence of some cross-cultural similarity regarding the nature of support is not necessarily evidence for noncultural causes of such similarity. Common cultural problems facing people everywhere can produce similarity, just as can biological inheritance, or functional requirements. Shweder and Bourne (1981), for example, presents a list of 10 themes about social existence that they propose as cultural dilemmas that need to be resolved everywhere.

1. The problem of personal boundaries—what's me versus what's not me.
2. The problem of sex identity—what's male versus what's female.
3. The problem of maturity—what's grown-up versus what's childlike.
4. The problem of cosubstantiality—who is of my kind and thus shares food or blood or both with me versus who is not of my kind.
5. The problem of ethnicity—what's our way versus what's not our way.
6. The problem of hierarchy—why people share unequally in the burdens and benefits of life.
7. The problem of nature versus nurture—what's human versus what's animallike.
8. The problem of autonomy—am I independent, dependent, or interdependent?
9. The problem of the state—what I want to do versus what the group wants me to do.
10. The problem of personal protection—how can I avoid the war of all against all?

Parents face the common problem of training children in the culturally given answers to these dilemmas. Offering support to children, and training children to give support to others, crosscuts several of the culturally universal problems on Shweder and Bourne's proposed list. For example, having other children offer support through sharing resources like food or shelter simultaneously provides knowledge to the child regarding cosubstantiality. Decisions regarding which persons to help and which not to help involve cultural rules regarding the problem of hierarchy, the state, and personal protection. Although social support varies in form and substance around the world, common issues regarding how and when to provide support are being resolved by every community.

The form of cultural solutions to these universal questions of development varies, but cultural variation is not unconstrained. All societies have to protect the young and helpless, and both cultural and biological evolution have established some patterns for how this occurs. These patterns include both evolved signalling and response systems such as crying and comforting, as well as common cultural problems such as the meaning and resolution of inequality, and the dominance of some over others.

One implication of this view of universals in social support is that each new culture is not unique, and does not require an entirely new analysis of every aspect of social support in childhood. Behaviors an observer in another culture *thinks* are indicators of social support quite probably will not have to be given an entirely new, local cultural interpretation in every new culture. But this presumption is only an initial hypothesis, which always will require modification. It is the task of the analyst to identify which instances of social support or help or nurturance are more or less cross-culturally recognizable, and what it is about each culture that makes some of these patterns of support appear more or less often, in an unexpected form, or with unexpected associated meanings and feelings.

Cultural Patterns of Support

Understanding both the universal and local meanings of social support for children is a complex task. Data reduction and analysis of field notes and behavior observation protocols among the Abaluyia illustrate the complexity.

The data for studying social support in the present study come from field observations of Abaluyia children's social behavior. These observations were written by trained African students during naturally occurring interactions in and around the children's homes. The raw field observations were in episodic, short-sentence form, focused on a particular target child. (An example is reproduced in Edgerton & Langness, 1974, pp. 39–43.) Each observation lasted 30 minutes, and African student field-workers completed 323 of these visits. Due to the time involved in the transcription of these protocols onto computer, I sampled 30%, or 97, for the present study. This gave a total of 48 1/2 (97 half-hour protocols divided by 2) hours of children's activities.

American researchers and the African students who did the original observations jointly coded each protocol, using a version of the observational scheme developed by John and Beatrice Whiting and colleagues (B. Whiting & J. Whiting, 1975; B. Whiting & Edwards, 1988). This coding scheme judges each interaction between a child and others according to the intentions and goals of the actors and the resources given or received. Social behaviors coded in this system include nurturance, prosocial behavior, commands and other attempts to change others' behavior, aggression, seeking and offering help, sociability, and others. Coding reliability was assessed using a minimum criterion of 70% or higher agreement between coders.

I began by rereading each of the 30-minute observation protocols, and pulling out every event that had already been identified by this coding scheme as involving supportive, nurturant, or helpful behaviors. Other events were added, particularly events in which delayed or deferred help occurred as part of a longer sequence of interactions. This screening produced 574 events that were then used in further qualitative study of social support.

These continuous running records of children's behavior offer a rich sample of events and contexts in everyday life within which social support and help occur for Abaluyia children. They were observed and judged by native speakers of the language who are members of the culture. But they were not collected in such a way as simultaneously to assess the folk meanings of support, inquire about the subjective interpretations of the supportive events during or immediately following their occurrence, or capture in the Luluyia language the discourse, motivations, and meanings of each supportive interaction. However, the method which was used is strongest in the breadth of the data, its careful sampling, the sheer number of instances of support captured, and the joint interpretation of the events by culture members and researchers.

In one sense, every one of these events, social support or not, occurring as they did in the midst of an African horticultural society speaking a Bantu language, has a cultural meaning different from what the same event would mean in North American middle-class families. But every socially supportive event is not equally different or distinctive, and some of these events fit with wider Abaluyia cultural themes more than others.

For instance, some events did not fit with western schemata of what help and support should "look like" for young children. Yet they were identified as supportive by the African participants and researchers. An example would be a child being given a job to do in response to distress, without any dialogue regarding the child's needs or feeling states or the causes of the distress. (Being given such a job subsequently resulting in evident calming and satisfaction for the child and others.) Another example would be situations in which support occurs with little empathic questioning and dialogue between children and adults. This is characteristic of adult–child interaction patterns in a variety of contexts other than support networks, and is connected with the gerontocratic, age-graded structure of Abaluyia society, and the importance placed on training children to monitor and respond to their environment, rather than attempting to change the environment around the child (cf. Ochs, 1982).

Other kinds of support were unusually frequent or rare. Thus offering food to placate a child occurs everywhere in the world, but seems to be unusually common in the Abaluyia observations. Similarly, dominance and teasing combined with support appear frequently. By contrast, empathic dialogue involving questions regarding the inner states and feelings of the child is virtually absent.

In most cultures, there are special names or terms used for certain kinds of support, which code for culturally special features which would also indicate possibly important cultural patterns. Although there are Luluyia terms for help, support, or assistance (*obukhonyi; obubeera*), doing things for the sake of others (*khulwa*), or giving to others (*beelesia*) (Donohew, 1962), these in fact are not routinely used by Abaluyia in soliciting help and support, and so could not be used to mark special kinds of help.

Any one or a combination of these conditions would qualify a given socially supportive event as a possible instance of a wider cultural pattern of social support, or as indicating a cultural theme in how support and help are offered to children. But then to provide that cultural interpretation requires an understanding of the cultural context, and its important features for social support for children.

Ecocultural Contexts of Social Support

Ecocultural features that influence the provision of support everywhere include children's, mothers', and other caretakers' work loads; the physical health and safety of the family within the local community; the availability of family and nonfamily personnel to assist in help and support; the personnel likely to be with children throughout their day; the sex and age composition of children's play and neighborhood groups; cultural beliefs regarding appropriate parental roles; and beliefs and values regarding the proper developmental course for children (Super & Harkness, 1980, 1982, 1986; Weisner, 1984; B. Whiting, 1980; B. Whiting & Edwards, 1988).

These ecocultural conditions in turn produce differences in the everyday *activity settings* around children. Activity settings are defined as the personnel, goals, motives, tasks, and culturally appropriate scripts for conduct that constitute children's daily routines (Cole, 1981; Weisner & Gallimore, 1985; Wertsch, 1985; B. Whiting, 1980). These activity settings are both the instantiation of ecocultural presses on the family and child, and the framework within which meaningful behavior occurs and is constituted by culture members. Using the activity setting as the unit of analysis for studying social support is a basic assumption of the ecocultural model. It is essential for understanding cultural differences. Support happens in the midst of the ordinary, mundane cultural routines of everyday life. The ecocultural–activity setting model presumes this, and assumes that this everyday context is crucial in interpreting social support for children.

THE ABALUYIA OF KENYA

The Abaluyia are an Interlacustrine Bantu-speaking group living north of Lake Victoria. They are, in fact, a collection of historically independent subtribes, and include groups such as the Kisa (Abashisa), the Maragoli (Munroe & Munroe, 1980; Wagner, 1948), Wanga (Were, 1967), and the Tiriki (Sangree, 1966). The Abaluyia numbered over 2.2 million by 1979 and the Kisa, the group I studied, some 50,000. They are patrilocal and patrilineal, living in dispersed lineage and clan groupings. Inheritance is fixed (e.g., clan-held land) rather than in the form of liquid or easily movable assets. The Kisa subsist today by growing maize, millet, manioc, cassava, beans, potatoes, plantains, and bananas. They also raise some cash crops (sugarcane, maize) and livestock for sale, engage in extensive trading activities, and work for wages in the region and in the major cities throughout Kenya. In cases where men are away from their rural homes working for wages, wives and children often will visit the cities and live there for varying periods.

Shared-Management Contexts for Support

The Abaluyia, like many other societies around the world (Gallimore, Boggs, & Jordan, 1974; Weisner, 1986, 1987), incorporate children as active coparticipants in managing the daily routine of the family. Children receive and provide support by doing chores and tasks for the family, caring for younger siblings, participating in a large and complex hierarchy of authority and direction, and sharing resources between related kin. Very early on, Abaluyia parents are preparing their children to share and exploit jointly held resources such as livestock, land, a business or trade.

Shared-management families emphasize interdependence more than autonomy, affiliation rather than individual cooperation, and child-managed rather than adult-managed activity. Children are learning through "enterprise-engagement" (Jordan & Tharp, 1979) by gradually performing tasks that they observe going on around them, more than through verbal directions regarding tasks given by adults.

Social support, including nurturance and helping behaviors toward children within large networks of kin, is a rather common occurrence in Kisa. Between 12 and 16% (depending on children's age and sex, and the family's urban or rural residence) of mothers' interactions with their children involve either direct care or some form of nurturant support (Weisner, 1979, 1986). Girls' percentages of nurturance and care toward other children were as high as for mothers: 9 to 17%. Boys' percentages ranged between 1 and 7. Offers of comfort provide roughly half of all the support: Mothers' proportions range from 5.5 to more than 9%, girls' from 0.5 to 9.5%, and boys' from 0.5 to 7%. Nurturant or supportive behaviors by children toward others rank between fourth and ninth out of the 15 most common behaviors in rural and urban Abaluyia households, within the Whitings' coding scheme.

The qualitative character of these supportive behaviors often differs from western expectations. (In my corpus a third clearly did, and others did in part.) These characteristics can be grouped into five *cultural themes* or patterns of support: (1) *Work* and support for children constantly co-occur. Giving a child work to do often seems to "mean" providing support to that child. (2) *Aggression, teasing, and dominance* often occur along with support, even when the same individuals are involved in both aggressive and supportive behaviors. (3) There are *chains of indirect support* among children's networks: Child A responds to help from child B by soon thereafter assisting child C; but there are no immediate thanks or direct acknowledgments between A, B, and C. (4) Children quietly scan their social environment for other persons to give assistance to and be assisted by; they are as or more likely to receive such *assistance from other children* as from their mothers or other adults. (5) *Food* is a constant concern and a medium by which adults and children soothe one another.

The next section illustrates each of these themes or patterns of support in more detail. The vignettes have been fleshed out in full sentences for readability, but are otherwise what was recorded in the field protocols. They give a glimpse of the normal, everyday social activities of Abaluyia children in which various kinds of social support occur. Sometimes, data on context have been used, from additional ethnographic information available on these families. These data include information on the activity setting in which the event is occurring (the personnel present, motivations, goals, tasks, and scripts for appropriate conduct).

FIVE CULTURAL THEMES IN ABALUYIA SOCIAL SUPPORT FOR CHILDREN

1. Co-participation in work signals social support.

Assigning a task, asking for help from rather than offering help to a child, and having a child participate in work all seem comforting and supportive for Abaluyia children. Work seems to signal not only task pressure or obligation, but also integration into the family network. Six percent of the 574 events in the sampled pool of supportive interactions involved work (including "mock work" in some cases for the younger children).

Children's work activity networks are a major context for offering or receiving assistance. The following example shows a very characteristic Abaluyia social network context for offering and receiving support and security. Older and younger siblings and other kin are present; maternal or other adult availability is intermittent; and work and play are going on simultaneously. The older children in this homestead are doing tasks and work, while younger children are caring for an infant, helping out with some planting, collecting food, and playing.

Outside a large Kisa homestead, a 1-year-old boy playfully hits his 3-year-old sister (the focal child in the observation) with a stick. The girl then walks over to her older sister, age 10, and tells her to sit down. She starts eating a guava and her mother asks how they taste—are they sweet? Mother then leaves the homestead to carry sheaves of grass to thatch the roof of another house located several hundred meters away, leaving her 13-year-old daughter to care for the 1-year-old and manage the home.

The 3-year-old girl and her 4-year-old brother call to their older sister (age 7) to come home, and both run down the path to lead her home. (The 13-year-old earlier had told the 7-year-old to come home.) The 3-year-old girl and the 4-year-old then take the baby and walk around carrying her, laughing and bouncing the baby in their arms. The 3-year-old talks to the baby (content unrecorded) along with her brother. She then tells her brother (age 3) to take his turn carrying the baby around and he does so. They laugh at the baby and talk to it and to each other while carrying it around. Girl then takes baby back, but baby does not want to climb onto her back and then into a sling arrangement. They ultimately succeed at putting the baby into the sling. The three young children then walk down a path into the garden, where the 13-year-old girl is planting sugarcane stalks in the prepared soil. The girl then starts helping her teenage sister by handing her each stalk as she is bending down to plant them. After awhile, the 4- and 3-year-olds go off into the bush alongside the field and urinate; they continue talking to each other regarding planting, where their mother is, and about the observer recording their behavior. [later on] They see some termites coming out of holes in the ground in the garden. (These are delicacies to eat live.) The children (all of them have collected together in the garden at this point) are helping to collect these termites (for their mother to cook later on).

The next vignette might be interpreted as a "pretend task request" episode, combined with teasing of a 2-year-old. But the child's crying, in the Abaluyia interpretations, was due to the boy not being able to do the chore being requested of him. Abaluyia students doing these observations saw the mother's request as a request for chore performance; they saw this as responsive, nurturant support for the crying child. The older sister's role is viewed the same way.

A boy 2 years and 9 months old is standing outside of his grandmother's (father's mother's) house, crying. Present are his grandmother, his mother, an 11-year-old sister, 8-year-old brother, and 3-year-old neighbor boy. Grandmother talks to the 2-year-old boy about getting ready to eat. Mother calls out to the 2-year-old boy to take some maize from his grandmother's house to hers, which is just down a small path about 40 meters away. The boy continues crying. The grandmother tells him to be quiet and not to cry. Mother then comes over and offers the boy some maize to eat. He takes the food, quiets down, and starts to eat. Neighbor boy, age 3, starts talking with the boy about the maize he is eating, and follows the younger boy around as he eats, asking if he can have some of the maize.

2. Support often co-occurs with teasing and aggression, yet still is seen as support.

Support and nurturance often are provided to children in the context of *cultural messages regarding dominance and the importance of the family social hierarchy.* Although the words *aggression* and *support,* or *teasing* and *help,* or *dominance* and *nurturance* may not go together, these *behaviors* co-occur in Abaluyia observations. The first vignette presented earlier in this chapter is an example of this pattern. Eight percent of all supportive events co-occurred with aggression or teasing. A child will often be involved in sequences involving harm and support, or dominance–conflict and support, either simultaneously or in quick succession. The support network for African children is in this respect like the adult support network they are preparing for: It is filled with conflict; it requires an understanding of hierarchy and deference; it is likely both to need help from children and to provide help to them.

The affective tone accompanying support or help is subdued, with mixed positive, negative and neutral emotional feelings. Expressions of warmth or empathy do not necessarily accompany support. Teasing and support have a closely connected cultural and emotional meaning for Abaluyia children. African mothers and children know how to use each one to get what they want or to assist others. As the breastfeeding example presented at the beginning of the chapter shows, mothers will openly "train" children to combine nurturance and teasing, and the training starts early.

Sometimes the intermixing of teasing, work, help, and nurturant support can get dangerous, as in the next example from an Abaluyia family living in Nairobi. A 5-year-old girl (the focal child), a sister, 8, and a 2-year-old sister are all playing outside the home while the mother cooks inside. Note in this sequence how the older sister takes on playful and caretaking roles with *both* the 5-year-old and the 2-year-old, but modulates her help for each one. Note also the indirect role of the mother: The mother monitors family activities, but without active interaction or direct involvement.

The focal child in this observation (a 5-year-old girl) is helping and playing in the home along with her older sister. The sister (age 8) has several nails and is hammering them into the ground with a stick. The 5-year-old girl gives her 8-year-old sister a stick, and then takes the stick back and hammers a nail with it. The 8-year-old agrees to this (at first). The 5-year-old looks over at her mother, who is stirring porridge inside the house. She tells her mother that earlier that day she went to a neighbor's room and was jumping over some thick ropes that were there. Her 2-year-old sister now comes over, and the 5-year-old shows the sister how to hammer a nail with the stick, and then lets younger girl do it. The 2-year-old ignores her sister at first, but then takes a stick and hits the nail. The 5-year-old and her older sister praise the 2-year-old, and smile. The 2-year-old then takes one of the nails and hits the 5-year-old with it. The 5-year-old starts crying, and calls out that the sister has "knifed" her. The 8-year-old sister then picks up the 2-year-old and carries her away, as 5-year-old continues to cry. (Mother does not respond to the situation.) The 8-year-old sister tells the 5-year-old she is okay and not to cry, while at the same time getting the younger child to stop fussing.

3. Response to support from others is often indirect, in the form of helping still another child.

Offering help or support to an Abaluyia child is often followed by that child's offering help to yet another child fairly soon thereafter. Requesting assistance from an older child is not infrequently followed by the child who was assisted giving help to a younger one; helping another child is often followed by receiving help from a yet older child. In perhaps a third of the field observations, this pattern of indirect or delayed chains of support seemed to occur. It is difficult to arrive at a precise estimate, however, since adequate information is not always available from observations of this type. Since use of *please* or *thank you* is rare as are any other forms of direct acknowledgment of assistance, the beginnings or endings of episodes are not easy to mark, nor are they supposed to be, in Abaluyia interactions. But the future availability of help seems to be an understood substitute for such acknowledgment. Support seems to "flow through" the network around children, and through the child being helped on to others.

The next example gives at least a partial glimpse of these chains of support. The ultimate recipient of nurturance and social support in this vignette (the 2-year-old boy) sees others making varied attempts to talk with, assist or help, using various styles. Other children offer support as an *indirect* response to an adult's comment or question to a younger child about what is wrong, before any adult becomes involved.

A boy, 2 years and 9 months old, is standing in the path outside his homestead, crying. A 15-year-old male cousin and his 8-year-old brother alternately tell him to come into the compound and/or to stop standing along the main path outside. Nothing happens. . . . His 13-year-old sister then comes over and gives the 2-year-old boy some maize, and this stops the crying. (later in this observation) The boy is crying again, and his mother calls him into her hut and asks him what he has to say about his crying. He just stands there and scratches himself. An 11-year-old half-sister, the boy's 4-year-old sister, and the mother's sister, age 40, are in the home during this conversation. The boy just looks at them. His 4-year-old sister (a frequent companion of the younger boy) smiles at the 2-year-old, and he laughs back in return, and they walk outside.

In a second example, a 5-year-old girl (the focal child in this observation) is with her 10-year-old sister and infant sister in and around their one-room Nairobi home; their mother is away from the house at the market. As in earlier vignettes, the children are mixing chores, teasing, and nurturance. There is also a sense here of the rhythm of alternating help and support in a large child network.

A 5-year-old girl is wandering around "in search of food or toys or anything that would interest her" (in the words of the field observer). She is eating a slice of bread, and asks her older sister for more. The sister gives her some of her bread. The girl notices that there is something in it, and the sister tells her that it is a sandwich—there is meat in it. The baby sister, a girl age 1, toddles up and asks for bread, and the 5-year-old gives her some of hers. The girl then gives the baby some bottle caps to play with. The girl takes her baby sister's nursing bottle and plays with it. The toddler then demands to have the bottle, and so the 5-year-old takes it and opens the top, but the baby ultimately refuses it. The 5-year-old girl then takes a tin of margarine and starts playing with it; the toddler starts to take the tin away; the 5-year-old girl refuses, and the toddler starts to cry. The older sister, age 10, says that the 5-year-old had better leave the margarine tin alone, or the toddler will beat her up and take it from her. The 5-year-old then asks for more bread from older sister, who gives her some more, and helps her.

4. Children look to other children for support as much as or more than to the mother. Indeed, children actively scan the environment for help and for others needing help.

Mothers were the *exclusive* providers of social support in only 23% of all supportive acts in the sample. The remainder of the support either included other children or occurred in the absence of the mother.

In the next vignette, many elements of the shared-management family system are in action. Work and assistance occur at the same time; and many children play a pivotal role between being a supporter of others and being helped by others. In addition, the attractiveness of entertainment and mutual play of infant and toddler care for these children is apparent. The children are orienting to one another and to their child-care tasks or play, and offer assistance and help to each other as needed.

A 6-year-old boy is in a fallow, recently harvested maize field surrounding his rural homestead, with his brother, 4, his older brother, 10, and his sister, 19. He is attempting to cut some sticks from the bushes and hedges for use as firewood. The children are all helping to do this, although the 4-year-old is not really contributing too much to the pile. His assistance is tolerated and encouraged. The 10-year-old runs down the path and the 6-year-old hides in the grass next to him. The older boy spots the younger and hits him. The 6-year-old runs after the older brother again, and the episode is repeated. The younger child starts to cry. The older sister says that she is going to beat the 10-year-old. The children then carry the wood back to their homestead and start to spread it out to dry in the sun. The 6-year-old and the 4-year-old help in this task and also watch the older boys working. Some of the children begin preparing maize for cooking out in the yard. Their baby sister is lying on a mat outside the homestead, and the 4-year-old goes over and smiles at the baby, and then laughs and licks the baby's hand. The children sit outside for a few minutes; the 4-year-old plays with the baby's hair. After a few minutes, a 16-year-old sister, a neighbor boy, 9, and a girl, 15, come in to the compound from the main path about 50 meters away. At first they say nothing, and then the 9-year-old comes over and touches the 6-year-old on the back in greeting.

5. African children and families cook and share food, and use food to comfort children, a great deal of the time.

Nineteen percent of the 574 supportive exchanges directly involved the exchange of food. Many more had cooking or subsistence-related tasks that involve food (such as imaginary cooking, children playing with food, or work being done to prepare food, etc.) going on in the background. The high percentage of instances in which food was used to comfort children may well be related to its perceived scarcity and uncertainty about future availability. When mothers and fathers were asked to describe the most important social problems in their community, two-thirds of the parents mentioned famine, insufficient food supplies, or lack of security of their food supply as their number one concern.

Providing and sharing food is both a sign of hospitality and a form of assistance to kin. Support and sociability amongst Abaluyia children routinely includes exchanging and sharing food, as the next two very typical examples illustrate.

A 4-year-old girl, her 3-year-old sister, an infant under a year old, and their mother are sitting on the veranda outside the door of their rural house. They occasionally tend to food cooking inside. The 4-year-old entertains the baby by juggling it, talking, and smiling. The girl then takes a candy that the baby was sucking on. The baby tries to grab it back, fails, and starts to cry. The girl gives it back to the baby, and then takes it again. The baby crawls toward the girl to try and get the sweet, and starts to cry. The girl then gives back the sweet and plays with the baby, along with her younger sister. Her mother calls to her to go and feed the hens in the yard, and she goes to do this and then returns with an empty plate, which she gives back to the mother. She then squats in the doorway singing to the baby, who starts to eat dirt, which the girl stops baby from doing while continuing to sing with her. She moves the baby around the room and outside the home, while laughing and talking to her and talking to her sister. The girls go and get their maize meal and vegetables from the fire and start eating. The 4-year-old asks if the 3-year-old is being burned by cooked maize and the younger sister says no. She then goes and gets more maize meal for her younger sister, and some for the baby to nibble on. She then gets some water and drinks it, and then gives water from her cup to her sister and to the baby—and between them they manage to spill the remaining water in the dirt.

A 4-year-old girl gets a cloth and spreads it on the ground so that she and four other girls (ages 2 through 6) can sit together under the veranda of their house in Nairobi. The girls start pretending to cook food together, and they simultaneously entertain the 2-year-old boy by clapping hands and clapping his hands. The 4-year-old girl then shows all of them various imaginary cooking objects, such as pots, leaves, and spoons, and they all look at these. The girl then gets some water and starts to pour it out into a (real) pan. The older girl tells her to be careful. The girls talk together about food; the 4-year-old pushes an older girl who told her to be careful with the water, and the older girl does nothing in return.

CULTURAL DIFFERENCES IN SUPPORT FOR CHILDREN: THE ECOCULTURAL CONTEXT

What in the ecocultural context around Abaluyia families leads to these kinds of social support and social networks? Some important features are consequences of demography, such as high fertility and a declining child mortality rate among the Abaluyia, which results in children close in age to one another living together. Other econiche features result from the rules of patrilineal descent and patrilocal residence, which ensure that kin will be nearby and available for assistance in child care.

In addition, subsistence horticulture, supplemented among the Abaluyia by pastoralism and wage labor, influences the contexts for support, since it drives the tasks and work loads of these families. The division of labor, for instance, expects that children contribute by doing daily chores, such as obtaining water, fuel, and fodder; cooking and cleaning; and hoeing and preparing food crops. Social support later in life will require similar kinds of shared work activity, something children see around them every day.

In fact, Abaluyia children generally see and experience the full adult world of work and adult networks of support around them, including roles of adult sibs of parents; clan elders; churches; local political struggles; and women's support groups. The understanding that support and support networks in childhood are closely linked to those of adulthood is very vivid for these children.

Many Abaluyia male siblings are preparing to inherit fixed resources (farms, animals, shops) in a permanent residence that at least some of them will share together all their lives. Their sisters are preparing to become managers of their future husbands' lands and other resources in other communities; this is a task they will have to do jointly with their new affinal kin. This pattern of future shared resource allocation is reflected in the ways support is tied to joint work, or the placing of children in a work group network as a form of support.

Social support among Abaluyia children often is provided in the context of learning through actual performance of a task with others. The social context within which support occurs in the Abaluyia observations often involves such activity. Support for young children was often instrumental in form (e.g., giving food or objects, giving work to do, accompanying others while involved in work), and seldom associated solely with play or fantasy activities, or combined with empathic adult attention directed to an individual child. This use of work roles for socialization of culturally valued beliefs and behaviors has been recognized as important for sex-role training (e.g., Ember, 1981; B. Whiting & Edwards, 1973) or for responsibility and compliance training (e.g., B. Whiting & J. Whiting, 1975), but not for social support.

Family routines involving shared management diffuse support and responsibility for children across many people. This happens for several reasons: task efficiency in situations of high family work loads, insurance in the event that the parent dies, a need for the child's help in the home of another relative, or wage labor migration by family members. Twenty-three percent of the homesteads in the Kisa community, for instance, had one or more children living in them who were not full siblings to the other children in that home. Most of these "visitor" children were there to assist their aunts, uncles, and cousins with work or child care, to attend school, or to do wage work.

Abaluyia parents' developmental goals for their children include giving and receiving social support. Abaluyia mothers use evidence that a child had the ability to give and receive social support, and assist others, as markers of a child's more general developmental level, much as an American parent might use literacy skills such as knowing the alphabet, or verbal facility, to show how grown-up or precocious his or her child is. Mothers include helpfulness and task competence as evidence that their children are maturing successfully. I asked 54 Abaluyia mothers about such goals, and they emphasized skills such as greeting visitors, knowing kinship relationships and terminology, being able to run errands, being able to manage the daily domestic routine, cooking (for girls), caring for infants and toddlers, and good school comportment (a more recent addition to this list). The use of literacy skills as developmental markers in our own ecocultural setting is equivalent to the use of domestic chores, skills in child care, interpersonal competence, and being supportive of others for the Abaluyia setting.

The mothers also emphasized a family *hierarchy* of control and support. These mothers certainly do expect joint, enterprise-engaged help from younger children, but also are quite aware that exclusive responsibilities do not begin until children reach 7 or 8 or older. Mothers also emphasized that even children between 7 or 8 and 16 or so still require overseeing and the mother's direction. Hence there are many instances in the field observations in which children under 7 are providing help and support, and receiving it, yet older children are also around in responsible roles, while mothers or other adults remain in indirect control.

Such experiences reflect what these children will probably experience later when they themselves become parents. These parents are training their children early in life for future parental roles. A girl is likely to marry by age 16 to 18, and to move to her husband's family's home. But the new couple is not likely immediately to have any significant degree of economic independence or autonomy in the rural economy, or to have their own homestead compound to manage at that point in the life cycle. Resource control normally will take many more years for young Abaluyia parents to acquire. Receiving support within indirect hierarchies of family authority, monitoring others needing assistance, and being involved in chains of direct and indirect assistance all will be familiar circumstances for them when they become parents themselves.

Marta Wenger (this volume) describes the basis of Giriama children's support as rooted in companionship. Feelings of fear, loss, or loneliness accompany separation from the Giriama child's extended kin network, or companionship group. Giriama complain of feelings of separation and lack of social support when their companionship group is lost to them even when alternative kinds of support might be available (from nonkin, for instance).

The Abaluyia have the same cultural theme (that the essence of what is felt or experienced as supportive is family and community companionship), although they do not have the same intensity of extra-homestead companionship groupings that the Giriama appear to have. The cultural origins of such feelings are apparent in the contexts in which support is given and offered, as revealed by the naturalistic observations.

Abaluyia do not have to provide reasons to one another explaining how or why these kinds of interactions and responses are signs of help and support—such an interpretation goes without saying in their everyday world. The low incidence of empathic, conversational dialogues regarding support, the absence of *please, thank you,* and other overt forms for acceptance of help, and the scanning or monitoring of the surroundings by children for help are other indications that these themes are culturally understood and shared.

But this pattern of less verbally mediated social support among the Abaluyia is more than a sign of culturally shared understanding about support. The Abaluyia supportive events often contain no sign of a verbal response in circumstances where American middle-class families would expect one. For instance, the 48.5 hours of observations in this sample do not contain *any* episodes of discourse between parents and children in which children were presumptive coequal interlocutors to adults, or in which scaffolded, empathic questioning occurred in the context of supportive acts. Parents are rarely heard asking for their children's views regarding what they want or what should be done. Children are seldom heard in conversations in which their parents ask about their needs, why they need help, and so on. Nonverbal, socially mediated means often (but not always, as some examples show) have been substituted for dyadic, verbal means of assistance.

These Abaluyia families have been in the midst of major social changes lasting for many decades. Western schooling and Christian mission activity are in their fourth generation in this community, for instance. The rural horticultural economy of the Abaluyia has been partially incorporated into the larger world economy since the 1920s (Kitching, 1980; Leys, 1974). Ninety-three percent of the homesteads in a complete survey of the rural Kisa community had at least one member working away from the homestead, or had had one within the previous 5 years. The Kisa social support and network system is, therefore, already adapted to these larger forces. These observations of social support, and mother interviews, reflect *current* behavior and modes of thought already adapted to such changes, not the remnants of a "traditional" cultural system that is fading away.

These patterns continue to change rapidly. One clear effect of urban migration, for instance, is that it divides the sibling group into urban and rural part-time residents (Ross & Weisner, 1977). School-age children, from 7 to about 18 or so, are likely to live in Nairobi only for relatively brief periods due to several factors: Children's labor is needed on their rural homesteads; adults prefer that their children attend rural schools; one-room urban accommodations violate cosleeping prohibitions; and food and travel costs of maintaining residence in the city are very high. Young men are increasingly likely to live apart, to be less dependent on shared family resources as adults, and to work in a Kenya wage economy that does not require cooperative support among kin (although obtaining such work and living arrangements continues to depend heavily on kin networks). This dispersal of the family group across multiple locations, along with land scarcity and marginal wage income dependency, is steadily changing many of the features that have sustained the Abaluyia peer socialization system and shared-management model of social support.

Cultures around the world face some common dilemmas regarding support: how to protect the small, young, and relatively helpless; how to balance the power some members of society have over others, with the inclusion of all in the common group; and how to provide assistance to children, while also showing them the limits of help. Indeed, a cultural dilemma everywhere is to support children in such a way that children later in their lives will become supporters of others in ways that culture finds appropriate.

REFERENCES

Belle, D., Burr, R., & Cooney, J. (1987). Boys and girls as social support theorists. *Sex Roles, 17*(11/12), 657–665.

Cohen, S., & McKay, G. (1984). Social support, stress and the buffering hypothesis: A theoretical analysis. In A. Baum, J. E. Singer, & S. E. Taylor, (Eds.), *Handbook of psychology and health* (Vol. 4). Hillsdale, NJ: Erlbaum.

Cole, M. (1981). The zone of proximal development: *Where culture and cognition create each other.* Report 106, Center for Human Information Processing, University of California, San Diego.

Donohew, G. (1962). *A first course in Luyia grammar.* Typescript.

Edgerton, R., & Langness, L. L. (1974). *Methods and styles in the study of culture.* San Francisco: Chandler & Sharp.

Edwards, C. P. (1985). Rationality, culture, and the construction of "ethical discourse": A comparative perspective. *Ethos, 13*(4), 318–339.

Ember, C. (1981). A cross-cultural perspective on sex differences. In R. Munroe, R. Munroe, & B. Whiting (Eds.), *Handbook of cross-cultural human development.* New York: Garland.

Gallimore, R., Boggs, J. W., & Jordan, C. (1974). *Culture, behavior and education: A study of Hawaiian-Americans.* Beverly Hills: Sage.

Jordan, C., & Tharp, R. (1979). Culture and education. In A. Marsella, R. G. Tharp, & T. Ciborowski (Eds.), *Perspectives in cross-cultural psychology,* (pp. 265–286). New York: Academic.

Kitching, G. (1980). *Class and economic change in Kenya. The making of an African petite-bourgeoisie, 1905–1970.* New Haven: Yale University Press.

Leys, C. (1974). *Underdevelopment in Kenya. The political economy of neo-colonialism, 1964–1971.* Berkeley: University of California Press.

Lin, N., Dean, A., & Ensel, W. M. (Eds.). (1986). *Social support, life events, and depression.* New York: Academic.

Munroe, R. H., & Munroe, R. L. (1980). Infant experience and childhood affect among the Logoli: A longitudinal study. *Ethos, 8,* 295–315.

Ochs, E. (1982). Talking to children in Western Samoa. *Language in Society, 11,* 77–104.

Ross, M., & Weisner, T. (1977). The rural-urban migrant network in Kenya: Some general implications. *American Ethnologist, 4,* 359–375.

Sandler, I., & Barrera, M., Jr. (1984). Toward a multimethod approach to assessing the effects of social support. *American Journal of Community Psychology, 12,* 37–52.

Sangree, W. (1966). *Age, prayer and politics in Tiriki, Kenya.* London: Oxford University Press.

Shweder, R., & Bourne, E. (1981). Does the concept of the person vary cross-culturally? In A. J. Marsalla & G. White (Eds.), *Cultural conceptions of mental health and therapy.* Boston: D. Reidel.

Super, C. M., & Harkness, S. (Eds.). (1980). *Anthropological perspectives on child development. New directions for child development* No. 8. San Francisco: Jossey Bass.

Super, C. M., & Harkness, S. (1982). The infant's niche in rural Kenya and metropolitan America. In L. L. Adler (Ed.), *Issues in cross-cultural research.* New York: Academic.

Super, C. M., & Harkness, S. (1986). The developmental niche: A conceptualization at the interface of child and culture. *International Journal of Behavior Development, 9,* 1–25.

Wagner, G. (1948). *The Bantu of Western Kenya* (Vol. 1). London: Oxford University Press.

Weisner, T. (1979). Urban–rural differences in sociable and disruptive behavior of Kenya children. *Ethnology, 18*(2), 153–172.

Weisner, T. (1984). Ecocultural niches of middle childhood: A cross-cultural perspective. In W. A. Collins (Ed.), *Development during middle childhood: The years from six to twelve.* Washington, DC: National Academy Press.

Weisner, T. (1986). Implementing new relationship styles in American families. In W. Hartup & Z. Rubin (Eds.), *Relationships and development.* LEA Press.

Weisner, T. (1987). Socialization for parenthood in sibling caretaking societies. In J. B. Lancaster, J. Altman, A. S. Rossi, & L. R. Sherrod (Eds.), *Parenting across the lifespan: Biosocial dimensions.* New York: Aldine De Gruyter.

Weisner, T. & Gallimore, R. (1985, December). *The convergence of ecocultural and activity theory.* Paper presented at a meeting of the American Anthropological Association.

Were, G. S. (1967). *A history of the Abaluyia of Western Kenya, c. 1500–1930.* Nairobi: East African Publishing House.

Wertsch, J. (1985). *Vygotsky and the social formation of mind.* Cambridge, MA: Harvard University Press.

Whiting, B. (1980). Culture and social behavior: A model for the development of social behavior. *Ethos, 8,* 95–116.

Whiting, B., & Edwards, C. (1973). A cross-cultural analysis of sex differences in the behavior of children aged three through 11. *Journal of Social Psychology, 91,* 171–188.

Whiting, B., & Edwards, C. (1988). *Children of different worlds. The formation of social behavior.* Cambridge, MA: Harvard University Press.

Whiting, B., & Whiting, J. (1975). *Children of six cultures. A psycho-cultural analysis.* Cambridge, MA: Harvard University Press.

CHAPTER 4

Work, Play, and Social Relationships Among Children in a Giriama Community

MARTHA WENGER

In the process of studying the factors that lead to individual differences in social behavior among children, we often leave unexamined the broader sociocultural context in which those factors operate for the majority of children. Indeed, it is difficult to identify, much less gain perspective on, the features that typify the social experience of children living in a single cultural setting without examining children from culturally distinct groups. In this chapter, I use naturalistic observational data, collected over the course of 2 years' field work in a rural community in Kenya, to examine the relationship between how and where children spend time and with whom they spend it. The community is called Kaloleni, and its residents are predominantly Giriama. My goal is to consider how these aspects of social ecology are shaped by the culture and economy of community residents and, in turn, influence the development of children's social relationships. In so doing, I hope to highlight some distinguishing features of children's social ecology that might serve a heuristic function in conceptualizing the development of social networks in our own society.

A significant body of cross-cultural research and theory informs the choice of focus for this discussion. My research is an extension of the work begun in *The Children of Six Cultures: A Psychocultural Analysis* (B. Whiting & J. Whiting, 1975) and subsequently expanded through several generations of researchers affiliated with the Laboratory of Human Development at the Harvard Graduate School of Education. One thrust of the accumulated evidence is that there are systematic differences in children's social ecology that are determined by culture. In a cross-cultural analysis of these data, B. Whiting and Edwards stress the theoretical importance of social ecology:

> [O]ur main hypothesis is that patterns of interpersonal behavior are developed in the settings one frequents, and that the most important characteristic

> of a setting is the cast of characters who occupy the set (as identified by their age, sex, and kinship relation to the actor). The settings one frequents are in turn related to the culturally determined activities that occupy males and females of various ages in the normal course of daily living, activities that are determined by economic pursuits, the division of labor, and organization of people in space. Our theory holds that knowing the company that children keep (the proportion of time they spend with different categories of individuals) makes it possible to predict salient aspects of their interpersonal behavior. . . . Ecology and the social and economic organization of society determine the daily routines of adults and children, the individuals who frequent the same settings, and the activities that are performed. The scripts for daily life of each age group are consonant with rules governing appropriate behavior in each of the settings. (1988, pp. 4–5)

One of the most striking differences between the children living in Kaloleni and American children lies in time spent contributing to the household economy. Differences in the underlying cultural meaning of children's task performance is evident from their prototypical responses to parents' requests. Many American children see the assignment of chores as the product of parental personal perogative. A chore, from this perspective, is a concession—of one individual to another—to be negotiated around and, possibly, resisted. In contrast, Giriama children participate, at some level, in the shared cultural understanding that the tasks requested are necessary to the well-being of household members, and thus they recognize that task assignment has a wider legitimacy than personal perogative. This aspect of Giriama children's lives is enormously important to the formation of their social networks for several reasons. Work provides a context for learning meaningful cooperation around a goal that benefits the domestic group. In the words of J. Whiting, Chasdi, Antonovsky, and Ayers (1966): "Certain aspects of the childrearing process seem to have the effect of, if not creating, at least strengthening values far beyond the conscious intent of the agents of socialization" (p. 83).

Many children in Kaloleni care for and supervise small children, and so from the earliest years youngsters develop strong bonds based on the mutuality of dependence and support. This has a significant long-term impact on the quality of children's relationships over time. In a discussion of sibling caretaking that is equally applicable to the entire range of chores presented here, Weisner (1982) underscores that the sharing of work and responsibilities promotes interdependence among siblings, parents, peers, and neighbors:

> Sibling caretaking is not an isolated and specialized institution that merely aids and supplements maternal care. It comes into being because it assists families in functioning in the wider community. It is adaptive not only in the sense of producing a more efficient family labor pool. It also encourages

> the sibling group towards the often strained interdependence I have described; it is part of a shared functioning family system and an affiliative rather than egoistic/individualistic style of achievement and competence. There is also an implicit model of status, hierarchy, and sex role obligations that will be continued later in adolescent and adult life. . . . The institution is part of a family circle that is perhaps less intensely sentimental than our own, but one that also isolates children less from the worlds of community and work and integrates them into the rhythms of the annual work cycle and a defined life-course. These characteristics of sibling groups do not stop at the end of childhood. On the contrary, they are intensified as children pass into adolescence and adulthood. (p. 326)

Giriama attach importance to providing children with duties that teach responsibility and mutuality. In their view, a mother who does not expect her children to help is remiss, even neglectful. A child so treated would inevitably emerge as an adult with few prospects and without the respect of the community.

Work imposes constraints on children's personal autonomy and choice of companions. Some kinds of work are very restrictive. One such task is the pounding of maize. The Giriama store maize kernels over the fire to reduce infestation by insects. Before grinding the kernels into flour, women pound the kernels, using a very large mortar and pestle, to remove the bitter, smoky outer shell. This is an arduous task performed at home. As a consequence, opportunities for sociability while pounding are very much limited. Other types of work, like running errands, are much less restrictive. Tasks of this type are often a break from drudgery, taking the child outside home, where there is scope for unsupervised sociability. Thus even within a community where children participate heavily in household work, there can be significant differences in its impact, depending on the tasks assigned for various categories of children.

My first objective in this chapter is to provide a brief cultural overview of the research site, with special emphasis on the features of community life that have a particular impact on the activities children engage in and the individuals they engage with. Next, I describe the methods of data collection. I will then turn to the analysis of children's activities and companionships based on naturalistic observations of youngsters 2 through 11 years old.

SOCIOCULTURAL CONTEXT

Kaloleni is a community of families who live around a small rural trade center located in the coastal interior of Kenya, some 35 miles northwest of the port city of Mombasa. The residents are predominantly Giriama, a patrilineal people who speak a Bantu language, as does the vast majority of Africa's population south of the Sahara. Like many East African peoples, the Giriama traditionally subsisted on hoe agriculture and pastoralism, supplemented by trade with neighboring peoples (see Brantley, 1981; Spear, 1979).

Giriama institutions historically were not differentiated into political, religious, and economic spheres. Patrilineal descent groups (*mbari*), varying in scope and size, provided the framework for all social organization; the extended family homestead (*mudzi* [s.]; *midzi* [pl.]) functioned as an autonomous unit of internal governance.

The *mudzi* constituted the primary unit of production, consumption, and inheritance. At its head was the patriarch (*mwenye mudzi*), who had full authority in all economic, social, political, and ritual matters affecting the domestic group. Other members of homestead included the patriarch's wives, their unmarried children, and their married sons, along with the married sons' wives and children. Except where external institutions intrude, the Giriama still have no villages in the sense of nucleated settlements of households, but rather their settlement pattern is characterized by dispersed homesteads. Relations between homesteads were the domain of the patriarchs and councils of elders. It is the goal of every Giriama male to marry, prosper, produce many progeny, and establish his own *mudzi*.

A cardinal feature of the Giriama domestic group is that it is virilocal. That is, the men, who constitute a minimal patrilineal descent group, are permanent members throughout the life cycle, but women, who must come from other clans, join the *mudzi* at marriage. In contrast to many other peoples living in the Highlands and western Kenya, the Giriama clans are not associated with tracts of land but are interspersed throughout the territory currently occupied. Thus it is possible, and even desirable, for a man to find a wife from his own immediate locality. As a consequence, homesteads in a locality often share multiple ties that are based on both genealogical and marriage links. A system of serial linking greatly extends the relationships between families (Parkin, 1972). With these ties comes a complex system of rights, responsibilities, and obligations that structure one's relationships throughout a lifetime.

Over the course of the past century, the Giriama have undergone significant social and economic change (Brantley, 1981; Parkin, 1972, 1979a). In earlier times, the region around Kaloleni was a sparsely populated pastoral area. Situated on the edge of the lush coconut palm belt, it is now densely populated, with most of the land taken up by coconut palms, the main cash crop. Residents continue to derive subsistence from their gardens, which are typically located several miles distant. Other sources of cash income include trade in the rapidly expanding local market and wage-earning jobs in the local hospital and Mombasa. Although most of the heads of household have not attended school, even the most traditional tend to view education as a good investment at least for their sons. This represents a dramatic change over the past two decades.

Despite change, the patrilineal extended family homestead remains the preferred living arrangement for most families. The majority of men old enough to have amassed sufficient wealth to marry a second wife are polygynists. The division of labor within the homestead continues to be based on gender and on age. Men's work includes clearing land and preparing soil, house building, caring for livestock, coconut palm tapping, and harvesting. It is primarily men who are involved in the cash sector. The married women of a homestead share the responsibility of providing household subsistence. Each wife is given her own garden, which she cultivates and from which she contributes to the domestic group's consumption. In addition to gardening, women's work includes storing, processing, and cooking food; collecting firewood and maintaining the fire; carrying water; transporting produce; washing clothing and utensils; caring for children; cleaning the houses and the homestead; and making minor house repairs. This is a heavy work load that is borne through the cooperative efforts of the women of the homestead with the assistance of children, who make a significant contribution to the domestic economy, primarily by performing chores that free adults' time to meet other demands.

Kinship continues to provide a framework for all primary social relationships. Even among the most educated youth, kinship supplies the metaphor for all significant social relationships. It is so pervasive that, in cases where a great "friendship" has developed (i.e., a relationship not based on ties of lineage or marriage), friends use kinship terms to refer to one another. Moreover, each friend's younger relatives will use the appropriate kin term to refer to their relative's friend.

Along with kinship, norms governing relationships between generations pervade all aspects of social exchange (cf. LeVine & LeVine, 1963). Interactions between members of adjacent generations (e.g., fathers and sons) are characterized by extreme respect and reserve, while relationships between members of alternate generations (e.g., grandfathers and grandsons) are intimate, playful, and free. Outside the domestic group, virtually all individuals may be categorized by generation according to a complex of considerations (see Parkin, 1980). The theme of generational seniority is expressed throughout social life—in the format of greetings, the content and style of conversation, the patterning of spatial positions occupied at both formal and informal occasions, and so forth—and can be observed to influence children's patterns of companionship.

Contemporary Giriama homesteads characteristically contain a number of buildings, oriented around a cleared "yard." It is common for each married man to have his own house, which he shares with his wife (wives), daughters, and young sons. Even married sons who might reside several hundred miles distant with their families will maintain a house in their father's *mudzi*. Unmarried youths usually have separate sleeping quarters. There is at least one building used for cooking, with grain storage arranged above the fire, and a place for the *mwenye mudzi* to receive visitors. There are also shelters made from thatching that provide privacy for personal hygiene. Although *midzi* are compactly arranged, they can be very sizable: even in a locality as densely populated as Kaloleni, some homesteads span a full acre.

Neighboring families typically have extensive contact with one another. This is not only because members of many households are related through marriage or descent, but also because Giriama *midzi* are linked by paths that run through, rather than around, their centers. Therefore, to move about within the locality, one must traverse the homesteads of others. This is typical of the entire region settled by the Giriama, where far and away the most dominant means of travel is by foot, along the intricate networks of paths that intertwine *midzi* and the occasional unpaved roadways that crisscross the territory.

At most times of the day, one finds various centers of activity within a *mudzi*. These clusters are often segregated by generation and gender, a pattern that reflects cultural expectations governing the responsibilities of males and females of differing degrees of seniority and norms governing social interaction between generations. Elder men usually sit in their own favored area, where they relax and receive visitors; likewise, senior women, who are no longer expected to participate in taxing duties, tend to relax apart. The other women and older girls work singly and in small groups around the compound and in adjacent gardens. Children form one or more play groups away from adults, where they can conduct their activities with greater freedom.

Given the number of people living in the average *mudzi* and the frequency of contact with neighbors, a Giriama child has a wide range of potential companions. Infants and young toddlers, when they are awake, remain near their mothers or caretakers. However, as soon as a toddler is old enough to walk confidently, he or she makes rounds to the various clusters of activity. Older children have a special appeal to the toddlers, who are readily incorporated into their play. Children as young as 4 or 5 years can adapt play to accommodate the toddler's capabilities. By 6 or 7 years of age, Giriama children are masters of distraction and enticement, the strategies that most effectively manipulate a toddler's behavior without triggering noisy protests and attendant disapproval from adults and elder siblings.

Once a very young child is mature enough to sustain play with other children, he or she displays a marked preference for the company of children over adults. Again, this pattern reflects the rules of respect that constrain adjacent generation interactions. Giriama mothers never involve themselves in the activities of children as western mothers often do. Children, for their part, are reluctant to attract adult attention, since this often incurs an undesirable consequence, such as the assignment of some task.

CHILDREN'S DAILY LIVES

In order to characterize the everyday social world of Kaloleni children, I selected a neighborhood of 23 homesteads situated just north of the trade center. The total population was 357, with the smallest homestead comprising 6 and the largest 35 members. Altogether, there were 105 children 2 through 11 years old living in these *midzi.*

Quantifiable data on how, with whom, and where Kaloleni children spend time were collected using the spot observation procedure developed by Munroe and Munroe (1971; Rogoff, 1978). This technique utilizes randomized visits to a homestead to record what a specified child is doing at the first moment of observation, when the observer initially approaches the *mudzi.* The goal of the observation technique is to take a mental "snapshot" of the people immediately surrounding the focal child and the activities he or she is engaged in. The observer records this information without including any modifications in position, activity, or social group that take place after the initial "sighting." Once the observer has made the appropriate greetings to family members, he or she collects additional items of interest, such as the location of the mother if she is not visible. If the preselected child is not at home, the observer records where the child has gone, with whom, and why he or she went there.

The spot observations collected in Kaloleni were distributed across daylight hours during the planting, weeding, and harvesting seasons. A total of 1328 observations, collected over a 5-month period, are included in this analysis. All 105 children were observed at least 10 times each. Members of the community served as the observers in order to ensure that behaviors were recorded and interpreted in a culturally meaningful way. The observers also coded their own observations, each of which was subsequently coded again by another observer. Agreement between all possible pairs of observers on the substance and the coding of observations exceeded 90%.

The two dimensions of Kaloleni children's social ecology for examination are the *activities engaged in* and the *individuals engaged with.* The analysis is framed in terms of the age and sex of the child observed. Ages were collapsed into the following groups: 2–3, 4–5, 6–7, and 8–11 (see Table 4.1). My goal was to focus on normative patterns rather than individual differences. Thus comparisons between girls and boys at the four age points were made using group proportion scores. These were calculated by dividing the frequency of occurrence of a selected social ecology variable for an age-by-sex group by the total number of observations made on that group.

Children's Activities

The first dimension of social ecology to be examined is *activity.* During the process of adapting the spot observation instrument to the field

TABLE 4.1. Distribution by Age and Sex of the Children Observed

	Age Group			
Gender	2–3 Years	4–5 Years	6–7 Years	8–11 Years
Females	16	13	12	13
Males	12	13	11	15
Total	28	26	23	28

setting, we developed a dictionary and coding scheme for the activities characteristic of children. These activities were grouped for this analysis into *work, social play, general sociability, individual activity,* and a residual category, *other,* which includes very infrequent activities that do not fit into the other categories. Descriptions of the activity variables are presented in Table 4.2.

Work

Work is the activity that increases most dramatically with age. For the four age groups, from youngest to oldest, the percentages of times observed working are 1, 8, 18, and 38%. Though typical for East African children and not unusual for children from other nonindustrialized societies (e.g., Rogoff, 1981; B. Whiting & Edwards, 1988; B. Whiting & J. Whiting, 1975), these percentages are substantially higher than one would observe for children living in the United States or Europe. It could be hypothesized that the linear increase in work with age reflects underlying developmental change (see Rogoff, Sellers, Pirrotta, Fox, & White, 1975) in children's abilities to perform tasks.

In the Giriama language the term for a child roughly 2 through 3 years in age is *kahoho kuhuma madzi:* a youngster who can be sent to fetch a cup of water. What is interesting about this term is that it is not gender specific (*kahoho* means "little child") but refers to a distinguishing feature of this age group's capabilities. Children of this age take enormous pleasure in being sent on small errands, and everyone enjoys their satis-

TABLE 4.2. Activity Variables Described

Type of Activity	Description
Work	Chores or tasks contributing to the household maintenance or economy; can be performed alone or in the company of others
Social play	Play involving others that is unique to childhood
General sociability	Miscellaneous sociability that is not play; includes activities such as chatting
Individual activity	Nonsocial activities (individual is not engaged with another) that are not categorized as work; includes sitting alone, playing alone

faction at completing the task. Mothers report that they consider these small errands to be preparation for carrying out orders that involve greater responsibility.

Terms referring to somewhat older children distinguish between females and males by reference to the division of labor by sex. A girl, from about 8 years until approximately puberty, is a *muhoho wa kubunda,* a child who pounds maize; a boy of this age is a *muhoho murisa,* a child who herds. Again, the term *muhoho* is not gender specific. In contrast to the behavior used to characterize the younger child, these activities—pounding maize and herding—are very strongly associated with gender. Just at this age, there emerge marked differences in the activities of girls and boys, especially with regard to work. Among children 8 through 11 years old, girls were observed working approximately 51% of the time and boys some 26% (see Fig. 4.1).

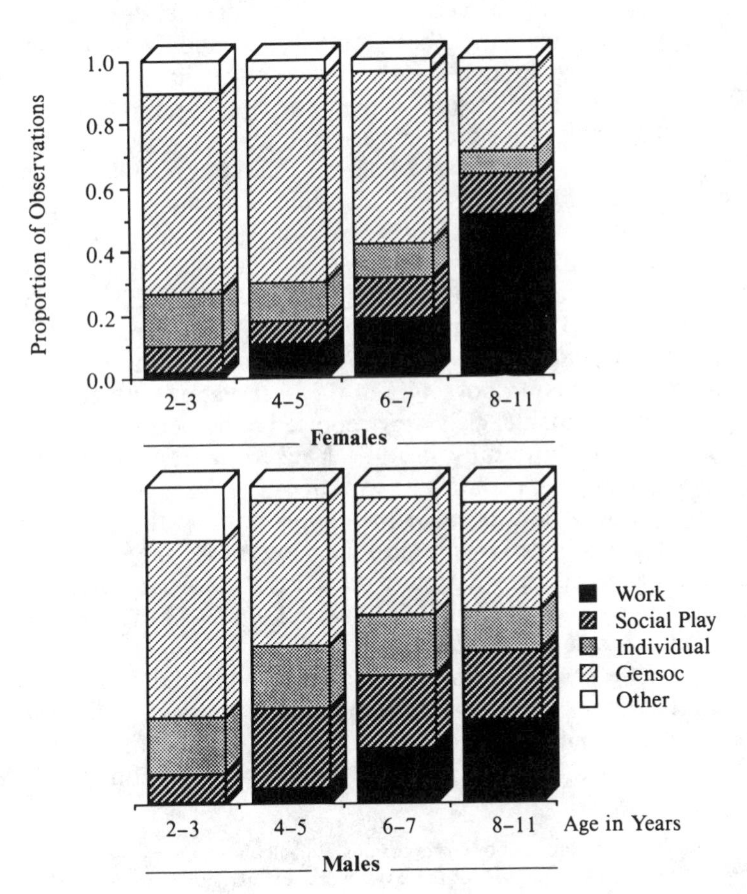

Figure 4.1. Profiles of children's activities, presented as proportions of the total times observed.

TABLE 4.3. Types of Work Performed by Children 8 Through 11 Years Old

Variable	Description
Gardening	Clearing land, preparing soil, cultivating, planting, weeding, scaring birds from crops, and harvesting
Errands	Running errands both inside and outside the homestead
Housework	Food processing, tending fire, cooking, serving food, cleaning house or yard, washing utensils, laundering, chopping wood, preparing thatching materials
Carrying	Collecting and carrying firewood; fetching water; transporting produce and palm wine
Child care	Supervising, feeding, dressing, soothing, carrying, and washing infants and toddlers

This gender difference pertains not only to the amount of work but also to the types of tasks performed (Table 4.3). Boys perform fewer types of tasks than girls. They do no "carrying" (of water, produce, and firewood)—tasks traditionally regarded as women's—and they do rather little child care; the most frequent chore boys do perform is the running of errands (Table 4.4).[1] Girls, on the other hand, do a greater variety of chores, with the most frequent being the carrying of loads and housework. The remainder of their time is fairly evenly divided between errands, child care, and gardening.

Clearly, after approximately 8 years of age, girls' time is more structured than boys', and it is structured around meeting the consumption, production, and reproduction needs of the household. This is highlighted by comparing two other aspects of time allocation. First, a comparison of percentages of observations when they were outside the *mudzi* shows that girls were out 37% and boys 44% of the observations. Of the observations when they were outside, girls were reported to be performing some type of task in 74% and boys only in 49%. Looked at from a slightly different angle, even within the context of work, boys' tasks gain them greater freedom from supervision, because the chores boys do take them outside the homestead. This is demonstrated by asking, of all the observations when the child was working, what percentage involved work outside the *mudzi*. Fifty-four percent of the girls' as compared to 82% of the boys' chores were performed outside the *mudzi*.

Most of the tasks performed by the sample children belong to the domain of women's work, and mothers tend to assign them, therefore, to girls who must one day be competent workers. Boys, in this sample, have little work to do that will prepare them for adulthood. While mothers

[1] It should be noted that the boys' proportions are calculated on a lower frequency of work. Consequently, even though 16% of the boys' work was gardening and only 11% of the girls' was, girls had a higher absolute frequency of gardening.

TABLE 4.4. Comparison of Girls' and Boys' Pattern of Task Performance at 8 to 11 Years Old

	Gender	
Type of Work	Females	Males
Gardening	10.9%	15.7%
Errands	16.5%	62.8%
Housework	33.0%	11.8%
Carrying	23.1%	——
Child care	15.4%	2.0%

report that, if necessary, they would require their sons to perform chores culturally defined as feminine, the need rarely arises since homesteads typically contain several women and mature girls. In former times and in areas where Giriama families keep small herds of livestock, a boy of this age would begin herding. Other forms of men's work, as these occur in Kaloleni, are too arduous and dangerous (e.g., palm tapping) or are restricted to adults (e.g., wage labor and trade).

Older girls routinely provide a meaningful proportion of the nurturance—"comforting," "helping," "caring for," and "protecting"—sought by younger children (Wenger, 1983). It is not at all unusual for a young child to be encouraged to develop a special bond with an older sister upon the arrival of a newborn. Very young Giriama children sleep in the same bed with their mothers. One of the traumatic events attendant upon the arrival of a new infant sibling is displacement from that sleeping arrangement. This trauma is commonly eased by shifting the displaced child into an older sister's bed. Recalling the special relationship he had with his older sister, one young man said that he was so greatly distressed when she went off to school at age 8 that he was allowed to go with her for 2 weeks, even though it was a walk of several miles. He remarked, "I respect my mother, but I love my sister." He also commented that he will always seem like a foolish young child to her.

The relatively greater burden of task performance placed on girls prepares them for their future roles as wives and mothers. It should be recalled that the Giriama homestead is patrilineal and virilocal. That is, a woman "marries in" to her husband's *mudzi.* In many East African societies, there is an expectation that the bride, who arrives as an outsider, will have difficult relationships with the other women of her husband's father's homestead. The Giriama, however, tend to view these relationships as cooperative, with the women of the *mudzi* sharing the responsibilities for farming, cooking, and raising children. This view of the relationships among married women in the homestead is expressed in the term used both for cowife and for sister-in-law, *mukakazi.* Based on the root *kazi,* a word that is often translated as "work," *mukakazi* expresses the notion that the wives of all the men of the same generation within a *mudzi* are co-workers. Moreover, Parkin (1979b) notes that *kazi* is a widespread suffix in Bantu languages that suggests a deep association between female reproductive fertility and female-induced fertility of the soil, thus indicating an implicit understanding that women's "work" is fundamental to sociocultural continuity.

Social Play

Boys' activity patterns reveal a larger portion of unstructured time and can be seen as providing them with some types of experience that could serve as preparation for the role of *mwenye mudzi.* The successful Giriama patriarch must strike a delicate balance between enterprising expansion and customary reciprocity among kin and neighbors. In short, he must counter dominance with sociability. Social play, with its rapid shifts from mutual sociability to dominance, is a context in which children learn to manage dominance in order to sustain play. The activity profiles depicted in Figure 4.1 indicate that, from approximately age 4, boys engage in social play more than girls. By 8 through 11 years, boys play outside the homestead (37%) more than girls (27%). This gives them more experience dealing with children who are related through marriage rather than blood or who are unrelated neighbors. Thus boys' social play offers a most relevant context for learning formative lessons in balancing dominance against cooperative sociability, a skill honed and polished by experience and plied in the role of *mwenye mudzi* and neighborhood elder.

Since social play has been so widely observed to increase with age during early and middle childhood, it is surprising in these data that the difference between ages 2 through 3 and 6 through 7 for girls is only 4%. Quite evidently this does not reflect social maturation for the girls in this particular sample, since their pattern of work clearly indicates that they have mastered the relevant social and cognitive skills. Nor is it likely that girls' lower rates of social play imply less interest in social interaction than boys, since their rates of general sociability are higher than boys' until 8 through 11 years old (Wenger, 1983). Rather, it appears that boys and girls in this sample express mutual sociability in different activities. These two distinct activity contexts for sociability parallel different companionship preferences: Boys spend more time with peers and girls spend more time with infants and adults. Social play occurs most frequently, in this sample, when children are in exclusively peer groups; general sociability occurs most frequently in mixed-age groups.

Individual Activity

The second type of activity in which boys' percentages, after 2 through 3 years old, are consistently higher than girls' is individual activity. This classification denotes activities that involve no one else but are not work (e.g., whittling a stick or playing alone). Indeed, the two sexes display rather unrelated patterns in individual activity, with girls' steadily decreasing and boys' remaining approximately the same until the oldest age group, when there is a decrease (see Fig. 4.1).

This gender difference, though less striking than that of social play, complements it in its implications for socialization. Boys, it appears, have or take more opportunities to engage their attention in activities of their own. Combined with their rather more frequent absence from the homestead,[2] this pattern suggests that boys experience less external constraint from the scrutiny of older girls and women and from the demands of labor. It would seem that boys are engaged in the process of negotiating dominance relations among the members of their age grade. Evidence from the companionship variables, presented next, further supports this interpretation.

Children's Companionship

The comparison of companionship comes from data on whom the child was engaged with at the time of the spot observation. The fact that a variety of people might be within the *mudzi* but not engaged with the child suggests a culturally constrained choice: In accordance with the norms of society, the child and members of his or her family choose to engage in some types of activities and with some classes of individuals rather than with others. This is especially apparent with regard to the segregation of "generations" of the two sexes. Moreover, norms influence the kind and degree of interchange between separate clusters of individuals. As I pointed out earlier, children are reluctant to draw the attention of adults to themselves, both because of respect and out of the desire to avoid the potentially negative consequences. When they do need attention, they do not call out to an adult—as many American children do—but instead go to the adult and speak politely. In order to treat the presence of a given category of companion as a choice in the analysis, a child was excluded from comparisons if no choice was possible.

The child's companionship was coded according to how many people were with her or him, the types of individuals present, and their gender distribution. For this discussion the following variables were selected to characterize companionship: the presence of women[3] or of infants in the child's interactional group, participation in exclusively peer and same-sex peer groups, and incidence of observations when the child was alone. These were chosen because they provide markedly distinct opportunities for exchanges that involve helping, supporting, and comforting and because they

[2] At ages 8 through 11, boys' general sociability also occurred outside the homestead more than girls': 30% as compared to 15%.

[3] Incidences of men present in children's social interactional space were much too infrequent to include.

highlight significant features of the Giriama child's social ecology. Adults were selected because they are the most likely class of individual to offer help, comfort, and support to children; infants because they are the most likely to elicit those resources; and peers because they are the least likely to do either (B. Whiting & Edwards, 1973, 1988; B. Whiting & J. Whiting, 1975). The category *adult females* includes women 16 years or older; *infants* includes children up to 18 months in age; *peers* includes any child within 2 years in age of the focal child. Since there were no observations in which a child was the only person in a homestead, *alone* always refers to being off by oneself (cf. individual activity in which a child was not engaged with others but could have been in their company). If a child was outside the homestead, *alone* means that the child is reported to have gone by himself or herself.

Peers

The first variable to be examined is association with peers as companions. Because of the minimum and maximum ages of peers, potentially fewer children qualify as peers for the youngest and oldest children. Moreover, given the increasing probability that older children will be outside the homestead, the chances of being observed in the company of a peer at home are decreased still further for older children. With these provisos in mind, I turn to the age trends in girls' and boys' association exclusively with peers (Fig. 4.2). Girls display a linear decrease between ages 2 through 3 (23%) and 8 through 11 (12%) in the percentage of observations in which they were in the company of only peers. This was not expected,

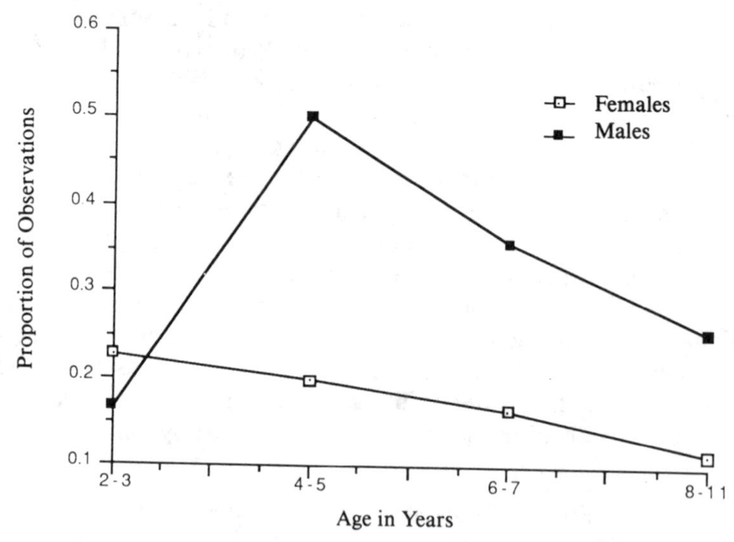

Figure 4.2. Child's companionship composed entirely of peers, presented as proportions of the total times observed.

since in most societies children of this age increase their peer contacts. Boys, on the other hand, display the expected and dramatic increase in their exclusively peer associations between ages 2 through 3 (17%) and 4 through 5 (50%). The overall age trend for boys, however, is quadratic, peaking at ages 4 through 5 and declining thereafter to 36% at ages 6 through 7 and 26% at ages 8 through 11. An explanation of the decrease in exclusively peer companions for older children is that they have more responsibilities and therefore less time for play and that peers are less available in the home.

In any case, the most important conclusion to draw from comparing girls' and boys' patterns of association with peers is that boys have substantially more exposure to the most extreme version of the peer environment. That is, boys spend more time with groups of children who are all close in age and whose interactions are characterized by horizontal (affiliation, competition, and egoistic dominance) rather than vertical reciprocity (prosocial dominance and egoistic dependence). These differences complement those reported earlier for social play and further substantiate the argument that boys' social ecology provides a context for learning how to manage the interplay of egoistic dominance and sociability.

Infants

If boys have more experience than girls with the interactions characteristic of peers, then girls have more experience with those characteristic of infants (Fig. 4.3). At each point, girls' percentages of observations with infants are greater than boys' (cf. B. Whiting & Edwards, 1973, 1988). The trend for girls is linear, increasing from 18% at ages 2 to 3 to 27% at ages

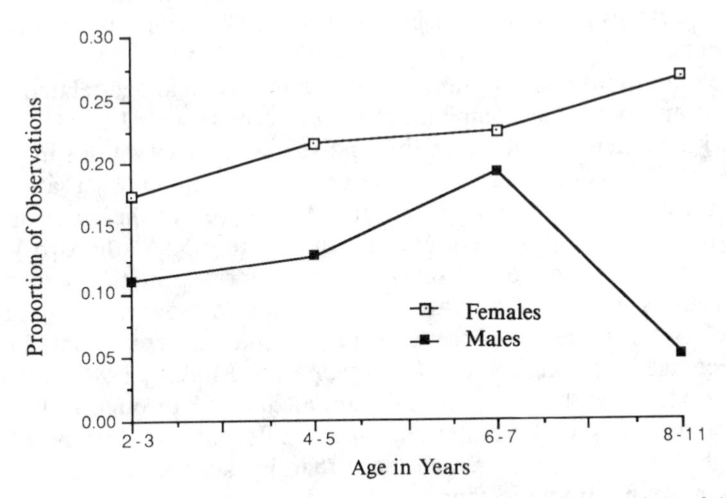

Figure 4.3. Child's companionship includes an infant, presented as proportions of the total times observed.

8 through 11. Boys, in this case, display the quadratic trend: between ages 2 through 3 and 6 through 7 their percentages increase linearly from 11 to 19%, but at ages 8 through 11 boys were in the company of infants only 5% of the observations.

Throughout the age range of 2 through 11, then, girls spend more time with a category of companion who elicits nurturance. At least for children 2 through 3, this cannot be explained by girls' association with women, because boys spend as much time with women. It would seem that girls are more attracted to infants than boys, though not dramatically so, and that this attraction is evident at a remarkably early age. The dramatic drop in contact with infants for boys 8 through 11 can be explained unequivocally by social norms. As discussed earlier, it is at this age that girls are seriously incorporated into the work activities of women; and, at least traditionally, the Giriama terms for children of this age make explicit reference to the division of labor between females and males. The implications of this division in terms of the companionship of girls and boys is evident at ages 8 through 11. Infants are cared for by females, and thus older boys are around them only for comparatively brief playful exchanges.

So far, the data indicate that from ages 4 through 5 boys spend more time than girls in exclusively peer environments and girls spend somewhat more time than boys with infants, a discrepancy that could be termed substantial by ages 8 through 11. Another way to consider these companionship patterns is to examine the ratio of observations in which an infant was present or peers were exclusively present. This allows us to compare relative exposure to individuals who by status elicit nurturance to those who by status elicit reciprocity in the form of sociability and egoistic dominance. The group proportions for girls and boys in each of the four age groups are presented in Figure 4.4. This graph demonstrates how divergent are the age patterns in companionship for girls and boys with respect to infants and peers.

The data on exclusively same-sex companions yield age-related patterns for girls and boys that complement the patterns reported later for association with women. The focus in this analysis is on observations in which all of the child's companions were other children. Of these observations, what percentage involved only children of the same sex as the child observed? The group proportions are presented in Figure 4.5. At the two youngest ages, both girls and boys display a linear increase in the percentage of observations in which there are gender-exclusive groups. The greatest increase for boys was 19 percentage points and occurred when expected, between ages 2 through 3 and 4 through 5 (cf. Morelli, 1986). Subsequent increases for boys, however, are substantial, and at 8 through 11 years some 70% of their all-child companionship is male only. Girls, who at ages 2 through 3 display a greater preference than boys for same-sex companions (32%), make no dramatic change at ages 4 through 5. Their greatest change

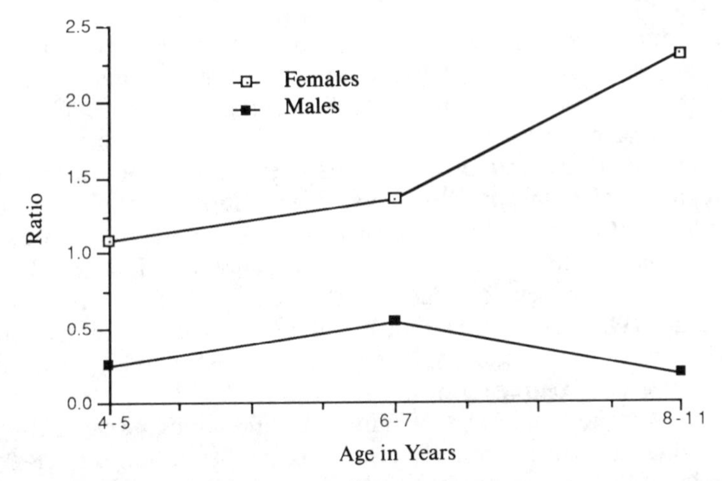

Figure 4.4. Comparison of infant versus peer companionship, presented as a ratio of proportions of times observed with an infant to times observed exclusively with peers.

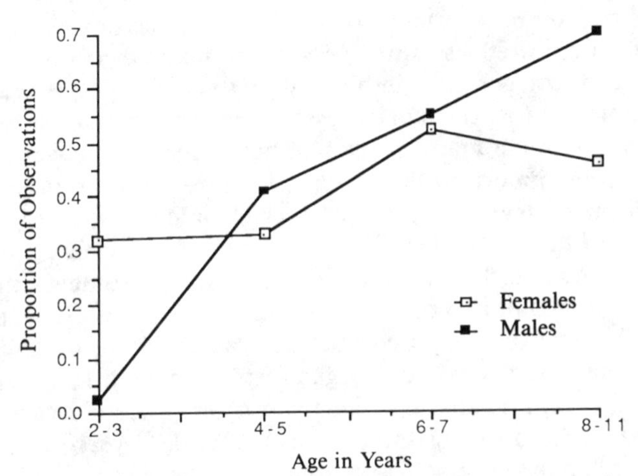

Figure 4.5. Proportion of exclusively same-sex companionship in observations in which all companions were other children.

occurs between ages 4 through 5 (33%) and 6 through 7 (52%). At the oldest age point, girls' rates of same-sex companionship drop, so that at this age boys' percentages are substantially higher than girls'.

The divergence of girls' and boys' preference for same-sex companions at ages 8 through 11 can be explained in terms of girls' responsibilities. By this age, a substantial portion of their time is devoted to household chores, which, as compared to social play, often place them in charge of small children or in the company of women. Thus if girls have a preference for sex segregation, the opportunity to express it is limited. Evidence in support of this explanation can be found by examining girls' and boys' rates of sex segregation with peer companions. Percentages of exclusively same-sex companions were calculated on the basis of the total number of observations when only peers were present. As can be seen in Table 4.5, an increasing percentage of both girls' and boys' peer groups are segregated by sex, until at the oldest age group more than 90% of these are gender exclusive and the rates for the sexes are roughly comparable (cf. Ellis, Rogoff, & Cromer, 1981; Harkness & Super, 1985; Rogoff, 1978, 1981; B. Whiting & Edwards, 1988). Assuming that of all types of companions peers are most likely to be freely chosen, these data give testimony to girls' inclination toward gender segregation.

What makes the preference for same-sex child companions so illuminating is its relevance to hypotheses regarding the formation of gender identity. Luria (1979) sees as aspects of the development of gender identity the use of gender-explicit nouns and pronouns, the choice of same-sex playmates, and gender-encoded toys. In the Giriama language, as in all Bantu languages, pronominal forms are not distinguished by sex. As a consequence, when children use third-person pronominal forms, they are not simultaneously categorizing individuals by sex. Thus it seems that the use of pronominal forms is not necessarily related to other aspects of gender identity. Although many of the families in the sample were large, children had fewer opportunities to choose same-sex peer playmates than children in the typical American research sample observed in classrooms. Compared to Ellis and colleagues' (1981) sample of American children 1 through 12 years old, the Giriama children display a somewhat higher rate of same-sex companion choices. And, even though the Giriama children have very few toys as compared to American children, by around age 3, the boys in the spot observations began displaying a marked preference for "male" toys, including the ingenious and often graceful "cars" (*magari*) constructed by boys out of found objects. While 2-year-old boys would cooperate as "babies" (i.e., allowing themselves to be carried on the back) when girls played "mothers," 3-year-old boys were not observed to do so. Girls were more flexible in their play choices. However, on occasions when

TABLE 4.5. Percentage of Peer-Only Observations That Involved Exclusively Members of the Same Sex as the Child Observed

	Gender	
Age Group	Females	Males
2–3 Years old	43.6%	31.6%
4–5 Years old	52.0%	40.0%
6–7 Years old	53.3%	67.9%
8–11 Years old	92.0%	95.0%

they attempted to play with *magari,* they were menaced by boys, who claimed that these were not the toys of girls. Thus despite cultural, linguistic, and demographic differences, the data reported here on sex segregation are compatible with Luria's discussion of the manifestations of core gender identity.

Women

Though the age-by-sex trends for time with women are not divergent, the sexes again display different rates of association with women (Fig. 4.6). The percentage of observations in which children were in the company of women declines from 41% at ages 2 through 3 to 18% at ages 8 through 11. This pattern is hardly surprising since with maturity children increasingly forsake caretakers to spend time with other children. Moreover, the norms of respect governing the relations between adjacent generations would strengthen this tendency to some extent. As expected, the decline for boys is more dramatic than it is for girls, and the timing of the decrease is different for the two sexes. Between ages 2 through 3 and 4 through 5, boys decrease the time they spend with women by more than 50%; thereafter the decrease is steady but not precipitous. Girls, in contrast, spend virtually the same amount of time with women at ages 4 through 5 as at ages 2 through 3. The major decrease for girls occurs between ages 4 through 5 and 6 through 7, when the percentages drop from 36 to 21%. A possible reversal of this trend occurs at the oldest age point, when girls were observed with women 26% of the observations and when they have begun to participate more extensively in the work of the homestead.

Age-related difference in the percentage of occasions girls and boys were observed with women could be interpreted to derive from the distinct

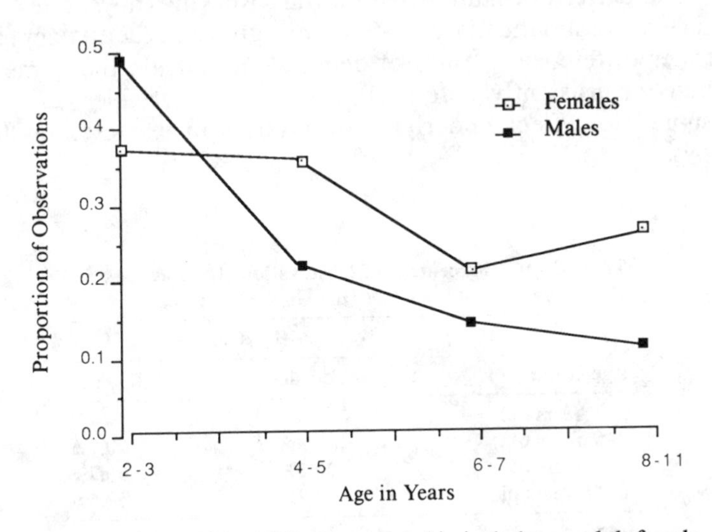

Figure 4.6. Observations in which child's companionship includes an adult female.

issues hypothesized by Chodorow (1974) to surround the consolidation of feminine and masculine identity. By ages 4 through 5, theoretically after the consolidation of core gender identity, boys clearly reduce the amount of time they spend with women. Chodorow theorizes that in order to consolidate their masculine identification boys must negate their primary attachment to their mothers and, consequently, everything "feminine." Feminine identification does not involve rejection of the primary relationship of infantile dependence on the mother; rather, it is continuous with early childhood identifications and attachments. Hence girls have no need to withdraw from their mothers at the time when they have consolidated their gender identities. Their overall pattern of decrease could be explained as part of the broader pattern of increasing association with other children, which is somewhat modified at the oldest age point by the incorporation of the girls into the domestic work force.

Alone

The final companionship variable analyzed is the percentage of observations in which the child is alone. This variable could be interpreted to represent freedom from the scrutiny of others. When at home, the sex differences between girls and boys were marginal, with boys scoring consistently but minimally higher after ages 2 through 3. However, when outside the homestead, boys are reported alone more often than girls (see Table 4.6). The gender differences are substantial and are consistent with earlier findings about activities: Boys spend more time than girls beyond the range of scrutiny. The first explanation of this phenomenon is that the nature of work that girls do outside the homestead requires the cooperation, and therefore the presence, of others. This, however, does not explain the pattern because when they are working, boys' rates of being alone are not dramatically different from girls'. In fact, it appears that the gender difference in rates of being alone outside the homestead is distributed consistently across all the activity variables, and it must be assumed to reflect underlying differences in expectations for girls and boys.

TABLE 4.6. Percentage of Observations Outside the Homestead When the Child Had Gone Out Alone

	Gender	
Age Group	Females	Males
2–3 Years old	—	—
4–5 Years old	5.8%	20.7%
6–7 Years old	20.5%	35.7%
8–11 Years old	40.9%	57.5%

CONCLUSIONS

This examination of the social ecology of Kaloleni children's everyday lives has revealed several important themes that warrant further attention. The first is that Giriama society is characterized by formalized social networks and relationships, based primarily on kinship but cross-cut by generation and gender, which permeate all facets of Kaloleni children's developing relationships. Second, these relationships, forged in the natal household and community, will endure until death and express shared cultural expectations governing rights, roles, responsibilities, obligations, and privileges.

In addition to their being enduring, another important feature of these emerging relationships among the children of Kaloleni is their double-edged quality. Those youngsters who offer each other, on a daily basis, the greatest sources for support—whether through the camaraderie of play, the bonds of caretaking and being cared for, or the shared responsibilities of chores—also present each other with the greatest sources of conflict. Even in a community where an age-based hierarchy among children is recognized and legitimates the use of authority between youngsters, what begins as prosocial interaction can quickly dissolve into a self-centered bid for dominance, whether by intent or perceived intent. This potential for conflict among those who constitute one's primary support group may be aggravated as the individual moves along his or her life course, with critical points at key transitions when rights over property and other valued resources are at stake. Thus, relationships developed in childhood endure over a lifetime and display an unfolding commitment, marked by reciprocity and conflict.

In sharp contrast to the experience of Kaloleni children, many youngsters growing up in industrialized societies have a radically different experience of childhood social relationships. Outside the household, often comprised solely of the parent(s) and children, social relationships typically develop and dissolve according to the exigencies of ephemeral situational contexts, such as day care or school.

Having reviewed in some detail the daily activities and companionship patterns of the children of Kaloleni, it is useful to return to the original purpose of this chapter, which is to consider how these patterns are shaped by the larger sociocultural context. It would be difficult to overstate that the persistent gender differences in both activity and companionship patterns mark divergent paths of preparation for female and male adulthood in Giriama society. The activity profiles clearly suggest that girls' time is more structured to meet the needs of others than boys': Girls display consistently higher rates of work than boys; and by 8 through 11 years of age, the girls were observed working in more than half the observations. The chores that girls perform represent a range of tasks typically performed by women. The chores performed by boys are narrower in range and fewer in incidence than girls', and boys' chores include few of men's productive activities. Boys' activity profiles display a higher frequency of social play and individual activity, activities that imply greater freedom to structure time according to one's own goals. In their cross-cultural analysis of children's activities, B. Whiting and Edwards (1988) also report that boys spend more time in undirected or unstructured activities than girls. Boys' relatively higher rate of social play, I argue, gains them valuable experience in managing the balance between cooperative sociability and egoistic dominance, a skill ultimately practiced in the future role of *mwenye mudzi.*

The gender differences in companionship complement those found for the activities. Girls spend more time than boys with women and infants, categories of persons who elicit, respectively, egoistic dependence and nurturance. Further, the presence of women implies constraint and scrutiny, surely evidence of still another way in which girls' time is organized rather more frequently to meet the needs of others. The presence of women also implies that girls have abundant exposure to adult sex-role models, while the presence of infants and the high rate of work suggest that girls practice many of the skills necessary to becoming competent Giriama women. The girls must certainly experience a sense of continuity in their development as females and legitimacy in their authority within the sphere of domestic activities. The pattern of girls' differential exposure to women is reported for other samples (Rogoff, 1978; B. Whiting & Edwards, 1988), as is their association with infants (cf. Berman, Monda, & Myerscough, 1977; Frodi & Lamb, 1978; Konner, 1976; Melson & Fogel, 1982; Rogoff, 1981b; B. Whiting & Edwards, 1988; B. Whiting & J. Whiting, 1975).

Between ages 2 through 3 and 8 through 11, boys' companionship patterns evidence some discontinuities. Initially, they spend considerable time with women and infants. However, by ages 4 through 5, their time with women is considerably reduced. At the same age point, their time with peers, who theoretically elicit sociability and egoistic dominance, increases dramatically. By 8 through 11 years old, boys spend very little time with infants. Indeed, considering their relatively higher rates of absence from the home, occasions during which they are less likely than girls to work and more likely to be alone, the patterning of boys' activities and companionship suggests ample opportunity for autonomy and fewer demands for responsibility. Boys have less exposure than girls to adult sex-role models and less practice in sex-stereotyped duties. There is an excellent case for arguing that sex-role modeling for boys takes place within the peer group and, increasingly with age, outside the home, a pattern certainly consistent with what one might expect in a patrilineal society where vestiges of an age-graded generational system still operate, and where there are few forms of work boys can learn to prepare them for adulthood. Although these gender differences are continuous with the divergent but complementary career trajectories of women and men in Giriama society, specific aspects of these differences appear to reflect potentially universal dimensions of gender differences. These include the preference for sex segregation in exclusively child groups (see Hartup, 1983; B. Whiting & Edwards, 1988; Morelli, 1986; cf. Harkness & Super, 1985), girls' higher rates of work and greater involvement with infants (Munroe, Munroe, & Shimmin, 1984; Rogoff, 1981b; B. Whiting & Edwards, 1988), and boys' higher rates of absence from the home. The patterning of boys' companionship choices evokes a psychological explanation like Chodorow's (1974). One can see in their systematically diminished association with women and infants and their increased association with peers and same-sex children the need to negate attachments to womanly nurturance to affirm those with male behaviors. Given the lack of opportunity to gain practical competence in men's work, boys must be understood to form a more positional type of identification than girls.

In this chapter, I have attempted to lay out a set of sociocultural features that, on the one hand, influence the patterns of companionship and, on the other hand, will evolve into the support networks of adulthood in a Giriama community. The activity chosen for special consideration because of its mediating influence and far reaching impact on the development of relationships is children's work. It is vital to stress that "work" is not simply a *variable* that, as an isolated factor, distinguishes the experience of the children of Kaloleni from, for example, children of an industrialized society. Rather, "work" is an embedded phenomenon that is tightly woven into community life, and it bears multiple and complex layers of cultural meaning. Indeed, "work," both as an activity and as a cultural construct, appears to be linked to fundamental dimensions of the experience of being male or female. Finally, the challenge remains to researchers studying American children to identify those processes that shape normative experience within socioculturally distinct groups and impart meaning into a host of individual differences in the formation of social relationships.

REFERENCES

Berman, P., Monda, L., & Myerscough, R. (1977). Sex differences in young children's responses to an infant: An observation within a daycare setting. *Child Development, 48,* 711–715.

Brantley, C. (1981). *The Giriama and colonial resistance in Kenya, 1800–1920.* Los Angeles: University of California Press.

Chodorow, N. (1974). Family structure and feminine personality. In M. Rosaldo & L. Lamphere (Eds.), *Women, culture, and society* (pp. 43–66). Stanford, CA: Stanford University Press.

Ellis, S., Rogoff, B. & Cromer, C. (1981). Age segregation in children's social interactions. *Developmental Psychology, 17,* 399–407.

Frodi, A., & Lamb, M. (1978). Sex differences in responsiveness to infants: A developmental study in psychophysiological and behavioral responses. *Child Development, 49,* 1182–1188.

Harkness, S., & Super, C. (1985). The cultural context of gender segregation in children's peer groups. *Child Development, 56,* 219–224.

Hartup, W. (1983). Peer relations. In E. Mavis Hetherington (Ed.), *Socialization, personality, and social development,* Vol. IV, (pp. 103–196). New York: Wiley.

Konner, M. (1976). Maternal care, infant behavior and development among the !Kung. In R. Lee & I. De Vore (Eds.), *Kalahari hunter gatherers.* Cambridge, MA: Harvard University Press.

LeVine, R., & LeVine [Lloyd], B. (1963). *Nyansongo: A Gusii community in Kenya.* New York: John Wiley.

Luria, Z. (1979). Psychosocial determinants of gender identity, role, and orientation. In H. Katchadourian (Ed.), *Human sexuality* (pp. 163–193). Berkeley, CA: University of California Press.

Melson, G., & Fogel, A. (1982). Young children's interest in unfamiliar infants. *Child Development, 53*(3), 693–700.

Morelli, G. (1986). Social development of 1, 2, and 3 year old Efe and Lese children within the Ituri Forest of Northeastern Zaire: The relation amongst culture, setting, and development. Ph.D. diss., Department of Psychology, University of Massachusetts at Amherst.

Munroe, R., & Munroe, R. (1971). Household density and infants care in an East African community. *Journal of Social Psychology, 83,* 3–13.

Munroe, R., Munroe, R., & Shimmin, H. (1987). Children's work in four cultures: Determinants and consequences. *American Anthropologist, 86,* 369–379.

Parkin, D. (1972). *Palms, wine, and witnesses: Public spirit and private gain in an African farming community.* San Francisco, CA: Chandler.

Parkin, D. (1979a). Along the line of road: Expanding rural centres in Kenya's Coast Province. *Africa, 49,* 272–282.

Parkin, D. (1979b). The categorization of work. Cases from coastal Kenya. In S. Wallman (Ed.), *The social anthropology of work.* (pp. 317–336). New York: Academic.

Parkin, D. (1980). The creativity of abuse. *Man* (New Series), *15,* 45–64.

Rogoff, B. (1978). Spot observation: An introduction and examination. *Quarterly Newsletter of the Institute for Comparative Human Development, 2,* 21–26.

Rogoff, B. (1981a). Adults and peers as agents of socialization: A Highland Guatemalan profile. *Ethos, 9,* 18–36.

Rogoff, B. (1981b). The relation of age and sex to experiences during childhood in a highland community. *Anthropology UCLA, 11,* 25–41.

Rogoff, B., Sellers, M., Pirrotta, S., Fox, N., & White, S. (1975). Age of assignment of roles and responsibilities to children: A cross cultural survey. *Human Development, 18,* 353–369.

Spear, T. (1979). *The Kaya complex.* Nairobi: Kenya Literature Bureau.

Weisner, T. (1982). Sibling interdependence and child caretaking: A cross-cultural view. In M. Lamb & Sutton-Smith, B. (Eds.), *Sibling relationships* (pp. 303–327). Hillsdale, NJ: Erlbaum.

Wenger, M. (1983). *Gender role socialization in an East African Community: Social interaction between 2 to 3-year-olds and older children in social ecological perspective.* Unpublished doctoral dissertation, Harvard University.

Whiting, B. (1980). Culture and social behavior: A model for the development of social behavior. *Ethos, 8,* 95–116.

Whiting, B., & Edwards, C. (1973). A cross-cultural analysis of sex differences in the behavior of children 3 to 11. *Journal of Social Psychology, 91,* 171–188. Society for Research in Child Development, San Francisco.

Whiting, B., & Edwards, C. (1988). *Children of different worlds.* Cambridge, MA: Harvard University Press.

Whiting, B., & Whiting, J. (1975). *Children of six cultures: A psychocultural analysis.* Cambridge: Harvard University Press.

Whiting, J., Chasdi, E., Antonovsky, H., & Ayers, B. (1966). The learning of values. In E. Vogt & E. Albert (Eds.), *People of Rimrock: A study of values in five cultures* (pp. 83–125). Cambridge, MA: Harvard University Press.

PART 2

Characteristics of Children's Social Networks

CHAPTER 5

The Social Networks of Girls and Boys from Early Through Middle Childhood

CANDICE FEIRING AND MICHAEL LEWIS

The social network construct has been discussed extensively, and several definitions of social networks exist (Bott, 1971; Cochran & Brassard, 1979; Leinhart, 1977; Lewis & Feiring, 1978). One aspect common to all definitions is the reference to the linkages between social units, both persons and groups, with which an individual has contact. The social network framework conceptualizes social relations, social opportunities, and social constraints by providing a schematic representation of how significant others and less central social contacts can be characterized, organized, and interrelated.

At any given point in an individual's life, a description of the person's network may be viewed as an index of the person's social world or life space. This includes descriptions of people in the network and the types of activities in which they are engaged. The infant is born into a social network, the most immediate and important component of which is the family. Initially through parents and later on his or her own initiative as well, the child's network will include significant others beyond the family such as friends, teachers, and eventually mates. The infant learns to adapt to a changing array of people, behavior, goals, and institutions, and it is within this array that the development and socialization of the individual take place. To some extent, socialization is learning to become a member of a social network (Cochran & Brassard, 1979; Lewis & Feiring, 1978). Beginning in infancy and then across the life span, it is of interest to explore the relationship between people and what they do. What people constitute the social network and what they do within the network, their social functions, can be conceptualized as the social network matrix (Lewis & Feiring, 1979).

Preparation of this paper was made possible through funds from the William T. Grant Foundation. We would like to thank John Jaskir for help with data analysis.

THE SOCIAL NETWORK MATRIX

Given the varied functions and the likelihood of multiple relations in the life of an individual, it is useful to think of a model that describes how multiple people and functions operate from given points in development. The matrix depicted in Figure 5.1 illustrates the hypothetical social network matrix of a 3-year-old child, Julia.

In Figure 5.1, $P_1 \ldots P_n$ represents the set of social network members and includes Julia (self), mother, father, older sister, grandparents, two girls and one boy friend, and any other persons to be considered. The array of network members is determined by a variety of factors such as the child's age, sex, culture, and social class. Of particular interest in this chapter is the relationship between a person's age, sex, and the nature of the network

	Social Network Members	Social Functions					
		F_1	F_2	F_3	F_4	F_5	F_n
		Protection $B_{11}B_{12}B_{13}$	Caregiving $B_{21}B_{22}B_{23}$	Nurturance $B_{31}B_{32}\ldots$	Play	Learning	B_n
P_1	Self-Julia				10	20	
P_2	Mother	50	50	50	5	15	
P_3	Father	5	5	20	10	15	
P_4	Older brother				15	15	
P_5	Grandma						
P_6	Grandpa						
P_7	Aunt						
P_8	Female cousin						
P_9	Girl friend				15	10	
P_{10}	Girl friend				5	5	
P_{11}	Boy friend						
P_{12}							
P_{13}							
P_{14}							
P_{15}							
P_n							

Figure 5.1. The social network matrix of social network members and functions for a hypothetical 3-year-old child, Julia. (Note that the numbers are hypothetical to indicate relative amounts of activity by a particular person in a particular function.)

matrix. The functions labeled $F_1 \ldots F_n$ consist of protection, caregiving, nurturance, play, and learning. This list of functions is not meant to be exhaustive but rather is suggestive of the type of broad categories that can describe social activities and their intended goals (Lewis, Feiring, & Kotsonis, 1984). The behaviors $B_{11}, B_{12} \ldots, B_n$ represent the set of behaviors that can be measured and that are subsumed under the broad heading of a particular function. For example, under nurturance, emotional behaviors such as verbal and nonverbal expressions of affection and acceptance might be considered. For play, the behaviors of making up stories, playing games, running, and riding a bicycle might be included. From a developmental perspective, any of these functions and the goals they represent can change or remain the same. It is clear, however, that the particular behaviors that comprise the function generally change. With development one also would expect to observe changes in which people are involved in which function as well as which functions predominate. The relative importance of particular functions and the people involved in the exchanges related to particular functions change with development. These shifts in the social network have to do with changes in centrality of people by function units (Connell & Furman, 1984). It should be noted that some researchers have conceptualized functions and their behavior somewhat differently, referring to goals for activities as functions and the processes by which functions are achieved as resources (Hirsch, 1981; Shumaker & Brownell, 1984).

Furman (this volume) in his chapter discusses the theories of developmental change that are concerned with the emergence of social needs and social motives. These theories may provide useful ways of specifying the functions of the social matrix. For example, Sullivan's five basic needs, tenderness, companionship, acceptance, intimacy, and sexuality, could be examined longitudinally across an array of changing social network members. In his own work, Furman (1984; this volume) uses the concept of social provisions, and pinpoints seven particular functions of the social network (e.g., enhancement of worth, companionship, instrumental help) that are particularly important for social development.

The general form of the social network model provides a framework for considering the complete array of social network members and functions that describe the person's social network. By examining the matrix, one can determine which social network members are present, what functions are being satisfied, and which functions are achieved by which social network members. By observing the vertical axis of the matrix, one can study the people characterizing the network of a particular child. The vertical axis will change so that the presence or absence of certain people will be related to the individual's time point in the life cycle, for example, an increase in the number of peers as the child gets older.

By examining the horizontal axis of the matrix, one can obtain an idea of what functions are characteristic of a particular social network. This type of analysis would also involve looking at global aspects of network changes

(Furman, this volume). While all the listed functions are presumed to be important, it might be that for some children the caregiving and nurturance functions predominate, while for others nurturing, play, and learning are equally important. Developmentally, the salience of certain functions will change depending on the age of the child being studied. Thus for infants we may find that caregiving and nurturance are predominant while for the young child play emerges as equally important. At least in terms of the amount of time spent in a given function, play represents a function that occurs often in the beginning of the life cycle but declines after adolescence. Nurturance appears to be a consistently exchanged function across the life cycle, although who nurtures whom changes considerably (e.g., Troll, 1987; Furman, this volume). Obviously, it is important to consider the person by function interaction or what people play what roles. For example, in childhood nurturance may be fulfilled in exchanges with parents, while in adolescence same-sex best friends may be an added resource for this function (Hunter & Youniss, 1982). Play may be particularly characteristic of father–infant exchanges while in childhood and adolescence play will become most characteristic of same-sex friends but not parents (Buhrmester & Furman, 1987). In regard to general roles, female network members may be more likely to be involved in the functions of nurturance and caregiving (Belle, 1987).

CASE EXAMPLE OF DEVELOPMENTAL CHANGES IN A CHILD'S SOCIAL NETWORK MATRIX

Figures 5.1, 5.2, and 5.3 show the social network matrix of the same child, Julia, at ages 3, 6, and 9, respectively. These hypothetical matrices attempt to illustrate some of the developmental shifts apparent in the social network as a child moves from a more home-centered, kin-oriented existence toward a more school-oriented, nonkin peer existence. In Figure 5.1, the vertical axis shows a large number of kin with a few peers present. On the horizontal axis, the functions of protection, caregiving, and nurturance are prevalent and mother is stipulated as mostly fulfilling these functions. Play and learning are also noted with play particularly characterized by father, older sibling, and peers. The tendency to have more same-sex peers has emerged.

At 6 years (Fig. 5.2) the vertical axis shows an increase in network members that is mostly due to an increase in friends. This is in part due to the fact that Julia attends school on a daily basis, something which she did not do at 3 years. In the kin dimension, there has been the loss of a grandparent and the addition of a baby sister. The social functions of caregiving and protection have shifted away from almost exclusive maternal predominance to include father and older brother. The functions of play and learning have become more salient. At 6 years, one sees a strong same-sex preference in

	Social Network Members	Social Functions					
		F_1	F_2	F_3	F_4	F_5	F_n
		Protection $B_{11}B_{12}B_{13}$	Caregiving $B_{21}B_{22}B_{23}$	Nurturance $B_{31}B_{32}$ . . .	Play	Learning	B_n
P_1	Self-Julia		15	5	20	30	
P_2	Mother	20	30	50	5	15	
P_3	Father	10	10	20	5	15	
P_4	Older brother		5	20	10	15	
P_5	Younger sister						
P_6	Grandma						
P_7	Aunt						
P_8	Female cousin						
P_9	Girl friend			20	20	20	
P_{10}	Girl friend				20	15	
P_{11}	Girl friend				5	15	
P_{12}	Boy friend					15	
P_{13}	Teacher					30	
P_{14}							
P_{15}							
P_n							

Figure 5.2. The social network matrix of social network members and functions for a hypothetical 6-year-old child, Julia. (Note that the numbers are hypothetical to indicate relative amounts of activity by a particular person in a particular function.)

peers in the network. At 9 years (Fig. 5.3) Julia's network has continued to grow in size especially in peer and nonrelative adult contact. The function of caregiving has shifted to self as well as parents. The function of nurturance is now satisfied by a best friend as well as family members. In general, learning and play are particularly salient. While the case example of Julia is fictitious, it illustrates some of the trends we have observed in children's networks (Bryant, 1985; Cochran & Riley, 1987; Feiring & Lewis, 1987a, 1987b; Furman & Buhrmester, 1985). It also illustrates how some functions may correspond closely to particular people (e.g., mother and caregiving in early childhood) while other functions may be less person specific (e.g., play with friends, siblings, and cousins). To a certain extent the broadening of the number of people who are involved in a variety of functions relates to the

	Social Networks Members	Social Functions					
		F_1	F_2	F_3	F_4	F_5	F_n
		Protection $B_{11}B_{12}B_{13}$	Caregiving $B_{21}B_{22}B_{23}$	Nurturance $B_{31}B_{32}\ldots$	Play	Learning	B_n
P_1	Self-Julia		40	10	20	40	
P_2	Mother		5	40		20	
P_3	Father		5	30		20	
P_4	Older brother		5	10	5	10	
P_5	Younger sister				10		
P_6	Grandma			10	5	5	
P_7	Aunt						
P_8	Female cousin						
P_9	Best girl friend			30	40	20	
P_{10}	Girl friend			5	30	10	
P_{11}	Girl friend			10	20	10	
P_{12}	Girl friend			5	20	10	
P_{13}	Boy friend				5	5	
P_{14}	Teacher			5		40	
P_{15}	Soccer coach					10	
P_n							

Figure 5.3. The social network matrix of social network members and functions for a hypothetical 9-year-old child, Julia. (Note that the numbers are hypothetical to indicate relative amounts of activity by a particular person in a particular function.)

development of autonomy, while a consistency in network membership in multiple functions (Zelkowitz, this volume) relates to a sense of belonging and security.

General Characteristics of Network Membership

In specifying the nature of the social network matrix, the structural characteristics of the network are important to take into account. Structural aspects of the network include descriptive factors such as size, personal connectedness or density, frequency of contact with network members, as well as the characteristics of the persons known (Lee, 1979). In regard to the characteristics of the network members, we have argued that as early as infancy the individual is capable of representing the social network membership in terms of three basic dimensions: age, kinship, and sex of network members (Lewis & Feiring, 1978; Lewis & Rosenblum, 1975; B. Whiting, 1980). Research suggests that for children, the social array can be constructed in terms of whether people are adults or peers, male or female, and kin or nonkin (Blyth, 1982; Coates, 1985; Cochran & Riley, 1987; Feiring & Lewis, 1987a, 1987b; Lewis, 1987; Lewis et al., 1984).

The distribution of individuals by age, sex, and kinship provides important information concerning activities and social roles. Cross-cultural research suggests that the age and sex of the person with whom the child interacts has a strong relationship to social behavior (B. Whiting & J. Whiting, 1975). For example, for boys access to setting with a higher ratio of peer to adults may be related to greater opportunity and incidence of aggressive behavior (B. Whiting & Edwards, 1973; Smith & Connolly, 1980).

The Social Network as Socialization Template

The structure of the network provides a social map that identifies the location of an individual within a specific social world. This structure defines with whom the person has the opportunity to interact. It also defines opportunities for observing others in interaction, as well as delimiting access to situations and activities involving social or nonsocial stimulation. Lewin (1951) suggested that the personal life space defines who a person is by delineating the structure of the social world. It is entirely feasible to argue that cultural rules and conformity to these rules are established and maintained not only through direct reinforcement of role-appropriate behavior but also by network composition. Sameroff (1987) has referred to the concept of *environtype* to suggest that certain environmental structures can constrain the limits of and possibility for behavior and development. Just as parents structure the home environment, for example, by providing sex-typed toys, and books, and separate rooms for siblings, so do they and other members of society structure the social network to encourage the development of appropriate behavior patterns. It has been suggested that the power of parents and other socialization agents to influence social behavior resides more in their social network composition (Cochran & Brassard, 1979; Cochran & Riley, 1987; Filsinger & Lamke, 1983) and the assignment of children to settings than in their providing direct instruction and reinforcement (Cochran & Riley, 1987; Garbarino, Burston, Raber, Russell, & Crouter, 1978; Whiting, 1980; Parke & Bhavnagri, this volume).

By being a member of a social network, young children learn who they are in relation to other people. They can learn this directly through adult-initiated instruction or child-initiated inquiry, and they can learn this more indirectly through observation of who is present in their networks, who does what, and in what location (Feiring & Coates, 1987; Whittemore &

Beverley, 1988). The social network matrix provides structure within which both direct interaction and indirect influences such as the observation of roles and rules take place (Feiring & Lewis, 1987c). In American society mothers in particular determine with whom and where young children have social contact. Particularly in regard to the kin network mothers have more influence on their children early on in life and later on in the life cycle (Cochran & Riley, 1987; Oliveri & Reiss, 1987; Reiss & Oliveri, 1988; Troll, 1987). In middle childhood and later on, fathers may have more influence on the nonkin-related network factors—such as peer and nonrelative adults (Oliveri & Reiss, 1987). Of course as children become more capable of making social contacts on their own, their own personal preference comes to exert a greater influence on network structure.

NETWORK STRUCTURE AND THE TRANSITION FROM HOME TO SCHOOL

Our work is concerned with describing the attributes of children's social networks as they change over age from the preschool period to the beginning of formal schooling and middle childhood. The nature of children's social network should change with age, reflecting the changes in developmental tasks (Cochran & Brassard, 1979; Lewis & Feiring, 1979). The process of development requires an increased complexity in the child's life space (Lewin, 1951). As children grow up they expand their capabilities to do more things with more people in a widening variety of settings (Garbarino & Gilliam, 1980). Of particular interest is how the social network changes as children move from a more home-centered existence at 3 years of age to a more school-centered existence at 6 and 9 years. Entwistle and Hayduk (1982) label this period the *school-child* stage, distinguished by the transition from home child to school child. Around 6 years of age, when the child enters formal school, the social network expands to include a new set of adults (teachers, principals, other school staff) and a new set of peers (students). Also, as children move from 3 to 6 years and even more so at 9 years of age, they become more independent of their parents in seeking and initiating social contact.

In regard to the age changes in the network structure, of particular interest was the nature of change, transition, and stability that might be reflected in the data. Specifically, we expected that from 3 to 6 years there would be a change in network structure reflecting the move to formal school. Six years was viewed as a transition period, as around this age children would be adapting to the expanded social world and increased demands of school life. In contrast, 9 years was viewed as an age point that might be more characterized by consolidation of trends noted at 6 years. Therefore we expected to see more stable patterns from 6 to 9 years than from 3 to 6 years. Stability in network structure should be more observable from 6 to 9 than from 3 to 6 years since from 3 to 6, a transition was taking place, while from 6 to 9, consolidation of change might be more expected.

SEX AND NETWORK STRUCTURE

The nature of the social network was also expected to vary as a function of the child's sex. Male children have been found to have more extensive peer and adult networks compared to those of females (Berndt, 1981; Bryant, 1985; Tietjen, 1982; Waldrop & Halverson, 1973). Males are more likely to use space and visit settings outside the home than are females (Bryant, 1985; Moore & Young, 1978), and this may lead males to a broader range of social network contacts. Sex differences in this sample have been found at 3 and 6 years such that children were more likely to have same- than opposite-sex peers in their networks (Feiring & Lewis, 1987a; Lewis et al., 1984). Others have found that children show a preference for same-sex friends as early as 33 months (Jacklin & Maccoby, 1978), and this preference may persist into childhood (Tietjen, 1982) and adolescence (Douvan & Adelson, 1966; Hartup, 1983; Savin-Williams, 1980).

Sex differences were also expected to interact with age, with differences becoming more pronounced as children moved from a home-based to a more school-based life space. In general, it has been found that as children emerge from infancy into early and then middle childhood the number and degree of sex differences in behavior increase, especially those related to sex-role-appropriate activities (Maccoby & Jacklin, 1978; Weinraub & Brown, 1983; Wolfe, 1978).

In order to explore the social network structure of children as they make the transition from a home-centered to a more school-centered existence, data from the Robert Wood Johnson Medical School Longitudinal Study were examined. The social networks of girls and boys at 3, 6, and 9 years of age were assessed for the number of and daily contact with adults, peers, kin, nonkin, and male and female network members. The data enable us to describe the quantitative and qualitative changes in the same children's networks as they presumably become increasingly capable of choosing their social network members within the opportunities and constraints set by parents and society.

A LONGITUDINAL ANALYSIS OF CHILDREN'S NETWORKS

Study Participants

The sample consisted of 75 children and their mothers who participated in a longitudinal study that began in infancy. The children were primarily from two-parent American families of European descent. The social network data were collected when the children were 3, 6, and 9 years of age. Of the 75 children, 38 were male and 37 were female. Thirty-seven families were upper-middle SES and thirty-eight were middle SES (see Feiring & Lewis, 1981). Socioeconomic status was determined by education and occupation of both parents in an adaptation of the Hollingshead Scale. The middle-SES parents had completed, on the average, 13 years of education while the upper-middle-SES parents completed 17 years of education. The majority of middle-SES mothers had been secretaries or had held clerical positions. The fathers in this group were in middle-level management positions or were skilled tradesmen. The majority of upper-middle-SES mothers were teachers while the fathers in this group tended to be professionals or held upper-level management positions.

Procedure

At 3, 6, and 9 years, the children and their mothers came to the laboratory for observation and were given questionnaires, and an interview assessment was also conducted. At 3, 6, and 9 years, while the child was being tested alone, the mother completed the network questionnaire. At 6 years during the laboratory testing, mother and child were interviewed separately concerning the child's friends, using a birthday party situation. At 9 years the child was interviewed in the laboratory concerning number and frequency of contact with friends.

Measuring the Social Network in Early and Middle Childhood

The problem of how best to describe the child's social network is not a simple one to solve. It involves issues of accessibility of information, the child's cognitive capacity to provide information, self-report and situation bias, conceptualization of network variables of interest, and veridicality of parent and child report. No measurement technique is without problems, and it is the task of the researcher to select the method that will provide the best alternative given the constraints of the situation under study. Reports by mothers regarding the networks of their children will undoubtedly be from the mother's perspective. However, for 3-year-old children, obtaining questionnaire data would be impossible, interview data unreliable (Zill, 1977; in press), and observation data too time-consuming and restricted to settings proximal in location to the child's home (e.g., would not pick up kin living far away). At 6 years children may be somewhat more able to report on their social networks, although the problems of attention span, inconsistency, and orientation toward current experience still exist at this age. Reliance on maternal reporting as the primary source for describing the young child's social network was used in this study because it was felt that this single method would yield the most complete picture of the young child's kin–nonkin, adult–peer, male–female network structure. Other investigators have also selected this method for use with young children (e.g., Cochran & Riley, 1987; Tietjen, 1982), although as children get older (Bryant, 1985) and especially in adolescence, self-report is the preferred method (e.g., Blyth, 1982; Blyth & Foster-Clark, 1988; Blyth, Hill, & Thiel, 1982; Coates, 1987; Garbarino et al., 1978). While we relied on maternal report we also obtained data on the peer network of children at age 6 using the child report birthday party situation and at 9 years using an interview of child peer contacts. These data enabled us to address the issue of similarity between mother and child report of peer networks at 6 and 9 years. The intention of presenting these data is not to examine friendship patterns, but rather to provide a means for comparing mother and child report of peer contacts. Maternal report of the peer network at 6 and 9 years, as compared to earlier ages, may be more open to report bias since children's contact with peers may more frequently occur without mothers' knowledge. As children enter more settings and make the transition toward more out-of-the-home social interaction, mothers may be less able to monitor or be aware of peer contacts. On the other hand, presence of or contact with kin in the child's network is more likely to be available to mothers, especially since they tend to be the family's kin keeper (Oliveri & Reiss, 1987).

Mothers' Report of the Child's Network

Mothers were asked to complete an adapted version of the Pattison Psychosocial Network Inventory (Pattison, Defrancisco, Wood, Frazier, & Crowder, 1975) when the child was 3, 6, and 9 years of age. In questionnaire form, the mother was asked to list the persons in the child's social network in the categories of immediate family residing in the same household as the child, relatives of the child not residing in the same household, friends of parents, and friends of the child whom the child knew in the past year. The mother was asked to specify each person's age, sex, the relationship of each person listed to the child (e.g., for the relatives category, cousin, grandparent, etc.), and the amount of contact the person had with the child. Contact was reported as daily, weekly, monthly, semi-yearly, or yearly and was defined to include face-to-face contact, phone contact, or letter. Daily contact was defined as people the child saw or communicated with either by phone or letter at least four times a week. While the daily contact measure does not allow us to determine length or quality of contact, it does give us a rough estimate of how many people were the most frequently in contact with the child. From the mother's report, we were thus able to obtain (1) the number of people in the network, and (2) daily contact defined as the number of people the child had contact with at least four times in a week.

Specific Measures

When we had collected data on the identity of people and the number and frequency of social contact children experienced in their social network, the child's network members were grouped by categories that have been proposed to represent the young child's perception of understanding of the social world. These included the categories of age, gender, and kinship, those attributes of the social world that the child recognizes early (Lewis, 1985; Lewis & Feiring, 1978, 1979). In the analyses to follow, people were classified in terms of: (1) kinship status—relatives (all kin except nuclear family) and nonrelatives (all nonkin adults and peers); (2) age—adults (all network members of age 18 or older, excluding the subjects' parents) and peers (all persons under age 18, excluding the subjects' siblings); and (3) gender—males (all male adults and peers excluding the subjects' father and brothers) and females (all female adults and peers, excluding the subjects' mother and sisters). The data also were coded to obtain the number of and frequency of contact with male peers (all male children excluding brothers) and female peers (all female children excluding sisters).

Proportion measures[1] were also used since they allow for the estimation of the relationship between two subsets of people within a given category (e.g., the number of peers divided by the number of peers plus adults). A proportion measure may be a more sensitive index to developmental shifts compared to raw frequency in a given category. For example, as children get older they make the shift away from adult to more peer contact. While older children may still show a higher frequency of adult compared to peer contact, the proportion of peer to adult contact will reflect this increase in the relative presence of peers to adults in the child's life space. Total number and daily contact proportion measures were obtained for: peers/peers + adults; kin/kin + nonkin; male/male + females; and male peer/male peer + female peer.

Birthday Party at 6 Years

The mother and child were interviewed separately concerning the people whom the child would invite to a birthday party. The experimenter recorded the child's list and the mother wrote down whom she thought her child would want to attend. The mother's and child's responses were compared for the total number of people invited, the number of male friends, female friends, male relatives, and female relatives.

The Friendship Questionnaire at 9 Years

To measure friendship patterns the 9-year-old child was interviewed on the following series of open-ended questions: "What friends do you play with

[1] Daily contact and number proportion scores were calculated as follows: (1) for the kin category, relatives divided by relatives plus nonrelatives; (2) for the age category, peers divided by peers plus adults; (3) for the gender category, males divided by males plus females; and (4) for the sex of peer category, male peers divided by male plus female peers. Proportion scores are calculated within subject and therefore overall means for groups cannot be used to estimate proportions. Prior to analyses, arc sign transformations were performed on the proportion scores.

when you're not at school and how often [daily, weekly, monthly]?" "What friends do you play with at school?" "Who are friends that you sleep over each other's house?" and "Who are your best friends?" From this interview we examined (1) the total number of friends, and (2) the total number of male and female friends reported by the child.

CHARACTERISTICS OF CHILDREN'S NETWORKS

The network membership categories of kin versus nonkin, adults versus peers, males versus females, and male peers versus female peers are contrasted, and the results are presented in terms of the age and sex of the children.[2] In addition, the 6-year birthday party results and the 9-year friendship data are presented in order to compare mother and child peer network reports. It should be noted that the focus of this study was the nature of the young child's network beyond the immediate family system. Consequently, we did not include in our analyses the parents and siblings of the children. Inclusion of nuclear family members increased the size of the network for relatives (parents and siblings), adults (parents), peers (siblings), males (fathers and brothers), and females (mother and sisters). In most cases, inclusion of nuclear family in the analyses did not change the nature of the results.

Tables 5.1, 5.2, 5.3, and 5.4 present the mean number of people in the network, while Tables 5.5, 5.6, and 5.7 present the mean number of network members with whom subjects have daily contact by age and sex of the subjects. For simplicity, the average number is referred to as *number* and average daily contact is referred to as *daily contact.*[3] All differences discussed in the text are significant unless otherwise noted.

[2] A repeated-measure analysis of variance design with Sex as the between-subject factor and Age as the within-subject factor was used to test for the differences between the various categories of network members, that is, adults and peers, relatives and nonrelatives, males and females, male peers and female peers, for total number, daily contact, and proportion measures. Repeated measures were used to determine whether changes in the network variables occurred between 3, 6, and 9 years of age for the sample as a whole and for each sex. When it was of interest to test for differences within Age for Sex, appropriate t tests were performed.

[3] For each subject, the number of people in each category was calculated by summing across all people mentioned in a given category (e.g., peers) regardless of frequency of contact. Each subject then had a total number score for each category. The mean numbers shown in Tables 5.1 through 5.4 were calculated by summing across the total number score for each subject in a given group (e.g., female subjects) and dividing by the sample size of that group. Mean daily contact was calculated by taking the number of people with whom the child had daily contact in a given category (e.g., peers), summing across all subjects in a given group (e.g., female 3-year-old subjects), and dividing by the sample size of that group.

TABLE 5.1. Total Mean Number of People in Network by Age and Sex of Child: Relatives and Nonrelatives

	Relatives			Nonrelatives			Relatives / (Relatives + Nonrelatives)		
	3	6	9	3	6	9	3	6	9
Total sample	8.71	9.08	10.28	12.80	12.65	28.44	0.42	0.42	0.26
Boys	8.45	8.97	9.90	12.68	12.34	27.90	0.42	0.43	0.26
Girls	8.97	9.19	10.68	12.92	12.97	29.00	0.42	0.42	0.26

TABLE 5.2. Total Mean Number of People in Network by Age and Sex of Child: Peers and Adults

	Peers			Adults			Peers / (Adults + Peers)		
	3	6	9	3	6	9	3	6	9
Total sample $N = 75$	6.99	6.44	9.52	14.52	15.28	21.57	0.35	0.30	0.30
Boys $N = 38$	6.71	6.39	8.84	14.42	14.92	21.61	0.34	0.30	0.28
Girls $N = 37$	7.27	6.49	10.22	14.62	15.65	21.54	0.36	0.29	0.32

TABLE 5.3. Total Mean Number of People in Network by Age and Sex of Child: Female Friends and Male Friends

	Female Friends			Male Friends			Male Friends / (Male Friends + Female Friends)		
	3	6	9	3	6	9	3	6	9
Total	2.68	2.85	3.71	2.99	2.64	3.32	0.51	0.48	0.48
Boys	2.11	1.45	1.53	3.50	3.82	5.08	0.60	0.74	0.79
Girls	3.27	4.30	5.95	2.46	1.43	1.51	0.41	0.22	0.17

TABLE 5.4. Total Mean Number of People in Network by Age and Sex of Child: Males and Females

	Males			Females			Males / (Males + Females)		
	3	6	9	3	6	9	3	6	9
Total	8.71	8.53	16.64	12.92	13.27	21.63	0.40	0.38	0.43
Boys	9.08	9.42	18.66	12.32	11.82	19.39	0.43	0.44	0.48
Girls	8.32	7.62	14.57	13.54	14.76	23.92	0.38	0.33	0.37

TABLE 5.5. Daily Contact by Sex and Age: Relatives and Nonrelatives

	Relatives			Nonrelatives			Relatives / (Relatives + Nonrelatives)		
	3	6	9	3	6	9	3	6	9
Total	0.31	0.17	0.19	3.15	4.07	7.50	0.17	0.05	0.03
Boys	0.26	0.16	0.05	2.68	3.82	8.00	0.09	0.06	0.005
Girls	0.35	0.19	0.32	3.62	4.32	6.90	0.25	0.04	0.05

TABLE 5.6. Daily Contact by Sex and Age: Peers and Adults

	Peers			Adults			Peers / (Peers + Adults)		
	3	6	9	3	6	9	3	6	9
Total $N = 75$	1.53	2.67	3.20	1.92	1.60	4.31	0.43	0.56	0.38
Boys $N = 30$	1.55	2.50	3.21	1.40	1.50	4.79	0.48	0.57	0.36
Girls $N = 37$	1.51	2.83	3.19	2.46	1.70	3.81	0.43	0.55	0.40

TABLE 5.7. Daily Contact by Sex and Age: Female Friends and Male Friends

	Female Friends			Male Friends			Male Friends / (Male Friends + Female Friends)		
	3	6	9	3	6	9	3	6	9
Total	0.76	1.47	1.63	0.77	1.20	1.56	0.49	0.44	0.48
Boys	0.63	0.66	0.68	0.92	1.84	2.58	0.55	0.74	0.81
Girls	0.89	2.30	2.60	0.62	0.54	0.51	0.41	0.20	0.14

Age Differences

Kin and Nonkin

In early through middle childhood, that is at 3, 6, and 9 years, children have a greater number and more daily contact with nonkin than kin (see Tables 5.1 and 5.5). Examination of age difference for number of relatives shows a small but significant increase with age in number of kin in the network (see left half of Fig. 5.4, Table 5.1). Inspection of the network records suggests this is mostly due to an increase in cousins. Although the trend is not significant (the standard deviations are quite large), there is some suggestion that daily contact with kin decreases from 3 to 6 years and remains at the lower level at 9 years (see right half of Fig. 5.4).

Age affects number and daily contact with nonkin. While there is little change from 3 to 6 years, from 6 to 9 there is a large shift (see Fig. 5.5).

At 9 years, there is more than a 100% increase in the number of nonkin in the network, and for the contact measure the increase approaches 100%.

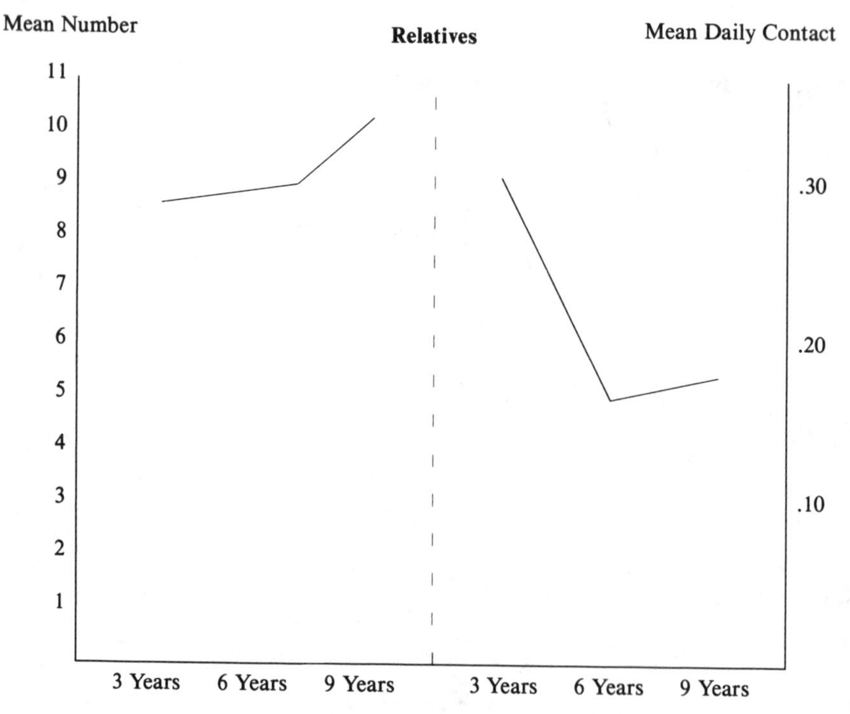

Figure 5.4. Relatives in the network at 3, 6, and 9 years.

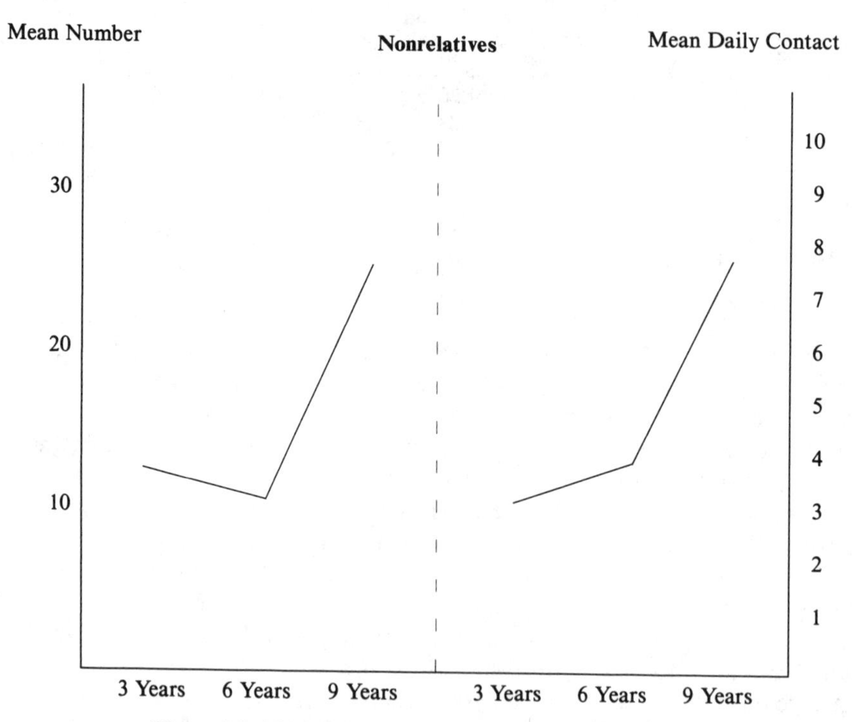

Figure 5.5. Nonrelatives in the network at 3, 6, and 9 years.

The proportion measure of number of kin to nonkin shows the effects of this steep acceleration of nonkin contact at 9 years (see Table 5.1). The proportion of daily contact with kin to nonkin also shows a significant association with age with the significant drop occurring between 3 and 6 years of age (see Table 5.5).

Peers and Adults

At 3, 6, and 9, children have a greater number of adults than peers in their networks. At 3 years, children have about the same amount of daily contact with peers and adults, at 6 years they have more daily contact with peers, but by 9 years, the level of adult daily contact is somewhat higher than that of peer contact (see Tables 5.2, 5.6).

For number of daily contact with adults, the 3- and 6-year levels are similar, with an increase occurring at 9 years (see Fig. 5.6). Number of peers shows a similar significant age effect (see Fig. 5.7). The age effect is significant for peer daily contact as well, but the trend is more gradual, showing a small linear increase from 3 to 6 to 9 years. The proportion of daily contact with peers to adults shows an increase in contact from 3 to 6 years and then a decrease from 6 to 9 years (see Table 5.6). Note that it is only at 6 years that daily contact with peers is slightly more than with adults (i.e., the proportion score goes above .50).

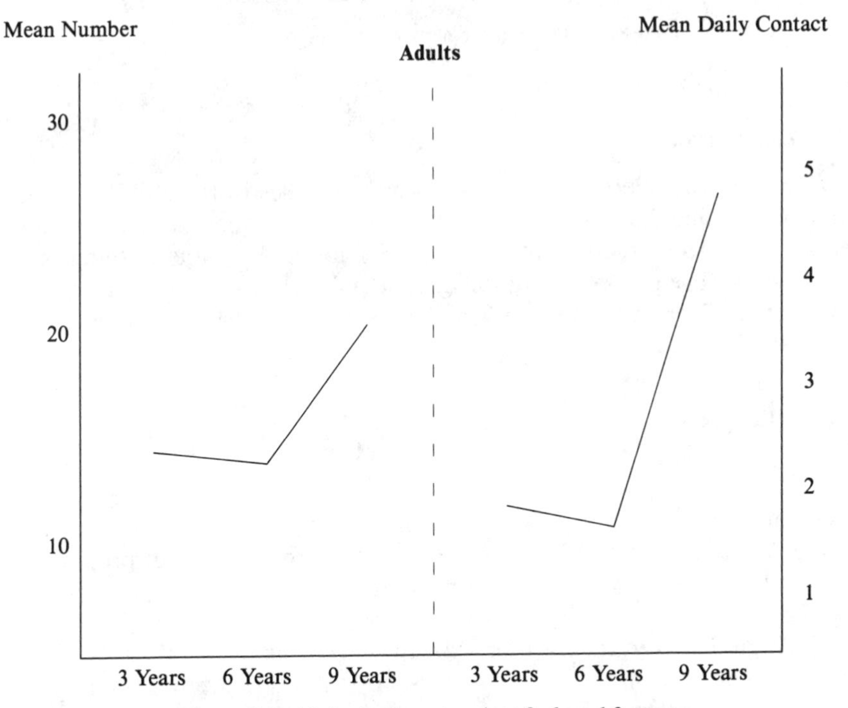

Figure 5.6. Adults in the network at 3, 6, and 9 years.

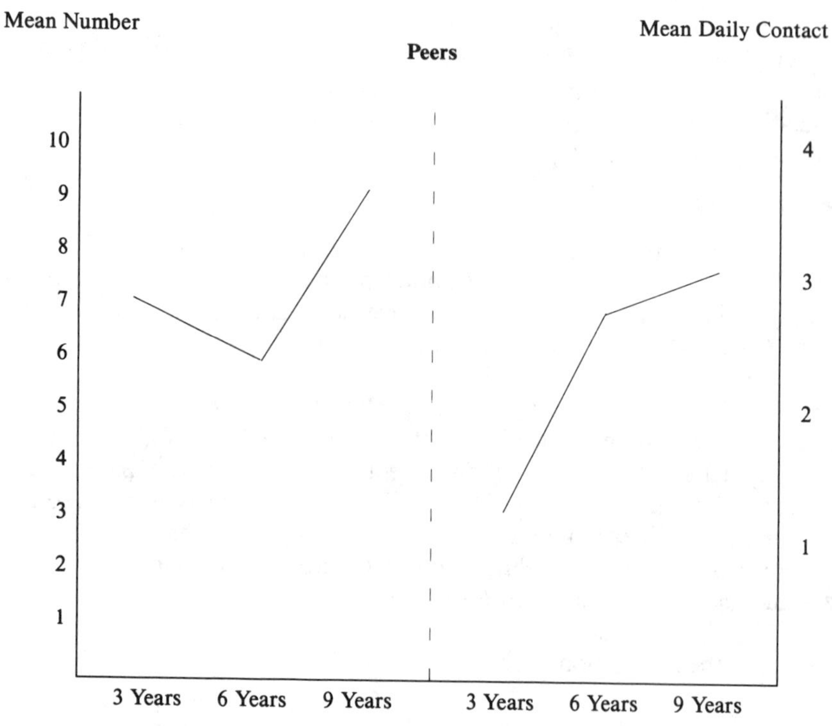

Figure 5.7. Peers in the network at 3, 6, and 9 years.

Male and Female

At all three ages, there are more females than males in the children's networks (see Table 5.3). While there are no changes from 3 to 6 years, at 9 years there is an increase in the number of males and number of females in the network. The proportion of males to females shows a changing pattern with a small drop in the proportion from 3 to 6 years and an increase at 9 years (see Table 5.3).

Sex Differences

Kin and Nonkin

There are no sex differences in the kin–nonkin proportion for number of people (see left half of Fig. 5.8). However, the daily contact proportion data show an interaction of age with the sex of the child (see right half of Fig. 5.8).

While girls at 3 years see more kin to nonkin than they do at 6 and 9 years, with little change from 6 to 9 years, boys show lower proportion scores than girls at 3 years and their scores show a small linear decline at each

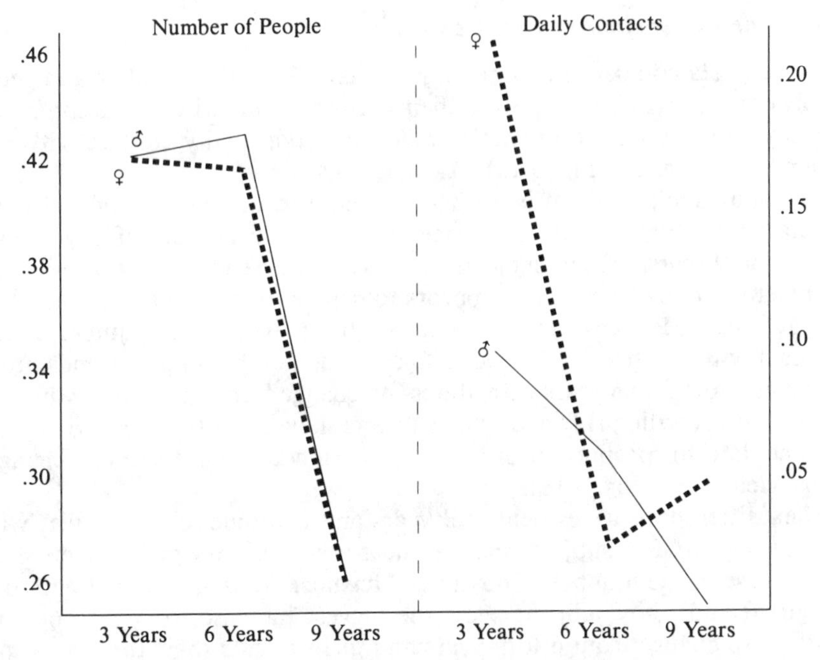

Figure 5.8. The distribution of relatives and nonrelatives by sex of child at 3, 6, and 9 years.

subsequent age point. Except for girls at age 3, the proportion of daily contact with kin to nonkin is very small for most children in this sample. Note that for the number of kin to nonkin girls and boys show similar trends (see left half of Fig. 5.8), so that it is only for proportion of daily contact that gender-related network experience may be conveyed.[4]

Males and Females

Across age, boys compared to girls have more males in their networks, with the difference most evident at 9 years (see Table 5.3). On the other hand, girls compared to boys have a greater number of females, and this difference is apparent at 6 and 9 years of age. For the proportion of males to females, boys compared to girl subjects have a higher proportion of males to females in their networks. While at 3 years, there is a 5% difference in boy and girl proportion scores, at 6 and 9 years, the difference widens to 10 and 11% respectively.

There were no significant effects for sex of child on the peer or adult measures. However, there were significant effects of sex of subject on sex of peer contact measure.

[4]While the sex effect for daily contact with kin is not significant ($p = .20$), in part due to the large standard deviations, there is an interesting trend that shows girls having more kin daily contact than boys.

Same- and Opposite-Sex Peer Contact

Boy subjects compared to girl subjects have a greater number and more daily contact with boy friends in their networks and girl subjects compared to boy subjects have a greater number and more daily contact with girl friends (see Fig. 5.9, Fig. 5.10).

For boy subjects there is a linear increase in the number of and daily contact with boy friends. The biggest change is in number of boy friends from 6 to 9 years. For girl subjects there is a decrease in number of and daily contact with boy friends: this appears to happen from 3 to 6 years, leveling off at 9 years. For girl subjects there is a linear increase in number of and contact with girl friends. For boy subjects, the number of girl friends drops the most from 3 to 6 years with almost no change from 6 to 9 years while for daily contact with girl friends, boy subjects show a flat function over age.

The data for proportion of boy to girl friends reveal these age changes most clearly (see Fig. 5.11).

Sex differences are evident at 3 years and continue to grow wider with increasing age. Boy subjects show a linear increase while girl subjects show a decrease in the number of boy to girl friends. For daily contact with boy to girl friends, boy subjects show the biggest increase from 3 to 6 years with little change from 6 to 9 years and girl subjects show the biggest decrease from 3 to 6 years with little change at 9 years.

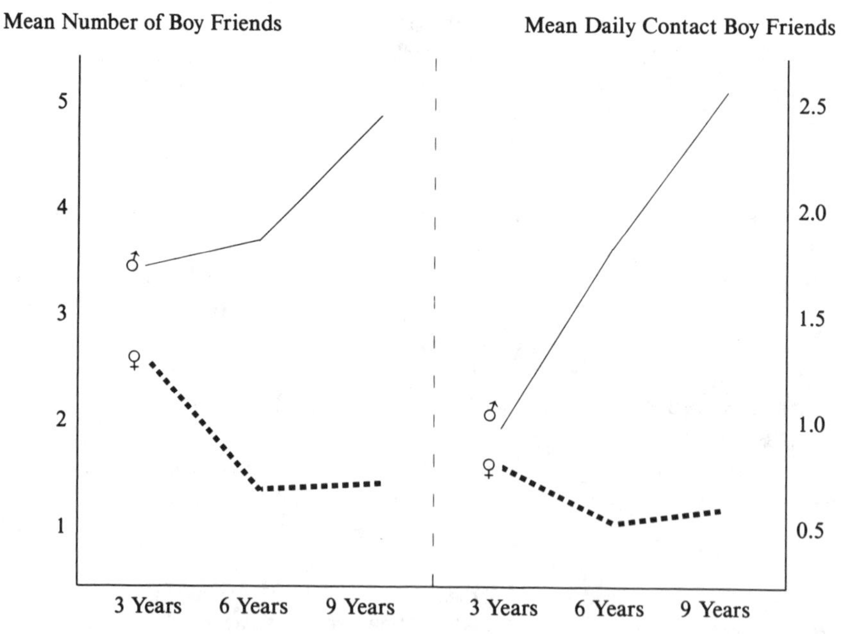

Figure 5.9. Boy friends by sex of subjects at 3, 6, and 9 years.

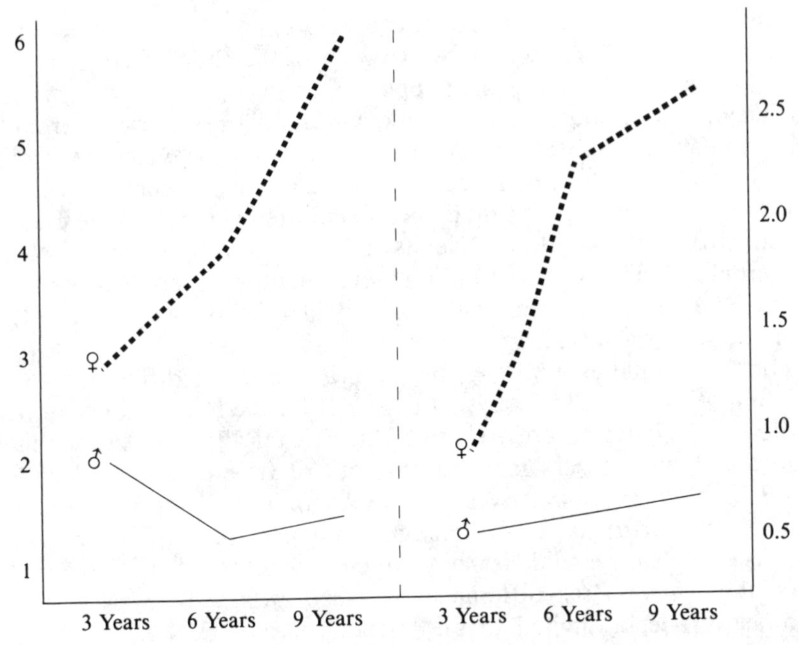

Figure 5.10. Girl friends by sex of subjects at 3, 6, and 9 years.

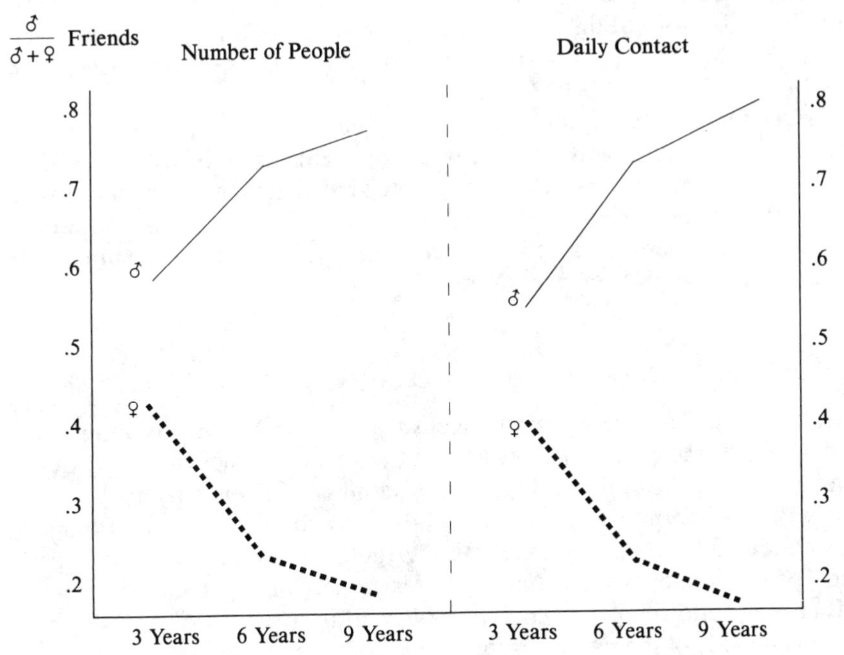

Figure 5.11. The distribution of boy to girl friends by sex of subjects at 3, 6, and 9 years.

Mother and Children Reports of the Peer Network at 6 Years

When the children were 6 years of age we attempted to get some estimate of the extent to which mothers were aware of the child's friends by asking each to give us a listing of the people the child would invite to his or her birthday party. In most cases the child and mother listed friends from both the home and school setting. Comparing the extent to which the mothers' and the children's lists matched showed an overlap in identity of friends listed at 65%. This suggests mothers and children agree, to some extent, on the identity of the children's friends and that mothers are aware of many of their children's friends. Examining total number of people listed by children and mothers (as opposed to actual identity of people named) also supports this conclusion.

For the sample as a whole, there is no significant difference between children ($\overline{X} = 7.30$) and mothers ($\overline{X} = 8.80$) for the total number of people invited to the party. There are also no significant differences between children and their mothers for total number of friends ($\overline{X} = 6.28$ children; $\overline{X} = 7.18$ mothers) or relatives ($\overline{X} = 1.02$ children; $\overline{X} = 1.62$ mothers) invited to the birthday party. As might be expected, children invite more friends than relatives to their party. Much as was the case with the network data, there are no sex differences between girls and boys for the total number of friends invited to the birthday party ($\overline{X}♂ = 6.09$; $\overline{X}♀ = 6.50$). However, when sex of friend invited to the party is examined, significant differences are found by sex of child for both the children's and mothers' data. Boys ($\overline{X} = 4.86$) invite more boy friends to the party than girls ($\overline{X} = 1.18$) while girls ($\overline{X} = 4.86$) invite more girl friends to their party than boys ($\overline{X} = 1.19$).

The mothers' data parallel that for their children. Mothers of boys estimate that their sons will invite more boy than girl friends ($\overline{X}♂ = 5.25$; $\overline{X}♀ = 1.84$) while mothers of girls estimate that their daughters will invite more girl than boy friends ($\overline{X}♂ = 1.93$; $\overline{X}♀ = 5.36$). In general, these data suggest that mothers are a reliable source of information concerning their 6-year-old children's peer networks.

Mothers' and Children's Report of the Peer Network at 9 Years

When the children were 9 years of age, we asked them to tell us about their friends in order to get an idea of the number and frequency of peer contact. Comparisons of the children's reports of number of friends from the interview with the mothers' reports of friends from the network questionnaire were conducted in order to estimate the mothers' awareness of their children's peer network. We did not expect extremely high agreement between mother and child report, since 9-year-old children should be making peer contacts outside of the parents' sphere of awareness, more so than at 6 years. Further, we expected a greater similarity between mother and daughter compared to mother and son reports of friends. This was so because: (1) we expected girls to confide in their mothers to a greater extent than boys about their friends; (2) if girls have less extensive peer networks, it would be easier for mothers to know about a smaller number of friends; and (3) if girls play closer to home, then mothers might be more aware of their peer activities.

For the total sample, children report more friends ($\overline{X}$ = 10.74) than their mothers ($\overline{X}$ = 7.03). Children report a greater number of boy friends than their mothers ($\overline{X}$ child = 5.35; $\overline{X}$ mom = 3.35) and a greater number of girl friends ($\overline{X}$ child = 5.39; $\overline{X}$ mom = 3.68). These results are very similar to the analyses done separately for mothers and daughters and mothers and sons. The biggest discrepancy between child and mother is for same-sex friends. Mothers of daughters significantly underestimate the numbers of same-sex friends ($\overline{X}$ daughter's girl friends = 10.33; $\overline{X}$ mom = 5.94). This finding is equally true for mothers of sons, who significantly underestimate the numbers of same-sex friends ($\overline{X}$ son's boy friends = 9.50; $\overline{X}$ mom = 5.08). For opposite-sex friends, mothers of daughters ($\overline{X}$ daughter's boy friends = .97; $\overline{X}$ mom = 1.53) and mothers of sons ($\overline{X}$ son's girl friends = .71; $\overline{X}$ mom = 1.53) slightly overestimate number of friends.

Examination of these data further confirm the predominance of same-sex friends in children's networks. Although the absolute levels estimated by mothers are different from those of their children, we note that girls and boys agree with mothers that there are more same-sex friends in the children's networks. These results indicate that the structure of networks is similar from mother and child report. However, when it comes to absolute number of same-sex friends mothers report fewer friends than children do. Contrary to our expectations, mothers of daughters and mothers of sons are no different in this underreporting of same-sex friends. Thus while we thought mothers' knowledge of their children's friends would be gender related, it was not. It may be the case, that regardless of sex, children's expanding friendship networks are beyond most mothers' ability to keep track. At 9 years it may be the increased mobility of middle childhood more than child sex that is related to the number of friends. This brings us to another observation that violated expectations. Boys did not show more extensive, larger friendship networks than girls, either from self- or maternal-report. This reminds us that, while girls may engage in more one-to-one interactions, the size of their friendship networks may be as large as that of boys. While the nature of contact may be more important for social functions such as intimacy, breadth of contact may be important for a sense of belonging and exposure to new social experiences (Feiring & Coates, 1987).

GROWING UP: AN EXPANDING SOCIAL WORLD

Young children, at least as shown here by the age of 3 years, are embedded in a social network comprising a variety of individuals such as immediate family members, extended kin, adult friends of the parents, peers, teachers, and babysitters. At 3 years of age children in this sample are reported to have an average of 22 people in their networks beyond their immediate family members. While this network size does not change at 6 years, by 9 years the average network size has grown to 39 people. Changes are taking place in network structure in addition to increases in size. As children become older, the composition of their networks changes in terms of both the absolute number of and contact with people in specific categories. Still other characteristics of the network remain consistent across age.

In our society at this point in time from early into middle childhood, there are consistently more nonkin than kin in children's networks. In this middle-class culture, this network characteristic is to be expected in contrast for example to the Abaluyia of Kisa or the Mandinka culture where kin predominate (Weisner, 1984; Whittemore & Beverley, 1988). A social world where the child must learn early to adapt to social exchanges with less familiar people is reflected in the large number of nonkin in 3-year-olds' networks. Significant changes take place in the kin–nonkin network structure from 3 to 9 years. Even though the absolute number of kin increases from 3 to 9 years, the proportion of kin to nonkin gets smaller. The largest drop in number of kin to nonkin occurs from 6 to 9 years, while the contact measure shows the biggest change between 3 and 6 years. This suggests that a transition to relatively less kin contact occurs earlier than a change in numbers of kin to nonkin in the network. Between 3 and 6 years, there is a 12% drop in the proportion of kin to nonkin contact with little drop (2%) at 9 years. For number, the proportion of kin to nonkin does not change from 3 to 6 years and then drops 18% from 6 to 9 years. The movement away from kin contact and an increasing amount of time spent outside the home environment have been documented by others for middle childhood and adolescence (Blyth, 1982; Bryant, 1985; Konner, 1975).

It is well known that peer contact increases as children get older, especially during the early to middle childhood period (Hartup, 1983). The findings here show a gradual linear increase in daily contact with peers. In regard to number of peers, however, the biggest change occurs between 6 and 9 years with approximately a 70% increase. By 9 years of age children report an average of 9 to 10 friends in their network.

While the peer network is increasing with age, so is the adult network. Daily contact with adults shows a gradual linear increase from early to middle childhood while, much as is the case with the peer network, the number of adults shows the biggest increase from 6 to 9 years. Thus the findings suggest that children's networks are changing not only in terms of peers but in terms of adults as well. Recently, other investigators have noted an overemphasis on peer contacts and have indicated the necessity for some caution in overgeneralizing the importance of peers to the importance of adults (Bryant, 1985; Steinberg & Silverberg, 1986). As children move into middle childhood, it appears that they may have the opportunity for more elaborate sources of exchanges between network members of the same and older generations (Vaux, 1985).

In regard to the proportion of peers to adults, we note that at 3, 6, and 9 years there are always more adults than peers in the children's networks. For daily contact, peers show a small predominance at 6 years, but otherwise adult contact is more prevalent at 3 and 9. The pattern of results at 3 and 6 years fits our expectations. Developmentally, we would expect an increase in peer to adult contact along with an increase in peer orientation and the ability to make peer contact independent of the parent (Bryant, 1985; Hartup, 1982). However, the drop in peer to adult contact from 6 to 9 years violates our expectations. To some extent, the data at 9 years especially in regard to peer contact may reflect a maternal report bias. At 9 years, mothers do not list as many same-sex friends as the children do themselves. Consequently mothers may be less aware of the extent of peer contact by 9 years and may also be more likely to overestimate the extent of adult contact. While our data cannot unravel the specific report biases, they do suggest that by 9 years of age, especially in regard to peer contact, the perspectives of child and parent differ.

Considering the female and male structure of the network, we find that from early to middle childhood there are always more females than males in children's networks. Age changes do occur so that from 6 to 9 years we observe an increase in male and female network members. This is not surprising, as we noted an overall change in network size from 6 to 9 years.

Network changes with age appear to reflect different kinds of developmental functions. Some changes appear to be gradual, such as the gradual linear increase in the daily contact with peers. Other changes appear to occur between 3 and 6 years as children move from a home- to a school-based existence. In particular, the shift to very little kin to nonkin contact takes place at the school transition period. Other changes are most notable once the child has been in grade school for a period of time, especially in terms of an increase in the number of network members. Consequently our initial expectation that the major transition is from home to school, from 3 to 6 years, is only partially supported by the data. Perhaps the shift from 3 to 6 years is related to a change in the kin–nonkin dimension of the network while from 6 to 9 years there is a transition across nonrelative adult and peer categories in terms of an increased breadth in network membership.

SEX DIFFERENCES AND NETWORK STRUCTURE

Beginning in early childhood and continuing on into middle childhood, adolescence, and adulthood, the structure and function of social networks are sex related (i.e., Belle, 1987; Feiring & Coates, 1987; Lewis et al., 1984). From childhood through old age, women are more connected to kin than are men. For this sample, examination of the developmental trends for increased proportion of nonkin to kin contact shows a sex difference such that boys show this trend sooner than girls. The earlier exposure of boys to nonkin is consistent with the view of the male child as more independent, less restricted, and less tied to the family (Bryant, 1985; Newson & Newson, 1974). By 6 years, while frequent contact with kin to nonkin is very low in this sample, over all ages girls maintain more frequent contact with kin than do boys.

As expected, the greatest impact of sex of child is on those variables related to sex of network members. In regard to the distribution of total number of males and females of any age in the network, the proportion of males to females always indicates more females than males. However, boys have proportionately more males in their networks than do girls. By 9 years of age, boys show a 50:50 male–female distribution while for girls it is 37:63. Inspection of the network data indicates that it is a greater presence of male peers, adults, and kin that is associated with the proportion score for boys. For infants and toddlers, social networks are mostly defined by their family networks. In American society, mothers in particular may be influential in determining kin and nonkin, adult and peer contact. Mothers may in part influence the predominance of females in the young child's network as their own networks may be more likely to include a larger number of women. However, mothers, fathers, and other network members may also be responsive to the child's sex so that male kin, for example, may be more likely to interact with boys as compared to girl children (Riley & Cochran, 1987). Certainly as children grow older, they become more capable of seeking out same-sex contacts.

Sex differences in same- and opposite-sex peer contact were found at all ages. Other research shows that children of all ages associate more frequently with their own sex than the opposite sex (Hartup, 1983). It has been shown that same-sex peer play is the norm by 3 years of age at least in a preschool setting (Jacklin & Maccoby, 1978). Our data suggest that not only is same-sex compared to opposite-sex peer contact the rule as early as 3 years, but by 6 years and again at 9 years this pattern has become more pronounced. At 6 and 9 years, both the child and the mother are reporting friendship patterns that reflect same- as preferred to opposite-sex contact. It is interesting to note that the greatest change in opposite-sex contact, that is, in terms of the drop in number and daily contacts with the opposite sex, occurs between 3 and 6 years. However, the biggest change in regard to the increase in the number of same-sex peers occurs between 6 and 9 years. This suggests that perhaps the initial shift to formal school is related to how the social world is structured by adults, according to sex of child, while by 9 years, to a greater extent than at 6 years, child preferences are operating. Patterns of same- and opposite-sex peer network structure reflect in part the child's own choice of friends according to sex-appropriate role behavior, and also must reflect to some degree parents' and other social institutions' structuring of the social environment to provide "appropriate" contact opportunities (Cochran & Riley, 1987). The structure of the social environment as reflected in the social network may go beyond individual choices for playmate interaction. The young child's network structure may best be viewed as a function of the opportunity the parents and other social agents (e.g., teachers) provide as well as the individual proclivities of the child.

It may be the case that sex-role behavior is given environmental structure by sex contact differences in the network. The kind of adult and peer contact in the network structures the child's experiences. That male children have proportionately more male contact while female children have proportionately more female contact illustrates how the social network provides a social environment that defines the nature and perhaps range of the child's sex-role-related experiences. It is interesting to note that there were a few exceptions to the general rule of large predominance of same-sex to opposite-sex peers. As might be anticipated, it is more likely that girls as compared to boys will show this pattern. Girls are given greater flexibility to violate sex-role-stereotypic behavior.

Of those girls at 6 years who show almost as many boys as girl friends (no boys show this comparable distribution), their teachers are more likely to see them as more independent and aggressive than other girls. To what extent the teachers' impressions are influenced by the girls' specific behavior and may be amplified by the girls' deviant association with more boys is impossible to tell. However, it is likely that it is what expectations children fulfill and violate as well as whom they associate with that give shape to their social identity.

Before concluding, a comment is necessary regarding the comparison of mother and child report of the network. Our data reflect both an agreement as to peer network structure and a divergence as to absolute numbers, especially as the child gets older. At 6 and 9 years of age, mother and children report the predominance of same-sex compared to opposite-sex peer network members. However, at 9 years, children report almost twice as many same-sex friends as do mothers. To some degree, this must reflect the obvious fact that 9-year-olds are better able than their parents to report who they know, at least when it comes to peers. In doing the network peer interviews, the differences are striking between the 6- and 9-year-olds' capacity to be involved in and capable of reporting peer contacts. Age differences in network structure that show large changes in regard to increases in network membership suggest the expanding nature of the child's world beyond the parents' knowledge. By 9 years it appears important to get information on network structure from both the parent and child's perspective in order to obtain a complete picture of the child's social world.

Zelkowitz (this volume) discusses the importance of exploring the distinct perspective of parents and children regarding the children's network members and their functions. Mothers often include a broader array of people than children, who primarily focus on parents, siblings, and friends. The parent and child perspective of the network may be related to unique developmental outcomes. The mother's inclusion of kin connection and family friends in the child's network, even if the child does not mention them, may provide important information about the variety of people and experiences that affect the child's development. While children may not mention the importance of family friends, their presence and participation in family activities may be an important factor for the child's later success in school (Riley & Cochran, 1987). Extended kin may also not be included in the young children's description of their network (e.g., aunts, uncles, cousins) and yet there is some evidence to suggest that mothers' descriptions of the kin contacts, which go beyond the child report, may be related to children's later connectedness to kin (Oliveri & Reiss, 1987). In fact, parents' perception of children's network may yield important information in regard to their management of their children's social network. As Parke and Bhavnagri (this volume) point out, this parental management function can have far-reaching implication for a child's social development. Of course, understanding the child's network from the child's point of view is critical as we try to understand how children's perception of social network members and their relationships and functions affect developmental outcomes.

The child's characteristics are a product of and contribution to the social network structure. The child's social network changes with age and developmental level so that for example by 9 years of age, children's networks have grown considerably, increasing in number and contact with adults and peers. Early differences in the distribution of sex of network members get consolidated by middle childhood. In contrast, the predominance of nonkin to kin network member contact is consistent from early childhood onward. Changes occur in absolute numbers as well as the proportion of network member types. For all children, the numbers of males and females in the network increase with age while for boys, the gap narrows between number of male to female network members. The social network matrix varies by age and sex of the child, and these variations describe the child's opportunities for social contact and experience.

REFERENCES

Belle, D. (1987). Gender differences in the social mediators of stress. In R. Barrett, L. Biener, & G. Baruch (Eds.), *Gender and stress.* New York: Free Press.

Berndt, T. J. (1981). Age changes and changes over time in prosocial intentions and behavior between friends. *Developmental Psychology, 17,* 408–416.

Blyth, D. A. (1982). Mapping the social world of adolescents: Issues, techniques and problems. In F. Serafica (Ed.), *Social cognition, context and social behavior: A developmental perspective.* New York: Guilford.

Blyth, D. A., & Foster-Clark, F. (1988). Gender differences in perceived intimacy with different members of adolescents' social networks. In C. Feiring & D. L. Coates (Eds.), The social networks of males and females: A life span perspective [Special issue]. *Sex Roles: A Journal of Research, 17,* (689–718).

Blyth, D. A., Hill, J. P., & Thiel, K. S. (1982). Early adolescents' significant others: Grand and gender differences with familial and nonfamilial adults and young people. *Journal of Youth & Adolescence, 11,* 425–450.

Bott, E. (1971). *Family and social network: roles, norms, and external relationships in ordinary urban families,* (2nd ed.). New York: Free Press.

Bryant, B. K. (1985). The neighborhood walk: Sources of support in middle childhood. *Monographs of the Society for Research in Child Development, 50,* 11985.

Buhrmester, D., & Furman, W. (1987). The development of companionship and intimacy. *Child Development, 58,* 1101–1113.

Coates, D. L. (1985). Relationship between self-concept measures and social network characteristics for Black adolescents. *Journal of Early Adolescence, 5,* 319–338.

Coates, D. L. (1987). Gender differences in the structure and support characteristics of Black adolescents' social networks. In C. Feiring & D. L. Coates (Eds.), The social networks of males and females: A life span perspective. Special Issue of *Sex Roles: A Journal of Research, 17,* (667–688).

Cochran, M. M., & Brassard, J. A. (1979). Child development and personal social networks. *Child Development, 50,* 601–616.

Cochran, M. M., & Riley, D. (1987). Mother reports of children's social relations: Agents, concomitants and consequences. In J. Antrobus, S. Salzinger, & M. Hamner (Eds.), *Social networks of children, adolescents and college students.* Hillsdale, NJ: Erlbaum.

Connell, J. C., & Furman, W. (1984). Conceptual and methodological issues in the study of transitions. In R. Harmon & R. Emde (Ed.), *Continuity and discontinuity in development.* New York: Plenum.

Douvan, E., & Adelson, J. (1966). *The adolescent experience.* New York: Wiley.

Entwisle, D. R., & Hayduk, L. A. (1982). *Early schooling: Cognitive and affective outcomes.* Baltimore: Johns Hopkins University Press.

Feiring, C., & Coates, D. L. (1987). The social networks of males and females: A life span perspective [Special issue]. *Sex Roles: A Journal of Research, 17.*

Feiring, C., & Lewis, M. (1978). The child and the family system. *Behavioral Science, 23,* 225–233.

Feiring, C., & Lewis, M. (1981). Middle class differences in the mother–child interaction and the child's cognitive development. In T. Field (Ed.), *Culture and early interactions* (pp. 63–91). Hillsdale, NJ: Erlbaum.

Feiring, C., & Lewis, M. (1987a). The child's social network: Sex differences from three to six years. In C. Feiring & D. L. Coates (Eds.), The social networks of males and females: A life span perspective [Special issue]. *Sex Roles: A Journal of Research, 17,* (621–636).

Feiring, C., & Lewis, M. (1987b). The child's social network: The effects of age, sex and socioeconomic status from 3 to 6 years. In S. Salzinger, S. Antrobus, & M. Hammer (Eds.), *Social networks of children, adolescents and college students.* Hillsdale, NJ: Erlbaum.

Feiring, C., & Lewis, M. (1987c). The ecology of some middle class families at dinner. *International Journal of Behavioral Development, 10*(3), 377–390.

Filsinger, E. E., & Lamke, L. K. (1983) The lineage transmission of interpersonal competence. *Journal of Marriage & the Family, 45,* 75–80.

Furman, W. (1984). Some observations of the study of personal relationships. In J. C. Masters & K. Yarkin-Levin (Eds.), *Interfaces between developmental and social psychology.* New York: Academic.

Furman, W., & Buhrmester, D. (1985). Children's perceptions of the personal relationships in their social networks. *Developmental Psychology, 21,* 1014–1024.

Garbarino, J., Burston, N., Raber, S., Russell, R., & Crouter, A. (1978). The social maps of children approaching adolescence: Studying the ecology of youth development. *Journal of Youth & Adolescence, 7,* 417–428.

Garbarino, J., & Gilliam, G. (1980). *Understanding abusive families.* Lexington, MA: Lexington Books.

Hartup, W. (1982). Peer relations. In C. Kopp & K. Krakow (Eds.), *The child.* Reading, MA: Addison Wesley.

Hartup, W. (1983). Peer relations. In P. H. Mussen (Ed.) & E. M. Hetherington (Series Ed.), *Handbook of child psychology: Vol. 4. Socialization, personality and social development* (pp. 103–196). New York: Wiley.

Hirsch, B. (1981). Social networks and the coping process: Creating personal communities. In B. H. Gottlieb (Ed.), *Social networks and social support* (pp. 149–170). Beverly Hills: Sage.

Hunter, F. T., & Youniss, J. (1982) Changes in functions of three relations during adolescence. *Developmental Psychology, 18*(6), 806–811.

Jacklin, C. N., & Maccoby, E. (1978). Social behavior at 33 months in same-sex and mixed-sex dyads. *Child Development, 49,* 557–569.

Konner, M. (1975). Relations among infants and juveniles in comparative perspective. In M. Lewis & L. Rosenblum (Eds.), *Friendship and peer relations* (pp. 99–130). New York: Wiley.

Lee, G. R. (1979). Effects of social networks on the family. In W. R. Burr, R. Hill, F. Nye, & I. Neiss (Eds.), *Contemporary theories about the family: Vol. 1. Research-based theories.* New York: Free Press.

Leinhart, S. (1977). Social networks: A developing paradigm. In S. Leinhart (Ed.), *Social networks: A developing paradigm* (pp. xiii–xxxiv). New York: Academic.

Lewin, K. (1951). *Field theory in social science: Selected theoretical papers.* New York: Harper.

Lewis, M. (1985). Age as a social dimension. In T. Field & N. Fox (Eds.), *Social perception in infants* (pp. 299–319). New York: Academic.

Lewis, M. (1987). Social development in infancy and early childhood. In J. Osofsky (Ed.), *Handbook of infancy* (2nd ed., pp. 419–493). New York: Wiley.

Lewis, M., & Feiring, C. (1978). The child's social world. In R. M. Lerner & C. D. Spanier (Eds.), *Child differences on marital and family interaction: A life-span perspective* (pp. 47–69). New York: Academic.

Lewis, M., & Feiring, C. (1979). The child's social network: Social object, social functions, and their relationship. In M. Lewis & L. Rosenblum (Eds.), *The child and its family: The genesis of behavior* (Vol. 2, pp. 9–27). New York: Plenum.

Lewis, M., Feiring, C., & Kotsonis, M. (1984). The social networks of the young child. In M. Lewis (Ed.), *Beyond the dyad* (pp. 129–160). New York: Plenum.

Lewis, M., & Rosenblum, L. (Eds.). (1975). *Friendship and peer relations: The origins of behavior.* New York: Wiley.

Maccoby, E. E., & Jacklin, C. N. (1978). *The psychology of sex differences.* Stanford, CA: Stanford University Press.

Moore, R., & Young, D. (1978). Childhood outdoors: Toward a social ecology of the landscape. In I. Altman & J. F. Wohlwill (Eds.), *Children and the environment* (pp. 83–130). New York: Plenum.

Newson, J., & Newson, E. (1974). School aged children in an urban community, cited in C. Maccoby, & C. N. Jacklin, *The psychology of sex differences.* Stanford: Stanford University Press.

Oliveri, M. E., & Reiss, D. (1987). Social networks of family members: Distinctive roles of mothers and fathers. In C. Feiring & D. L. Coates (Eds.), The social networks of males and females: A life span perspective [Special issue]. *Sex Roles: A Journal of Research, 17,* (719–736).

Pattison, E. M., Defrancisco, D., Wood, P., Frazier, H., & Crowder, J. (1975). A psychosocial kinship model of family therapy. *American Journal of Psychiatry, 132,* 1246–1251.

Reiss, D., & Oliveri, M. E. (1988). The family's construction of social reality and its ties to its kin network: An exploration of causal directions. *Journal of Marriage & Family, 45,* 81–91.

Riley, D., & Cochran, M. (1987). Children's relationships with non-parental adults: Sex specific connections to early school success. In C. Feiring & D. L. Coates (Eds.), The social networks of males and females: A life span perspective [Special issue]. *Sex Roles: A Journal of Research, 17,* (637–656).

Sameroff, A. J. (1987). Developmental systems: Contexts and evolution. In P. H. Mussen (Ed.) & W. Kessen (Series Ed.), *Handbook of child psychology: Vol. 10. History, theory and methods.* New York: Wiley.

Savin-Williams, R. C. (1980). Dominance hierarchies in groups of middle to late adolescent males. *Journal of Youth & Adolescence, 9,* 75–85.

Shumaker, S. A., & Brownell, A. (1984). Toward a theory of social support: Closing conceptual gaps. *Journal of Social Issues, 40,* 11–36.

Smith, P. K., & Connolly, K. J. (1980). (Eds.). *The ecology of preschool behaviour.* Cambridge, England: Cambridge University Press.

Steinberg, L., & Silverberg, S. B. (1986). The vicissitudes of autonomy in early adolescence. *Child Development, 57,* 841–851.

Tietjen, A. M. (1982). The social networks of preadolescent children in Sweden. *International Journal of Behavioral Development, 5,* 111–130.

Troll, L. (1987). Gender differences in cross generation networks. In C. Feiring & D. L. Coates (Eds.), The social networks of males and females: A life span perspective [Special issue]. *Sex Roles: A Journal of Research, 17,* (751–766).

Vaux, A. (1985). Variations in social support associated with gender, ethnicity and age. *Journal of Social Issues, 41,* 89–110.

Waldrop, M. F., & Halverson, C. F. (1973). *Intensive and extensive peer behavior: Longitudinal and cross-sectional analyses.* Unpublished manuscript, Child Research Branch, Washington, DC.

Weinraub, M., & Brown, L. M. (1983). The development of sex role stereotypes in children: Crushing realities. In V. Ranks & F. Rothblum (Eds.), *The ailing feminine stereotype: Sex roles and women's mental health.* New York: Springer.

Weisner, T. (1984). The social ecology of childhood: A cross cultural view. In M. Lewis (Ed.), *Beyond the dyad* (pp. 43–58). New York: Plenum.

Whiting, B., & Edwards, C. (1973). A cross cultural analysis of sex differences in the behavior of children aged 3 to 11. *Journal of Social Psychology, 91,* 171–188.

Whiting, B., & Whiting, J. (1975). *Children of six cultures: A psychocultural analysis.* Cambridge, MA: Harvard University Press.

Whiting, D. B. (1980). Culture and social behavior: A model for the development of social behavior. *Ethos, 2,* 95–116.

Whittemore, R. D., & Beverley, E. A. (1988). Trust in the Mandinka way: Cultural context and sibling caregiving.

Wolfe, M. (1978). Childhood and privacy. In I. Altman & J. F. Wohlwill (Eds.), *Children and the environment.* New York: Plenum.

Zill, M. (1977). *National survey of children: Summary of preliminary results.* Unpublished manuscript, Foundation for Child Development, New York.

Zill, M. (in press). *Learning to listen to children.* New York: Cambridge University Press.

CHAPTER 6

The Development of Children's Social Networks

WYNDOL FURMAN

As children grow up, there are many significant persons in their lives. Mothers, fathers, siblings, relatives, teachers, friends, and peers all play important parts in shaping the course of development. The social support provided by these relationships can have a major impact on psychological health and adjustment (Furman, 1987; Werner & Smith, 1982; Wolchik, Sandler, & Braver, in press).

Of course, one would expect children's relationships and social networks and their impact to change over the course of development. In the present chapter, the literature on developmental changes in school-age children's and adolescents' social networks will be selectively reviewed. Particular emphasis will be placed on research describing changes in a number of different relationships or the network as a whole, because comprehensive reviews already exist concerning the development of specific relationships, such as those with parents or peers (see Hartup, 1983; Maccoby & Martin, 1983).

CARVING UP SOCIAL NETWORKS

Even a young child's social network is a complex set of pieces that defy easy categorization. A child has relationships with a range of different people; each relationship involves a number of different types of interactions. Networks can be carved up in terms of three primary dimensions—level, facet, and perspective.

Several studies described in this research were supported by funding from the National Institute of Child Health and Human Development or from the W. T. Grant Foundation. Preparation of this chapter was made possible by a W. T. Grant Faculty Scholar award.

Level

First, four levels of a network can be distinguished: the interactional level, the dyadic relationship level, the group level, and the global network level (Buhrmester, 1983). Interactions are face-to-face encounters. Dyadic relationships subsume such interactions, but they are ongoing phenomena that incorporate more than particular interactions. Similarly, groups are coherent sets of relationships, such as the peer group or family, but they are more than the simple sum of specific relationships. Finally, the global network incorporates the entire set of relationships.

Different pictures of social support or social networks are revealed by examining the different levels (Buhrmester, 1983). Studies of interactions can indicate how social support is manifested in specific interactions with specific people. Studies of relationships will provide us information that cannot be obtained at the interactional level. Children have expectations or wishes about the social support various relationships should provide. Many of these expectations refer to face-to-face interaction, but some refer to the general characteristics of a relationship. For example, a boy may feel that most interactions with his father are supportive, but he may feel that the relationship is not very supportive because he does not see his father very often. Relationships can also continue in the absence of interactions; for example, before the days of worldwide communication, two distant lovers might have no contact with each other for years. One might even want to argue that relationships can continue even if there never will be interactions in the future (e.g., a widow's relationship with a deceased spouse), or they may develop without any interactions ever occurring (e.g., with a movie or musical idol). Whether one considers these last examples relationships depends upon how restrictive one's definition is; certainly, they are not prototypical relationships.

A group is also more than a simple aggregate of dyadic relationships. For example, some children may have a few supportive friendships, but they may not feel accepted by the peer group as a whole. A dyadic relationship may also be part of more than one group. For instance, some sibling relationships are part of both family and peer group relationships. Analogous differences exist between the overall network level and the other levels. For example, a perception of not being supported by anyone may not be based on any particular relationship.

These considerations indicate that the different levels are distinct from each other and cannot be reduced to a single level. The four levels are, however, interrelated. The most obvious way is that the higher levels are partially, but not completely, made up of the lower levels. For example, the set of relationships help make up the network.

At the same time, the lower levels are influenced by the nature of the higher levels. Salzinger (1982) persuasively argued that the character of a relationship, or even whether such a relationship develops, is affected by the nature of the individuals' social networks. For example, Salzinger proposes that members of high-density networks know fewer individuals than members of low-density networks. Moreover, high-density networks become increasingly connected over time; new relationships are likely to develop with members of the network, whereas those with outsiders are likely to dissolve. Salzinger thought that relationships in high-density networks were generally more stable than those in low-density networks, except for those with outsiders where the reverse was the case. Not only is the stability of relationships thought to be affected by the degree of structural interdependence of the network, but also the quality of the relationships may be influenced. For example, Salzinger thought that the relationships in high-density networks would be more multiplex in nature—that is, serving more functions. At the same time, she thought that, because their relationships tended to be more intense, individuals in high-density networks would develop more stringent criteria for defining friendships. Although the literature is not extensive, most of Salzinger's hypotheses have been supported by empirical research (see Milardo, 1986).

Facet

Each level is also multifaceted in nature. First, one can differentiate on the basis of the person or persons involved in the interaction, relationship, or group. Children interact with or are involved in relationships or groups with many different people. The number of groups or relationships, their density or interconnectedness, and other structural properties are also important to describe. The overall network or any particular group, relationship, or interaction with a person is also multifaceted in nature. For example, one can describe a number of different facets or qualitative features in a relationship with a father.

What are the different facets? There are certainly many ways of carving up interactions or relationships, but we believe that four general facets of relationships need to be addressed in any description (Adler & Furman, in press). These are: (1) the degree of warmth or support in the interaction, relationship, or group; (2) the degree of conflict; (3) the distribution of power and status; and (4) the relative nature or status of the relationship or group in the participants' networks (e.g., parental treatment of different children, exclusivity of a friendship).

Warmth and support and conflict factors have consistently emerged in our own research on children's relationships with siblings, friends, and parents. Although the issue of power is important in all relationships, it does not always appear as a factor. For example, in friendships, no such factor is found, perhaps because friendships are inherently egalitarian. Studies of specific relationships have also revealed a fourth factor that seems to reflect the quality of a relationship relative to others (e.g., rivalry in sibling relationships, exclusivity in friendships, and protectiveness in parent–child relationship).

Perspective

Finally, one could distinguish among the different perspectives various people may have on interactions, relationships, groups, or networks (Furman, Jones, Adler, & Buhrmester, in press; Olson, 1977). Insiders or participants in an interaction, relationship, or group may each have different perspectives or views of it. A second set of perspectives may be obtained from participant observers or individuals who are indirectly involved. For example, parents would be considered to be participant observers of their children's relationships with each other. Finally, outsiders, such as social scientists, may provide another set of perspectives.

THEORIES OF DEVELOPMENTAL CHANGE

Most theories of social development have not focused on changes in social networks, although such changes are often implied. Typically, theorists have been concerned with the emergence of social needs or social motives. For example, Sullivan (1953) believed that individuals' preferences for specific types of interactions or relationships are derived from their social needs or *integrative tendencies.* He hypothesized that social needs are biologically based tensions, which are roughly equivalent to negative emotions, such as fear or loneliness. The tensions can be avoided or reduced by engaging in particular types of interactions. For example, an infant can avoid feeling frightened by seeking out the tender care of a parent.[1]

Sullivan hypothesized that there were five basic social needs: tenderness, companionship, acceptance, intimacy, and sexuality. Each of the five needs emerges at a different developmental stage. Figure 6.1 depicts the stages, corresponding needs, and key relationships for each need at each stage.

In the first stage, the infant is helpless and must depend on caretakers for all bodily needs. The need for *tenderness* or protective care develops in the context of the caregiving provided by parents. When the need is fulfilled, the child feels secure; when it isn't, the child feels frightened or distressed. In the stage of childhood (2 to 6 years of age), the need for adult participation is added. That is, the child desires the interest or participation of a significant adult in his or her play. Sullivan recognized that young children also play with peers and siblings, but he thought that play with parents was particularly valued in this stage. We believe it is best to characterize the desire for adult participation as the first manifestation of the need for *companionship.* Throughout the rest of life, children and adults seek the participation

[1] The description of Sullivan's theory is based on Buhrmester and Furman's (1986) interpretation. Sullivan's theoretical writings were not very systematic. We have had to fill in certain gaps in his model, but we believe that the present description is consistent with the thrust of his thinking.

Emergent Needs and Key Relationships

Infancy (0 to 2 yrs.)	Childhood (2 to 6 yrs.)	Juvenile Era (6 to 9 yrs.)	Preadolescence (9 to 12 yrs.)	Early Adolescence (12 to 16 yrs.)
				SEXUALITY Opposite-Sex Partner
			INTIMACY Same-Sex Friend	Opposite-Sex Friend/Romance Same-Sex Friend
		ACCEPTANCE Peer Society	Friendship Gang	Heterosexual Crowd Friendship Gang
	COMPANIONSHIP Parents	Compeers Parents	Same-Sex Friend Parents	Opposite-Sex Friend/Romance Same-Sex Friend
TENDERNESS Parents	Parents	Parents	Same-Sex Friend Parents	Opposite-Sex Friend/Romance Same-Sex Friend

Figure 6.1. Neo-Sullivanian model of developing social needs (adapted from Buhrmester & Furman, 1986). Used with permission.

of others in activities of mutual interest and enjoyment. When the need for companionship is fulfilled, the child feels enjoyment or amusement; when it isn't, he or she feels bored or isolated.

Companionship with peers becomes particularly important with the emergence of the juvenile stages or the beginning of formal schooling. As a result of the increased contact with each other, juveniles become aware of individual differences in appearance, background, personality, and social behavior. These differences are used to judge their peers' desirability as playmates. Consensus develops concerning what is and is not desirable and social status hierarchies emerge. With the emergence of these evaluations develops a need for *acceptance*. If accepted, a child feels a sense of pride; if not, he or she feels rejected or ostracized.

The best known stage in Sullivan's theory is preadolescence (approximately 9 to 12 years of age). At this time, there emerges a need for *intimacy* or for friendship with or love of another person. The target of this need for intimacy is usually a same-sex agemate. What is distinct about this relationship is that it is the first time the child develops a sensitivity to the needs of the other. The needs of the other and one's own becomes increasingly similar, and a genuinely interdependent relationship develops. These intimate exchanges lead to a sense of being loved; when absent, the child feels lonely.

In early adolescence, lust or *sexuality* emerges in relationships with opposite-sex peers. The need for intimate exchange also begins to emerge in these relationships. Thus opposite-sex peers suddenly take center stage and the key issue becomes integrating the needs for sexuality and intimacy. Sullivan briefly discussed a stage of late adolescence in which relationships that fulfill the range of different needs are established. The specific nature of this stage and subsequent development in adulthood are not addressed extensively, however.

Veroff and Veroff (1980) have also proposed a developmental theory of social incentives. In the course of the life span, individuals are believed to encounter certain developmental tasks that universally elicit certain incentives. Four primary tasks are encountered in the following order: (1) differentiation of self from others; (2) differentiation of relationship to significant others; (3) differentiation in one's relationship to social systems; and (4) differentiation of interdependence of self with other social systems. Each task involves two successive stages—an engagement stage in which exploration occurs and a consolidation stage in which learning is solidified. Each stage of each task elicits a different social incentive, resulting in eight different motives. The eight are listed in Table 6.1.

Some parallels with Sullivan's stages seem apparent. The details may differ, but the attachment incentive seems to correspond to the need for tenderness. The Veroffs' social relatedness motive of childhood actually consists of three developmentally sequenced incentives, which are: (1) authoritarian social approval; (2) affiliation; and (3) altruism. The three all involve evaluation of one's social relatedness, but the source of information for norms varies (e.g., authority, peer, or objective event). For authoritarian social approval, it is parents initially, and later, it may include other authorities, such as teachers, as well. For affiliation, it is peers, whereas for altruism it is the objective social event. Authoritarian social approval seems to resemble

TABLE 6.1. Veroff and Veroff's Stages of Universal Incentives

Developmental Period	Basic Social Developmental Task	Motivational Mode	Stage
Infancy	Differentiation of self and others	Engagement Consolidation	Curiosity Attachment
Childhood	Differentiation of relationship to others	Engagement Consolidation	Assertiveness Social relatedness
Adolescence	Differentiation of relationship to social organization	Engagement Consolidation	Belonging Consistency
Adulthood	Differentiation of interdependence of self with others or society	Engagement Consolidation	Interdependence Integrity

Source: Veroff and Veroff (1980). Used with permission.

Sullivan's motive of adult participation and involvement in play, although more emphasis is placed on the evaluative component and it doesn't seem specific to play. The affiliation motive bears some resemblance to companionship and acceptance by peers.

Certainly, the similarities between the Veroffs' and Sullivan's theories can be overstated. Several of the motives in each theory do not have corresponding ones in the other theory. For example, the Veroffs' belongingness motive refers to a participation in peer groups that is not well captured by Sullivan. Although the construct of motivation is central in both systems, the two have approached the issue of social development from different perspectives. The Veroffs focus on the self and its relations to the world. Sullivan focuses on the social relationships that a person has. The Veroffs emphasize the role of cognitive development, whereas Sullivan discusses the role of dynamic processes in development (e.g., collisions of dynamisms, developmental arrests). Despite these differences, however, their descriptions of development resemble each other. An integrative picture of development should be able to draw upon the insights of the complementary approaches.

Robert S. Weiss (1974) also proposed a list of relational provisions that people seek in their relationships with others. The six are: (1) attachment—security, affection, and intimate disclosure; (2) reliable alliance—a lasting, dependable bond, though not necessarily an emotional one; (3) social integration—companionship and the sharing of experience; (4) enhancement of worth—affirmation of one's competence or value; (5) opportunity for nurturance—taking care of another; and (6) guidance—tangible aid and advice.

In a recent chapter, Weiss (1986) speculated about the developmental course of these provisions or "bonds." Using Bowlby's (1969) conceptualization of attachment, he believed that the attachment bond remains throughout childhood, but it is less frequently expressed in behavior because separation distress occurs less frequently. Although there may be a primary figure, attachment in some form can develop to parents and often to siblings. In late adolescence or early adulthood, strong feelings of affection may continue, but one is not likely to turn to family figures for security. Instead, these bonds are thought to be transformed into attachment to a romantic partner (see Hazan & Shaver, 1987).

Social integration or affiliation emerges out of exploratory impulses and is primarily manifested in peer relationships. As children grow older and the attachment bond is activated less frequently, the affiliation bond increases in saliency and takes primacy. The situation, however, is reversed in early adulthood when attachment bonds to romantic figures become the chief concern.

Reliable or persistent alliance is primarily found in relationships with kin. In childhood, relationships with siblings would be expected to be the most important of those based on this bond. As adults, relationships with parents would also be based on this type of bond once the attachment bond has withered.

Originally, Weiss thought that enhancement of worth usually occurred in relationships in the workplace. In his developmental paper (1986), he reconceptualized this provision and referred to it as collaboration or a bond based on feeling of shared commitment to the achievement of a goal. It still, however, occurs primarily with colleagues, teammates, or partners with whom one's own efforts are coordinated. Weiss believed that the ability to take the perspective of others would be required to develop such collaborative bonds. It is not clear what the developmental course of these bonds is. On the one hand, the description of these relationships resembles Sullivan's (1953) characterization of collaborations that began to emerge in preadolescent chumships. On the other hand, Weiss hypothesized that the enhancement of esteem may occur in young children's play or in work-oriented collaborations with parents or other adults.

Weiss's descriptions of the other bonds were brief. Nurturance could be manifested in interactions with younger siblings, pets, or dolls. The developmental competencies required for such interactions, however, are not known. Weiss also expected instrumental aid or help obtaining to be an important component of parent–child relationships, but it is unclear what the developmental course is. One might expect this bond to be less important as children grow older and become more independent. On the other hand, some research suggests that older children are sometimes more likely to seek or accept necessary help than younger children (see Nelson-Le Gall, Gumerman, & Scott-Jones, 1983).

Compared to the other theories discussed here, Weiss's description of developmental changes and the bases for such is not as comprehensive. Such is to be expected because his theory originated in his research with adults. On the other hand, he is more explicit about the specific relationships in which children obtain different provisions. In fact, one of his fundamental points is that different provisions are obtained in different relationships. This is an important insight, particularly when placed in a developmental framework that recognizes that the sources also change over development. In the subsequent sections, we'll review the empirical studies that have examined the developmental changes at the global, group, and relationship levels.

CHANGES AT THE GLOBAL LEVEL

Although both Sullivan's and the Veroffs' theories seem to predict developmental changes at the global level, the issue has received relatively little attention. Instead, most of the research has focused on changes at the dyadic level, which will be discussed in a subsequent section. In a recent study of approximately 300 fourth-, seventh-, and tenth-grade students, we examined changes at the global, as well as dyadic, level. In our Global Network Inventory, 7 social provisions are examined: (1) enhancement of worth; (2) reliable alliance; (3) instrumental help (guidance); (4) companionship (social integration); (5) affection; (6) intimacy; and (7) nurturance. These generally correspond to Weiss's list, but a distinction was made between affection and intimacy. Weiss included both as part of attachment, but we distinguished them because we believe that individuals, particularly children, may have strong feelings of affection for others without necessarily engaging in much intimate disclosure with them. Four other qualities were examined as well: (1) conflict; (2) punishment; (3) the relative amount of power the child has in interactions with others; and (4) satisfaction. To assess children's perceptions at the global level, we asked them to rate how much they experienced each of the provisions or other qualities in their social relationships in general. For example, a companionship item read: "How much do you go places and do things with other people?" Each of the 11 was assessed with three 5-point Likert items (1 = little or not at all; 5 = the most possible).

Table 6.2 depicts the means of the qualities at each of the three grade levels. There are indications of both change and stability in the perceptions of the various qualities. Overall satisfaction decreases with age, as does a sense of reliable alliance and enhancement of worth ($p < .06$). For boys, perception of intimacy also decreased, but for girls it showed increases. Even with these decreases, it doesn't appear, however, that social life is becoming unappealing or aversive, in that perceptions of conflict and punishment also decrease, particularly between the seventh and tenth grade. Perhaps students are becoming more autonomous and relying less on their interpersonal relationships to fulfill various needs or goals.

TABLE 6.2. Developmental Changes at the Overall Level

	Grade		
Feature	4	7	10
Reliable alliance	3.70[a]	3.26[b]	3.29[b]
Enhancement of worth	3.37[a]	3.22[a,b]	3.12[b]
Instrumental help	2.88[a]	2.70[a]	2.68[a]
Companionship	3.56[a]	3.52[a]	3.50[a]
Affection	3.60[a]	3.49[a]	3.52[a]
Intimacy	2.72[a]	2.70[a]	2.74[a]
Nurturance	3.08[a]	3.09[a]	3.17[a]
Conflict	2.08[a]	2.12[a]	1.86[a]
Punishment	2.05[a]	2.25[a]	1.94[a]
Relative power	2.72[a]	2.81[a]	2.94[a]
Satisfaction	3.78[a]	3.55[b]	3.51[b]

Note: Sex effects and interactions with sex are described in the text. Higher scores indicate perceptions of more of a quality. Higher scores on relative power indicate greater perceptions of power by the child. The letters in superscripts indicate the rank order of means across grade levels within each type of relationship. Means with different letters in the same row are significantly different from each other.

What is also noteworthy is the absence of increases in the various provisions. Sullivan and the other theorists would have expected an increase in intimacy. Girls displayed such an increase, but the boys showed the opposite trend. Even the supportive findings for girls must be interpreted cautiously, because we failed to find changes in either another sample of children in fourth through twelfth grade, or a sample of second-, fifth-, and eighth-grade children (Buhrmester & Furman, 1987b). Perhaps developmental changes in needs or provisions are not reflected by changes in the *desires* for different provisions—or at least in subjective self-reports of such desires. Alternatively, changes may not occur at the overall level as much as in specific group or dyadic relationships, the topics we turn to next.

CHANGES AT THE GROUP LEVEL

Several investigators have been concerned with developmental changes in peer groups, particularly during adolescence. An early description of these changes was provided by Dunphy (1963). Based on case studies, he outlined five stages of development. During the first stage, unisexual cliques emerge, consisting of four to six close friends. The cliques are organized around leaders who have traits admired by the other group members. Throughout most of adolescence, they are the basic social units, offering closeness and support to the members. In the second stage, two cliques begin to socialize with one another in a group context, marking the first step toward heterosexual relationships. Then in the third stage heterosexual crowds begin to appear, consisting of large groups containing members of both sexes. High-status members in each clique begin to date one another. In the fourth stage, there is a fully developed crowd with several heterosexual cliques in close association. Finally, boys and girls begin to form couples. As a result, the crowd begins to disintegrate, leaving loosely associated groups of couples.

Dunphy's ideas receive some support from Csikszentmihalyi and Larson's (1984) study of how adolescents spend their time. High school students carried pagers for a week. During every 2-hour block of time, the pager would beep and students were asked to indicate what they were doing and with whom. Between the freshman and sophomore year, there was a decrease in the amount of time spent interacting with members of a same-sex group and a concomitant increase in time interacting with members of an opposite-sex group. Such findings could reflect the emergence of crowds. The emergence of couples was also found with an increase in the junior and senior year in the amount of time spent with one member of the opposite sex. The amount of time spent in same-sex dyads remained relatively stable over the 4 years.

In our own research (Gavin & Furman, 1987), we also found marked changes in peer groups during the adolescent years. In this study, 306 students in the fifth through twelfth grade were asked to rate their interactions with members of their groups and other students who were not part of their groups. Consistent with other research (Brown, Eicher, & Petrie, 1986), being part of a group was reported to be more important in early (seventh and eighth grade) and middle (ninth and tenth grade) adolescence than before or after. Being part of a group may fulfill a need to belong, as Veroff and Veroff (1980) would suggest, or it may help bolster adolescents' sense of identity as they seek to separate from the family (Blos, 1967).

As the groups increased in importance, they appeared to become more cohesive units with clear boundaries and standards for expectations. In particular, negative interactions with those outside the group occurred more frequently during early and middle adolescence. The permeability of the group was lower than during late adolescence, and conformity to group norms was higher. Erickson (1968) suggested that this conformity and clannishness may help them cope with their difficulties in developing an autonomous identity.

Interestingly, the interactions with peer group members were not necessarily rewarding. A significant quadratic effect was found for positive or supportive interactions with group members. In particular, scores dropped from preadolescence (fifth and sixth grade) to early adolescence (seventh and eighth grade) and middle adolescence (ninth and tenth grade), and rose again in late adolescence (eleventh and twelfth grade). A complementary pattern was found for negative interactions with group members, with negative interactions occurring most frequently in early and middle adolescence. The negative interactions may enforce group similarity; when someone does not conform to the expected norms, he or she may be criticized or punished. Sullivan (1953) observed that some individuals can bolster their own sense of worth by disparaging or criticizing others. Being critical of one's peers then may help keep others in their place. Antagonistic interactions within the group may also help establish group status hierarchies. In fact, students reported that status hierarchies were more characteristic of their groups during this period than before or after.

In the later years of high school, being part of a peer group became less important. Group conformity decreased and the boundaries became permeable. Positive interactions increased with those both in and out of the group, whereas negative interactions decreased. It appears that, as adolescents become self-reliant and establish a sense of identity, being part of a group becomes less critical, and yet they are able to reap the benefits of positive peer group interactions. These changes are also consistent with Blos's (1967) idea that the peer group serves as a transitional object for adolescents as they separate from their families.

Although these studies begin to sketch out the changes in peer groups during adolescence, less is known about the evolution of groups earlier in childhood. Clearly, peers are a major source of companionship for school-age and preschool children, and children prefer some playmates to others.

It does not appear that young children's peer groups are really cohesive units, however; instead, they appear to be simple collections of dyadic relationships. In a laboratory study, H. W. Smith (1973) found that preschool children's groups tend to break into subgroups of two or three children. As children got older, there were increases in the cohesiveness of the group; the frequency of positive interactions increased, and antagonism and tension decreased. Other laboratory research has also shown increases in task orientation and interdependence during the elementary school years (Smith, 1960).

In preadolescence, children become more peer oriented and the norms and standards of peers become more clear, consensually valid, and differentiated (Bowerman & Kinch, 1959; Emmerich, Goldman, & Shore, 1971). There is also greater consensus about the reputations of peers, and sociometric status shows less fluctuation (Horrocks & Buker, 1951). At the same time, Selman (1980) found that it is not until adolescence that children began to describe a peer group as a whole structure in which there is shared community of common interests and beliefs and consensus concerning norms. Preadolescents usually conceive of peer groups as either unilateral or bilateral partnerships. Children may, however, experience groups as cohesive units prior to developing such conceptualizations. Thus it appears that groups begin to emerge during the elementary school years, especially the later years, but the nature of their development has not been carefully specified.

Little work has been done on groups other than the peer group. One can think of the family as a group, but most of the research has examined specific dyadic relationships, rather than the family as a whole (see Handel, 1965, for an exception). Moreover, relatively little is known about the role formal organizations, such as sports teams or activity clubs, play in social development. In their study of children's lives outside school, Medrich, Roizen, Rubin, and Buckley (1982) provide interesting descriptive information about sixth graders' experiences in organized activities, but investigators have apparently not examined developmental trends.

CHANGES AT THE DYADIC LEVEL

A significant amount of research has been conducted on developmental changes in dyadic relationships. In most instances, however, investigators have only examined changes in one type of relationship at a time. A few studies of changes in the network of relationships have, however, been conducted.

In one of the few studies of changes during the elementary school years, Belle and Longfellow (1984) examined patterns of confiding in children 5 to 12 years old. As children grew older, they increasingly confided in siblings and friends, and turned less often to fathers. Throughout this age span, however, mothers were the most favored confidants.

In a study of older children and adolescents, Hunter and Youniss (1982) examined changes in friendships and mother–child and father–child relationships. Students in the fourth, seventh, and tenth grades and college were asked to rate the degree of nurturance, intimacy, and control in each of the three relationships. Nurturance by both parents was high at all ages, but it increased with age in friendships so that by the tenth grade, the scores for friends and parents were comparable. Intimacy with mothers remained relatively consistent across ages. Intimacy with fathers was also relatively consistent across ages except for a surprising peak in the seventh grade. In contrast, intimacy with friends increased consistently across the four ages. In the fourth grade, intimacy with friends was less frequent than with mothers (and comparable to that with fathers), but by the tenth grade, friendships were the most intimate relationships. For all three relationships, perceptions of controlling behavior by the other peaked in the seventh and tenth grade.

In a subsequent study Hunter (1985) examined developmental changes in adolescents' discussions with parents and friends about academic–vocational, social–ethical, family, and peer issues. In general, academic–vocational and family issues were discussed more with parents, whereas peer issues were discussed with friends. Social–ethical issues were discussed most often with mothers. The frequency of discussions with parents in the various domains was relatively stable from early to late adolescence. In contrast, as they got older, adolescents talked more frequently with friends about academic issues and social–ethical issues. In early adolescence, these were primarily parental domains, but by late adolescence, discussions with parents and friends were equally common.

In our own research, several studies have examined developmental changes in school-age children and adolescents' relationships (Buhrmester & Furman, 1987; Furman & Buhrmester, 1987). The study described in the previous section on global changes included an assessment of changes at the dyadic level as well as at the overall level. Specifically, approximately 550 students in the fourth, seventh, or tenth grade or college completed Network of Relationship Inventories describing their relationships with parents, siblings, grandparents, teachers, friends, and boyfriends or girlfriends. For each relationship, the students rated the same 11 characteristics they had rated in their descriptions of the overall network.

A series of factor analyses of scores for each relationship usually revealed three factors: (1) support provisions, which comprised the seven provisions and the satisfaction ratings; (2) negative interactions, which contained the conflict and punishment scales; and (3) relative power, which contained the relative power scale and secondarily nurturance of the other. As can be seen, these are three of the four facets that were previously asserted to be important elements that should be included in description of a relationship. The fourth element, the relative nature of a relationship in the network, is not examined on this inventory. It is also interesting to note that one exception to the factor pattern was friendships, where a relative power factor did not emerge. An egalitarian distribution of power seems to be a defining feature of friendships, and not a dimension along which friendships vary—at least not same-age friendships.

When the scores for all the relationships were simultaneously factor-analyzed, the scores for different relationships generally fell on different sets of factors with each set of factors usually containing the three groupings described previously. For example, there was a sibling support factor, a sibling negative interaction factor, and so on. Few factors contained scores from more than one relationship; those factors that did contain more than one were quite interpretable; for example, the punishment scores from both parents loaded on one factor, and the nurturance of mother and father loaded on another. Thus these results not only provide support of the facets previously proposed, but also underscore the importance of distinguishing among relationships in the network.

A similar picture arises when one examines the correlations across corresponding scores for different relationships. For example, support scores for different relationships tended to be moderately correlated with each other ($M\ r = .38$) with scores among family relations being more highly related than those between familial and nonfamilial relations. Whereas the magnitude of these correlations indicates that the different relationships are distinct from one another, the fact that most relationship scores were positively correlated with one another is consistent with the recent emphasis on the interrelations among relationships (see Dunn, in press; Sroufe & Fleeson, 1986). Interestingly, the size of correlations tends to decrease as the students get older, suggesting that the relationships become differentiated and perhaps specialized (see Furman & Buhrmester, 1987, for further information).

Table 6.3 depicts the mean scores for each relationship at each grade level. The seven provisions displayed similar patterns of change with a few noteworthy exceptions; thus changes at the factorial level are primarily presented.[2] Conflict and punishment are presented separately because the punishment measure was not administered to the college students.

The first noteworthy pattern is that parents are perceived as less supportive with the onset of adolescence. The largest change is between the fourth and seventh grade, but further decreases occur between the seventh and tenth grade. Parental conflict and punishment also increase between the fourth and seventh grade. Finally, compared to the fourth graders, the seventh- and tenth-grade students report having less power in their interactions with parents, even though they are older. All of these changes are consistent with the idea that adolescence is the period of individuation. As part of this process, adolescents begin to rely less on their parents and become more independent from them. The increase in independence may lead to

[2] For the sake of conceptual clarity, satisfaction scores were not included in the calculation of the support provision factor.

TABLE 6.3. Developmental Changes at the Dyadic Level

	Grade			
	4	7	10	13+
		Support		
Mother	$3.90^{1,a}$	$3.51^{1,b}$	$3.32^{2,c}$	$3.42^{1,b,c}$
Father	$3.89^{1,a}$	$3.39^{1,b}$	$2.98^{3,c}$	$3.16^{2,c}$
Sibling	$3.43^{2,3,a}$	$2.99^{2,c}$	$3.11^{3,b,c}$	$3.22^{1,2,b}$
Grandparent	$3.64^{2,a}$	$3.01^{2,b}$	$2.75^{4,6,c}$	$2.68^{3,c}$
Teacher	$2.61^{5,a}$	$1.86^{3,b}$	$1.93^{5,b}$	—
Same-sex friend	$3.41^{3,a,b}$	$3.61^{1,a}$	$3.57^{1,a}$	$3.37^{1,b}$
Romantic friend	$2.77^{4,c}$	$3.08^{2,b,c}$	$3.19^{2,a,b}$	$3.50^{1,a}$
		Conflict		
Mother	$1.98^{2,b}$	$2.37^{2,a}$	$2.30^{2,a}$	$2.07^{1,b}$
Father	$1.94^{2,b}$	$2.26^{2,a}$	$2.30^{2,a}$	$1.98^{1,b}$
Sibling	$2.01^{1,a}$	$1.94^{1,a}$	$2.66^{1,b}$	$1.60^{1,b}$
Grandparent	$1.59^{3,a}$	$1.38^{4,b}$	$1.20^{4,b}$	$1.30^{2,b}$
Teacher	$1.64^{3,a}$	$1.81^{3,a}$	$1.36^{4,b}$	—
Same-sex friend	$2.01^{2,a}$	$1.94^{3,a}$	$1.66^{3,b}$	$1.54^{2,b}$
Romantic friend	$1.68^{3,a,b}$	$1.47^{3,4,b}$	$1.74^{3,4,b}$	$1.88^{1,a}$
		Punishment		
Mother	$2.28^{1,b}$	$2.83^{1,a}$	$2.60^{1,a}$	
Father	$2.25^{1,b}$	$2.84^{1,a}$	$2.66^{1,a}$	
Sibling	$1.97^{2,a}$	$2.15^{3,a}$	$1.55^{2,b}$	
Grandparent	$1.71^{2,a,b}$	$1.82^{2,a}$	$1.51^{2,b}$	
Teacher	$1.85^{2,b}$	$2.09^{3,a}$	$1.64^{2,c}$	
Same-sex friend	$1.39^{3,a}$	$1.51^{4,a}$	$1.32^{2,a}$	
Romantic friend	$1.35^{3,a}$	$1,30^{4,a}$	$1.51^{2,a}$	
		Relative power		
Mother	$2.19^{2,a}$	$1.91^{2,b}$	$1.84^{4,b}$	$2.30^{4,a}$
Father	$2.18^{2,a}$	$1.97^{2,a,b}$	$1.73^{4,b}$	$2.04^{5,a}$
Sibling	$2.93^{1,b}$	$2.98^{1,b}$	$3.34^{1,a}$	$3.24^{1,a}$
Grandparent	$2.33^{2,a}$	$2.28^{2,a}$	$2.26^{3,a}$	$2.50^{3,a}$
Teacher	$2.07^{1,a}$	$1,71^{3,b}$	$1.90^{4,a}$	—
Same-sex friend	$2.84^{1,b}$	$2.95^{1,a,b}$	$3.04^{2,a}$	$3.09^{2,a}$
Romantic friend	$2.97^{1,a}$	$2.85^{1,a}$	$2.85^{2,a}$	$3.05^{2,a}$

Note: Higher scores indicate perceptions of more of a quality. Higher scores on relative power indicate greater perceptions of power by the child. The numbers in superscripts indicate the rank order of the means across relationships within each grade. Means with different number ranks in the same column are significantly different from each other. The letters in superscripts indicate the rank order of means across grade levels within each type of relationship. Means with different letters in the same row are significantly different from each other. Sex effects and interactions with sex are described in the text.

conflict with their parents, who are likely to disagree with some of their decisions. The amount of support provided by parents is still great in an absolute sense, however. As Youniss and Smollar (1985) point out, adolescents do not sever their relationships with parents, but instead they transform them; they are still responsive to parental authority, but they experience greater freedom from it. Parents also contribute to this transformation by giving them more freedom.

Relationships with parents undergo a different change when students leave home and begin college. Conflict was perceived as decreasing, whereas feelings of power increased. Students perceived a decrease in companionship and nurturance of the other, but increases were perceived in instrumental help, intimacy, admiration, and reliable alliance. It seems unlikely, however, that some of these supportive behaviors underlying help or intimacy actually increased because most college students lived away from home. Thus the changes seem to reflect a subjective reappraisal, rather than objective changes. Subjective or not, the changes are quite real. In fact, the same pattern of changes has been found in an earlier longitudinal study of the transition to college (Shaver, Furman, & Buhrmester, 1985).

What accounts for the changes? They do not seem to be a simple case of "absence makes the heart grow fonder." In the other study, relationships with high school friends and romantic partners were described less positively when the students began college. (As we'll see shortly, romantic relationships with *college* peers are perceived more positively.) It may be that the positive changes reflect the status accorded being a "grown-up college student." Daily hassles and conflicts are less frequent, and the students may perceive the advice and financial aid to be helpful, rather than constraining. Alternatively, the difficulties of establishing a new network of friends may have led the students to appreciate their stable family relationships. Another potential explanation was proposed by Pipp, Shaver, Jennings, Lamborn, and Fischer (1985), who also found that college students described their current relationships with parents as more loving and closer than their relationships with parents had been in the past. They suggested that the sense of an adult self may develop optimally and least distressingly when the adolescent's move toward autonomy is balanced by a strong sense of love in the relationship. That is, the increased feeling of love counters fears of separation.

Developmental changes in relationships with siblings and grandparents bore some similarities to the changes with parents. The perceptions of support declined in the seventh grade, and the ratings for relationships with grandparents were even lower in the tenth grade. The ratings of conflict and punishment did not, however, peak during these periods. To the contrary, they were actually lower than the fourth-grade ratings. Similar changes were found in a study of developmental changes in sibling relationships (Buhrmester and Furman, 1987a). Thus as was not the case with the relationships with parents, these changes reflect not so much an increase in conflict or strife as a loss in intensity. The relationships with grandparents and siblings seem less important to adolescents, although with the advent of college, sibling relationships are perceived more positively once again.

The changes in peer relations provide a marked contrast with the changes in family relations. The overall support scores followed a quadratic function, with scores tending to rise between the fourth and seventh grade and drop between the tenth grade and college. More detailed analyses revealed that the changes from fourth to seventh grade primarily occurred in intimacy and affection, and not the other provisions. The specific nature of these changes is quite consistent with Sullivan's (1953) description of the development of chumships.

The decreases from the tenth grade to college were also provision specific. Companionship and nurturance of the other decreased, whereas the others remained stable or even increased in the case of reliable alliance. Perhaps simple companionship is less central to friendships among college students, or perhaps they have fewer opportunities for contact with their friends. Alternatively, they may spend more time with others, such as romantic partners.

Some support for the last explanation is provided by the changes in romantic relationships. As students got older, they described their romantic relationships as increasingly supportive. By college, the ratings for this relationship were as high as or higher than those for any other relationship. These changes are consistent with Sullivan's (1953) idea that the needs for sexuality and intimate exchange begin to merge in relationships with opposite-sex peers during late adolescence. The changes also fit Dunphy's (1972) description of the development of couples and the accompanying disintegration of the crowd.

It is interesting to contrast the differences in the developmental trajectories for peer group relationships and relationships with friends and romantic partners. Interactions in the general peer group became less supportive and more conflictual in early adolescence, whereas the dyadic relationships became more supportive. Apparently, these relationships provide shelters in the storm of early adolescent popularity wars. Certainly, these findings underscore the importance of distinguishing between friendships and peer group processes (Furman & Robbins, 1985).

Although not depicted in Table 6.2, children's relationships with their pets were also examined. Compared to the other relationships described here, these may seem trivial to most of us. We decided to examine them, however, because of elementary school children's repeated assertion that their pets were important "people" in their lives (see Bryant, 1982). The fourth-grade children reported that they turned frequently to their pets for companionship, alliance, intimacy, and particularly opportunities to provide nurturance. In fact, they reported providing more nurturance to their pets than to anyone else in their network. These relationships are primarily special for the young children. Marked developmental decreases between fourth and seventh grade were found for each of the provisions listed previously in this paragraph. Make no bones about it! The potential significance of pets in the younger children's lives does warrant further attention.

Changes at the Interactional Level

Although it is important to distinguish between interactions and relationships, social scientists usually do not examine changes at the interactional level per se. Instead, they study interactions with a particular person or persons. In this sense, the relevant research has been discussed in the previous sections.

A related concept is the idea of changes in the manifestations of relationship qualities. That is, over the course of development, a relationship quality or process may be expressed differently in interactions. For example, young infants may seek proximity by physical contact, whereas older infants may seek it by visual contact (Marvin, 1977). The essence of the process and its function may be the same, however. Parents may change from using physical punishment to using verbal punishment, but they both may reflect efforts to control children's behavior. In effect, this is the classic developmental issue of phenotypic and genotypic continuity (Connell & Furman, 1984; Kagan, 1969). In some respects, the literature on children's conceptions of friendships or other relationships addresses this issue (see Bigelow, 1977; Furman & Bierman, 1984; Livesley & Bromley, 1973). Consistent, marked changes have been found, but it is unclear whether these reflect changes in the manifestations of an underlying quality or the emergence of new qualities in a relationship. For example, young children may tell of daily experiences, whereas older children may share deep interpersonal feelings with friends. Should we consider these to reflect the same process of personal sharing or should we treat them as two different phenomena? Longitudinal research may prove valuable here by helping us examine potential continuities among phenotypically different behaviors.

FUTURE DIRECTIONS

The research that has been discussed here has been somewhat restricted by the chapter's scope. In particular, I did not systematically review the various literatures describing developmental changes in particular relationships, such as in friendships (see Berndt, 1982; Furman 1982).

Aside from this restriction, however, the limitations of the research described here reflect the current state of the field. Surprisingly little is known about the evolution of family relationships beyond early childhood, even if one includes research on one type of family relationship (but see Maccoby & Martin, 1983; Roberts, Block, & Block, 1984). Other relationships, such as those with relatives, teachers, or other adults, have not yet received much attention. In fact, we know very little about what these relationships are like or what their significance is, let alone their changes over the course of development.

Most of the work is also based on self-reports or family members' reports. These perceptions provide invaluable information about relationships (Furman, 1984; Furman et al., in press), but observational studies are needed as well. To date, relatively few observational paradigms have been developed for studying school-age children's relationships. Particularly needed are paradigms that can be used to examine multiple types of relationships.

Finally, we need more longitudinal studies to examine changes or stability in social networks. In fact, we need to broaden our concept of change or development. In a recent paper (Connell & Furman, 1984), we proposed three types of change: (1) level change; (2) structural change; and (3) changes in centrality. The first refers to the mean level of a variable for an individual or groups of individuals. Structural change refers to changes in the degree and pattern of relationships between measured variables (manifest variables) and underlying constructs (latent variables). It refers to the idea that an underlying variable may have different behavioral manifestations at different times or that any specific behavior's meaning may change with development (Baltes & Nesselroade, 1970; Coan, 1966; Kagan, 1969). Finally, changes in centrality refer to changes in the degree and pattern of interrelatedness of a variable. Almost all the research on this topic or other developmental topics has focused on changes in level. In the prior section, some research on changes in the behavioral manifestations of relationship properties was described, but such structural changes have remained relatively unexplored. Changes in centrality have been virtually untouched. One might expect such changes as some relationships come to center stage or move into the background as others do. For example, relationships with friends may become more strongly linked to self-esteem or adjustment as such relationships become more intimate in adolescence. By broadening our perspectives on change and relationships both conceptually and methodologically, we should be able to obtain a more comprehensive picture of children's social networks and their functions at different points in development.

REFERENCES

Adler, T., & Furman, W. (in press). A model for close relationships and relationship dysfunctions. In S. W. Duck (Ed.), *Handbook of personal relationships: Theory, research, and inventions.* London: Wiley.

Baltes, P. B., & Nesselroade, J. R. (1970). Multivariate longitudinal and cross-sectional sequences for analyzing ontogenetic and generational change: A methodological note. *Developmental Psychology, 2,* 163–168.

Belle, D., & Longfellow, C. (1984, August). *Turning to others: Children's use of confidants.* Paper presented at the meetings of the American Psychological Association, Toronto.

Berndt, T. J. (1982). The features and effects of friendship in early adolescence. *Child Development, 53,* 1447–1460.

Bigelow, B. J. (1977). Children's friendship expectations: A cognitive-developmental study. *Child Development, 48,* 246–253.

Blos, P. (1967). The second individuation process of adolescence. *The Psychoanalytic Study of the Child* (Vol. 12, p. 162).

Bowerman, C. E., & Kinch, J. W. (1959). Changes in family and peer orientation of children between the fourth and tenth grades. *Social Forces, 37,* 206–211.

Bowlby, J. (1969). *Attachment and loss: Vol. 1, Attachment.* New York: Basic.

Brown, B. B., Eicher, S. A., & Petrie, S. (1986). The importance of peer group ("crowd") affiliation in adolescence. *Journal of Adolescence, 9,* 73–96.

Bryant, B. K. (1982). Sibling relationships in middle childhood. In M. E. Lamb & B. Sutton-Smith (Eds.), *Sibling relationships: Across the lifespan.* Hillsdale, NJ: Erlbaum.

Buhrmester, D. (1983). *Toward a model of socioemotional development in preadolescence and adolescence.* Unpublished dissertation, University of Denver.

Buhrmester, D., & Furman, W. (1986). The changing functions of friends in childhood: A Neo-Sullivanian perspective. In V. J. Derlega & B. A. Winstead (Eds.), *Friendship and social interaction* (pp. 145–166). New York: Springer-Verlag.

Buhrmester, D., & Furman, W. (1987a). *Developmental changes in children's perceptions of their sibling relationships.* Manuscript in preparation.

Buhrmester, D., & Furman, W. (1987b). The development of companionship and intimacy, *Child Development, 58,* 1101–1113.

Coan, R. W. (1966). Child personality and developmental psychology. In R. B. Cattell (Ed.), *Handbook of multivariate experimental psychology.* Chicago: Rand McNally.

Connell, J. C., & Furman, W. (1984). Conceptual and methodological issues in the study of transitions. In R. Harmon & R. Emde (Ed.), *Continuity and discontinuity in development.* New York: Plenum.

Csikszentmihalyi, M., & Larson, R. (1984). *Being adolescent: Conflict and growth in the teenage years.* New York: Basic.

Dunn, J. (in press). Interrelations among relationships. In S. W. Duck (Ed.), *Handbook of personal relationships: Theory, research, and inventions.* London: Wiley.

Dunphy, D. C. (1963) The social structure of urban adolescent peer groups. *Sociometry, 26,* 230–246.

Emmerich, W., Goldman, K. S., & Shore, R. E. (1971). Differentiation and development of social norms. *Journal of Personality & Social Psychology, 18,* 323–353.

Erickson, E. H. (1968). *Identity: Youth and crises.* New York: Norton.

Furman, W. (1982). Children's friendships. In T. Field, G. Finley, A. Huston, H. Quay, & L. Troll (Eds.), *Review of human development.* New York: Wiley.

Furman, W. (1984). Some observations on the study of personal relationships. In J. C. Masters & K. Yarkin-Levin (Eds.), *Interfaces between developmental and social psychology.* New York: Academic.

Furman, W. (1987). *Social support, stress, and adjustment in adolescence.* Paper presented at the meeting of the society for Research in Child Development, Baltimore.

Furman, W., & Bierman, K. L. (1984). Children's conceptions of friendship: A multimethod study of developmental changes. *Developmental Psychology, 20,* 925–933.

Furman, W., & Buhrmester, D. (1987). *Developmental changes in children and adolescents' perceptions of their social network.* Unpublished paper, University of Denver.

Furman, W., Jones, L., Buhrmester, D., & Adler, T. (in press). Children's parents', and observers' perspective on sibling relationships. In P. G. Zukow (Ed.), *Sibling interaction across culture.* New York: Springer-Verlag.

Furman, W., & Robbins, P. (1985). What's the point? Issues in the selection of treatment objectives. In B. Schneider, K. Rubin, & J. Leddingham (Eds.), *Children's relations: Issues in assessment and intervention.* New York: Springer-Verlag.

Gavin, L., & Furman, W. (1987). *The development of cliques in adolescence.* Under review.

Handel, G. (1965). Psychological study of whole families. *Psychological Bulletin, 63,* 19–41.

Hartup, W. W. (1983). The peer system. In P. H. Mussen (Ed.-in-Chief) & E. M. Hetherington (Ed.), *Carmichael's manual of child psychology* (4th ed., Vol. 4). New York: Wiley.

Hazan, C., & Shaver, P. (1987). Romantic love conceptualized as an attachment process. *Journal of Personality & Social Psychology, 52,* 511–524.

Horrocks, J. E., & Buker, M. E. (1951). A study of the friendship fluctuations of preadolescents. *Journal of Genetic Psychology, 78,* 131–144.

Hunter, F. T. (1985). Adolescents' perceptions of discussions with parents and friends. *Developmental Psychology, 21,* 433–440.

Hunter, F. T., & Youniss, J. (1982). Changes in functions of three relationships during adolescence. *Developmental Psychology, 18,* 806–811.

Kagan, J. (1969). The three faces of continuity in human development. In D. A. Goslin (Ed.), *Handbook of socialization theory and research.* Chicago: Rand McNally.

Livesley, W. J., & Bromley, D. B. (1973). *Person perception in childhood and adolescence.* London: Wiley.

Maccoby, E. E., & Martin, J. A. (1983). Socialization in the context of the family: Parent-child interaction. In P. Mussen (Ed.-in-Chief) & E. M. Hetherington (Ed.), *Carmichael's manual of child psychology* (4th ed., Vol. 4). New York: Wiley.

Marvin, R. S. (1977). An ethological cognitive model for the attenuation of mother–child attachment behavior. In T. Alloway, L. A. Kramos, & P. Plinor (Eds.), *Advances in the study of communication and affect: The development of social attachment.* New York: Plenum.

Medrich, E. A., Roizen, J. A., Rubin, V., & Buckley, S. (1982). *The serious business of growing up: A study of children's lives outside school.* Berkeley, CA: University of California Press.

Milardo, R. M. (1986). Personal choice and social constraint in close relationships: Applications of network analysis. In V. J. Derlega & B. A. Winstead (Eds.), *Friendship and social interaction*. New York: Springer-Verlag.

Nelson-Le Gall, S., Gumerman, R. A., & Scott-Jones, D. (1983). Instrumental help-seeking and everyday problem-solving: A developmental perspective. In B. M. DePaulo, A. Nadler, & J. D. Fisher (Eds.), *New directions in helping*. (Vol. 2, pp. 265–283). New York: Academic.

Olson, D. H. (1977). Insiders' and outsiders' view of relationships: Research strategies. In G. Levinger & H. L. Raush (Eds.), *Close relationship: Perspectives on the meaning of intimacy*. Amherst: University of Massachusetts Press.

Pipp, S., Shaver, P., Jennings, S., Lamborn, S., & Fischer, K. W. (1985). Adolescents' theories about the development of their relationships with parents. *Journal of Personality & Social Psychology, 48,* 991–1001.

Roberts, G. C., Block, J. H., & Block, J. (1984). Continuity and change in parents' child-rearing practices. *Child Development, 55,* 586–597.

Salzinger, L. L. (1982). The ties that bind: The effect of clustering on dyadic relationships. *Social Networks, 4,* 117–145.

Selman, R. L. (1980). *The growth of interpersonal understanding: Developmental and clinical analyses*. New York: Academic.

Shaver, P., Furman, W., & Buhrmester, D. (1985). Aspects of a life transition: Network changes, social skills and loneliness. In S. Duck & D. Perlman (Eds.), *The Sage series in personal relationships* (Vol. 1). London: Sage.

Smith, A. J. (1960). A developmental study of group process. *Journal of Genetic Processes, 97,* 29–39.

Smith, H. W. (1973). Some developmental interpersonal dynamics through childhood. *American Sociological Review, 38,* 543–552.

Sroufe, L. A., & Fleeson, J. (1986). Attachment and the construction of relationships. In W. W. Hartup & Z. Rubin (Eds.), *Relationships and development*. Hillsdale, NJ: Erlbaum.

Sullivan, H. S. (1953). *The interpersonal theory of psychiatry*. New York: Norton.

Veroff, J., & Veroff, J. B. (1980). *Social incentives: A life-span developmental approach*. New York: Academic.

Weiss, R. S. (1974). The provisions of social relationships. In Z. Rubin (Ed.), *Doing unto others*. Englewood Cliffs, NJ: Prentice-Hall.

Weiss, R. S. (1986). Continuities and transformations in social relationships from childhood to adulthood. In W. W. Hartup & Z. Rubin (Eds.), *Relationships and development* (pp. 95–111). Hillsdale, NJ: Erlbaum.

Werner, E. E., & Smith, R. S. (1982). *Vulnerable but invincible: A longitudinal study of resilient children and youth*. New York: McGraw-Hill.

Wolchik, S. A., Sandler, I. N., & Braver, S. L. (in press). In N. Eisenberg (Ed.), *Contemporary topics in developmental psychology*. New York: Wiley.

Youniss, J., & Smollar, J. (1985). *Adolescent relations with mothers, fathers, and friends*. Chicago: University of Chicago Press.

CHAPTER 7

Gender Differences in Children's Social Networks and Supports

DEBORAH BELLE

Gender differences in children's social relations, particularly within the peer group, have interested child development researchers for many years. Only recently, however, has this interest broadened to include the child's entire social network, including nonrelated adults and children, siblings, parents, and other relatives. Meanwhile, social network and social support researchers have been primarily concerned with adults. These researchers have given little attention to gender differences in the structure and function of social networks until the last few years.

Yet there is a growing body of theory and research suggesting that gender is one of the key variables in shaping our social networks and our ways of relating to network members (Belle, 1982, 1987; Feiring & Coates, 1987; Vaux, 1985; B. Whiting & Edwards, 1988). Women have been found to have smaller, more local, and more familistic networks, although these effects are strongly modified by stage in the life cycle (Fischer, 1982). Children at home tend to constrict the social networks of mothers more than those of fathers, and middle-aged women have been found to have particularly large and active networks, while older men are unusually isolated (Fischer, 1982).

Women's social relationships have been found to be more dyadic, self-disclosing, and intimate than those of men, while men's friendships tend to focus around shared activities and experiences such as sports (Booth & Hess, 1974; Candy, Troll, & Levy, 1981; Depner & Ingersoll, 1982; Weiss & Lowenthal, 1975). Both men and women tend to turn to persons of their own gender for support provisions (Fischer, 1982).

Research with adults has shown that women utilize both formal and informal sources of help more frequently than do men and that women turn to family members and friends in times of crisis more readily than do men

Preparation of this chapter was supported by a William T. Grant Foundation faculty scholar award.

(Brown & Fox, 1979; Chiriboga, Coho, Stein, & Roberts, 1979; Veroff, Douvan, & Kulka, 1981; Veroff, Kulka, & Douvan, 1981). While women turn to a variety of support providers and confidants, men tend to restrict themselves to one key support provider—the wife (Veroff, Douvan, & Kulka, 1981).

Vaux, Burda, and Stewart (1986) found that the disposition to utilize support resources in times of difficulty was linked to psychological femininity. Help seeking by men has been seen as a potential threat to men's sense of competence or independence (DePaulo, 1982), and as a violation of explicit social sanctions regarding appropriate male behavior, especially in the workplace (Weiss, 1985). Help seeking by women has been seen as compatible with female sex roles and with women's socialization (DePaulo, 1982).

Among adults, females have been found to provide nurturance and emotional support to others more frequently than do males. As wives, mothers, "kin keepers" to elderly and infirm relatives, neighbors, and friends, and even as professional support providers, such as nurses, day-care workers, social workers, and teachers, women provide considerable social support to others (Belle, 1987). Women are named disproportionately as counselors and companions by both men and women (Fischer, 1982), and as confidants and sources of affirmation and understanding by their own children (Belle & Longfellow, 1984), adolescents (Kandel & Lesser, 1972; Kon & Losenkov, 1978; Youniss & Smollar, 1985), and spouses (Campbell, Converse, & Rodgers, 1976; Lowenthal & Haven, 1968; Warren, 1975). Men, however, are named disproportionately as sources of financial aid, particularly older men, and especially fathers (Fischer, 1982).

These gender differences suggest that in adulthood, at least, males and females inhabit very different social worlds. While the cast of characters may be similar, men's and women's ways of relating to others are quite different. Do such gender differences exist in childhood? This chapter reviews what is known about gender differences and similarities in children's social networks, combining research conducted within the earlier child development tradition of studying children's peer relationships and friendships and that conducted more recently using the concept of the social network. Cross-cultural research on children's daily companions is also cited when appropriate. Trends apparent in this review of the literature are compared to gender differences in the social networks of adults. The limitations of current research are noted and future research directions are suggested.

SIZE AND STRUCTURE OF SOCIAL NETWORKS

In size and in structural properties, children's overall social networks appear quite similar, although gender differences have been found in several studies. Riley and Cochran (1987), relying on maternal report, found the composition of social networks quite similar for 6-year-old girls and boys. Boys and girls had networks of similar size, with similar numbers of kin and nonkin, adults, and children in the network. Both boys and girls had more adult females than adult males in their networks. Observational data from diverse cultures show that both boys and girls are more often in the presence of mothers than of fathers, and in the presence of adult females than of adult males (B. Whiting & Edwards, 1988). Garbarino, Burston, Raber, Russell, and Crouter (1978) found no sex differences in the number of persons sixth graders listed as members of their social networks, nor in the percentages of network members who were adults or who were institutional representatives. Similarly, no sex differences were found for measures of network density and contact frequency. Bryant (1985) found that school-age boys knew and interacted with more adults than did girls, and tended to interact with more peers as well. Tietjen (1982) reported that boys between the ages of 8 and 11 had a larger circle of friends than did girls of the same age. Many boys belonged to soccer or hockey teams, which regularly brought them into contact with large groups of other boys, and these sports teams probably provided boys with many of their friendships. Girls more rarely participated in such large, single-sex activity groups.

Tietjen also found an important interaction between child gender and household composition (two-parent vs. single-parent mother households). Daughters of single mothers and sons of married mothers reported knowing the greatest number of adults who were not their relatives. Several of the single mothers and daughters reported that the daughters were often included in their mothers' activities with adult friends. Boys from two-parent families tended to name the coaches of their sports teams and their fathers' friends as adults they knew. Boys in single-parent families had less access to both of these sources of adult companionship.

Coates (1987) found that among Black middle-class adolescents there were no gender differences in the overall size of social networks, in the proximity of social network members, or in the average length of time network members had been known. Coates did find that males tended to see network members more frequently than did females. Blyth, Hill, and Thiel (1982), however, who asked early adolescents to name the important people in their lives (i.e., "people you spend time with or do things with, people you like a lot or who like you a lot or both, people who make important decisions about things in your life, people you go to for advice or people you would like to be like"), found that females named more such "significant others" than did males. Oliveri and Reiss (1987), who analyzed kin and friendship networks separately, found no gender differences even approaching statistical significance in the size, density, and contact frequency of adolescents' networks.

Taken together, these studies are most convincing in conveying the similarities between the social networks of boys and girls. While Bryant, Tietjen, and Coates find evidence of greater size or activity level within boys' networks, Blyth and colleagues find that girls report more network members.

Such discrepancies may reflect differences in the ways network membership is assessed or differences among the samples of young people surveyed. The clearest evidence for gender differences in network size was found for preadolescent children, and there may be a developmental effect operating here, with boys' networks larger in preadolescence, but not in the early school years or during adolescence. Further research is needed to clarify this issue.

Further research should also pursue Tietjen's finding that sons of single mothers had less access to the companionship of unrelated adults than did daughters of single mothers or children in two-parent households. As Tietjen notes, sons of single mothers have been found in many studies to be a high-risk group. It is interesting, in this light, that Riley and Cochran (1987) discovered that the number of adult male relatives who took the child on outings away from home was positively related to the child's report card score. This effect, however, was restricted to the subgroup of one-parent (mother only) boys, the particular subgroup pinpointed in Tietjen's research as vulnerable to a dearth of adult companionship. Are outcomes other than school success related to supplemental adult companionship for boys in single-parent households? Would daughters in households headed by single fathers experience a similar lack of companionship from nonkin adults?

SEX CLEAVAGE

One of the most well documented effects of gender on social networks is *sex cleavage,* the tendency to associate differentially with members of one's own sex. Children have been found to show a preference for same-sex peers as early as 33 months (Jacklin & Maccoby, 1978), and this preference apparently grows stronger over the preschool and early school years. A recent longitudinal study found that children were more likely to have same- than opposite-sex peers in their social networks at 3 years (Lewis, Feiring, & Kotsonis, 1984), and that this tendency intensified by the time the same children had reached age 6 (Feiring & Lewis, 1987). Sex cleavage remained strong at age 9 as well as in this sample of children (Feiring & Lewis, this volume). Riley and Cochran (1987) found that 6-year-old children had more same-sex than opposite-sex peers in their social networks. In Riley and Cochran's sample there was also a nonsignificant trend for children to have more same-sex social ties to adults.

Hartup (1970) reported that isolation between the sexes reaches a peak during the late elementary and early junior high school years. One study of 11 classrooms in the fourth through sixth grades found that friendship cliques were completely segregated by sex, with not a single clique containing both boys and girls (Hallinan, 1977, cited in Schofield, 1981). Tietjen noted that only 15% of the Swedish preadolescents she studied named any opposite-sex children as friends. During adolescence sex cleavage is still marked, with boys and girls continuing to associate primarily with same-sex peers

(Douvan & Adelson, 1966; Hartup, 1983; Savin-Williams, 1980). Blyth and colleagues (1982) found that two-thirds of the "important others" listed by both male and female adolescents were of the same sex as the respondent.

Thorne (1986) describes the rituals, many adult invoked, that serve to perpetuate gender segregation in the elementary school. She notes that there are also occasions when gender diminishes in importance as an organizing principle and boys and girls are able to play together in comfortable ways. Such occasions are most likely to arise, for instance, when an absorbing task encourages cooperation, when adults organize and thus legitimize mixed-sex encounters, when grouping principles other than gender are explicitly stated, and when children are in private, uncrowded settings so that scarcity may require that one interact with a child of the other sex and so that few witnesses are present to ridicule this.

Studies of children's networks in nonwestern societies have found evidence of sex cleavage, but have also demonstrated that such patterns are responsive to specific culturally mandated expectations for boys and girls. B. Whiting and Edwards (1988) report that sex segregation is more common after the beginning of middle childhood and that sex segregation is more typical of same-age than of mixed-age groupings. Research by Harkness and Super (1985) among the Kipsigis people of western Kenya showed that children's peer groups were essentially undifferentiated by gender at ages under 6, but that in later childhood boys and girls were strongly sex segregated. Wenger (this volume), who observed children in another Kenyan group, the Giriama, discovered that children's involvement in same-sex groups increased sharply during childhood, especially for boys. These patterns of sex segregation appear to be related to parental expectations and children's customary duties around the homestead (Harkness & Super, 1985; Wenger, this volume). In one explicit comparison of a western and a nonwestern society, Tietjen (this volume) found in her studies of preadolescent children in Sweden and among the Maisin of Papua, New Guinea that the Swedish children had friendship networks that were substantially more gender segregated than those of the Maisin. While the Maisin children named, on average, 1.64 friends of the opposite sex, the Swedish children named only 0.25.

Harkness and Super also note that, while children over 6 spend increased proportions of their time with same-sex peers, they do not differentially choose children of their own sex as targets of social interaction (p. 221), suggesting that the sex segregation that exists is a product more of parental authority than of children's preferences. However, B. Whiting and Edwards (1988) report that in 10 cultures for which appropriate data were available two-thirds of the interactions of children 4 to 5 years old and 80% of the interactions of children 6 to 10 years old with children other than siblings were with children of the same sex. Further analysis suggested that sex segregation was least pronounced in societies in which children did not range far from home and were therefore limited in their choice of companions, while sex segregation was most pronounced in societies where children could find more peers to play with in public places. B. Whiting and Edwards argue that beginning around the age of 4 or 5 children are strongly motivated to behave in ways that announce their gender and demonstrate their mastery of sex-appropriate behavior. The single-sex group provides an environment that supports children's emerging gender identity, and it is therefore deeply appealing to children, particularly to boys, who have had less opportunity than girls to model their sex-role behavior on routinely available same-sex adults.

These studies suggest that children and adolescents live in social worlds that are highly sex segregated, and that this sex segregation tends to increase during the childhood years, to peak in late childhood or early adolescence, and to stabilize in adolescence at a fairly high level. The research suggests both that adults encourage this sex cleavage and that children actively seek out same-sex peers. Future research can focus on examining the situations that allow some relaxation of the pervasive sex cleavage among children, and the consequences for children's development of participation in networks that are more or less gender segregated.

MODES OF INTERACTION

Beyond the sex cleavage that characterizes the networks of children, there is evidence that boys and girls differ in their modes of interaction with network members. Studies have reported a tendency for boys to play in groups of three or more, which allows for more elaborated games and team sports, and for girls to prefer dyadic interaction, with its opportunities for emotional intimacy (Lever, 1976; Tietjen, 1982; Waldrop & Halverson, 1975). Tietjen (1982) reported that, among Swedish children between 8 and 11, girls reported spending more time in peer dyads, while boys reported having contact with more peers more often. Not only do girls prefer dyadic over large-group interactions, there is evidence that girls' dyadic friendships are more exclusive than those of boys (Eder & Hallinan, 1978).

In her study of middle-class Black adolescents, Coates (1987) found that a greater proportion of females than males reported special "chum groups" of less than five members, while a greater proportion of males than females reported chum groups of more than five members. In addition, females tended to report seeing network members in significantly more private settings than did males.

In accordance with their preference for dyadic interaction and for private settings, girls have been found to value intimate conversations and intimate knowledge of friends as part of friendship more than do boys (Berndt, 1982). Girls are more likely to confide their experiences in at least one other person than are boys (Belle & Longfellow, 1984). Bryant (1985) found that girls were more likely than boys to engage in intimate talks with peers and tended to have more such talks with adults and even with pets. During adolescence, girls have been found to report more intimacy in friendship than do boys

(Blyth & Foster-Clark, 1987; Hunter & Youniss, 1982; Kon & Losenkov, 1978; Youniss & Smollar, 1985) and to disclose more about themselves than do boys (Dimond & Munz, 1967; Youniss & Smollar, 1985).

Even when boys and girls behave identically and disclose information about themselves to others, they may have different goals and expectations in mind. One study of children's reasoning about confiding found that girls were more likely than boys to imagine a child in a hypothetical situation as confiding in others in order to seek practical help with the problem at hand. Boys, on the contrary, were marginally more likely than girls to imagine a child telling someone about an experience simply to convey factual information or because the other person would find out anyway or ought to be told (Belle, Burr, & Cooney, 1987). Such findings suggest that girls more than boys may self-disclose in order to solicit social support, while boys may do so simply to satisfy external expectations.

There is also strong evidence that girls are more inclined than boys to seek instrumental help and emotional comfort from others and to be comfortable with the support they receive. In their cross-cultural research B. Whiting and V. Whiting (1975) found that girls seek more help from others in early childhood than do boys. Nelson-LeGall, Gumerman, and Scott-Jones (1983) showed that when facing problems girls are more likely than boys to seek help. Wallerstein and Kelly (1980) found that in the transitional period following parental divorce more girls than boys had friends and more girls used their friends as a support system (p. 166). Similarly, Wolchik, Sandler, and Braver (1984) found that among children experiencing parental divorce girls reported more family members who provided emotional support and positive feedback and more individuals from outside the family who provided advice, goods and services, and supportive feedback than did boys. Girls also felt more positively than did boys about the individuals who provided this support. Interestingly, Wallerstein and Kelly (1980) also found that during the initial crisis of parental divorce, a time when children did not seem to be able to derive comfort from friends or family members, boys more than girls made use of their peers for distraction, to help them distance themselves from the turmoil in the home.

Among adolescents, girls name more informal sources of support, such as friends and other adults, than do boys (Cauce, Felner, & Primavera, 1982) and are more likely to turn to their peers for support than are boys (Burke & Weir, 1978).

These gender differences suggest that social relationships among girls are more dyadic, exclusive, intimate, and self-disclosing than those of boys, from childhood through adolescence. From childhood to adolescence, girls appear to seek more help and support from others than do boys. Boys may also utilize network members in times of stress, but perhaps more as sources of alternative satisfactions and as distractions from problems than as direct providers of emotional comforting and instrumental assistance. These differences parallel those previously found for adult men and women.

These differences in the ways boys and girls relate to members of their networks may well have important consequences for children of both sexes. Gilligan (1982) has argued that girls' experiences with intimate, dyadic play lead them to develop a style of moral reasoning that gives weight to empathy and sensitivity, and to "knowing the other as different from the self" (p. 11), while boys' involvements in large groups such as sports teams lead them to a style of moral reasoning that respects rules and relies on a more abstract view of human relationships.

Girls' tendencies to self-disclose and to favor exclusive dyadic relationships may account for girls' greater concern about the faithfulness of friends, and greater anxiety about rejection by friends, since girls' self-disclosure may leave them vulnerable to their peers should friendships sour (Berndt, 1982). Kon and Losenkov (1978) note of girls' friendships, "the intense need for shared confidences can be a potential source of misunderstandings and conflicts, which are fewer in the more restrained masculine friendship" (p. 150). Belle and colleagues (1987) also found that girls more than boys thought that a child in a hypothetical situation might want to be alone to work out a solution to a problem. The authors speculate that girls may feel themselves so thoroughly connected to others that they may need to make special provision for sufficient privacy and independence to master a situation on their own.

Recent research on depression suggests that a ruminative style may contribute to the preponderance of women among those who are depressed, while men's more typical pattern of engaging in distracting behaviors when distressed may contribute to their lower risk of depression (Nolen-Hoeksema, 1987). This argument implies that the tendency of girls to disclose problems and seek out emotional and instrumental assistance may, by encouraging further thinking about the problem at hand, be less useful in escaping depression than the tactic boys display more often, namely, using others as sources of distraction.

Conversely, boys may have ample opportunity to confront the challenges of childhood on their own, but may lack sufficient opportunities to turn to others for emotional comfort and instrumental assistance. In childhood boys appear to be more vulnerable than girls to many psychosocial stressors (Longfellow & Belle, 1984; Rutter, 1979). It is possible that this greater vulnerability is related to boys' relative lack of access to intimate, disclosing, and supportive relationships within their social networks.

These alternative but not mutually exclusive possibilities deserve further research attention.

Other research findings suggest that the different modes of interaction with network members that girls and boys tend to prefer may be differentially beneficial to them. Waldrop and Halverson (1975) found that social maturity and facility with peers had very different correlates for boys and girls. Among boys, those who had a greater *number* of friendships were found to be more socially mature, while among girls, those who had more *intense and intimate* friendships were rated as more socially mature. Furthermore, peer sociability at age 2½ tended to predict these very different patterns of social involvement at age 7½ for boys and girls. Ten years later Bryant (1985) discovered a similar pattern, finding that, among boys, social perspective-taking skill, internal locus of control, and empathy were linked to *extensive, casual involvements* with many adults, while among girls such involvements were associated with negative outcomes. Instead, *intimate involvements* with adults predicted positive socioemotional development for girls, but not boys.

This striking convergence in findings may be interpreted to suggest that boys and girls find different types of social involvements inherently beneficial, or to suggest that socially adept boys and girls are more successful than their less accomplished peers in determining the kinds of social relationships that are considered socially appropriate for their gender.

It would be interesting in future studies to examine the relationship between membership in sports teams and network dimensions for both boys and girls. As girls increasingly become involved in athletic activities and competitive sports, it may be that earlier differences found between the networks of girls and boys diminish. Studies might be designed to compare schools in which team sports are emphasized for both sexes and those in which sports remain essentially the domain of boys. Children's networks could be followed longitudinally to examine the impact of team involvement on network size and functioning. Such studies might help to clarify whether boys' networks are sometimes different from those of girls because the boys happen to be on sports teams, or whether boys seek out sports teams because they prefer to be with large groups of friends.

SPECIFIC SUPPORT FIGURES

Gender differences also emerge when we examine the types of individuals who act as support figures to girls and boys. Riley and Cochran (1987) reported that boys had approximately equal numbers of men and women who involved them in adult tasks or took them on outings, while girls had about twice as many female as male adults who interacted with them in these ways. Observational research in diverse cultures shows that girls spend more time with mothers than do boys, while boys spend more time with fathers than do girls (B. Whiting & Edwards, 1988). Studies have also highlighted a tendency for girls to spend leisure (e.g., weekend) time with families while boys spend leisure time with friends (Coates, 1987; Tietjen, 1982). Cross-culturally, boys are typically found farther away from their homes, both when performing errands for their families and when on their own at play (B. Whiting & Edwards, 1988).

Coates (1987) found female adolescents to prefer family members, particularly female family members, rather than peers as sources of emotional and instrumental support, while males tended to favor peers and nonfamily adults as support providers more than did females. Coates also found a tendency to prefer same-gender family members (parent, sibling) as supports. Blyth and Foster-Clark (1987) showed that female adolescents were much more likely than male adolescents to name a female extended family adult as a significant other.

In comparing the intimacy experienced in family relationships versus those with close friends, however, the data suggest that it is girls, not boys, who find that emotional intimacy outside the family. Blyth and Foster-Clark (1987) found that adolescent girls experienced a higher level of intimacy with the most intimate same-sex friend than with mother or father, while boys reversed this picture, reporting more intimacy with both mother and father than with the closest male friend. Similar findings were reported by Buhrmester and Furman (1987). In their study, fifth-grade girls rated the intimacy of the closest same-sex friendship as highly as the intimacy of relationships with parents, and eighth-grade girls rated the same-sex friendship significantly more intimate than relationships with parents, while boys rated the same-sex friendships less intimate than parental relationships in the fifth grade and nonsignificantly different from relationships with parents in the eighth grade. Within the bounds of the household, Youniss and Smollar (1985) discovered that girls were emotionally closer to their mothers and emotionally more distant from their fathers than were boys.

This research on support figures does not conform to the simple notion that girls are more "familistic" in orientation, while boys are more focused on peers. Girls do appear to spend more leisure time with family members and to experience closeness to relatives, particularly those of their own gender. However, two recent studies now confirm that for adolescent girls the same-sex friend may be a more important source of intimacy than either mother or father. Furthermore, girls appear to be somewhat emotionally distanced from their fathers in comparison to boys.

In adulthood, it is men who tend to restrict their confiding and support seeking to their spouses, while women turn to an array of confidants inside and outside the family. Similarly, it is adolescent girls, not adolescent boys, who appear more likely to find important sources of intimacy outside the family. There is thus some continuity in the importance to females of nonfamily sources of support.

SUPPORT GIVING

There is some evidence for a gender difference in support giving among children as well as adults. Weisner (this volume) reports that Abaluyia girls exhibit as much nurturance and care to other children as do mothers in the

Abaluyia culture, while boys display a lower frequency of nurturant acts. In their cross-cultural work B. Whiting and J. Whiting (1975) found that girls offer more help and support to others in the preadolescent years than do boys. Cross-culturally, girls are more often responsible for the care of infants and toddlers than are boys (B. Whiting & Edwards, 1988), which may reflect girls' greater interest in nurturing children and in performing aspects of the maternal role as well as parents' interest in preparing daughters for motherhood.

B. Whiting and Edwards also note that taking care of infants provides training in nurturance and in sensitivity to nonverbal cues. Infants and toddlers elicit nurturant behavior universally, and boys and girls who spend time with them engage in more nurturant behavior than children who do not. This behavior then appears to generalize, so that children who have been caretakers of very young children behave nurturantly to their peers more often than do children who have not spent much time with infants and toddlers (B. Whiting & Edwards, 1988). A recent American study found, similarly, that young adult women who had taken care of siblings during childhood tended to continue their nurturant relationships with brothers and sisters into adulthood and to extend this supportive and protective style of relating to other family members as well (Warschausky, 1988). The study also found a tendency, which was not statistically significant, for the sibling caretakers to choose professions that offered opportunities for nurturance as well.

Bryant (1985) discovered that older sisters were named frequently on younger children's lists of important others, more frequently than were older brothers and even more frequently than either mothers or fathers. In indirect corroboration of such a gender difference, Blyth and Foster-Clark (1987) found that, when reporting about relationships with younger siblings of both the same and the opposite sex, girls reported greater intimacy than did boys. Girls were also significantly more likely than boys to list such siblings when asked about the significant persons in their own lives. However, Furman and Buhrmester's study of fifth- and sixth-grade children (1985) did not confirm the special supportiveness of older sisters. In this study children named older and same-sex siblings as particularly important support figures. Instrumental aid was seen as coming more frequently from brothers than from sisters.

Research on children's social networks has frequently focused on children as support receivers, rarely on children as support providers. Future research should examine this important function within children's social networks and should investigate gender differences and similarities in the provision of social support resources to others. Research with adults suggests that, while women derive some of their deepest satisfactions and much of their sense of identity in their roles as providers of support to others, these roles also are major sources of stress in the lives of women (Belle, 1982, 1987). Very little is known about the childhood antecedents of such roles.

SUMMARY

Reviewing research on gender differences in children's social networks and supports suggests that many of the gender differences found for adults are evident in childhood as well. There is suggestive evidence that boys' social networks are somewhat larger and more active than those of girls. However, the research is far from unanimous on these points. There is much stronger evidence that the style of relationships within children's social networks tends to differ by sex, with girls maintaining more intimate, self-disclosing, and dyadic relationships and boys preferring larger chum groups and friendships focused on shared activities rather than verbal self-disclosure. Just as in adulthood, there is also evidence that females seek out more social support than do males, both from within and from outside the family, and that females provide more social support to others, such as younger siblings, than do males. Just as in adulthood, research shows some tendency for males and females to prefer same-sex persons as companions and confidants. These are provocative gender differences, and they have implications for the well-being of boys and girls, and for the well-being of the men and women these children will grow up to be.

FUTURE RESEARCH

Many specific directions for future research have already been suggested, and these will not be summarized here. Instead, two overarching research directions will be discussed. One promising direction would be to examine situational factors that promote either gender differences or gender similarities in social networks. One such factor that already has been mentioned is the encouragement of sports teams for both girls and boys. Since boys' greater involvement in such teams seems to be associated with several gender differences in social networks, such as network size, chum group size, and preferences for shared activities versus intimate self-disclosure, it would be interesting to compare settings that foster team sports for girls with other settings that do not encourage such activities to see whether social network functioning also varies with team involvement. A less rigorous test of this hypothesis would be to compare the networks of boys and girls involved in team sports and those of boys and girls who are not similarly involved. Examining school climate for team sports would help one to tease out self-selection factors as well.

Research in future might also examine characteristics of children whose networks are atypical for their gender: children with more than the usual number of opposite-sex friends in their networks, children whose style of network functioning is more typical of the opposite sex (e.g., boys who prefer dyadic interaction and verbal self-disclosure, girls who prefer large chum groups and shared activities), and children whose major support figures are more typical of the opposite sex (e.g., girls who are emotionally closer to father than mother, boys who are especially close to female kin).[1] One might examine the perceptions others have of such children, situational factors that might help to account for their network patterns, and the relationships between network characteristics and other personal characteristics. Such research could help to inform us about the origins of these gender-linked patterns of network involvement and about the significance to children of such patterns.

REFERENCES

Belle, D. (1982). The stress of caring: Women as providers of social support. In L. Goldberger & S. Breznitz (Eds.), *Handbook of stress: Theoretical and clinical aspects* (pp. 496–505). New York: Free Press.

Belle, D. (1987). Gender differences in the social moderators of stress. In R. Barnett, L. Biener, & G. Baruch (Eds.), *Gender and Stress* (pp. 257–277). New York: Free Press.

Belle, D., Burr, R., & Cooney, J. (1987). Boys and girls as social support theorists. *Sex Roles, 17* (11/12), 657–665.

Belle, D., & Longfellow, C. (1984, August). *Turning to others: Children's use of confidants.* Paper presented at the annual meeting of the American Psychological Association, Toronto.

Berndt, T. J. (1982). The features and effects of friendship in early adolescence. *Child Development, 53,* 1447–1460.

Blyth, D. A., & Foster-Clark, F. S. (1987). Gender differences in perceived intimacy with different members of adolescents' social networks. *Sex Roles, 17* (11/12), 689–718.

Blyth, D. A., Hill, J. P., & Thiel, K. S. (1982). Early adolescents' significant others: Grade and gender differences in perceived relationships with familial and nonfamilial adults and young people. *Journal of Youth & Adolescence, 11*(6), 425–450.

Booth, A., & Hess, E. (1974). Cross-sex friendship. *Journal of Marriage & the Family, 36,* 38–47.

Brown, P., & Fox, H. (1979). Sex differences in divorce. In E. Gomberg & V. Frank (Eds.), *Gender and disordered behavior: Sex differences in psychopathology.* New York: Brunner/Mazel.

Bryant, B. (1985). The neighborhood walk: Sources of support in middle childhood. *Monographs of the Society for Research in Child Development, 50*(3, Serial No. 210).

Buhrmester, D., & Furman, W. (1987). The development of companionship and intimacy. *Child Development, 58,* 1101–1113.

Burke, R. J., & Weir, T. (1978). Sex differences in adolescent life stress, social support, and well-being. *Journal of Psychology, 98,* 277–288.

[1] I am grateful to Candice Feiring for suggesting this line of research.

Campbell, A., Converse, P., & Rodgers, W. (1976). *The quality of American life: Perceptions, evaluations, and satisfactions.* New York: Russell Sage.

Candy, S. G., Troll, L. W., & Levy, S. G. (1981). A developmental exploration of friendship functions in women. *Psychology of Women Quarterly, 5,* 456–472.

Cauce, A. M., Felner, R. D., & Primavera, J. (1982). Social support in high-risk adolescents: Structural components and adaptive impact. *American Journal of Community Psychology, 10*(4), 417–428.

Chiriboga, D. A., Coho, A., Stein, J. A., & Roberts, J. (1979). Divorce, stress and social supports: A study in help-seeking behavior. *Journal of Divorce, 3,* 121–135.

Coates, D. L. (1987). Gender differences in the structure and support characteristics of Black adolescents' social networks. *Sex Roles, 17* (11/12), 667–687.

DePaulo, B. (1982). Social-psychological processes in informal help seeking. In T. A. Wills (Ed.), *Basic processes in helping relationships.* New York: Academic.

Depner, C., & Ingersoll, B. (1982). Employment status and social support: The experience of the mature woman. In M. Szinovacz (Ed.), *Women's retirement: Policy implications of recent research.* Beverly Hills: Sage Yearbooks in Women's Policy Studies, Vol. 6.

Dimond, R. E., & Munz, D. C. (1967). Original position of birth and self-disclosure in high school students. *Psychological Reports, 21,* 829–833.

Douvan, E., & Adelson, J. (1966). *The adolescent experience.* New York: Wiley.

Eder, D., & Hallinan, M. T. (1978). Sex differences in children's friendships. *American Sociological Review, 43,* 237–250.

Feiring, C., & Coates, D. (1987). Social networks and gender differences in the life space of opportunity [Special issue]. *Sex Roles, 17* (11/12).

Feiring, C., & Lewis, M. (1987). The child's social network: Sex differences from three to six years. *Sex Roles, 17* (11/12), 621–636.

Fischer, C. (1982). *To dwell among friends: Personal networks in town and city.* Chicago: University of Chicago Press.

Furman, W., & Buhrmester, D. (1985). Children's perceptions of the personal relationships in their social networks. *Developmental Psychology, 21,* 1016–1022.

Garbarino, J., Burston, N., Raber, S., Russell, R., & Crouter, A. (1978). The social maps of children approaching adolescence: Studying the ecology of youth development. *Journal of Youth & Adolescence, 7*(4), 417–428.

Gilligan, C. (1982). *In a different voice: Psychological theory and women's development.* Cambridge, MA: Harvard University Press.

Hallinan, M. T. (1977). *The development of children's friendship cliques.* Paper presented at the American Sociological Association convention, Chicago.

Harkness, S., & Super, C. (1985). The cultural context of gender segregation in children's peer groups. *Child Development, 56*(1), 219–224.

Hartup, W. (1970). Peer interaction and social organization. In P. H. Mussen (Ed.), *Carmichael's manual of child psychology* (Vol. 2). New York: Wiley.

Hartup, W. (1983). Peer relations. In E. M. Hetherington (Ed.), *Handbook of child psychology: Vol. 4. Socialization, personality and social development.* New York: Wiley.

Hunter, F. T., & Youniss, J. (1982). Changes in functions of three relations during adolescence. *Developmental Psychology, 18*(6), 806–811.

Jacklin, C., & Maccoby, E. (1978). Social behavior at 33 months in same-sex and mixed-sex dyads. *Child Development, 49,* 557–569.

Kandel, D. B., & Lesser, G. S. (1972). *Youth in two worlds: U.S. and Denmark.* San Francisco: Jossey-Bass.

Kon, I. S., & Losenkov, V. A. (1978). Friendship in adolescence: Values and behavior. *Journal of Marriage & the Family, 40,* 143–155.

Lever, J. (1976). Sex differences in the games children play. *Social Problems, 23,* 478–487.

Lewis, M., Feiring, C., & Kotsonis, M. (1984). The social networks of three-year-old children. In M. Lewis, (Ed.), *Beyond the dyad* (pp. 129–160). New York: Plenum.

Longfellow, C. & Belle, D. (1984). Stressful environments and their impact on children. In J. H. Humphrey (Ed.), *Stress in childhood* (pp. 63–78). New York: AMS Press.

Lowenthal, M. J., & Haven, C. (1968). Interaction and adaptation: Intimacy as a critical variable. *American Sociological Review, 33,* 20–30.

Nelson-LeGall, S., Gumerman, R. A., & Scott-Jones, D. (1983). Instrumental help-seeking and everyday problem-solving: A developmental perspective. In B. DePaulo, A. Nadler, & J. Fisher (Eds.), *New directions in helping: Vol. 2. Help-seeking* (pp. 265–283). New York: Academic.

Nolen-Hoeksema, S. (1987). Sex differences in unipolar depression: Evidence and theory. *Psychological Bulletin, 101*(2), 259–282.

Oliveri, M. E., & Reiss, D. (1987). Social networks of family members: Distinctive roles of mothers and fathers. *Sex Roles, 17* (11/12), 719–736.

Riley, D., & Cochran, M. (1987). Children's relationships with non-parental adults: Sex-specific connections to early school success. *Sex Roles, 17* (11/12), 637–655.

Rutter, M. (1979). Protective factors in children's response to stress and disadvantage. In M. W. Kent & J. E. Rolf (Eds.), *Primary prevention of psychopathology: Vol. III. Social competence in children.* Hanover, NH: University Press of New England.

Savin-Williams, R. C. (1980). Dominance hierarchies in groups of middle to late adolescent males. *Journal of Youth & Adolescence, 9,* 75–85.

Schofield, J. W. (1981). Complementary and conflicting identities: Images and interaction in an interracial school. In S. R. Asher & J. M. Gottman (Eds.), *The development of children's friendships.* Cambridge, England: Cambridge University Press.

Thorne, B. (1986). Girls and boys together . . . but mostly apart: Gender arrangements in elementary schools. In W. W. Hartup & Z. Rubin (Eds.), *Relationships and development* (pp. 167–184). Hillsdale, NJ: Erlbaum.

Tietjen, A. (1982). The social networks of preadolescent children in Sweden. *International Journal of Behavioral Development, 5,* 111–130.

Vaux, A. (1985). Variations in social support associated with gender, ethnicity, and age. *Journal of Social Issues, 41*(1), 89–110.

Vaux, A., Burda, P., & Stewart, D. (1986). Orientation towards utilizing support resources. *Journal of Community Psychology, 14,* 159–170.

Veroff, J., Douvan, E., & Kulka, R. (1981). *The inner American: A self-portrait from 1957–1976.* New York: Basic.

Veroff, J., Kulka, R., & Douvan, E. (1981). *Mental health in America: Patterns of help-seeking from 1957 to 1976.* New York: Basic.

Waldrop, M., & Halverson, C. (1975). Intensive and extensive peer behavior: Longitudinal and cross-sectional analysis. *Child Development, 46,* 19–26.

Wallerstein, J., & Kelly, J. (1980). *Surviving the breakup.* New York: Basic.

Warren, R. (1975). *The work role and problem coping: Sex differentials in the use of helping systems in urban communities.* Paper presented to the annual meeting of the American Sociological Association, San Francisco.

Warschausky, J. S. (1988). *Sibling caretaking and its impact on the caretaker's relationships and aspirations in young adulthood.* Unpublished doctoral dissertation, Boston University.

Weiss, L., & Lowenthal, M. (1975). Life-course perspectives on friendship. In M. L. Lowenthal, M. Thurnher, & D. Chiriboga (Eds.), *Four stages of life.* San Francisco: Jossey-Bass.

Weiss, R. (1985). Men and the family. *Family Process, 24,* 49–58.

Whiting, B. B., & Edwards, C. P. (1988). *Children of different worlds: The formation of social behavior.* Cambridge, MA: Harvard University Press.

Whiting, B. B., & Whiting, J. W. M. (1975). *Children of six cultures: A psychocultural analysis.* Cambridge: Harvard University Press.

Wolchik, S., Sandler, I., & Braver, S. (1984, August). *The social support networks of children of divorce.* Paper presented at the American Psychological Association meeting, Toronto.

Youniss, J., & Smollar, J. (1985). *Adolescent relations with mothers, fathers, and friends.* Chicago: University of Chicago Press.

PART 3

Measurement Issues

CHAPTER 8

Mapping Children's Support Networks: Conceptual and Methodological Issues

SHARLENE A. WOLCHIK, JANETTE BEALS, AND IRWIN N. SANDLER

INTRODUCTION

Over the past few years, interest in children's social support has blossomed. The research in this area is still in its infancy and thus many challenges face researchers who are intrigued by the complexities inherent in mapping children's networks and in understanding how social support may enhance adjustment. This chapter focuses on one of the basic challenges: how to conceptualize and operationalize the construct of social support. In the first section, we discuss conceptual issues in the definition and assessment of social support. Next, we review inventories that are currently available and suggest ways to improve our assessment approaches. In the final section, we discuss advantages of using structural equation modeling in studying support and illustrate how this type of data-analytic strategy can help us understand the relations between various dimensions of social support and between social support and adjustment.

CONCEPTUALIZING SOCIAL SUPPORT

Social support has been conceptualized in many different ways. Definitions vary in their degree of specificity, breadth of transactions encompassed, and the importance attributed to the stability of interpersonal relationships. For example, Caplan (1974) defined social support as "continuing social aggregates that provide individuals with opportunities for feedback about themselves and for validations of their expectations of others" (pp. 4–5). More specifically, Caplan noted that, in times of need, information and cognitive guidance, tangible resources, and emotional sustenance are provided by these

Partial funding for the writing of this paper was provided by grant #MH39246-01 from the National Institute of Mental Health to establish a Preventive Intervention Research Center.

supportive others. Similarly, Barrera, Sandler, and Ramsey (1981) suggested that social support includes activities directed at helping others in mastering emotional distress, sharing tasks, giving advice, teaching skills, and providing material assistance. In contrast to Barrera and colleagues' focus on the provision of specific resources, Cobb (1976) defines social support as information that leads a person to believe that she or he is cared for and loved, is esteemed and valued, or belongs to a network of communication and mutual obligations.

Recently, Barrera (1986) has argued that the global concept of social support should be abandoned for more precise, narrower constructs. Barrera proposed that researchers use the following terms, which reflect important differences in how support is conceptualized: *social embeddedness* (connections with significant others); *perceived support* (quality of support); and *enacted support* (frequency of supportive behaviors). Support for employing more refined definitions is provided by research indicating that intercorrelations among measures of these three concepts are low (cf. Barrera, 1987; Cohen & Wills, 1985; Sandler, Wolchik, & Braver, 1985) and that measures of psychological and physical health relate differentially to these dimensions of support in adults (cf. Barrera, 1986; Cohen & Wills, 1985).

In the following discussion of the ways in which children's social support has been operationalized, we use the conceptual categories suggested by Barrera (1986). However, we have renamed the category of perceived support *perceived quality of support* to highlight the unique aspect of this construct. Whereas all three categories represent perceptions of an individual's experience of social support, perceived support measures reflect an individual's assessment of the *quality* or *adequacy* of social support.

Social Embeddedness

The concept of social embeddedness refers to the connections or linkages between an individual and the people in the environment. These connections indicate that a relationship exists but do *not* specify the adequacy or frequency of the helping exchanges that occur. There are two types of social embeddedness measures: those that assess characteristics of the social network, regardless of whether or not specific support transactions occur within these relationships, and those that assess the occurrence of support from network members. In other words, although most social embeddedness measures do not examine the content of helping exchanges, some recently developed measures provide information on content by assessing the provision of specific types of supportive functions by various network members. For example, some measures assess the social network that provides one type of support, such as emotional support (Belle & Longfellow, 1983; Bryant, 1985), whereas others include several kinds of support, such as cognitive guidance, tangible assistance, positive feedback, and recreation (Barrera, 1981; Hirsch & Reischl, 1985; Wolchik, Sandler, & Braver, 1984; Zelkowitz, 1984).

Measures of social embeddedness may be as simple as the presence or absence of a specific type of tie or may describe structural aspects or patterns of social ties. Examples of simple social embeddedness measures include whether or not a child has an older sibling or a father in the household (Sandler, 1980), and the total number of social ties or network size (Wolchik et al., 1984). More complex social network measures include network density, or the degree to which the network members interrelate with one another independent of their relationship with the subject (Wellman, 1981), and conflicted network size, or the number of supporters who are also sources of interpersonal conflict (Barrera, 1981). For support measures that include assessment of network size for specific support functions, multiplexity, or the number of different types of supportive exchanges provided by a network member, can be assessed. These more complex social network structural measures generally have not been used with children. However, they may be important in furthering our understanding of how social support may impact on children's adjustment and our understanding of the relations between different dimensions of social support. For example, children may feel more satisfied with the support they receive when the typical supporter provides many rather than few support functions.

Perceived Quality of Support

This type of measure reflects appraisals of subjective dimensions of support such as satisfaction with support that was actually received, perceptions of whether adequate support would be provided if needed, and feelings toward particular network members. Ratings of the helpfulness of various kinds of supporters (Cauce, Felner, Primavera, & Ginter, 1982) and satisfaction with specific kinds of support received (Barrera, 1981; Wolchik et al., 1984) have been used in research with children and adolescents. Other measures of perceived quality of support include satisfaction with particular relationships (Furman & Buhrmester, 1985) and perceived closeness of relationships (Zelkowitz, 1984).

Because these types of measures are most clearly cognitive, they are most directly tied to theoretical models of the impact support has on adaptation to stress in which cognitions play a central role. For example, Lazarus, Averill, and Opton (1974) propose that response to stressful situations is in part a function of individuals' judgments about whether their social resources are sufficient to cope with a situation that is perceived to be threatening.

Enacted Support

This type of measure refers to the *frequency* of supportive transactions that have taken place. Only a few researchers have assessed enacted support among children. For example, Zelkowitz (1984) examined the frequency of the supportive transactions of maintenance, nurturance, and recreation whereas Furman and Buhrmester (1985) assessed the frequency of several different kinds of support (enhancement of worth, instrumental help, companionship, affection, and intimacy).

Comparison of Dimensions of Support

Like Barrera (1986), we believe that social support is a multidimensional construct and that each of the ways of operationalizing support just mentioned provides different information about an individual's social relationships. Further, as Barrera (1986) has noted, each of these ways of operationalizing support has unique strengths and limitations. For example, social embeddedness measures provide an index of connectedness. However, some measures of this type do not specifically assess whether supportive transactions occur within these social connections; rather they focus on whether there is a relationship between two individuals. The cognitive nature of the perceived quality measures provides an important evaluative perspective. However, relative to other constructs of support, these measures may be affected most strongly by psychological functioning and thus the measurement of support and distress may be confounded. Finally, enacted support measures are unique in that they assess the frequency of recent exchanges that have occurred within the network. However, the meaning of different levels of enacted support is complex. Higher levels of enacted support may reflect the presence of greater amounts of stress, because support is more likely to be sought in times of stress. On the other hand, high levels of enacted support at times of low stress may reflect a dependent orientation toward the person's social network.

Because of the different information that is provided by these constructs, we recommend that researchers employ more than one method of operationalizing support. Attention to the interrelations between these dimensions should further our understanding of how children conceptualize their social worlds.

MEASURES FOR ASSESSING CHILDREN'S AND ADOLESCENTS' SOCIAL SUPPORT

In this section, we will examine several social support inventories that have been used with children and school-age adolescents. More specifically, we will summarize the conceptual framework used in defining social support (in the cases where authors have provided this information), the dimensions of social support that the inventory assesses, the content and format of the inventory, and information on reliability and validity. We will first discuss scales in which only one social support concept is assessed, and then we will examine those inventories that assess support more broadly.

Using Saunder's (1977) Nurturance Scale, Belle and Longfellow (1983) have operationalized social support as confiding in others. This scale provides a measure of social embeddedness for one type of supportive transaction: confiding about both positive and negative events. Children list the people whom they might tell about nine situations, and the support score for a particular person consists of the total number of these situations about which a child confides.

As shown in Table 8.1, the stability of children's reports of confiding over a 3-month period varied across type of confidant (Belle & Longfellow, 1984). Belle and Longfellow noted that the agreement may have been so low because the first interview occurred during the school year and the second during the summer. Thus opportunities to spend time with particular classes of confidants may have changed markedly between the assessments. The average internal consistency reliability for confiding scores is .68.

Belle and Longfellow (1983, 1984) conducted two studies of the relations between choice of confidant and children's mental health. Children who reported more often confiding in their mothers exhibited significantly higher self-esteem, more internal locus of control, and less loneliness. Confiding in friends was significantly associated with less loneliness, while confiding in no one was significantly related to lower self-esteem and a more external locus of control.

Bryant (1985) conceptualizes support as including both experiences of relatedness to others and experiences of autonomy from others. In Bryant's inventory, information about three major categories of support is obtained: others as resources (persons in the peer, parent, and grandparent generation; pets), intrapersonal sources of support (hobbies, fantasies, skill development), and environmental resources (places to be by oneself, formal organizations, unsponsored meeting places). Given our view of social support as involving transactions between people, only the 10 subscales that are interpersonal in nature will be considered. These subscales are measures of social embeddedness that are derived separately for supporters within the peer, parent, and grandparent generation (e.g., number of adults in parents' generation whom the child knows and interacts with; number of times peers are named as a resource for intimate talks).

Unlike all other available measures, this inventory is administered during a walk around the child's neighborhood. Bryant selected this method of administration because she believed that reliability would be enhanced by the visual and kinesthetic cues and because this format would not seem like a test. As indicated in Table 8.1, 2-week test–retest reliabilities are highly satisfactory.

Bryant (1985) has examined the relations between support and several measures of psychological well-being in 7- and 10-year-olds. The pattern of findings is complex and thus cannot be reviewed in detail here. The most

TABLE 8.1. Internal Consistency and Test–Retest Coefficients for Social Support Inventories

Scale and Authors	Dimension of Support Measured	Scores	Internal Consistency	Test–Retest
Nurturance Scale (Belle & Longfellow, 1984; Saunders, 1977)	Social embeddedness	Confiding		
		Mother	.61	.35
		Father	.85	.69
		Sibling	.78	.39
		Friend	.65	.14
		No one	.50	.37
Neighborhood Walk (Bryant, 1985)	Social embeddedness	Network size		
		Knowledge and interaction		
		Intimate talks		
		10 most important individuals		>.85[a]
	(above scores computed separately for peer, parent, and grandparent generations)			
		Special talks with adults		
Social Support Rating Scale (Felner, Aber, Primavera, & Cauce, 1985)	Quality	Family support Formal support Informal support	high 70s to low 80s	
Berndt & Perry's (1986) Inventory	Enacted	Play, Prosocial		
		Intimacy, Loyalty, Attachment		
		Absence of conflicts		
			Friend/acquaintance	
	Hybrid of social embeddedness and quality	Play	.73/.81	
		Prosocial	.76/.83	
		Intimacy	.74/.80	
		Loyalty	.71/.72	
		Attachment,	.54/.66	
		Absence of conflicts	.64/.69	
Zelkowitz's Inventory (1984)		Nurturance	.85	.57
		Maintenance	.92	.48
Child's section	Social embeddedness			
	Enacted	Recreation	.70	.76
Parent's section	Social embeddedness	Total network size		
	Quality	Closeness of relationship		
	Enacted	Recreation	.91	.90
		Occasional maintenance	.94	.83

TABLE 8.1. *(continued)*

Scale and Authors	Dimension of Support Measured	Scores	Internal Consistency	Test–Retest
		Daily maintenance	.96	.98
		Nurturance	.95	.91
Network Relationship Inventory (Furman & Buhrmester, 1985)	Quality	Satisfaction with relationship	>.60 [b]	
		Reliable alliance	$M = .80$ [a]	
	Enacted	Affection		
		Enhancement of worth	$M = .80$ [a]	
		Companionship		
		Instrumental help		
		Intimacy		
	(Separate scores computed for mother, father, grandparent, older brother, younger brother, older sister, younger sister, best friend, and teacher.)			
Buhrmester & Fuhrman's Inventory (1987)	Enacted	Companionship	.44–.79	
		Intimacy	.34–.67	
Social Relations Questionnaire (Blyth, Hill, & Thiel, 1982)	Social embeddedness			
	Hybrid of enacted support and quality	Intimacy	>.77 [2]	
Hirsch & Reischl's Inventory (1985)	Social embeddedness	Cognitive guidance		
		Emotional support		
		Tangible guidance		
	(Separate scores are derived for family and school problems.)			
		Boundary density		
		Reciprocity (for friendships only)	.22	
	Enacted	Activities with friends	.64	
		Confiding in friends	.69	
Arizona Social Support Interview Schedule (Barrera, 1980)	Social embeddedness	Total network size		.88 (college sample)
		Unconflicted network size		

TABLE 8.1. Internal Consistency and Test–Retest Coefficients for Social Support Inventories *(continued)*

Scale and Authors	Dimension of Support Measured	Scores	Internal Consistency	Test–Retest
		Conflicted network size		.54 (college sample)
	Quality	Satisfaction with support	.50 (adolescent sample)	.69 (college sample)
		Need for support	.70 (adolescent sample)	.80 (college sample)
Inventory of Socially Supportive Behaviors (Barrera, Sandler, & Ramsey, 1981)	Enacted	Frequency of supportive activities	.92 (adolescent sample)	.88 (college sample)
Children's Inventory of Social Support (Wolchik, Sandler, & Braver, 1984)	Social embeddedness	Total number of support functions		
		Family adults	.83	.52
		Nonfamily adults	.81	.53
		Family children	.90	.63
		Nonfamily children	79	.85
	Quality	Satisfaction with support		
		Family	.52	.77
		Nonfamily	.71	.50
My Family and Friends (Reid, Landesman, Jaccard, & Rabkin, 1987)	Social embeddedness	Emotional Instrumental Informational Companionship	range = .28 – .97 (all but 2 scores >.58)	Segment[1] median = .70
				Segment[2] median = .65
	(Scores derived separately for mother, father, sibling(s), relative(s), friend(s), and teacher.)			
	Quality	Satisfaction		Segment[1] median = .71
	(Scores derived separately for mother, father, sibling(s), relative(s), friend(s), and teacher.)			Segment[2] median = .66

[1] Reliabilities for individual scores are not reported.

[2] Exact values are not reported.

important general conclusion is that the relations between support and several aspects of psychological functioning were moderated by family size, developmental level, and sex of child.

Felner, Cauce, and colleagues (Cauce et al., 1982; Felner, Aber, Primavera, & Cauce, 1985) have used a measure of perceived quality of support in their work with adolescents. Their inventory, the Social Support Rating Scale, consists of 10 items that assess the helpfulness of a number of individuals (e.g., parents, teachers, friends). Factor analysis has revealed the following three factors: family support, formal support, and informal support. Cauce (personal communication, May 13, 1987) has obtained test–retest reliabilities of high .70s to low .80s. Cauce and colleagues (1982) reported that children with a higher level of family support had higher scholastic self-concept scores than did adolescents low on this type of support. Adolescents high in formal school support reported higher levels of peer self-concept than those low on this type of support. Adolescents with high levels of peer support reported higher peer self-concept but lower grade-point averages and greater school absences than those low in peer support.

Recently Berndt and Perry (1986) have examined supportive aspects of children's relationships with close friends and acquaintances using an interview that taps six features of friendship. This 30-item scale assesses play/association, prosocial behavior, intimacy, loyalty, attachment/self-esteem enhancement, and absence of conflicts. For some items, children rate the occurrence of specific interactions (e.g., "When you want someone to have fun with, do you get together with [friend's name]?"), whereas for other items, children make judgments about whether specific interactions would occur in a particular context (e.g., "If other kids were teasing you, would [friend's name] tell them to stop it?"). Children then rate the frequency of those interactions that did or might occur on a 4-point scale. Given that the questions concern both perceptions of actual and available support and frequency of supportive interactions, all three dimensions of support are assessed.

Cronbach alpha coefficients for subscale scores of ratings for close friends ranged from .54 to .76, and the alpha for a scale consisting of the mean ratings on all aspects of friendships was .89. Alpha coefficients for subscale scores of ratings of acquaintances ranged from .66 to .83, and the alpha for the mean ratings of all dimensions was .88. Use of this scale with second, fourth, sixth, and eighth graders showed that friends were perceived as more supportive than acquaintances. Also, factor analyses revealed increases across grade level in differentiation between support and conflict dimensions of relationships.

Berndt (personal communication, July 13, 1987) recently developed a questionnaire version of this measure that assesses intimacy (informational support), prosocial interactions (instrumental support), and self-esteem enhancement (emotional support). Psychometric data are not currently available for this inventory.

In Zelkowitz's (1981) examination of social support among preschoolers, support was defined as the gratification of basic needs such as material needs, love, attention, acceptance, and training for social responsibility. As described in the chapter by Phyllis Zelkowitz, both mothers and children report the children's social networks.

The maternal version includes measures of social embeddedness, enacted support, and perceived support, whereas social embeddedness and enacted support measures can be derived from the children's version. (More detailed information on the format and content of this scale is provided in Phyllis Zelkowitz's chapter of this volume.) Test–retest coefficients (over an interval of 1 to 2 months) for scale scores for maternal and children's reports averaged .90 and .60, respectively. As shown in Table 8.1, alpha coefficients for the scale scores are acceptable.

Although the construct validity of this measure has not yet been examined, Zelkowitz (1981) used scores on a very similar inventory to assess the relations between support from adults other than mothers and aggression among preschoolers. Support scores were based on maternal and children's reports and on observational data. Results indicated that support from fathers was significantly inversely associated with aggression. Also, Zelkowitz reported that support from adults buffered the effect of stress on adjustment.

In Furman and Buhrmester's (1985) Network of Relationships Inventory, both perceived quality of support and enacted support are assessed. In developing this inventory, the authors relied extensively on Weiss's (1974) theory of social provisions. The following kinds of social support are assessed: affection, intimacy, reliable alliance, enhancement of worth, companionship, and instrumental help. Also, the relative power, conflict, importance, and satisfaction in the relationship are assessed. Children provide information for each of the following relationships: mother, father, grandparent, older and younger brother, older and younger sister, best friend, and teacher; separate scores are derived for each relationship.

Test–retest reliabilities for this inventory have not yet been reported. Internal consistency reliability figures are satisfactory, with an average alpha of .80. Consistent with Weiss's theory, results of a validation study (Furman & Buhrmester, 1985) indicated that children reported seeking different types of social support from different individuals. Furman (personal communication, July 10, 1987) has recently modified the Network of Relationships Inventory; Nurturance and Punishment scales have been added and the Importance scale has been deleted. Psychometric data on these scales are not yet available.

Buhrmester and Furman (1987) adapted items on the Companionship and Intimacy scales of the Network of Relationships Inventory to provide an overall index of social support. Using a 5-point scale, children rate the frequency of intimate disclosures and companionship or shared activities they experience in their social relations (e.g., "How much do you go places and do things with other people?"). Coefficient alphas for the intimacy scores were

.34, .67, and .66 for second, fifth, and eighth graders, respectively, and alpha coefficients for the companionship scores were .44, .64, and .79 for second, fifth, and eighth graders, respectively (Buhrmester, personal communication, March 14, 1988). Buhrmester and Furman (1987) have also used these scales to assess supportive interactions in eight specific dyadic relationships (e.g., mother, father, most important grandparent, best same-sex friend, best opposite-sex friend). In this study, Buhrmester and Furman reported developmental shifts in the importance of specific providers of support. For example, family members were important providers of companionship for second and fifth graders but became significantly less so for eighth graders. Similarly, parents were less important providers of intimacy for adolescents than for the younger children.

The Social Relations Questionnaire (Blyth, Hill, & Thiel, 1982) can be used to assess social embeddedness, enacted support, and quality of support. The scale has been used with adolescents in grades seven to ten. Unlike most measures, in this inventory social relations are viewed as occurring within domains of functioning. More specifically, subjects list young people and adults who are important within the contexts of family, school, neighborhood, outside-of-school activities, and miscellaneous. Importance is defined by the person meeting one of the following conditions:

> People you spend time with or do things with; people you like a lot or like you a lot, or both; people who make important decisions about things in your life; people who you go to for advice; or people you would like to be like. (Blyth et al., 1982, p. 430)

Subjects also complete questions about the important person's age, gender, type of relationship, residence, frequency of contact, and the quality of the relationship. Four of the questions about the quality of the relationship comprise an Intimacy Scale, which is best described as a hybrid measure of enacted support and quality of support in which both the frequency of supportive interactions and qualitative judgments about supportive interactions are assessed. Alphas of over .77 were obtained for the Intimacy Scale (Blyth & Foster-Clark, 1987). Test–retest reliabilities for scores on this inventory have not been reported. Blyth and Foster-Clark (1987) note that the scale validly discriminated between relationships that presumably differ on degree of intimacy (e.g., mom vs. uncle).

Hirsch and Reischl (1985) have employed an inventory that includes several measures of social support. Respondents list those individuals who have provided cognitive guidance, emotional support, or tangible assistance for a family and a school "hassle." The social embeddedness measures derived from this scale include the total number of supporters for each type of support and boundary density (how well her or his parents and friends know each other). Enacted support within friendships is assessed as the frequency of shared activities and confiding. Stress in friendships is assessed with four questions about conflict, trust, contact, and geographic distance. Reciprocity of the friendship is also assessed. Alpha coefficients for the scores for reciprocity, confiding, and activities within friendships averaged .52. Test–retest reliabilities have not yet been reported. Examining the relations between social support and adjustment of school-age adolescents with depressed, arthritic, and normal parents, Hirsch and Reischl found that higher amounts of support, stronger friendships, and more parent–friend linkages were associated with *better* adjustment in the normal group but with *poorer* adjustment among the depressed and arthritic groups.

Barrera has developed two inventories that reflect his view that support is a multifaceted construct including specific helping transactions, subjective appraisals of the support received, and the social relationships within which support occurs. The Arizona Social Support Interview Schedule (ASSIS; Barrera, 1980, 1981) assesses structural aspects of support networks (e.g., network size, conflicted network) and satisfaction with and need for support. The following support functions are included: material aid, physical assistance, intimate interaction, guidance, feedback, and social participation. Research with college samples has indicated adequate test–retest and internal consistency reliabilities of scores on this scale. The Inventory of Socially Supportive Behaviors (ISSB, Barrera, Sandler, & Ramsey, 1981) assesses enacted support. Subjects rate the frequency of 40 supportive activities (e.g., "helped you understand why you didn't do something well") that occurred during the last month. Internal consistency and test–retest reliabilities in college student samples are adequate (Barrera et al., 1981), and results of several studies with college students have provided evidence of the construct validity. For example, ratings of supportive behaviors provided by family members are positively associated with measures of cohesiveness of the family (Barrera et al., 1981).

Although the ASSIS and the ISSB are typically used with adults, these measures have been employed with adolescents (Barrera, 1981; Newbrough, Dokecki, & Simpkins, 1986). Table 8.1 provides internal consistency reliabilities for scores derived from the ASSIS and ISSB in Barrera's (1981) sample of pregnant adolescents. For these adolescents, support satisfaction was significantly negatively related to several indices of symptomatology, whereas scores for enacted support, support need, and conflicted network size were *positively* related to several indices of symptomatology. Barrera also examined whether support interacted with stress in predicting adjustment. When depression served as the criterion variable, the relation between stressful events and depression was smaller for adolescents with large total and large unconflicted networks than for adolescents with small total and small unconflicted networks. None of the other indices of social support interacted significantly with stress.

In developing the Children's Inventory of Social Support (CISS), we adapted the content and format of the ASSIS to make the scale appropriate for younger children. On the basis of previous conceptual work on the content of support (Barrera & Ainlay, 1983; Cochran & Brassard, 1979), five support functions were assessed: recreation/play, advice/information, goods/services, emotional, and positive feedback. Children list all the people inside and outside their family who have provided this kind of support during the past 3 months, rate their satisfaction with each kind of support they have received from family and nonfamily members, and rate their feelings toward each network member. Children also list individuals who sometimes make them feel "angry, bad or upset."

Several measures of social embeddedness have been derived from the CISS, including total network size, network size for each function, total number of support functions received, degree of multiplexity, and conflicted network size. Perceived quality of support measures include satisfaction with specific kinds of support and feelings toward supporters.

Given that researchers studying children have shown that characteristics of the supporter influence the relation between support and adjustment (e.g., Bryant, 1985; Cauce et al., 1982), we have computed scores separately for different categories of supporters. More specifically, because support from peers has been nonsignificantly or negatively related to children's adjustment (Bryant, 1985; Cauce et al., 1982) whereas support from adults is positively related to adjustment (e.g., Bryant, 1985; Guidubaldi & Cleminshaw, 1983; Santrock & Warshak, 1979), we have computed scores separately for adults and children. In our work with children of divorce, we have further categorized supporters by family versus nonfamily status because one of the central adaptive tasks of divorce concerns the restructuring of family interaction patterns, and thus whether the supporter was a family member might influence the relation between adjustment and support. Support from family members may be particularly important because of the centrality of the task of redefining family relationships. Alternatively, support from people outside the family may be useful because these people are less personally involved in the divorce-related stressors that are occurring and thus may provide an outside perspective or distraction from these stressors.

We have computed alpha coefficients and test–retest reliabilities for the following summary scores in a sample of children of divorce: number of functions provided by family adults, number of functions provided by family children, number of functions provided by nonfamily children, number of functions provided by nonfamily adults, satisfaction with support from family members, and satisfaction with support from nonfamily supporters. The scores for number of functions were computed by summing the number of supporters within a specific category (e.g., family adults) across the five support functions. With the exception of satisfaction with support from family, the internal consistency of these measures was acceptable. Test–retest reliabilities, which were assessed over a 2-week interval, are shown in Table 8.1.

We have recently revised the CISS to include identification of a specific time marker (e.g., end of summer vacation) that begins the 3-month interval about which the child reports supportive transactions, frequent reminders about this time interval, and frequent follow-up questions that include use of visual prompts that list the various types of supporters (e.g., brothers, sisters, aunts, etc.). However, we have not yet assessed test–retest on scores from this revised inventory.

The construct validity of the CISS has been assessed in a sample of children of divorce ranging in age from 8 to 15 years by examining relations between social support and children's psychological adjustment and their social competence (Wolchik, Sandler, & Braver, 1987). Social competence as measured using the social competence score on the Perceived Competence Scale for Children (Harter, 1982) was significantly positively correlated to several measures of peer support. Relations between social support from network members who are not sources of interpersonal conflict and psychological adjustment differed, depending on the source of support, such that higher levels of support from family adults were significantly positively related to parental report of children's adjustment whereas support from family children, support from nonfamily children, and support from nonfamily adults were nonsignificantly related to adjustment. For children's reports of symptomatology, significant Stress × Support interaction effects occurred for adult family support and nonfamily adult support. Interestingly, the pattern of these interactions was not a prototypical stress-buffering effect (Cohen & Wills, 1985). Under conditions of high stress, children who reported higher levels of support were better adjusted than were children with low support. However, under conditions of low stress, children with high support reported *more* adjustment problems than did children with low support. It may be that children who have extremely helpful networks but few stressors with which to cope interpret the overresponsiveness of their networks as indicative that they must need help and thus perceive themselves as less healthy than children with less helpful networks.

The relations between adjustment and another social embeddedness measure, multiplexity (average number of functions provided), was assessed in a sample of children whose parents were receiving treatment for alcoholism (Beals, Roosa, Sandler, Short, & Gehring, 1986). Both children's and parental reports of children's depression and anxiety and parental reports of children's conduct problems were moderately and inversely correlated with the degree of multiplexity for nonfamily adult supporters and household supporters. In the next section of the chapter, we will present some additional data on the CISS.

Landesman and her colleagues have conceptualized social support as involving instrumental, informational, companionship, and emotional support (Landesman, Jaccard, & Gunderson, in press; Reid, Landesman, Jaccard, & Rabkin, 1987). Their inventory, My Family and Friends, uses a dialogue format that begins with the child listing family members, one or two relatives, one or two friends, and a teacher. These names are written on cards the children use to rank the order in which they would seek specific types of support from these people. Children rate how satisfied they usually feel after each interaction, using a barometer with a moving indicator. Children are also asked questions about age and role, frequency of contact, and types of shared activities for each of the people they listed initially as well as other people who are important to them. The inventory is administered in two segments on two occasions or on the same day but with a break of 10 minutes.

Social embeddedness and perceived quality of support measures can be derived from this scale. Median test–retest correlations, assessed within a 3-week period (mode = 10 days), for rankings of the network members were .70 and .65 for the first and second segments, respectively (M. Reid, personal communication, March 9, 1988). Median test–retest reliabilities for satisfaction with support were .71 and .66 for the first and second segments, respectively (Reid, personal communication, March 9, 1988). Internal consistency reliabilities ranged from .28 to .92. It should be noted, however, that only two of the reliabilities (instrumental support from teachers, instrumental support from friends) were below .58 (Reid, personal communication, March 9, 1988).

Summary

The assessment of social support among children and adolescents is in its infancy. Currently, there are only a few social support inventories whose psychometric properties have been examined. In general, the internal consistency reliabilities of most measures are acceptable. It is, however, difficult to draw definitive conclusions about the adequacy of test–retest reliabilities. This difficulty occurs in part because few researchers have assessed test–retest reliability. Only Bryant's (1985) inventory, which involves visiting the child's neighborhood, and the Social Support Rating Scale (Felner et al., 1982), which has been used with adolescents, provide highly stable scores. The stability of scores on other measures over time is less than adequate. However, it is important to note that, for four inventories, the test–retest intervals were lengthy, with test–retest intervals ranging from about 2 to 12 weeks. It is highly likely that the amount of support children receive *actually* changes over intervals of this length. Thus it is not possible to determine whether the low level of agreement in children's reports over time occurs because of problems with the inventories or because of true fluctuations in support. With shorter intervals of time (e.g., 2 to 3 days) between assessments, the impact of changes in level of support should be decreased and thus a more accurate assessment of test–retest reliability could be obtained.

What are other ways to increase the accuracy of children's reports of social support? Inclusion of an introductory section similar to that used by Landesman and her colleagues, in which children identify the individuals with whom they have regular contact, might be useful. More specifically, listing the names of nuclear and extended family members, teachers, counselors, baby-sitters, and friends might serve to prime the child to recall supportive interactions. For younger children in particular, it may be useful to have parents participate in listing potential supporters. This list could also be employed as a follow-up visual prompt throughout administration of the questionnaire. For example, after the child has responded to a question such as "Who tells you good things about yourself?" researchers might show this list and ask whether anybody else on the list has said good things. Alternatively, instead of using an open-ended question, the list might be used to elicit information about support from each network member. In the example just given, children might be asked whether or not each member of the social network has told the child good things about herself or himself. Clearly, an important issue for future research concerns the development of inventories that yield valid and reliable indices of support and that can be administered efficiently.

The available data on the construct validity of measures of social support indicate weak to moderate relations between social support and adjustment. These weak relations may be due in part to a lack of attention to variables that may influence the relations between support and adjustment such as age, sex of child, and family size (Bryant, 1985). Also, these weak relations may be due to the measurement problems. More specifically, measures with poor reliability will attenuate relations between indices of support and adjustment. The development of highly reliable inventories will allow us to address more adequately the issue of construct validity.

Given the recency of most research on the assessment of children's social support, it is not surprising that many measurement and conceptual issues remain to be explored. In the next section, we address two questions that we view as fundamental to furthering our understanding of children's social support. The first concerns the underlying organizing structure of our social support inventory, the CISS. The second concerns the interrelations between the two dimensions of support assessed by the CISS—social embeddedness and quality of support—as well as the relations between these dimensions of support and children's adjustment. Both of these issues are addressed with structural equation modeling, and thus we begin the section with a discussion of the advantages of this analytic approach.

ADVANTAGES OF USING STRUCTURAL EQUATION MODELING

Internal consistency has traditionally been assessed using Cronbach's alpha, which combines information on the number of items in the scale and the average correlation between them (O'Muircheataigh & Payne, 1977). The higher the alpha, the higher the possible correlation between scales. An internal consistency lower than 1.00 attenuates or deflates the size of the correlation between constructs. Although in theory the effects of attenuation may be accounted for by the calculation of disattenuated correlations, this is rarely done in practice.

Reliance on internal consistency measures may preclude researchers from investigating the structure of a particular scale given that use of Cronbach's alpha assumes that the correlations are not divisible into discrete subscales (O'Muircheataigh & Payne, 1977). Rather than simply assuming that a single-factor model is most appropriate, researchers should investigate whether alternative models better account for the pattern of correlations between the items. Factor analysis is commonly used to answer questions about the multidimensionality of scales. Although this method is well developed, it has been criticized on the grounds that it is highly exploratory in nature (Joreskog, 1969; Long, 1983).

The recent development of sophisticated structural equation modeling methods, specifically the confirmatory factor analysis utility within these methods, allows the more adequate investigation of the factor structure of particular scales (Bentler, 1985; Joreskog & Sorbom, 1979). Confirmatory factor-analytic methodology allows the researcher to specify, test, and often reject a given model of the factor structure (Long, 1983). The strongest use of this methodology is the testing of alternative factor structures (measurement models) against one another. Furthermore, these procedures allow one to test whether a given factor structure can be assumed to be equal across different groupings, for instance, gender.

Confirmatory factor analysis attempts to account for the correlations or covariances between variables by specification of three different matrices. First, the factor structure is proposed. In most cases, each variable is proposed to load on only one factor or construct. Second, the residual variance matrix must be specified. Confirmatory factor analysis allows the modeling of correlations between the residuals. Instances in which this might be appropriate include cases in which items share method variance or cases in which there is some other reason to expect that the relationships of the observed covariance matrix will be inadequately represented by the common factors. Finally, the variance–covariance matrix between the constructs must be specified: which constructs (if any) are expected to be correlated with one another. The researcher proposes a model, and if upon testing he or she finds that the data do not confirm the proposed model, the model is rejected.

DIMENSIONS OF CHILDREN'S SOCIAL SUPPORT NETWORKS: USE OF CONFIRMATORY FACTOR ANALYSIS TO ASSESS THE DIMENSIONAL STRUCTURE OF THE CISS

In this section, we explore the underlying organizing structure of the social support children receive. We have focused on examining two types of organizing mechanisms: a functional model and a structural or relationship model. In the social support literature on adults, much attention has been given to the distinctions between the structural and functional components of social support (cf. Cohen & Wills, 1985). For example, Leavy (1983) describes structure as the availability of helping relationships within the context of social links and functions as the quality or content of those relationships. Several other researchers (e.g., Barrera, 1986; Cohen, Mermelstein, Kamarck, & Hoberman, 1985; Marsella & Snyder, 1981; Thoits, 1982; Vaux & Harrison, 1985) have also discussed the importance of discriminating between the structural and functional components of support.

Most of the research in this area with adults had focused on the functional aspects of support. Barrera and Ainlay (1983) presented a conceptual analysis of the content of social support that yielded the following six categories: material aid, behavioral assistance, intimate interaction, guidance, feedback, and social interaction. Barrera and Ainlay also factor-analyzed the supportive transactions of undergraduates and reported four unique dimensions: directive guidance, nondirective support, positive social interaction, and tangible assistance. Stokes and Wilson's (1984) factor analysis of the same inventory revealed similar factors: emotional support, tangible assistance, cognitive information, and directive guidance.

The work on functional aspects of children's social support is exceptionally limited. Berndt and Perry (1986) factor-analyzed scores on the Friendship scale that includes the following supportive functions: play, prosocial behavior, intimacy, loyalty, and attachment. Among a sample of second, fourth, and eighth graders, these functions of friendship formed one general factor. Although we currently know little about the covariation of the receipt of different support functions among children and adolescents, the model that receipt of similar support functions should be related to each other seems quite plausible. For example, some children might be in need of emotional support during a given time period, and they may receive this kind of support from multiple providers (e.g., parents, friends).

Source of support or relationship category is an alternative organizing structure for social support. At a theoretical level, Caplan (1974) has argued that individuals' support networks are composed of various groups that, although they are separable, also overlap at times. More specifically, Caplan suggests that such support subsystems occur in the contexts of home, work, church, and so on. Weiss (1974) has elaborated on the notion of differences between relationships within a social network. More specifically, he argues that relationships are specialized such that different types of supporters provide specific and distinct kinds of support functions or provisions.

Most of the support measures for children and adolescents reviewed in the first section of this chapter assess supportive exchanges that occur within specific relationships (e.g., mother, father, friend) or within category of supporter (e.g., family adult, nonfamily adult). However, few studies have focused on studying the empirical relations between support provided by these relationships. In one of the few studies of this type, Cauce and her colleagues have examined subsystems of support networks among younger adolescents.

Factor analysis of the helpfulness of various supporters in an inner-city adolescent sample revealed three factors: formal supporters (primarily school personnel), family supporters, and friend supporters (Cauce et al., 1982). More recently, Cauce, Hannan, and Sargent (1987) replicated this factor structure using an upper-middle-class junior high sample. An alternative view of the dimensionality of children's support systems focuses on the functions provided rather than the perceived helpfulness. Although covariation of support by providers has not been investigated, it is seen as a plausible model. It may be that children are more likely to receive support from one type of provider than another, so that, for example, their receipt of emotional support is related to receipt of advice, play, goods and services, and so on from family.

In the research on adolescents' and children's social support described earlier, factor analyses have been conducted using scales that assess either relationship variables (Cauce et al., 1982; Cauce et al., 1987) or functions within these relationships (Berndt & Perry, 1986), thus precluding a comparison of these two alternative factor structures. As described earlier, the CISS (Wolchik et al., 1984) assesses receipt of five types of support from specific relationship categories of family and nonfamily and thus data from the CISS can be used to test alternative factor structures.

These data are based on interviews with 285 families in three stress situations: 92 had experienced the death of parent in the past 2 years, 94 had experienced a parental divorce in the past 2 years, and 99 of the children had moderate asthma. Also included are 74 matched community controls who had experienced none of these stressors. All children were between the ages of 8 and 16. The CISS was administered as part of a larger battery.

As discussed earlier, in the CISS children list all the people within the categories of family and nonfamily who provide five functions: play, advice, provision of goods and services, emotional support, and positive feedback. Scores for the five functions were calculated for each of five relationship categories: household adults, household children (siblings for the most part), extended family, nonfamily adults, and nonfamily children (or peers). These five provider relationship groupings were chosen because they encompass all possible supporters, and at the same time, there is empirical evidence that children make these distinctions in thinking of their support networks (Cauce & Srebnick, 1987). Ratio scores were calculated; that is, the number of supporters within that category providing a particular function was divided by number of supporters mentioned in the category.[1] For example, if a subject reported receiving advice from one adult

[1] Alternative scores would be counts of people providing each function within the relationship categories. However, because correlations between these counts would reflect number of supporters within the network as well as number of functions provided, these scores would necessarily yield higher correlations within network category and therefore be inappropriate for testing our alternative models.

and there were a total of four household adults in his network, his score would be .25 for household adults. A covariance matrix of the resulting 25 variables provided the basis for measurement models.

Several alternative models were entertained. In the first of these, the factors represent the types of support *functions* that are provided. More specifically, this function model of support utilizes the different functions (e.g., advice, emotional support, and positive feedback) as the critical constructs and assumes the factors are organized by these five functions. In other words, is the receipt of a given support function from one type of provider related to receipt of that same function from other providers? For example, in this model emotional support from household adults, household children, extended family, nonfamily adults, and nonfamily children would form an emotional support dimension and there would be separate analogous dimensions for each of the other functions.

The second model conceptualizes support networks according to the type of relationship the supporters have with children, that is, whether they are family or nonfamily, and whether they are children or adults. This provider model tests whether the relationship categories are in fact the underlying organizing structure. In this model, the assumption is that, if the adults in the child's family provide one function, they are also likely to provide other functions; the case is similar with other relationship categories.

Finally, the third alternative is a single-factor model in which the 25 scores were hypothesized to be equally correlated with one another. Here, provision of social support is considered a unitary construct, regardless of who the supporters are or what functions they are providing. That is, each of the function or provider scores would be equally correlated with each other, with these correlations not being higher within providers or functions.

The models were tested using LISREL VI (Joreskog & Sorbom, 1985) and the fit estimates are presented in Table 8.2. The null model is one that hypothesizes that there are *no* covariances between the items and forms the basis for the nonnormed and normed fit indices suggested by Bentler and Bonett (1980). Although the issue of assessment of fit for structural equation models continues to be debated in the literature (Tanaka, 1987), generally, a χ^2/df ratio of under 2.00 is considered acceptable and normed fit indices of

TABLE 8.2. Alternative Models of Social Support as Measured by the CISS

Model Level	df	χ^2	χ^2/df	Nonnormed	Normed
0: Null model	300	2915	9.92		
1a: Single-factor model	275	2032	7.39	.303	.255
1b: Function model	265	1432	5.40	.509	.455
1c: Provider model	265	1178	4.44	.596	.552
2b: Function model with correlated residuals	215	363	1.69	.875	.830
2c: Provider model with correlated residuals	215	307	1.43	.895	.856

.80 and above have been considered indications that the model is substantially compatible with the data (Tanaka & Huba, 1984; Marsh, 1986; Marsh & Hocevar, 1985). Although we are not able to test whether our alternative models are significantly different from one another because they are not "nested" or special cases of one another (Bentler & Bonett, 1980; Joreskog, 1979), the fit indices provide information on the fit of one model relative to another. While it is clear that none of the alternative models just proposed approach these levels, the provider model provides the best fit to the data (ratio = 4.44, normed fit index = .552), followed by the function model (ratio = 5.40, normed fit index = .455); the single-factor model fits poorly in comparison (ratio = 7.39, normed fit index = .255).

These fit indices for the provider and function models indicate, however, that the fit could be substantially improved. It is also clear that both mechanisms are operational; the covariances among the scores are explained both by the relationship category of the supporters and by the functions provided. In other words, when the common variance due to the provider factors is partitioned out, some residual covariance due to the functions remains. Therefore, allowing correlated residuals among the function items within the provider model should improve fit, as should allowing correlated residuals among the provider items in the function model. The results of the models allowing correlated residuals are also presented in Table 8.2. The fit of both models is significantly improved and provides an adequate to good fit to the data. Again, the fit of the provider model (ratio = 1.43, normed fit index = .856) is superior to that of the function model (ratio = 1.69, normed fit index = .830), reaffirming the evidence that the greatest proportion of common variance within the CISS is due to supporter category.

Table 8.3 presents the factor loadings and the correlations between the constructs for the provider model. Although all the loadings are significantly different from zero, it is interesting to note the loadings for the play function tend to be lower than those for other functions for extended family, nonfamily adults, and peers. In general, the correlations between the factors tend to be moderate in size with two exceptions. Support provided by siblings is significantly related only to that provided by household adults. Secondly, support provided by extended family is highly correlated with, but still distinguishable from, support provided by nonfamily adults.

The factor structures did not differ appreciably for boys and girls, nor across age for the children in our sample. More specifically, using the procedures suggested by Alwin and Jackson (1981), we found that the factor loadings were equal across both gender (difference χ^2 [25] = 22.5, $p < .50$). Differences in structure across age was examined by dividing the sample into two groups, those between 8 and 11 years of age and those between 12 and 16. The difference in χ^2 is not significant (difference χ^2 [25] = 41.9, $p < .10$), indicating that the factor loadings may be assumed equal across these age groups.

TABLE 8.3. Parameter Estimates of Provider Confirmatory Factor Model

	Household Family		Extended	Nonfamily	
	Adults	Children	Family	Adults	Children
		A: Factor Loadings			
		Family adult			
Play	.575	.0	.0	.0	.0
Emotional support	.648	.0	.0	.0	.0
Goods and services	.554	.0	.0	.0	.0
Positive feedback	.541	.0	.0	.0	.0
Advice	.738	.0	.0	.0	.0
		Family children			
Play	.0	.615	.0	.0	.0
Emotional support	.0	.668	.0	.0	.0
Goods and services	.0	.648	.0	.0	.0
Positive feedback	.0	.594	.0	.0	.0
Advice	.0	.670	.0	.0	.0
		Extended family			
Play	.0	.0	.284	.0	.0
Emotional support	.0	.0	.579	.0	.0
Goods and services	.0	.0	.610	.0	.0
Positive feedback	.0	.0	.619	.0	.0
Advice	.0	.0	.670	.0	.0
		Nonfamily adult			
Play	.0	.0	.0	.211	.0
Emotional support	.0	.0	.0	.579	.0
Goods and services	.0	.0	.0	.541	.0
Positive feedback	.0	.0	.0	.545	.0
Advice	.0	.0	.0	.453	.0
		Nonfamily children			
Play	.0	.0	.0	.0	.101
Emotional support	.0	.0	.0	.0	.633
Goods and services	.0	.0	.0	.0	.526
Positive feedback	.0	.0	.0	.0	.570
Advice	.0	.0	.0	.0	.524
		B. Correlations Between the Factors			
Family children:	.317***				
Extended family:	.390***	−.036[a]			
Nonfamily adult:	.321***	.066[a]	.747***		
Nonfamily children:	.305***	.138[a]	.178*	.202**	

***$p < .001$
** $p < .01$
* $p < .05$
[a] These correlations are nonsignificant.

The finding of the superiority of the fit of the provider model relative to that of other models suggests that the primary underlying organizing structure of the CISS involves relationship category. Children's social support networks appear to be organized in terms of the type of tie rather than the content of supportive exchanges that occur within these ties. These data are similar to those of Cauce and her colleagues (1982, 1987), suggesting that adolescents' social support is organized around type of supporter. However, the improvement in fit of this model, due to allowing correlated residuals among the function items, suggests that concluding that relationship variables are the only organizing structure is an oversimplification of children's social networks. It should also be noted that more elaborate models that include several kinds of relationship categories may better describe the underlying organization of children's social networks.

These results indicate that use of the CISS in a full structural equations model should utilize scores based on the provider model rather than the function model. Most directly, the confirmatory factor analysis could become the measurement modeling component of a full structural equations model. However, this is often impractical because of power considerations with scales involving a large number of items, such as the 25 scores that comprise the model of the CISS. Therefore, summary scores must be constructed, and these could take several forms. For instance, one set of scores could be the average number of functions provided by each type of supporter in each relationship category. This summary score would have a major disadvantage, however: It masks information on the number of supporters in the network, one consequence being that a child mentioning one person who provided four functions would receive the same score as someone reporting five persons providing an average of four functions each. An alternative summary score would be a count of functions provided by all supporters in each category. Although using counts was inappropriate in the factor analysis to ensure that the superior fit of the provider model was not simply an artifact (see footnote 1), for summary scores, the information on number of providers within the network is useful. In the following pages we present a causal model based on the "total number of functions" provided within each relationship category.

MODELS OF RELATIONS BETWEEN DIMENSIONS OF SOCIAL SUPPORT AND CHILDREN'S ADJUSTMENT

Clearly, the issue of most theoretical and clinical interest concerns how social support relates to children's adjustment. Is it important not only to examine which dimension(s) of support relates significantly to children's adjustment, but to identify how various dimensions of support may affect each other. Given the nascent state of research on children's social support, it is not surprising that few researchers have tested models of the impact of support on adjustment. Two other factors that have precluded measurement modeling approaches include small sample sizes and assessment of single dimensions of social support. In the model described in Figure 8.1, we tested the relations between social embeddedness measures, quality of support measures, adjustment, and demographic variables.

The summary measures of social embeddedness on the CISS are counts of number of supporters within each relationship category summed across the five functions: that is, number of functions provided by household adults, siblings, extended family, nonfamily adults, and peers. As noted earlier, quality of support is assessed on the CISS by measuring satisfaction with support provided by family members and with support provided by nonfamily members. Children's reports of symptomatology were based on the Child Depression Inventory (Kovacs, 1981), Children's Manifest Anxiety Scale (Reynolds & Richmond, 1978), Cook's Antisocial Scale (Cook & Braver, 1984), as well as the Depression, Anxiety and Conduct subscales of the Child Assessment Schedule (Hodges, Kline, Stern, Cytryn, & McKnew, 1982; West, Gersten, Beals, Sandler, & Wolchik, 1988). Finally, the following demographic variables were included as exogenous predictors: age of child, sex of child, family income, number of adults living in the household, and number of children living in the household. As in the confirmatory factor analysis, this sample includes the 285 children who have experienced a major stressful life event—either parental death, parental divorce, or chronic asthma—as well as the 74 matched control children.

The proposed model provides an adequate fit to the data (χ^2 [51] = 106.6, $\chi^2/df = 2.09$, nonnormed = .901, normed = .796). A number of the paths, especially those between sex and income to the social support and symptomatology variables, were not significantly different from zero. In a nested, "trimmed" model, in which these nonsignificant paths are set to zero, which in turn frees up degrees of freedom, the fit improves: χ^2 (62) = 108.3, $\chi^2/df = 1.74$, nonnormed = .899, normed = .830. The trimmed model is presented in Figure 8.1.

The model indicates that structural aspects of the network (e.g., number of functions provided by household adults) are meaningfully related to qualitative judgments about support received. More specifically, the higher the number of functions provided by the family subsystems of household adults and of "extended" family, the higher the satisfaction with support received. Similarly, the greater number of functions provided by nonfamily subsystems, the greater the level of satisfaction with support from nonfamily. Thus richer networks, in terms of number of functions, are associated with greater satisfaction. The model also suggests that higher levels of satisfaction with family support are associated with less depression and less conduct problems whereas higher levels of satisfaction with support from nonfamily are associated with less anxiety.

The pattern of relations between demographic variables and social embeddedness measures is not surprising and provides more evidence of the

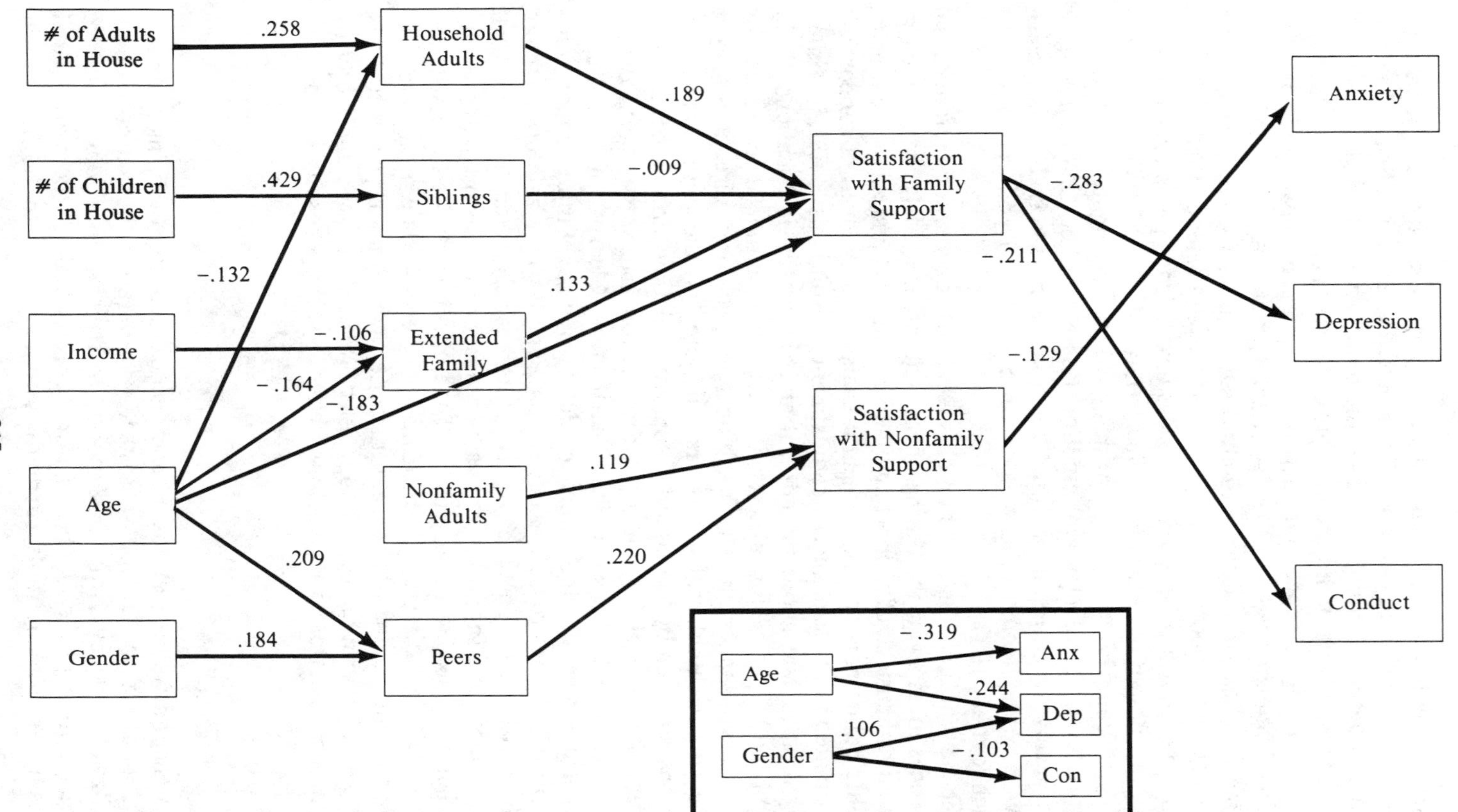

Figure 8.1. Causal model of relations between dimensions of support and children's adjustment. Gender is coded such that girls have a higher score.

construct validity of our measures of support. Not surprisingly, the path between number of adults in the household and number of functions provided by household adults as well as the path between the number of children in the household and the number of functions provided by siblings is of moderate significance. The negative association between income and support from extended family may reflect a greater reliance on kin in low-income families for assistance in child care. The negative association between age and support from household adults and extended family and the positive relationship between age and support from peers are consistent with Buhrmester and Furman's (1987) study on age differences in the frequency of companionship and intimacy, which are highly similar to our support functions of play and emotional support. The finding that girls report receiving more support functions from peers than do boys is consistent with some of our earlier work with a sample of children of divorce (Wolchik et al., 1987).

The current model is based on cross-sectional data and therefore causal inferences must await the testing of this and other models of the relations between dimensions of support and between support and adjustment using longitudinal designs and experimental trials in which levels of support are manipulated to assess changes in adjustment. Despite this caveat, it is interesting to speculate about the clinical and theoretical implications of the present model. At a clinical level, if satisfaction is indeed influenced by the richness of support, two useful clinical and preventive directions involve augmenting the number of supporters and increasing the number of support functions provided by the existing supportive relationships. One interesting theoretical issue raised by the present model concerns why richer networks are associated with higher levels of satisfaction. Clearly, multiple mechanisms of action are possible. It may be that the receipt of more support functions provides effective assistance in coping and thus the children are more satisfied with the support they receive. Alternatively, it may simply be that the receipt of more support reflects a more responsive network that provides aid when it is needed. Independent of the effectiveness of the assistance, children may be satisfied with their network because they see it as responsive to their needs. In either case, satisfaction with support relates to lower symptomatology while support functions provided are only indirectly related to symptomatology through their effects on support satisfaction.

SUMMARY

In this chapter we have discussed approaches to conceptualizing and measuring children's social support. Instead of reiterating the central themes, we will conclude by tying these points to fruitful directions for future research. Although the number of inventories is limited, there are several promising assessment tools currently available. It is to be hoped that researchers will build on our existing knowledge and choose to refine and expand the existing inventories rather than "reinvent the wheel." Only after the same inventory has been used with several samples that are either similar or different on individual (i.e., age) and environmental characteristics (i.e., experience of transitional life events such as school change, parental divorce) will we be able to address the critical issues of replicability of the impact of support on adjustment and of specifying the conditions under which support *is* and *is not* protective for children.

We have also illustrated how sophisticated data-analytic strategies such as measurement modeling can be useful in addressing measurement and conceptual issues. Our findings suggest that relationship categories provide the primary organizing structure for our measure of social support. Intriguing issues for future research involve the generality of this finding across different inventories and the identification of the developmental span in which functional aspects of support become important organizing structures.

Finally, continued efforts to develop and test theoretically based models of the causal relations between support and children's adjustment are needed. The model we have tested is based on a dynamic view of support, that receipt of functions from support providers leads to satisfaction, which in turn relates to lower symptomatology. Prospective longitudinal studies are needed in which the roles of stress and other processes are investigated to further our understanding of the processes by which support leads to better mental health of children. Such studies are made possible by the development of increasingly adequate measures of the different constructs of social support.

REFERENCES

Alwin, D., & Jackson, D. (1981). Application of simultaneous factor analysis to issues of factorial invariance. In D. J. Jackson & E. F. Borgatta (Eds.), *Factor analyses and measurement in sociological research.* Beverly Hills: Sage.

Barrera, M., Jr. (1980). A method for the assessment of social support networks in community survey research. *Connections, 3,* 8–13.

Barrera, M., Jr. (1981). Social support in the adjustment of pregnant adolescents: Assessment issues. In B. H. Gottlieb (Ed.), *Social networks and social support* (pp. 69–96). Beverly Hills: Sage.

Barrera, M., Jr. (1986). Distinctions between social support concepts, measures and models. *American Journal of Community Psychology, 14,* 413–441.

Barrera, M., Jr., & Ainlay, S. L. (1983). The structure of social support: A conceptual and empirical analysis. *Journal of Community Psychology, 11,* 133, 143.

Barrera, M., Jr., Sandler, I. N., & Ramsey, T. B. (1981). Preliminary development of a scale of social support: Studies on college students. *American Journal of Community Psychology, 9,* 435–447.

Beals, J., Roosa, M., Sandler, I., Short, J., & Gehring, M. (1986). *Predictors of psychopathology among children of alcoholics.* Poster presented at the Annual American Psychological Association meetings.

Belle, D., & Longfellow, C. (1983, April). *Emotional support and children's well-being: An exploratory study of children's confidants.* Paper presented at the biennial meeting of the Society for Research in Child Development, Detroit.

Belle, D., & Longfellow, C. (1984). *Confiding as a coping strategy.* Unpublished paper, Boston University.

Bentler, P. M. (1985). *Theory and implementation of EQS: A structural equations program.* Los Angeles: BMDP Software.

Bentler, P. M., & Bonett, D. G. (1980). Significance tests and goodness of fit in the analysis of covariance structures. *Psychological Bulletin, 88(3),* 588–606.

Berndt, T. J., & Perry, T. B. (1986). Children's perceptions of friendships as supportive relationships. *Developmental Psychology, 22,* 640–648.

Blyth, D. A., & Foster-Clark, F. (1987). *Gender differences in perceived intimacy with different members of adolescents' social networks.* Unpublished manuscript.

Blyth, D. A., Hill, J. P., & Thiel, K. S. (1982). Early adolescents' significant others: Grade and gender differences in perceived relationships with familial and nonfamilial adults and young people. *Journal of Youth & Adolescence, 11,* 425–450.

Bryant, B. (1985). The Neighborhood Walk: A study of sources of support in middle childhood from the child's perspective. *Monographs of the Society for Research in Child Development, 50* (3, Serial No. 210).

Buhrmester, D., & Furman, W. (1987). The development of companionship and intimacy. *Child Development, 58,* 1101–1113.

Caplan, G. (1974). *Support systems and community mental health: Lectures on concept development.* New York: Behavioral Publications.

Cauce, A. M., Felner, R. D., Primavera, J., & Ginter, M. A. (1982). Social support in high risk adolescents: Structural components and adaptive impact. *American Journal of Community Psychology, 10,* 417–428.

Cauce, A. M., Hanna, K., & Sargeant, M. (1987). *Structural characteristics of early adolescents' social networks.* Unpublished manuscript, University of Delaware.

Cauce, A. M., & Srebnik, D. S. (in press). Peer networks and social support: A focus for preventive efforts with youths. In L. Bond, B. Compas, & C. Swift (Eds.), *Primary prevention of psychopathology: Prevention in the schools.* Hanover, NH: University Press of New England.

Cochran, M. M., & Brassard, J. A. (1979). Child development and personal social networks. *Child Development, 50,* 601–616.

Cohen, S., Mermelstein, R., Kamarck, T., & Hoberman, H. (1985). Measuring the functional components of social support. In I. G. Sarason & B. Sarason (Eds.), *Social support: Theory, research, and applications* (pp. 73–94). The Hague: Martinus Nijhoff.

Cohen, S., & Wills, T. A. (1985). Stress, social support, and the buffering hypothesis. *Psychological Bulletin, 98,* 310–317.

Cook, C., & Braver, S. (1984). *Youth Self-Report Externalizing Scale.* Unpublished manuscript.

Felner, R. D., Aber, M. S., Primavera, J., & Cauce, A. M. (1985). Adaptation and vulnerability in high-risk adolescents: An examination of environmental mediators. *American Journal of Community Psychology, 13,* 365–379.

Furman, W., & Buhrmester, D. (1985). Children's perceptions of the personal relationships in their social networks. *Developmental Psychology, 20,* 277–290.

Guidubaldi, J., & Cleminshaw, H. (1983, August). *Impact of family support systems on children's academic and social functioning after parental divorce.* Paper presented at the annual meeting of the American Psychological Association, Anaheim, CA.

Harter, S. (1982). The Perceived Competence Scale for Children. *Child Development, 53,* 87–97.

Hirsch, B. J., & Reischl, T. M. (1985). Social networks and developmental psychopathology: A comparison of adolescent children of depressed, arthritic or normal parents. *Journal of Abnormal Psychology, 94,* 272–281.

Hodges, K., Kline, J., Stern, L., Cytryn, L., & McKnew, D. (1982). The development of a child assessment interview for research and clinical use. *Journal of Abnormal Child Psychology, 10*(2), 173–189.

Joreskog, K. H. (1969). A general approach to confirmatory factor analysis. *Psychometrika, 36,* 409–426.

Joreskog, K. H. (1979). *Advances in factor analysis and structural equation models.* Cambridge, MA: ABT.

Joreskog, K. H., & Sorbom, D. (1985). *LISREL VI: Analysis of linear structural relationships.* Mooresville, IN: Scientific Software.

Kovacs, M. (1981). Rating scales to assess depression in school-aged children. *Acta Paedopsychiatrica, 46,* 305–315.

Landesman, S., Jaccard, T., & Gunderson, V. (in press). The family environment: The combined influence of family behavior, goals, strategies, resources, and individual experiences. In M. Lewis & S. Feinman (Eds.), *Social influences on development.* New York: Plenum.

Lazarus, R. S., Averill, J. R., & Opten, E. M., Jr. (1974). The psychology of coping: Issues of research and assessment (pp. 249–316). In G. V. Coelher, D. H. Hamburg, & J. E. Adams (Eds.), *Coping and adaptation.* New York: Basic.

Leavy, R. L. (1983). Social support and psychological disorder: A review. *Journal of Community Psychology, 77,* 3–21.

Long, J. S. (1983). *Confirmatory factor analysis.* Beverly Hills: Sage.

Marsella, A. J., & Snyder, K. K. (1981). Stress, social supports, and schizophrenic disorders: Toward an interactional model. *Schizophrenia Bulletin, 7,* 152–163.

Marsh, H. (1986). Negative item bias in ratings scales for preadolescent children: A cognitive developmental phenomenon. *Developmental Psychology, 22*(1), 37–49.

Marsh, H., & Hocevar, D. (1985). Application of confirmatory factor analysis to the study of self-concept: First and higher order factor models and their invariance across groups. *Psychological Bulletin, 97*(3), 562–582.

Newbrough, J. R., Dokecki, P. R., & Simpkins, C. G. (1986). *Methodological development for a study of family factors affecting behavioral management and control of diabetes in juveniles.* Final report of a pilot and feasibility study funded by the Diabetes Research and Training Center, Vanderbilt University Medical Center.

O'Muivcheataigh, C. A., & Payne, C. (1977). *The analysis of survey data: Vol I. Exploring data structures.* New York: Wiley.

Reid, M., Landesman, S., Jaccard, J., & Rabkin, J. (1987, April). *Dialogues with children: The child as reporter for family and self.* Paper presented at the meeting of the Society for Research and Child Development.

Reynolds, C. R., & Richmond, B. O. (1978). What I think and feel: A revised measure of children's manifest anxiety. *Journal of Abnormal Psychology, 6,* 271–280.

Sandler, I. N. (1980). Social support, resources, stress, and maladjustment of poor children. *American Journal of Community Psychology, 8,* 41–52.

Sandler, I. N., Wolchik, S. A., & Braver, S. L. (1985). Social support and children of divorce. In I. G. Sarason & B. R. Sarason (Eds.), *Social support: Theory, research and applications* (371–389). Boston: Martinus Nijhoff.

Santrock, J. W., & Warshak, R. A. (1979). Father custody and social development in boys and girls. *Journal of Social Issues, 35,* 112–145.

Saunders, E. B. (1977). *The Nurturance Scale.* Unpublished report, Stress and Families Project, Harvard University.

Stokes, J. P., & Wilson, D. (1984). The inventory of social support behaviors: Dimensionality, predictability and gender differences. *American Journal of Community Psychology, 12,* 53–70.

Tanaka, J. S. (1987). "How big is big enough": Sample size and goodness of fit in structural equation models with latent variables. *Child Development, 58,* 134–146.

Tanaka, J. S., & Huba, (1984). Confirmatory hierarchal factor analyses of psychological distress measures. *Journal of Personality & Social Psychology, 46 (3),* 621–635.

Thoits, P. A. (1982). Conceptual, methodological, and theoretical problems in studying social support as a buffer against life stress. *Journal of Health & Social Behavior, 23,* 145–159.

Vaux, A., & Harrison, D. (1985). Support network characteristics associated with support satisfaction and perceived support. *Journal of Community Psychology, 13,* 245–268.

Weiss, R. S. (1974). The provisions of social relationships.. In S. Rubin (Ed.), *Doing unto others.* Englewood Cliffs, NJ: Prentice-Hall.

Wellman, B. (1981). Applying network analyses to the study of support. In B. H. Gottlieb (Ed.), *Social networks and social support* (171–200). Beverly Hills: Sage.

Wolchik, S. A., Sandler, I. N., & Braver, S. L. (1984, August). *The social support networks of children of divorce.* Poster presented at the annual meeting of the American Psychological Association, Toronto.

Wolchik, S. A., Sandler, I. N., & Braver, S. L. (1987). Social support: Its assessment and relation to children's adjustment. In N. Eisenberg (Ed.), *Contemporary topics in developmental psychology.* New York: Wiley.

Zelkowitz, P. (1981, April). *Children's support network: Their role in families under stress.* Paper presented at the biennial meeting of the Society for Research in Child Development, Boston.

Zelkowitz, P. (1984, August). *Comparing maternal and child reports of children's social networks.* Poster presented at the annual meeting of the American Psychological Association, Toronto.

CHAPTER 9

Parents and Children as Informants Concerning Children's Social Networks

PHYLLIS ZELKOWITZ

While the study of social networks and social support has gained increasing acceptance as a means to identify the significant social influences in the lives of both children and adults, there is as yet no consensus in the literature as to those aspects of the social network that are most important to measure. Among the variables considered in the adult literature are network size, density, reciprocity of relations between the individual and members of his or her network, as well as perceptions of supportiveness and types of support provided. Turner, Frankel, and Levin (1982) have argued that it is essential to consider not only the presence of social support resources (i.e., the fact that a person has contact with a variety of network members) but also the experience of social support (i.e., the person's perception of being supported). Studies employing multiple indices of social support have found that the subjective measures, such as satisfaction with support, were more closely related to outcomes such as adjustment or stress reduction than were quantitative measures such as network size (cf. Sandler & Barrera, 1984; Wolchik, Sandler, & Braver, 1984). Such findings tend to give rise to questions regarding the validity of self-report measures; in other words, happy or well-adjusted people may simply be more satisfied with their lot in life, including the support to be derived from their networks.

In studying the social networks of children, the issue of measurement becomes even more complex. Not only must we determine which features of the network to assess, but we must also decide upon whose report to rely—that of the parent or that of the child. Research with very young children (3 to 7) has tended to use maternal reports (cf. Feiring & Lewis, 1981; Lewis, Feiring, & Kotsonis, 1984; Zelkowitz, 1982). The assumption here is that the mother is best able to catalog the full membership of the child's social network. Such research shows that children have contact with a broad range of network members, including relatives, family friends, substitute caregivers, and the child's own friends.

Several recent studies of older children, ranging in age from 6 to 12 years, have been based on interviews with the children themselves regarding their relations with different categories of network members (Belle & Longfellow, 1984; Bryant, 1985; Furman & Buhrmester, 1985; Nair & Jason, 1985; Tietjen, 1982; Wolchik et al., 1984). This approach has the advantage of examining the network from the child's own perspective. This is of particular importance if our aim is to determine which aspects of the child's social network are psychologically salient to him or her. In terms of the individuals likely to be named by children as sources of support, mothers tended to figure most prominently in these reports, with fathers coming in a close second (Belle & Longfellow, 1984; Bryant, 1985; Furman & Buhrmester, 1985; Sandler, Wolchik, & Braver, 1985). Studies that examined not only network membership but also support provisions found that, in general, nuclear family members were important sources of emotional support, instrumental aid, and cognitive guidance (Furman & Buhrmester, 1985; Nair & Jason, 1985; Tietjen, 1982). Children were likely to turn to their own friends, and secondarily to siblings, for companionship and recreation (Furman & Buhrmester, 1985; Tietjen, 1982). Extended family and nonrelated adults were less frequently mentioned as sources of support. In Bryant's study, only 23% of the children included a nonrelated adult among their 10 closest network members. Furman and Buhrmester found that, while relationships with grandparents were rated highly in terms of providing affection and enhancing the child's self-worth, they were not often sources of companionship, intimacy, and concrete assistance. Thus while studies relying on parental report indicate that children come into contact with a broad range of network members, interviews with children suggest that their most important relationships are those with their parents, siblings, and friends.

Very few studies have compared maternal and child report. Garbarino, Burston, Raber, Russell, and Crouter (1978) asked a sample of preadolescents and their mothers to name the people who knew the children best, apart from nuclear family members. Congruence between maternal and child reports ranged from 57.1% overlap (among suburban children) to 39.9% (among rural children). Similarly, a greater level of congruence was found between parents and children of higher socioeconomic status (56%) than between those of lower socioeconomic status (37%). These data demonstrate a fair but by no means high degree of correspondence between parent and child perceptions of the child's network.

Feiring and Lewis (in press) used the device of listing birthday party invitees to compare the reports of a sample of mothers and their 6-year-old children. These authors found an overlap of 65% between the lists of the mothers and the children. Furthermore, both lists showed similar patterns of same- and opposite-sex friends, suggesting that mothers were well aware of the children's friendships.

Other research looks at the consistency between parent and child report in a less direct fashion. A study of elementary school children (Cohn,

Lohrmann, & Patterson, 1985) compared maternal and child reports of network size and composition as predictors of children's loneliness. The same pattern of relationship with the outcome measure was found for both maternal and child reports regarding the child's network, with somewhat stronger associations between network information from the mother and the child's reported loneliness.

That there is overlap between the mother's and child's reports regarding the child's social network is not surprising. The few comparisons that have been made tell us little about what determines the perceptions of parents and children. To what extent are the children influenced by the frequency of contact with network members, or by the support functions performed by network members?

The study of children's support networks is still in its early stages. Research has been undertaken with children of widely varying ages and with diverse measurement strategies. Detailed comparisons of maternal and child reports need to be made, with a view to mapping the degree of correspondence between them, as well as determining possible sources of congruence and divergence. My own research has made some first steps in this direction, by obtaining detailed information on network structure and functioning from both mothers and children. In this chapter I will review comparisons between maternal and child report, as well as explore some of the variables that may have an impact on the salience of network members to children.

METHODS

A sample of 60 children was recruited through nursery schools and daycare centers in a middle-class area of a large Canadian city. There were 31 girls and 29 boys in the sample, and the children ranged in age from 4.0 to 5.5 years, with a mean age of 4.4 years. All children attended group-care settings for an average of 5 hours per day, the range being 2.5 to 10 hours.

All but 2 of the children lived in two-parent families. Both of the children who lived with single mothers saw their fathers several times a week. The number of children in the sample families ranged from 1 to 5, with a modal value of 2 children. Half the children were firstborns, the rest laterborns. Sixty-five percent of the mothers were employed outside the home; 17 of these women worked less than 20 hours per week, and the others worked from 20 to 45 hours per week.

A set of instruments was designed to assess the structure and functioning of children's social networks. Both the mother and the child were interviewed with regard to the composition and task performance of the child's social network. The mother's form of the interview had two parts. In the first part, the composition of the child's network was elicited by asking about household residents (parents, siblings, extended family members, etc.), substitute caregivers, relatives residing in town, family friends and neighbors with whom the child has a relationship, and the child's own friends. In the second part of the interview, mothers were asked to complete a series of support scales for each network member. The support scales documented the performance of the following functions by network members:

Daily Maintenance. The frequency with which network members performed daily child-care tasks (e.g., meal preparation, supervision, bathing, bedtime), on a scale from "daily" to "never."

Occasional Maintenance. The frequency with which network members performed maintenance tasks that were not generally required on a daily basis, such as shopping for supplies, or transportation to extracurricular activities, on a scale from "always" to "never."

Nurturance. The frequency with which the target child would turn to each network member for nurturance or emotional support under different circumstances (e.g., to talk about problems or fears), on a scale from "always" to "never" (adapted from Saunders, 1977).

Recreation. The frequency with which network members engaged in recreational activities with the child (e.g., playing games, reading books, or going on outings), on a scale from "daily" to "never."

Mothers were also asked to indicate the frequency with which network members disciplined the child. Finally, mothers were asked to make a global rating (on a scale from 1 to 7) of the closeness of the child's relationship with each network member.

The child's interview comprised open-ended questions, covering the various functions of the child's social network. The children's interview data were analyzed in terms of scales that were conceptually related to those of the mother's interview. While many of the items on both interviews were the same, the child's version would be phrased in an open-ended fashion. Thus the child would be asked, "Who puts you to bed?" The mother would be asked to indicate how often each network member she mentioned would put the child to bed. Consequently, in the children's data, scale scores were not available for each individual, as they were from the mother's interview data. The following scales were derived from the children's data:

Maintenance Scale. Children were asked to name the people who performed several daily tasks—making breakfast and supper, taking the child to and from school, bathing the child, and putting him or her to bed. The number of mentions for each person comprised the Maintenance scale score.

Nurturance Scale. Children were asked to name the people to whom they would turn for nurturance and emotional support in different situations, with the number of mentions comprising the network member's Nurturance scale score (adapted from Saunders, 1977). In addition, the children were asked to name people, apart from their parents, with whom they had a special relationship.

Recreation Scale. Children were asked to rate the frequency with which each adult, nonparental network member who had been named by the mother performed various activities (e.g., reading books, playing games, and going on outings). The child was first asked whether a given network member ever engaged in each activity; if the child said yes, she or he was asked to say whether the network member did it "a lot," "sometimes," or "a little bit."

Children were not questioned about discipline, since pilot testing had found them to be unreliable in providing information regarding this function.

Both the maternal and child scales showed a high degree of internal consistency, with Cronbach's alpha ranging from .70 to .96; the reports were also found to be stable over a period of approximately 2 months (Zelkowitz, 1984).

The 60 children in the sample had a total of 854 network members (including parents and siblings). The mean network size was 13.5, and this did not differ by the sex of the child (Zelkowitz & Jacobs, 1985).

Mean scale scores for the various categories of network member are presented in Table 9.1. It may be seen that mothers were the primary support figures, according to both maternal and child report. Mothers were most likely to perform the maintenance functions, with fathers coming in a somewhat distant second. The level of support from fathers approached that of the mothers for nurturance and recreation. Frequency of discipline was virtually the same for both parents. After parents, siblings were the most important source of emotional support and recreation; nuclear family members were also given the highest closeness ratings by mothers. Substitute caregivers were also major support figures, being more involved in the maintenance, nurturance, and discipline functions than any other adult network members apart from the parents. This undoubtedly reflects their "in loco parentis" role while parents were away from home.

The roles of relatives and family friends and neighbors seemed to be confined to recreation and nurturance, although these network members were virtually never mentioned by the children on the Nurturance scale. Indeed, responses to this measure were limited almost entirely to mothers, fathers, siblings, and the child's own friends. More detailed analyses of the children's responses to the Nurturance scale will be undertaken on the pages to follow.

COMPARISON OF MATERNAL AND CHILD REPORTS

Intercorrelations of Scale Scores

A correlation of .89 ($p < .001$) was obtained between maternal and child reports of daily maintenance from network members. There was an association

TABLE 9.1. Mean Support Scale Scores for All Network Members

Scale	Network Member							
	Mother	Father	Grandparents	Aunts and Uncles	Family Friends and Neighbors	Substitute Caregivers	Siblings	Peers
Maternal Report								
Daily maintenance (range = 1–6)	5.03 (0.49)	2.58 (1.01)	1.23 (0.42)	1.05 (0.27)	1.15 (0.27)	2.22 (0.88)	1.35 (0.65)	not applicable
Occasional maintenance (range = 7–35)	32.57 (2.48)	18.06 (5.98)	9.30 (3.53)	8.02 (2. 04)	7.70 (1.55)	10.70 (4.25)	8.31 (4.13)	not applicable
Nurturance (range = 7–35)	31.57 (3.85)	27.64 (5.96)	15.19 (5.90)	12.16 (5.32)	12.65 (5.89)	17.72 (7.07)	19.75 (7.97)	12.13 (5.89)
Recreation (range = 9–36)	35.65 (5.37)	30.75 (6.12)	15.11 (5.46)	12.55 (3.96)	13.49 (4.73)	19.83 (6.74)	28.87 (9.42)	16.31 (5.50)
Discipline (range = 1–6)	5.47 (0.87)	5.15 (1.02)	2.13 (1.13)	1.45 (0.74)	1.67 (0.84)	3.05 (1.32)	2.12 (1.75)	not applicable
Closeness (range = 1–7)	6.93 (0.31)	6.81 (0.43)	5.21 (1.29)	4.22 (1.67)	4.23 (1.32)	4.71 (1.54)	6.64 (0.78)	4.92 (1.37)
Child Report								
Nurturance (range = 0–9)	4.97 (2.40)	3.03 (2.53)	0.06 (0.31)	0.02 (0.18)	0	0.29 (0.67)	1.72 (1.85)	1.11 (1.67)
Recreation (range = 0–24)	not applicable	not applicable	11.16 (4.25)	8.66 (4.39)	7.28 (3.92)	11.03 (5.32)	not applicable	not applicable
Maintenance (range = 0–6)	4.97 (1.18)	2.17 (1.70)	0.10 (0.55)	0	0	1.10 (1.42)	0	not applicable

Note: Numbers in brackets below the means are the standard deviations.

of .54 ($p < .001$) between the two reports of nurturance, and one of .30 ($p < .001$) between maternal and child Recreation scale scores. The striking correspondence between maternal and child reports with regard to maintenance is likely due to the fact that, according to both mothers and children, it was primarily mothers and fathers who performed this function. The other functions were performed by a broader range of people, thus allowing greater possibility for disagreement. The greater divergence between the two reports of recreation with network members may be accounted for in part by the fact that the mother and child scales had fewer overlapping items than was true for the measures of the maintenance and nurturance functions. Nonetheless, agreement between mother and child reports of network support can be seen to be far better than chance.

Comparison of Specific Items from the Scales

We can compare the mother and child reports on two specific recreation items—playing games and reading stories. An analysis of variance was performed using the child's rating of "never," "a little bit," "sometimes," and "a lot" as the independent variable, and the mother's frequency rating as the dependent variable. For both items there were significant differences between the means ($F[3,427] = 8.40$ for games; $F[3,427] = 21.80$ for reading; $p < .001$ in both cases). Post hoc comparisons indicated that it was the group rated by the children as "never" doing these activities that was different from the other groups, in that these individuals received lower frequency ratings from the mothers as well. However, there was no difference in maternal ratings among the individuals rated "a lot," "sometimes," or "a little bit." In other words, the children could differentiate between people who never did something and people who ever did it, but may have had difficulty making finer distinctions in frequency of task performance by network members.

Maternal and child reports were compared on specific items that comprised the Maintenance and Nurturance scales. Table 9.2 summarizes the percentage of agreement between mothers and children with respect to the people who performed specific supportive activities. These data indicate that there was very good agreement between mothers and children as to which network members performed the maintenance and nurturance functions.

Thus we have seen that maternal and child reports correspond quite closely. It remains to examine some of the factors that may affect the salience of specific categories of network members in the eyes of both mothers and children.

Frequency of Contact

Mothers were asked to indicate how often each network member came into contact with their children. A summary of this information is presented in

TABLE 9.2. Agreement Between Mother and Child on Individuals Performing Support Tasks

Task	Percentage of Agreement
Maintenance	
Breakfast	93.3
Takes to school	85.9
Brings from school	80.3
Supervises after school	79.3
Gives supper	91.9
Gives bath	89.9
Puts to bed	92.2
Nurturance	
Tells good news	94.2
Shows good product	95.5
Tells of fight with friend	87.5
Wants to be with when sad	68.6
Tells of fears	87.0
Tells of problems	85.9
Tells important things	92.0

Table 9.3. (Nuclear family members have been excluded, since they were of course all seen on a daily basis.) In a majority of cases, grandparents were seen at least once a week, and often more frequently than that. Substitute caregivers were also seen several times a week. However, next to substitute caregivers, the category of network member with whom the child was most likely to spend time was his or her own friends. Fully two-thirds of these friends were seen at least two to three times per week: From the interview data it is apparent that many children played with their friends five days a week at school or day care.

Is frequency of contact related to ratings of supportiveness by mothers and children? Correlations with support from nonnuclear family network members are presented in Table 9.4. In general, it may be concluded that, while mothers rated as more supportive network members who were seen more often, frequency of contact bore a somewhat less consistent relationship to the reports of the children. The mention of peers on the Nurturance scale was associated with frequency of contact, as were the Recreation scale scores of aunts and uncles. However, the Recreation scale scores of grandparents and substitute caregivers, who were seen more frequently than other relatives, were not related to frequency of contact. It is possible that lack of substantial variation in frequency of contact with grandparents and substitute caregivers rendered this variable less salient to the young children of this sample. Since these network members were usually seen often (be it once a week or several times a week), the recreation ratings given by the children may have been affected by

TABLE 9.3. Frequency of Contact with Network Members

Category	Frequency				
	Less Than Once a Month	Once a Month	Two to Three Times a Month	Less Than Once a Week	Two to Three Times a Week
Grandparents ($N = 152$)	7 (4.6%)	5 (3.3%)	29 (19.1%)	49 (32.2%)	62 (40.8%)
Aunts and uncles ($N = 121$)	15 (12.4%)	25 (20.7%)	29 (23.9%)	37 (30.6%)	15 (12.4%)
Substitute Caregivers ($N = 42$)	0	0	5 (11.9%)	5 (11.9%)	32 (76.2%)
Family friends and neightbors ($N = 72$)	2 (2.8%)	5 (6.9%)	11 (15.3%)	25 (34.7%)	29 (40.3%)
Child's friends ($N = 144$)	3 (2.1%)	9 (6.2%)	9 (6.2%)	27 (18.2%)	96 (66.7%)

TABLE 9.4. Relationship Between Frequency of Contact and Support from Network Members

	Network Member				
Scale	Grandparents ($N = 152$)	Aunts and Uncles ($N = 121$)	Family Friends and Neighbors ($N = 72$)	Substitute Caregivers ($N = 42$)	Peers ($N = 144$)
			Maternal Report		
Daily maintenance	.28***	.21*	.22*	.39**	not applicable
Occasional maintenance	.32***	.26**	.31**	.38**	not applicable
Nurturance	.30***	.33***	.14	.32*	.15*
Recreation	.30***	.33***	.08	.34*	.23**
Discipline	.25***	.26**	.08	.44**	not applicable
Closeness	.19**	.56***	−.24*	.29*	.18*
			Child Report		
Nurturance	[a]	[a]	[a]	[a]	.18*
Recreation	.12+	.24**	−.20+	.15	not applicable
Maintenance	[a]	[a]	[a]	.39**	not applicable

[a] Correlations are not reported since frequency of mention was too low to allow for meaningful analysis.
+$p < .10$
*$p < .05$
**$p < .01$
***$p < .001$

variables other than frequency of contact. In contrast, the children may have been better able to draw the distinction between aunts and uncles who were seen often and those seen more rarely, and thus rated the more frequently seen relatives more highly.

The negative correlation between frequency of contact and closeness to family friends and neighbors may be due to geography. Since by definition they lived in close physical proximity to the child and his or her family, neighbors might be seen more often than family friends, who did not necessarily live close by. Nonetheless, family friends may in fact have had closer ties to the children; this would produce the negative association that was found.

To summarize, frequent contact would seem to be a necessary though not sufficient condition for the provision of support by network members. Young children may not be as sensitive as their mothers to small differences in frequency of contact with network members when making judgments regarding supportiveness.

Uniplex Versus Multiplex Relations

Multiplexity, or the performance of more than one support function by network members, has been found to be associated with greater satisfaction of children with their networks (Nair & Jason, 1985; Sandler et al., 1985). We compared uniplex (i.e., the performance of one support function) and multiplex relationships with respect to the support ratings given by mothers and children. The results for this variable were uniform across support scales and for both respondents. Network members who had multiplex relations with the target child were assigned higher scale scores by both mothers and children. Multiplexity is an index of a more supportive relationship between network member and child: Not only did such a network member perform more functions, she or he also performed these functions more often. Both children and their mothers clearly distinguished between uniplex and multiplex relationships.

Children's Recreation and Nurturance Scale Scores and Mothers' Support Ratings

We have already determined that there is considerable correspondence between maternal and child ratings of individual network members for each scale. It is also of interest to examine interscale correlations. In other words, how do children's recreation and nurturance ratings relate to other scale scores assigned by their mothers? (Maintenance will not be considered as for the most part only mothers and fathers were said to perform this function.)

Looking first at children's Recreation scale scores for the relevant categories of network member,[1] we find that only for substitute caregivers was there a consistent relationship to support as assessed by mothers: Maternal scale scores and closeness ratings were highly positively correlated with Recreation scale scores (r's ranging from .39 for discipline to .61 for closeness). For grandparents, maternal report of daily maintenance was associated with recreation ($r = .28$, $p < .05$), while the correlation with frequency of discipline approached significance ($r = .12$, $p < .10$). For aunts and uncles, closeness ratings were correlated with recreation ($r = .16$, $p < .05$), but for family friends there were no significant relationships.

It is intriguing that only for substitute caregivers is there such a high degree of correspondence between maternal and child views. We can only speculate as to the source of this consistency. It is possible that the

[1] Children were asked to provide Recreation scale scores only for adult network members, excluding parents.

relationship between substitute caregivers and their charges is a very well defined one: The caregiver tends to be seen on a regular schedule, and is responsible for many of the same tasks as is the parent. For example, substitute caregivers were second only to parents in frequency of discipline, while few other network members performed this function. Furthermore, substitute caregivers were involved with the child when parents were not present, making their relationship with the child more exclusive. Children often spent time with relatives and family friends in the context of family activities, rendering their relationship more diffuse. While mothers may perceive these network members as supportive to the child, their support may not be as salient to the children.

The issue of salience becomes even more significant in the case of Nurturance scale scores. For this measure, children generated spontaneously the names of network members to whom they would turn for emotional support. As previously noted, with few exceptions the children named only parents, siblings, and their own friends in response to these questions. In terms of total responses to all 10 questions, mothers were most often mentioned (32.6% of responses). The child's own friends received 25.7% of the responses, fathers 19.6%, and siblings 11.6%. The remaining 10% were divided among teachers, substitute caregivers, grandmothers, other relatives, and "no one."

The children were also quite selective in terms of who was mentioned for a particular item. Table 9.5 presents a breakdown of the scale on an item-by-item basis, indicating the proportion of responses for each category of network member. Friends and siblings were selected when the child was looking for a playmate or wanting to share a cookie (cf. Feiring & Lewis's [in press] finding that children were more likely to invite friends than relatives to their birthday parties). Interestingly enough, these were also the network members of choice when the child felt sad. Mothers and fathers were chosen to discuss fears or problems, or to soothe a hurt. These children were clearly well able to distinguish among the roles played by different network members.

Did support from these network members bear a relationship to mentions on the Nurturance scale? The maternal Daily Maintenance scale was associated with mentions of mother, such that mothers who were above the mean on this scale were named more often than those below the mean.[2] For fathers, maternal reports of both daily and occasional maintenance, recreation, discipline, and closeness were all positively correlated with nurturance mentions by children, clearly indicating that more involved fathers were more important support figures in the eyes of the children. Sibling support was unrelated to any of the support scales, while mentions of the child's friends were related to the mother's closeness rating, with "closer" friends mentioned more often. Thus while paternal and to a lesser extent maternal supportive behavior were associated with the child's view of the

[2] The sample was split at the mean due to the lack of variation in this variable.

TABLE 9.5. Children's Responses to the Nurturance Scale

Question	Percentage of Responses for Each Network Member							
	Mother	Father	Sibling	Peer	Substitute Caregiver	Grandmother	Other Relative	No One
1. If you were tired of playing alone, who would you ask to play with you?	8.1	5.1	22.2	60.6	1.0	0	0	3.0
2. If something good happens to you, who do you tell about it?	31.7	19.8	13.9	25.7	4.9	0	1.0	3.0
3. If you have a fight with a friend, who do you tell about it?	36.7	13.9	7.6	15.2	13.9	2.5	0	10.2
4. If you are feeling sad or unhappy, who do you want to be with?	28.9	15.6	17.8	31.1	2.2	0	0	4.4
5. If you are afraid, or have a bad dream, who do you tell?	45.9	24.7	9.4	14.1	1.2	0	0	4.7
6. If you have a problem, or are worried about something, who do you talk to?	41.6	21.3	7.9	15.7	7.9	1.1	0	4.5
7. Who do you talk to about things that are important to you?	39.9	28.6	7.1	17.3	3.0	1.0	0	3.1
8. If you hurt yourself, who would you ask to help you?	48.3	30.8	3.3	8.8	7.7	1.1	0	0
9. If you have an extra cookie, who would you share it with?	9.8	9.8	17.1	53.6	0	0	1.2	8.5
10. If you do something nice at school, who do you tell about it?	35.9	25.0	11.6	14.6	6.8	1.0	1.0	3.9

parents as sources of nurturance, support from siblings and peers was not related to the nurturance ratings of these network members.

Nurturance scale scores of siblings and peers did seem to be related to support from the parents. Naming siblings was *negatively* correlated with maternal maintenance (both maternal and child report), recreation, and discipline, as well as paternal discipline. Similarly, the child was more likely to mention his or her own friends when mothers scored relatively low on maintenance and discipline, and when fathers were assigned low scores by mothers on nurturance, recreation, and discipline. It would appear that when parents were less supportive, siblings and peers loomed larger as support figures, according to the child's own report.

While sibling caretaking occurs commonly in other cultures (cf. Weisner, 1982), it is more rare in North American middle-class families. Cross-cultural data do indicate that, where sibling caretaking does occur, children tend to be highly peer oriented, spending relatively little time in the company of adults, and becoming accustomed to seeking help and information from other children. However, sibling caregivers often adopt child-rearing strategies that are more arbitrary and domineering than that of the parents (Weisner, 1982). This may account for the fact that in our study children's nurturance ratings of siblings were not related to the sibling support ratings of the mothers. Siblings who were more actively involved in caretaking may not necessarily have been perceived as more nurturant.

Another question that tapped the spontaneous views of the child was: "Is there anyone special, besides your mummy and daddy, that you like to visit or spend time with?" Here relatives fared somewhat better than on the Nurturance scale, with 16% mentioning a grandparent, and another 16% naming other relatives. However, the child's own friends were the top choice, mentioned by 40%. Siblings were named by 10%, and substitute caregivers by 4%. Fourteen percent said specifically "no one."

These "special relationships" did seem to differ from other network members in terms of supportiveness. These grandparents had higher Maintenance scale scores, and were rated as closer by mothers. Aunts and uncles were also rated as closer; in addition they received higher Recreation scale scores from mothers. There was a trend for these grandparents and other relatives to receive higher Recreation scale scores from the children as well. Siblings and peers named as having special relationships scored higher on the maternal Nurturance and Recreation scales; such peers were also rated as closer, and were mentioned significantly more often on the child's Nurturance scale. Thus there is good corroboration that individuals viewed by the children as having special relationships with them did in fact provide more support, as compared to other network members of the same category.

Both the children's Nurturance scale and the question on special relationships elicited only spontaneous mentions. There was no probing for other types of network members. Had the children been asked specifically about grandparents or other relatives, it is more than likely that they would have agreed that these were people that they might turn to with a problem or a bad dream. However, the people who were clearly uppermost in the minds of the children were nuclear family members and their own friends.

CONCLUSION

Detailed comparison of maternal and child reports of children's social networks indicates that there is substantial agreement between mothers and their preschool-age children, both as to composition and as to support provisions. Frequency of contact was related to the supportiveness judgments of both mothers and children, though the latter seemed able to make only gross distinctions with regard to frequency. Both respondents considered multiplex relations to be more supportive than uniplex ones.

Nonetheless, there would appear to be two distinct perspectives. Mothers described broad networks, including relatives, family friends, and substitute caregivers. In many cases, relatives (especially grandparents) were seen several times a week. Yet the children, in their spontaneous reports, mentioned primarily nuclear family members and their own friends. That nuclear family members were most important to these young children is consistent with other research on children's social networks (cf. Belle & Longfellow, 1984; Bryant, 1985; Furman & Buhrmester, 1985; Tietjen, 1982). Clearly, other network members played a role in the lives of these children—why were they not more prominent in the children's reports? One factor, affecting adult network members, might be the performance of the maintenance function. Grandparents who were named as having special relationships, and who received higher Recreation scale scores from children, had higher Maintenance scale scores. Similarly, substitute caregivers, who often performed maintenance tasks, had higher scores on the children's Recreation scale. Aunts, uncles, family friends, and neighbors were generally unlikely to be involved in maintenance. It is possible that for young children, performance of the basic daily child-care tasks gave network members a high profile. These were the tasks that parents were most likely to perform, and perhaps in the mind of the young child such care becomes equated with affection and concern. Five- and 6-year-olds are concrete thinkers whose judgments about love may well be based on the performance of physical care (cf. Saunders, 1979). In other words, network members who provide maintenance support may thus be communicating their devotion to the children in a fashion most readily understood by a young child. Daily child-care tasks such as supervision, transportation, and bathing may also provide occasions for nurturant interaction between caregiver and child, thus strengthening their relationship.

The child's own friends may have been particularly salient at least in part because they were seen very frequently, often on a daily basis at school or day care. As Youniss (1980) has noted, children today spend more time with agemates than with other people, which may enhance the significance of peer relationships. Youniss also pointed out that peer relations are important to children because they are mutual and reciprocal, in contrast to the status differential in dealings with adults. Even the very young children of this sample sought companionship and emotional support from their own friends. Sibling relationships seemed secondary to those with peers. Furman and Buhrmester (1985) found sibling relationships to be somewhat conflictual: Children were close to their siblings but also more ambivalent about them, possibly due to the competition for resources within the family.

The current study was largely descriptive in nature. A more structured approach to the study of children's reports of their social networks is warranted. Systematic questioning with regard to each category of network member might yield a different picture from that derived by analyzing children's spontaneous reports. Nonetheless, I would venture to say that mothers' and children's reports do represent different viewpoints, the implications of which might be seen when examining the effects of different types of network structure and functioning on children's developmental outcomes. It is possible that, in evaluating the supportive role of relatives, family friends, and substitute caregivers, mothers were reporting support that actually benefits *them,* by providing child-care assistance. Such support would therefore be salient to the mothers, but less so to the children. The support of adult network members might be particularly important in families under stress, by affording relief to the mother and necessary care to the child. Analysis of mother and child reports of network functioning in relation to maternal and child behavior would be of particular interest in this regard. Longitudinal study of children's reports would also be useful to see whether the emphases change with the child's age. Do older children become more appreciative of other relationships or do peers become even more important? These are among the questions that should be addressed in this rich area of research. In this manner we can begin to elucidate how different relationships come to influence children's social development.

REFERENCES

Belle, D., & Longfellow, C. (1984, August). *Turning to others: Children's use of confidants.* Paper presented at the meetings of the American Psychological Association, Toronto.

Bryant, B. K. (1985). The Neighborhood Walk: Sources of support in middle childhood. *Monographs of the Society for Research in Child Development, 50* (3, Serial No. 210).

Cohn, D. A., Lohrmann, B. C., & Patterson, C. J. (1985, April). *Social networks and loneliness in children.* Paper presented at the meetings of the Society for Research in Child Development, Toronto.

Feiring, C., & Lewis, M. (1981). *The social networks of three-year-old children.* Paper presented at the meetings of the Society for Research in Child Development, Boston.

Feiring, C., & Lewis, M. (in press). The child's social network: Sex differences from three to six years. *Sex Roles.*

Furman, W., & Buhrmester, D. (1985). Children's perceptions of the personal relationships in their social networks. *Developmental Psychology, 21,* 1016–1024.

Garbarino, J., Burston, N., Raber, S., Russell, R., & Crouter, A. (1978). The social maps of children approaching adolescence: Studying the ecology of youth development. *Journal of Youth & Adolescence, 7,* 417–428.

Lewis, M., Feiring, C., & Kotsonis, M. (1984). The social network of the young child: A developmental perspective. In M. Lewis (Ed.), *Beyond the dyad* (pp. 129–160). New York: Plenum.

Nair, D., & Jason, L. A. (1985). An investigation and analysis of social networks among children. *Special Services in the Schools, 14,* 43–52.

Sandler, I. N., & Barrera, M. (1984). Toward a multimethod approach to assessing the effects of social support. *American Journal of Community Psychology, 12,* 37–52.

Sandler, I., Wolchik, S., & Braver, S. (1985). Social support and children of divorce. In I. G. Sarason & B. R. Sarason (Eds.), *Social support: Theory, research and application.* The Hague: Martinus Nijhoff.

Saunders, E. B. (1977). *The Nurturance Scale.* Unpublished report, Stress and Families Project, Harvard University.

Saunders, E. B. (1979). *Children's thoughts about parents: A developmental study.* Unpublished doctoral dissertation, Harvard University.

Tietjen, A. M. (1982). The social networks of preadolescent children in Sweden. *International Journal of Behavioral Development, 5,* 111–130.

Turner, R. J., Frankel, B. G., & Levin, D. (1982). *Social support: Conceptualization, measurement and implications for mental health.* Health Care Research Unit, University of Western Ontario, London, Ontario, Canada.

Weisner, T. S. (1982). Sibling interdependence and child caretaking: A cross-cultural view. In M. E. Lamb & B. Sutton-Smith (Eds.), *Sibling relations* (pp. 305–327). Hillsdale, NJ: Erlbaum.

Wolchik, S. A., Sandler, I. N., & Braver, S. L. (1984). *The social support networks of children of divorce.* Paper presented at meetings of the American Psychological Association, Toronto.

Youniss, J. (1980). *Parents and peers in social development.* Chicago: University of Chicago Press.

Zelkowitz, P. (1982). *Children's support networks: Their role in families under stress.* Unpublished doctoral dissertation, Harvard University.

Zelkowitz, P. (1984). *Comparing maternal and child reports of children's social networks.* Paper presented at the meetings of the American Psychological Association, Toronto.

Zelkowitz, P., & Jacobs, E. (1985). *The composition of the social networks of preschool-aged children.* Paper presented at the meetings of the Society for Research in Child Development, Toronto.

PART 4

Building Supportive Networks

CHAPTER 10

Parents as Managers of Children's Peer Relationships

ROSS D. PARKE AND NAVAZ P. BHAVNAGRI

Our views of the family as an isolated social unit have undergone considerable shift over the past decade. Families are no longer isolated but are conceptualized as being embedded in a set of social systems outside the family, including formal and informal social networks as well as kin, peer, and friendship groups (Cochran & Brassard, 1979; Parke & Tinsley, 1982). It is recognized that the influence is bidirectional, with the family both influencing these outside systems and being influenced by these extra-familial social units. The aim of this chapter is to evaluate one aspect of this issue, namely, the ways in which the family is linked to children's peer groups. Specifically our task will be to explore alternative ways in which the family can potentially influence the child's competence in the peer context.

ALTERNATIVE APPROACHES TO THE ROLE OF FAMILY IN FACILITATING CHILDREN'S PEER RELATIONSHIPS

Families influence their children's peer relationships in a variety of ways. To facilitate our examination of this linkage between family and peer systems it is heuristically valuable to distinguish between direct and indirect paths of family influence. In the case of indirect influences the parents' goal is not explicitly to modify or enhance the child's relationships with other children and/or adults. Any effect on peer relationships may be an indirect carryover from the pursuit of another goal.

The most common and well researched way in which families indirectly influence their children's peer relationships is through the nature of

Preparation of this chapter and the research reported were supported in part by NICHD grant HD05951 and NICHD training grant HD07205. Thanks to Terry Sturdyvin and Kae Helms for assistance in the typing of this manuscript.

the parent–child relationship. In this case the goal is to develop and maintain a relationship with the child. Parents can have an indirect impact on their children's peer competency as a result of the quality of their interpersonal relationship with their child. Two research traditions illustrate this approach. First, in the attachment tradition, the focus has been on the impact of early infant–mother attachment on social adaptation to the peer group (for reviews see Jacobson, Tianen, Willie, & Aytch, 1986; Sroufe & Fleeson, 1986). The second tradition is illustrated by studies of the impact of either particular child-rearing styles (Baumrind, 1973; Hoffman, 1960) or parent–child interaction (MacDonald & Parke, 1984; Parke, MacDonald, Beitel, & Bhavnagri, 1987; Putallaz, 1987). In both research traditions, there is clear evidence that the quality of parent–child relationships is linked with the competence of children with their peers. A detailed review of studies in these traditions is beyond the scope of the present chapter.

The goal of direct influences, on the other hand, is explicitly to select, modify, or structure the child's physical and/or social environment in order to enhance the child's peer relationships. These types of influences often occur in the context of the parents' role as manager of their children's social lives. The concept of manager is receiving increased recognition in the recent social development literature (Hartup, 1979; Parke, 1978). In turn, these direct strategies can be conceptualized as two broad sets of activities. First, parents can be viewed as arrangers of opportunities for peer–peer interaction, such as providing safe neighborhoods, organizing play groups, or enrolling their children in activities involving other children (Rubin & Sloman, 1984). Second, parents can be viewed as facilitating peer relationships by directly monitoring and supervising their children's interaction with peers in order to facilitate the development of their children's social skills (Bhavnagri & Parke, 1985). The goal of this chapter is to examine these alternative direct pathways by which families influence peer–peer interaction.

PARENTS AS ARRANGERS OF OPPORTUNITIES

Young children, in particular, are dependent on their parents to provide opportunities for their social contacts. This can occur in a variety of ways, including the choice of neighborhood, the availability of child-centered activities, such as clubs, sports, accessibility to day-care or preschool facilities, or merely the presence of other children to permit informal contacts.

Neighborhoods as Settings That Influence Peer–Peer Relationships

Neighborhoods vary in terms of their opportunities for peer–peer contact. Especially in the case of young children who have limited mobility, the neighborhood forms a significant proportion of their social world (Moore & Young, 1978). The most systematic evidence concerning the impact of variations in the quality of neighborhood environments comes from the work of Medrich (Berg & Medrich, 1980; Medrich, Roizen, Rubin, & Buckley, 1982). These investigators isolated a number of factors, such as terrain, distance from commercial areas, child population density, and safety, that affect the amount and type of peer social experience. Based on interviews with sixth-grade children, they found that children in neighborhoods in which houses are widely separated with few sidewalks tended to have fewer friends and travel longer distances in order to make contact. Their friendship patterns were more formal and rigid. In contrast, children in neighborhoods with little distance and few barriers between houses reported a higher number of friends and a more informal and spontaneous play pattern.

Safety was a further determinant of peer access. Children in neighborhoods with safety hazards such as major thoroughfares and unregulated traffic reported much less autonomy to visit playmates and gain access to play areas. Safety restraints limit the number of friends and amount of large-group play and is associated with rigidity of friendships. To compensate, children with these restraints report more play with siblings than did children in less restrained neighborhoods. Children's access to public facilities such as parks and schoolyards affects their play interaction; children with less access report less large-group play and fewer friends than children with easy access to these facilities. Finally, the density of the child population is important. A neighborhood with high social density was related to higher number of friends, more large-group play, and more spontaneity in play. Children in neighborhoods with fewer children reported having a smaller number of friends and more formal friendship patterns.

More recently, Bhavnagri (1987) found that children's use of neighborhood varies with the age of the child. In an interview study of mothers of preschoolers 2 to 6 years old, this investigator found that younger children (2 to 3½ years old) were permitted less unsupervised access to neighborhood facilities and playmates than older children (3½ to 6 years old). Similarly, older children played significantly more outdoors with their friends in the neighborhood and were rated by their mothers as having more playmates in the neighborhood than younger children.

While this work clearly underscores the importance of the ecology of the neighborhood as a determinant of peer interaction patterns, what is the impact of these variations on peer competence? Some recent data from Bryant (1985) suggest that accessibility to neighborhood resources is an important correlate of socioemotional functioning. Children who could easily access (by walking or bike) such community resources as structured and unstructured activities at formally sponsored organizations were higher in their acceptance of individual differences, as well as higher in perspective taking.

Although it is argued that parents often choose residential settings in order to facilitate contact between their children and potential playmates, the reverse may also be valid. Specifically, parents could actively avoid neighborhoods that are densely populated with other children, especially if parents view these children as undesirable influences on their own offspring. For example, parents may reject neighborhoods that are characterized by high rates of juvenile delinquency or vandalism in order to limit their children's contact with potentially undesirable peer contacts. Family economic resources, however, obviously constrain the degree of choice. Parents, in any case, can serve as important gatekeepers in either facilitating or decreasing the amount of contact as well as the type of peers that children will have access to in their neighborhood contexts. Finally, the impact of neighborhoods on children of different ages merits more investigation, since only a limited age range has been explored to date.

Parental Participation in Children's Organized Activities

In addition to choosing a neighborhood as a way of increasing access to children, parents influence their children's social behavior by interfacing between children and institutional settings. More than 20 years ago Coser (1964) recognized this function:

> Through her activities in the PTA, Brownies, Cub Scouts and the like, a mother helps both to maintain the communal social network and to integrate her children in it—Hence the modern middle-class American mother performs a large share of the mediation between the community and the family; to use Parsons' phrase, she helps to adapt the family to the "external system." (p. 337, cited in O'Donnell & Stueve, 1983)

These mediational activities are important since they permit the child access to a wider range of social activities that may, in turn, contribute to their social and cognitive development.

As the early observations of Coser (1964) suggest, there are clear sex-of-parent differences in these activities. Joffe (1977) found that mothers communicate more regularly with child-care staff than fathers. Similarly, Lightfoot (1978) found that mothers had more regular contact with teachers in elementary schools than fathers. Finally, Bhavnagri (1987) found that mothers and fathers differ in their views of the importance of preschool as an opportunity to learn social skills. Although both mothers and fathers indicated that the learning of social skills was an important factor in their choice of a preschool and an important goal of the preschool experience for their children, mothers' ratings of these factors were higher than fathers'. Together these findings suggest not only that mothers are more involved in the interface between the family and social institutions, but also that mothers view these settings as being more important for the development of social relationships than fathers.

Moreover, there are clear social-class variations in this activity. O'Donnell & Stueve (1983) in an interview study of 59 families with children between 5 and 14 years of age found that 80% of the families were involved in community-based children's activities. Age determined to some extent the level of participation, with those families most involved in community-based activities having at least one child between the ages of 10 and 14 years of age. Moreover, only 22% of the mothers gave no evidence of volunteer activity, while 78% participated at least occasionally in one of the activities. There were marked social class differences both in children's utilization of community organizations and in the level of maternal participation. Working-class children were only half as likely to participate in activities as their middle-class peers, and working-class children were more likely to use the facilities on an occasional rather than a regular basis. Middle-class mothers were more likely to sign their children up for specific programs, whereas working-class mothers were less likely to involve their children in planned activities. The level of maternal participation varied by social class with better-educated and economically more advantaged mothers participating more heavily than working-class mothers.

> By virtue of their purchasing power and their ability to manipulate the system, middle-class mothers were better prepared to act as social agents, and to introduce their children into the broader range of organized activities and resources beyond the boundaries of their homes and schools. (O'Donnell & Stueve, 1983, p. 123)

Unfortunately we do not yet know how these opportunities for participation relate to children's social behavior with their peers. One exception is Bryant (1985), who found that participation in formally sponsored organizations with unstructured activities was associated with greater social perspective-taking skill among 10-year-old children, but had little effect on 7-year-olds. In light of the importance of this skill for successful peer–peer interaction (Hartup, 1983), this finding assumes particular significance. Moreover, it suggests that activities that "allow the child to experience autonomy, control and mastery of the content of the activity are related to expressions of enhanced social-emotional functioning on the part of the child" (Bryant, 1985, p. 65).

Although we do not know systematically how these activities vary as a function of children's age, it appears that there is an increase with age in participation in sponsored organizations with structured activities (e.g., clubs, Brownies, organized sports) with participation most prevalent among preadolescent children (Bryant, 1985; O'Donnell & Stueve, 1983). Finally, more attention to the ways in which fathers participate in these types of activities is needed, especially in light of their shifting roles (Parke & Tinsley, 1984).

Parent as Social Initiator and Arranger

Parents play an important role in the facilitation of their children's peer relationships by initiating contact between their own children and potential play partners. There is an emerging but still limited body of literature that addresses this issue. Schiavo and his colleagues (Schiavo & Solomon, 1981; Schiavo, Solomon, Evers, & Cohen, 1981) found that preschool classmates were more likely to have contact during summer vacation and remain friends over a 1-year period if their parents were friends than if they were not. As this research suggests, this type of parental activity probably is more critical for maintaining contact between peers for younger children who are less mobile and independent. Recent evidence indicates that this activity varies with the age of the child and with the sex of the parent but not with the sex of the child.

First, this type of activity is more likely to be undertaken on behalf of younger rather than older children. Bhavnagri (1987) recently interviewed mothers of children 2 to 6 years old, and in response to the question "How often do you contact other children for your child to play with?" there were significant differences as a function of the age of the child. Mothers reported significantly more invitations to their children's friends on behalf of younger rather than older children. In the case of older children (3½ to 6 years), the children themselves and/or their friends took the initiative to maintain their own friendship patterns. In view of the more limited mobility of younger children (2 to 3½ years) and their lower ability to gain access to other children, this strategy is particularly important for younger children.

Second, sex of the child does not influence this activity; Bhavnagri (1987) found no differences between the rates of maternal initiation on behalf of boys and girls. Similarly, Ladd and Golter (1988) in a recent study of parental initiation based on parental logs of children's daily social activities found no sex-of-child differences.

However, Ladd and Golter found that a third factor—sex of parent—did make a difference. They reported that mothers of children 4 to 5 were more likely to initiate contacts with other children than fathers (82% vs. 12% respectively). This finding is consistent with earlier portraits of mothers as mediators of social relationships outside the family, especially extended kin (Bahr, 1976; Gray & Smith, 1960). Moreover, it is consistent with other more recent data that suggest that mothers play an important role in the nature of children's social networks. Oliveri and Reiss (1987) found that the size of adolescents' kin network and the amount of direct contact with the kin network were significantly related to the mother's own kinship network characteristics. Similarly, there were striking parallels between the density of mothers' friendship networks and the density of their adolescents' friendship networks. In contrast there were fewer relationships between the structural characteristics of fathers' kin or friendship networks and the pattern of the social networks of their children. While these relationships suggest that mothers influence their offspring's networks, they underscore the important differences between mothers and fathers in their influence over children's patterns of social relationships.

Does active parental initiation of peer contact relate to children's social competence? Some indirect support comes from Murray, Webb, and Andrews (1983), who reported that mothers who had satisfying contacts in the community had socially competent children as measured by popularity, social behavior, and social-cognitive skills. Perhaps socially competent parents provide appropriate models for their offspring. To assess this issue further, Ladd and Golter (1987) examined children's relationships both outside school and within the school context. Children of parents who tended to arrange peer contacts had a larger range of playmates and more frequent play companions outside of school than children of parents who were less active in initiating peer contacts. In the school context, boys with parents who initiated peer contacts were better liked and less rejected by their classmates than were boys with noninitiating parents; girls did not differ in their acceptance by their classmates as a function of parental initiation activities.

Finally, Krappmann (1986) in a study of children 10 to 12 years old in Germany found that the extent to which parents stimulated and facilitated peer relationships and peer activities was related to several measures of the quality of peer relations, including the closeness and stability of the peer ties as well as the character of the peer links. Children whose parents facilitated and stimulated peer relationships had closer and more stable peer bonds and fewer problems in their peer relationships. These studies provide impressive evidence of the possible facilitative role of parents in the development of social competence with peers.

PARENTAL MONITORING AND SUPERVISION

Another way in which parents can affect their children's social relationships is through monitoring of their children's social activities. Monitoring refers to a range of activities, including the supervision of children's choice of social settings, activities, and friends. A number of studies of adolescents have examined the use of parental monitoring. These studies indicate that parents of delinquent children engage in less monitoring and supervision of their children's activities, especially with regard to children's use of evening time, than parents of nondelinquent children (Belson, 1975; Pulkkinen, 1981). Others (Gold, 1963) found that parents of delinquents perceive themselves as less in control of their sons' choice of friends. Although earlier studies relied on a single self-report from either parents or children, a recent study by Patterson and Stouthamer-Loeber (1984), using multiple informants, found significant relationships between lack of parental monitoring (defined as awareness of the child's whereabouts) and court-reported delinquency, attacks against property, delinquent life-style, rule breaking outside the home, and an antisocial disposition (e.g., fighting with peers, talking back to teachers, troublesome, breaking school rules) among seventh- and tenth-grade boys. Monitoring is a composite measure that indexes how well the parents track their children's whereabouts, the kinds of companions they keep, or the types of activities they engage in. Adolescents who were monitored by their parents exhibited less antisocial behavior. Consistent with this work is the recent work of Steinberg (1986), who found that children in sixth to ninth grade, especially girls who are on their own after school, are more susceptible to peer pressure to engage in antisocial activity (e.g., vandalism, cheating, stealing) than are their adult-supervised peers. Any adolescent who indicated that at least one adult was present in the after-school setting (regardless of whether there was face-to-face contact with the adult) was categorized as supervised. Not all forms of supervision are similar. As Steinberg noted:

> Adolescents who are at home after school without an adult present may be supervised distally by their absent parents through telephone calls, an agreed-upon schedule followed by the adolescent, or the power of internalized parental controls which may be heightened by the adolescent's being in his or her own house. (1986 p. 436)

In support of this distal monitoring, he found that adolescents who are on their own "hanging out" and not at home (e.g., unsupervised at a friend's house) are more susceptible to peer pressure than are adolescents who are on their own in their own homes. Further support for the distal monitoring notion is evident from the finding that adolescents whose parents know their whereabouts after school are less likely to be susceptible to peer pressure (Baumrind, 1978). Finally, Steinberg (1986) found that monitoring may be more important for some families than for others; specifically, children of parents who were high in their use of authoritative parenting practices (Baumrind, 1978) were less susceptible to peer pressure in the absence of monitoring. On the other hand, children of parents who were low in authoritative child rearing were more susceptible to peer pressure in nonsupervised contexts. The importance of monitoring varies with other aspects of the family environment, including child-rearing practices. Nor are the effects of monitoring limited to a reduction in negative aspects of peer relations. As Krappmann (1986) recently found in Germany, preadolescents of parents who were well informed about their children's peer relationships and activities had closer, more stable, and less problem-ridden peer relationships. Isolation of other conditions or variables that alter the impact of monitoring would be worthwhile. Developmental shifts may be important, since younger children are less likely to be left unsupervised than older children; moreover, it is likely that direct supervision is more common among younger children while distal supervision is more evident among adolescents.

Parental Supervisory Activities

Another form of parental management that has received only limited attention is the extent to which parents supervise their children's activities when they are with other children. Two strategies have been employed in research addressing this issue. In one approach, field-based assessments of the extent to which parental supervisory behavior is employed are utilized and the links between the use of these parental tactics and children's social behavior with peers are examined. A second approach, a laboratory-based strategy, the impact of parental supervision on the interactive competence of two peers, is explored, as well as the impact of stylistic variations in supervisory style.

Field-Based Assessments

Recently several investigators have examined the extent to which parents supervise the activities of their child with a peer in the home situation. These studies begin to provide descriptive information concerning the frequency of occurrence of this type of parental behavior as well as some insights concerning the personal factors such as sex of parent and child that determine this activity as well as the situational determinants of parental supervisory behavior.

Mothers and fathers vary in the extent to which they actively participate in the supervision of their children's play with peers in home settings. In one study, Ladd and Golter (1988) interviewed parents to assess parents' reported involvement in one or more of the following types of supervision: maintaining a presence during the period of contact between their child and a peer (i.e., remaining within the children's view), participating in the activity, and watching at a distance but checking on the children's activities on a regular basis. With their sample of 4- and 5-year-old children, they found that parents varied considerably in terms of the extent to which they engaged in supervisory activities. One-third of the parents had supervised all of their children's peer contacts and half of the sample had supervised 75% or more of their children's peer contacts. The remaining parents monitored between 0 and 71% of their children's contacts (median level = 25%). Moreover, monitoring was more often done by mothers than by fathers (67 and 33%, respectively) even after controlling for the extent to which the parents are available for monitoring. Similar sex-of-parent differences were recently reported by Bhavnagri (1987). While mothers and fathers did not differ in the extent to which they participated in low levels of supervision (e.g., "keep an eye on child but no direct involvement" or "start playing and then withdraw"), fathers were less likely than mothers to be actively involved in supervising and maintaining children's interaction with playmates at home (e.g., "actively participate in their play"). Furthermore, Bhavnagri (1987) reported that there were differences in mothers' and fathers' play styles during supervision, when they play with their child and a peer. Fathers when compared to mothers were more involved in physical play with their child and a peer. Mothers, on the other hand, were significantly more involved in verbal and cognitive teaching games when they supervised their child with a peer. Similar stylistic differences have been found in parent–infant dyadic play (Lamb, 1977; Power & Parke, 1982; Yogman, 1982). Thus the stylistic differences between mothers and fathers that are found in the parent–infant dyad are also present in triadic interactions when the parents are supervising their child with his or her peer. Neither Ladd and Golter nor Bhavnagri found sex-of-child differences; boys and girls were equally likely to experience this type of parental supervision of their social contacts.

Are there links between this type of parental behavior and children's peer relations? Ladd and Golter found no relationship between these types of activities and the children's nonschool peer relations. On the other hand, they found that parents who engaged in higher as opposed to lower levels of monitoring had children who spent less time in constructive solitary play during school and were rejected more by their classmates. In addition teachers rated children of high supervisory parents as higher in hostility–aggression and more hyperactive–distractible. As Ladd and Golter (1988) comment:

> It may be the case that children who display higher levels of social competence require less parental supervision than those who manifest interpersonal difficulties . . . conversely it may be that parental monitoring has some effect on children's ability to relate to peers in larger group settings such as classrooms. . . . [Children] who are constantly supervised in nonschool settings may be less well prepared for settings that afford less individual attention and respond to what may be perceived as lack of structure by becoming more disruptive or unruly. (1988, p. 116)

What are the situational determinants of parental supervisory behaviors? To answer this question Lollis and Ross (1987) observed 20- and 30-month-old children playing either in their own home with a peer or in the peer's home. This observational approach represents a significant advance over the earlier interview studies of Ladd and Golter and Bhavnagri. Mothers of both children were present and the frequency with which mothers intervened during different types of activities was examined. First, mothers intervened more during peer–peer conflict sequences (42%) than during other types of activities, such as games (20%) or pretense activities (25%). Second, during conflict sequences mothers addressed their own children almost exclusively; 82% of all interventions were addressed to their own children. Mothers intervened more in conflicts when their own children were the initiators of the conflict but only in their own homes. Mothers were much less likely to intervene when the other child started a conflict or when the setting was the other child's home. This is consistent with the earlier finding (Halverson & Waldrop, 1970) that mothers were more likely to use negative sanctions with their own 2½-year-old children than with unrelated children in a laboratory context.

Finally, Lollis and Ross found that mothers' interventions changed the relationships between the children. Under conditions of maternal intervention, children were more likely to settle their disputes by sharing resources more equally; in contrast, when left on their own children's disputes more often resulted in less equality of outcomes with one child winning the argument and another losing. In short, equality was higher when mothers intervened. Next, we turn to laboratory studies of parental supervisory behavior.

Lab-Based Studies of Parental Supervision

Parents can play a direct role in facilitating the interactions of their children with their peers. In this case, the parental managerial role is as a supervisor who directly assists the children to initiate their play together, maintains the interaction, and assists the children in resolving their difficulties and disagreements.

To date, there has been surprisingly little experimental examination of this aspect of parental management of peer relations. One illustration of parent-implemented training of social skills is provided by Powell, Salzberg, Rule, Levy, and Letzkowitz (1984). In this study the goal was to increase the play skills (e.g., sharing, play organizing, assisting, and affection) of four handicapped children with their nonhandicapped siblings. Although simple instructing of parents to try to increase the extent to which children played with each other failed, the provision of formal instruction in reorganizing, prompting, and reinforcing play behaviors led to increases in play behavior in structured training sessions. However, the small sample size, the specialized nature of the population, and the sibling focus limit the generality of this study for understanding the potential role of parents as supervisors of their children's play with extrafamilial play partners. In another one of the few studies in this domain, Levitt, Clark, and McDonnell (1983) found that mothers' interventions increased sharing between 3-year-old peers. None of the 3-year-olds spontaneously shared across physical barriers, while 65% did share when their mothers requested them to share. While this study does suggest that parents can facilitate some forms of social behavior between peers, the limited range of behaviors studied as well as the restricted examination of maternal strategies that were used to facilitate sharing clearly suggests the need for a more comprehensive exploration of the parental role in the development of peer interaction.

The Bhavnagri-Parke Investigations of Parental Supervision

In our laboratory we investigated how parents can function as facilitators of their child's interaction with an unfamiliar peer (Bhavnagri & Parke, 1985).

Study 1

The following paradigm was developed to permit examination of this issue. In a playroom, children's social competence with an unfamiliar peer was assessed under two conditions. In one condition, two children played without assistance from an adult. In this case, both mothers were present but were instructed not to assist or interfere with the children's play. In the contrasting condition, one mother was asked to play an active supervisory role with the specific instruction to "help the children play together." By comparing the quality of children's social play under these contrasting conditions, we were able to determine whether or not maternal supervisory behavior can facilitate peer–peer interaction and secondly identify which parental strategies were effective in facilitating peer social play.

The participants were 40 firstborn 24-month-old toddlers and their mothers. Children were matched for age and sex with their peer partners during the play sessions. Across a 30-minute play session, the two children played uninterrupted for the first 5 minutes in order to obtain a baseline concerning children's competence to interact with their peers. Thereafter each mother supervised the children's play for a 10-minute period. The order in which the mothers assumed the supervisory role was randomly determined. During periods when a mother was not actively supervising the children's play, she was asked to complete a questionnaire and not to interact with the children. The purpose of these two 10-minute periods was to determine the influence of parental supervision on peer–peer interaction. In the final 5 minutes of the play period the children again played without maternal supervision. The aim of the last period was to determine whether there was any carryover effect of parental supervision or whether the children returned to their baseline level of peer interaction. Periods two and three were twice as long as sessions one and four in order to provide adequate sampling for identifying parental supervisory strategies. Toys (a ball, a toy telephone, a push-and-pull "popcorn" toy, and a toy horse) were available throughout the session. The toys were developmentally appropriate, appealed to both sexes, and permitted the display of a wide range of social skills (e.g., turn taking, cooperative and simultaneous action upon the same object, and complementarity of actions on object). The entire 30-minute session was videotaped. Mothers' and children's behaviors were rated by independent coders for each of the four sessions using 5-point global rating scales. The items on the scales assessed the frequency, duration, intensity, and effectiveness of behaviors.

Does maternal supervision affect children's social competence? To find out, an analysis of variance with repeated measures involving four sessions and sex of child was executed. Not only was children's overall social competency rated higher during the periods of parental supervision, but there were significant differences in a variety of specific aspects of peer–peer interaction such as turn taking, the duration of play bouts, and the amount of cooperation as well. However, there were no sex differences. The next question concerns the specification of the maternal strategies that are most effective in facilitating peer–peer interaction. To assess this issue, correlational analyses of the relationship between specific maternal supervisory strategies and behavior were executed. Mothers' overall ability in expressing affect and their overall supervisory competence were positively related to children's overall social competence, as well as a variety of specific aspects of children's social behaviors directed toward their peers (e.g., turn-taking). Similarly, specific facets of maternal supervisory behavior were positively related to children's social competence. Mothers' ability to initiate interaction, their ability to sustain interaction, as well as their responsiveness, synchrony, and level of positive affect were all positively related to children's social behavior with peers. These findings clearly suggest a variety of specific ways in which variation in maternal supervisory style is linked with peer interactive competence.

Study 2: Replication and Extension

Our next study (Bhavnagri, 1987) extended the basic paradigm in several ways. First, both mothers and fathers were included as supervisory agents. Second, a wider age range of children was included, with 70 children from 2 to 6 years old participating in this study. Third, the basic design was modified to include alternating supervised and unsupervised sessions of equal duration. The specific design was as follows:

1. First 6 minutes: children play alone unsupervised
2. Second 6 minutes: one parent supervises play
3. Third 6 minutes: children play alone unsupervised
4. Fourth 6 minutes: other parent supervises play
5. Fifth 6 minutes: children play alone unsupervised

Mothers and fathers participated on separate occasions and same-sex parents participated together. The procedure followed the format of the earlier study. The results indicated that both fathers and mothers are effective facilitators of their children's play with their peers; second, supervision clearly enhances the quality of children's peer play. However, this finding is qualified by the age of the child. The effects of parental supervision were greater for the younger (2 to 3½ years) than the older (3½ to 6 years) group of children.

As Figure 10.1 shows, the older children are able to maintain the level of interaction achieved under the initial session of facilitation throughout the remainder of the experimental sessions even when parental facilitation is unavailable. In contrast, younger children do not sustain their levels of interaction when parental support is removed. This suggests that parental facilitation may be more important for younger than for older children; for young children who are beginning to acquire and practice emerging social skills this type of parental intervention may be most critical.

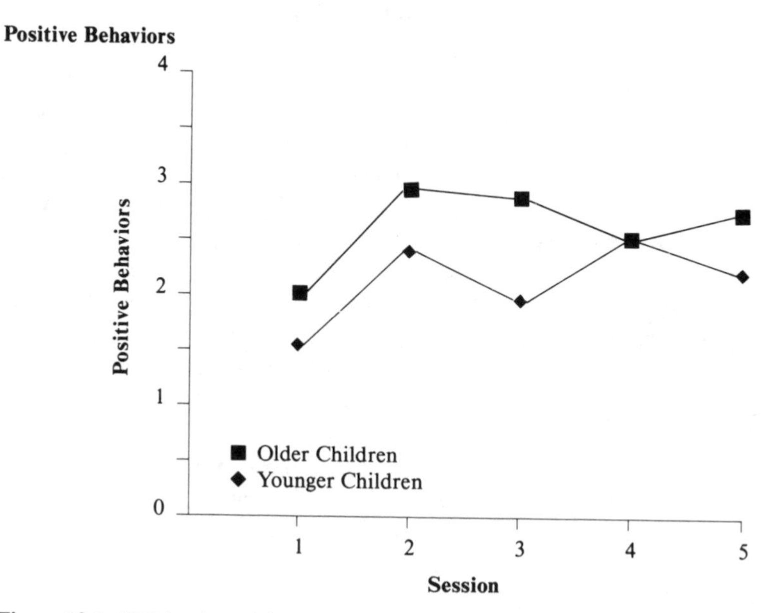

Figure 10.1. Children's positive social behaviors across sessions. (*Positive behaviors* refers to a composite of positive social skills, positive affect, and prosocial behavior.)

Do parental facilitative styles differ in their effectiveness in promoting peer interaction? As in Study 1, there are a variety of strategies that are significantly related to peer interactive competence, but some parental approaches were effective for children of both age groups, while others were more effective for younger or older children. Parental competence in sustaining interaction was positively related to a variety of peer behaviors for both younger and older children including children's ability to act simultaneously on toys, their ability to take turns, their level of cooperative play, and their duration of play together. In contrast, parental competence in teaching turn taking was positively related to a range of peer behaviors for younger children including their ability to act simultaneously on toys, cooperative play, and duration of play. On the other hand, mothers' competence in initiation of peer interaction was related more frequently to older children's peer play and less often to younger children's peer interactions. This pattern of findings is consistent with the general conclusion that older children may need assistance in initiating interaction with a peer, but once started, they have the social skills to maintain the interchange. Younger children, in contrast, require more sustained and continuing support (e.g., by directly teaching them turn taking) in order to maintain the interaction patterns.

As noted earlier, interviews with the parents in our study indicated that similar differences in the extent of parental supervision occurred at home for younger and older children. Specifically, parents reported higher levels of active supervision with their younger than their older children and allowed older children to play at further distances from home without supervision.

In addition, mothers' ratings of the frequency with which their children initiate interaction with their peers in their natural environment were positively correlated with a variety of children's positive behaviors in the laboratory. Moreover, ratings of children's sensitivity and cooperation with peers at home were negatively related to children's disruptive behaviors in the laboratory. These results provide support for the ecological validity of the laboratory findings.

In summary, our studies suggest that parental management in the form of supervision can significantly increase the social-interactive competence of preschool children, especially young children with emerging social skills. Older children can benefit as well, but need less sustained assistance to be effective social play partners. Fathers as well as mothers are effective and competent as supervisory agents. The findings illustrate the utility of examining parental management strategies as a way of increasing children's peer involvement. Finally, the study suggests that parents could potentially be used as intervention agents for increasing young children's social skills.

CONCLUSIONS AND UNRESOLVED ISSUES

The review suggests that parental management can assume a variety of forms. Each of these aspects of management may contribute to the development of the child's peer relationships, but in different ways.

A developmental perspective on this issue is necessary since it is unlikely that all forms of parental management will occur with equal frequency across different points of development, nor is it likely that all forms of management will be beneficial at all phases of development.

In terms of frequency, it is clear that parents play a decreasing role as active arrangers of children's social contacts. Similarly it is likely that parental supervisory behavior in the form of direct coaching or teaching will decrease across age. In contrast, parental monitoring of children's activities will continue throughout childhood, but the particular form that this type of parental behavior assumes may change as the child develops. Supervision may involve direct observation and tracking of a child's activities in the preschool period but may shift to involve merely being aware of a child's social plans and activities during adolescence.

Parental management can produce both positive and negative consequences for children's relationships with their peers. While we have emphasized the positive aspects, the negative consequences merit attention as well. Parents who persist in actively managing various aspects of their children's social relationships beyond the time that the children can competently perform the necessary tasks may be inadvertently curtailing or retarding their children's social growth by denying them the opportunity to learn, practice, rehearse, and implement their emerging social skills independently.

The issue of bidirectionality of effects needs more attention. While it is often assumed that parental management strategies modify children's social behavior, it is equally plausible that parents may shift or alter their behavioral approaches in response to alterations in the children's age situation, personality, or social competence. A variety of strategies could be utilized to investigate this issue. For example, the use of sibling designs would permit comparison of parental supervisory behavior with different children. Through longitudinal analyses, sibs could be assessed at similar age levels. Second, changes in parental strategies for managing children's relationships could be monitored across different unrelated children. Related to this approach is one in which the same children are seen with a variety of different adults. Experimental approaches are useful as well, in which child behavior is systematically modified through training or instruction to assess the impact on adult behavior. Alternatively, the effects of experimentally induced shifts in adult managerial strategies on children's social relationships with peers could be examined. Together these approaches would place the causal status of parental managerial strategies in relation to peer competence on a firmer basis.

Research that addresses more fully how parental management strategies vary across social classes, ethnic groups, and families of varying compositions (e.g., single vs. intact) is needed. Recent evidence (Cochran & Riley, 1988) that indicates that variations in children's social networks depend on ethnicity, education, and family structure may, in fact, be in part mediated by differences in parental managerial strategies that impact on children's peer relationships and social networks. Finally, the facilitative role of nonparental kin such as aunts, uncles, or grandparents as well as nonkin in serving as mediators between the family and the social worlds of both peers and adults needs increased attention. The role of these nonfamily agents may be especially important in families where there is a reduced number of parents (e.g., single-parent homes) or in families under stress (Cochran & Riley, 1988; Tinsley & Parke, 1984).

It is clear that the concept of parental management is useful in our understanding of how children develop their patterns of peer relationships and social networks. By moving beyond description to process, our understanding of the role of parents in the development of children's social relationships and social networks will be increased.

REFERENCES

Bahr, H. M. (1976). The kinship role. In F. Nye (Ed.), *Role structure and analysis of the family.* Beverly Hills: Sage.

Baumrind, D. (1973). The development of instrumental competence through socialization. In A. D. Pick (Ed.), *Minnesota Symposium on Child Psychology* (Vol. 7). Minneapolis: University of Minnesota Press.

Baumrind, D. (1978). Parental disciplinary patterns and social competence in youth. *Youth & Society, 9,* 239–276.

Belson, W.A. (1975). *Juvenile theft: The causal factors.* London: Harper & Row.

Berg, M., & Medrich, E. A. (1980). Children in four neighborhoods: The physical environment and its effect on play and play patterns. *Environment & Behavior, 12,* 320–348.

Bhavnagri, N. (1987). *Parents as facilitators of preschool children's peer relationships.* Unpublished doctoral dissertation, University of Illinois at Champaign-Urbana.

Bhavnagri, N., & Parke, R. D. (1985, April). *Parents as facilitators of preschool peer interaction.* Paper presented at the biennial meeting of the Society for Research in Child Development, Toronto.

Bryant, B. (1985). The Neighborhood Walk: Sources of support in middle childhood. *Monographs of the Society for Research in Child Development, 50* (3, Serial No. 210).

Cochran, M., & Brassard, J.A. (1979). Children's development and children's social networks. *Child Development, 50,* 601–616.

Cochran, M., & Riley, D. (1988). Mother reports of children's personal networks: Antecedents, concomitants and consequences. In S. Salzinger, M. Hammer, & J. Antrobus (Eds.), *The social networks of children, adolescents and young adults.* Hillsdale, NJ: Erlbaum.

Coser, R. L. (1964). Authority and structural ambivalence. In R.L. Coser (Ed.), *The family, its structure and functions.* New York: St. Martins.

Gold, M. (1963). *Status forces in delinquent boys.* Ann Arbor: University of Michigan Press.

Gray, R. M., & Smith, T.C. (1960). Effect of unemployment on sex differences in attitudes toward the parental family. *Marriage & Family Living, 22,* 36–38.

Halverson, C. F., & Waldrop, M. F. (1970). Maternal behavior toward own and the other preschool children: The problem of "oneness." *Child Development, 41,* 839–845.

Hartup, W. W. (1979). The social worlds of childhood. *American Psychologist, 34,* 944–950.

Hartup, W. W. (1983). Peer relations. In E.M. Hetherington (Ed.), *Handbook of Child Psychology,* (Vol. 4, pp. 103–196). New York: Wiley. pp. 103–196.

Hoffman, M. L. (1960). Power assertion by the parent and its impact on the child. *Child Development, 31,* 129–143.

Jacobson, J. J., Tianen, R. L., Willie, D. E., & Aytch, D. M. (1986). Infant–mother attachment and early peer relations: The assessment of behavior in an interactive context. In E. C. Mueller & C. C. Cooper (Eds.), *Process and outcome in peer relationships.* (pp. 57–78). New York: Academic.

Joffe, C. E. (1977). *Friendly intruders.* Berkeley: University of California Press.

Krappmann, L. (1986, December). *Family relationships and peer relationships in middle childhood: An exploratory study of the association between children's integration into the social network of peers and family development.* Paper presented at the conference "Family Systems and Life-Span Development" at the Max Planck Institute for Human Development and Education, Berlin, Federal Republic of Germany.

Ladd, F. W., & Golter, B. S. (1988). Parents' management of preschooler's peer relations: Is it related to children's social competence? *Developmental Psychology, 24,* 109–117.

Lamb, M. E. (1977). Father–infant and mother–infant interaction in the first year of life. *Child Development, 48,* 167–181.

Levitt, M. J., Clark, M. C., & McDonnell, P. (1983, April). *Mother child interaction, comprehension of emotions and sharing behavior in toddlers.* Paper presented at the meeting of the Society of Research in Child Development, Detroit.

Lightfoot, S. L. (1978). *Worlds apart: Relationships between families and schools.* New York: Basic Books.

Lollis, S. P., & Ross, H. S. (1987, April). *Mothers' interventions in toddler-peer conflicts.* Poster presented at the biennial meeting of the Society for Research in Child Development, Baltimore.

MacDonald, K., & Parke, R. D. (1984). Bridging the gap: Parent-child play interaction and peer interactive competence. *Child Development, 55,* 1265–1277.

Medrich, E. A., Roizen, J. A., Rubin, V., & Buckley, S. (1982). *The serious business of growing up: A study of children's lives outside school.* Berkeley: University of California Press.

Moore, R., & Young, D. (1978). Children outdoors: Toward a social ecology of the landscape. In I. Altman & J. F. Wohlwill (Eds.), *Children and the Environment,* (pp. 83–130). New York: Plenum.

Murray, K., Webb, S., & Andrews, D. (1983, April). *The relationship between child & parental social competence.* Paper presented at the biennial meeting of the Society in Child Development, Detroit.

O'Donnell, L., & Steuve, A. (1983). Mothers as social agents: Structuring the community activities of school aged children. In H. Lopata & J. H. Pleck (Eds.), *Research in the interweave of social roles: Jobs and families: Vol. 3. Families and Jobs.* Greenwich, CT: JAI.

Oliveri, M. E., & Reiss, D. (1987). Social networks of family members: Distinctive roles of mothers and fathers. *Sex Roles, 17,* 719–736.

Parke, R. D. (1978). Children's home environments: Social and cognitive effects. In I. Altman & J. F. Wohlwill (Eds.), *Children and the environment.* New York: Plenum.

Parke, R. D., MacDonald, K. B., Beitel, A., & Bhavnagri, N. (1987). The role of the family in the development of peer relationships. In R. DeV. Peters & R. J. McMahon (Eds.), *Social learning and systems approaches to marriage and the family.* New York: Brunner-Mazel.

Parke, R. D., & Tinsley, B. R. (1982). The early environment of the at-risk infant: Expanding the social context. In D. Bricker (Ed.), *Intervention with at risk and handicapped infants: From research to application* (pp. 153–177). Baltimore: University Park Press.

Parke, R. D., & Tinsley, B. J. (1984). Fatherhood: Historical and contemporary perspectives. In K. A. McCluskey & H. W. Reese (Eds.), *Life span developmental psychology: Historical and generational effects.* New York: Academic Press.

Patterson, G. R., & Stouthamer–Loeber, M. (1984). The correlation of family management practices and delinquency. *Child Development, 55,* 1299–1307.

Powell, T. H., Salzberg, C. L., Rule, S., & Letzkowitz, J. S. (1984). Teaching mentally retarded children to play with their siblings using parents as trainers. *Education & Treatment of Children,*

Power, T. G., & Parke, R. D. (1982). Play as a context for early learning: Lab and home analysis. In I. E. Sigel & I. M. Laosa (Eds.), *The family as a learning environment* (pp. 223–241). New York: Plenum.

Pulkkinen, L. (1981). Search for alternatives to aggression in Finland. In A. P. Medstein & M. Segall (Eds.), *Aggression in global perspective.* New York: Pergamon.

Putallaz, M. (1987). Maternal behavior and children's sociometric status. *Child Development, 58,* 32–340.

Rubin, Z., & Sloman, J. (1984). How parents influence their children's friendships. In M. Lewis (Ed.), *Beyond the dyad.* New York: Plenum.

Schiavo, R. S., & Solomon, S. K. (1981). *The effect of summer contact on preschoolers' friendships with classmates.* Unpublished manuscript, Wellesley College.

Schiavo, R. S., Solomon, S. K., Evers, C., & Cohen, W. (1981). *Maintenance of friendships among preschoolers.* Unpublished manuscript, Wellesley College.

Sroufe, L. A., & Fleeson, J. (1986). Attachment and the construction of relationships. In W. W. Hartup & Z. Rubin (Eds.), *Relationships and development.* Hillsdale, NJ: Erlbaum.

Steinberg, L. (1986). Latchkey children and susceptibility to peer pressure: An ecological analysis. *Developmental Psychology, 22,* 433–439.

Tinsley, B. R., & Parke, R. D. (1984). Grandparents as support and socialization agents. In M. Lewis (Ed.), *Beyond the dyad.* New York: Plenum.

Wilson, H. (1980). Parental supervision: A neglected aspect of delinquency. *British Journal of Criminology, 20,* 203–235.

Yogman, M. W. (1982). Development of the father–infant relationship. In H. Fitzgerald, B. Lester, & M. W. Yogman (Eds.), *Theory and research in behavioral pediatrics* (Vol. 1, pp. 221–279). New York: Plenum.

CHAPTER 11

The School–Nonschool Ecology of Early Adolescent Friendships

BARTON J. HIRSCH AND DAVID L. DUBOIS

There is no reason to believe that the developmental transition from childhood to adolescence is an easy one. Few areas of life are untouched. All kinds of bodily changes are detected, some of which are mysterious or downright embarrassing. The relatively protected elementary school environment is abandoned for the more demanding and impersonal setting of the junior high or middle school. Adolescent friendships pose new challenges of exploring intimacy and sexuality. And family ties must be renegotiated on the basis of increased independence. It is no wonder that Hamburg (1974) argued that, "even for the modal individual, early adolescence is intrinsically a period of great stress, impoverished coping skills, and consequent high vulnerability" (p. 101).

Most adolescents make it through this difficult period without serious impairment (e.g., Abramowitz, Petersen, & Schulenberg, 1984; Berndt & Hawkins, 1985; Hirsch & Rapkin, 1987; Nottelmann, 1987), but some do not. Moreover, since general adaptive failure during childhood and adolescence is among the best predictors of adult psychopathology (Sroufe & Rutter, 1984), problems during this transition may have more than short-term negative consequences for psychological well-being. It is therefore quite important to identify those adolescents who are not doing well and to specify underlying processes that account for differential outcome.

The quality of peer social support may well have an important effect on adaptive success. Findings from recent research consistently reveal a beneficial impact for social support (Cohen & Syme, 1985; Sarason & Sarason, 1985), though little of this research was conducted with adolescent samples. The omission is striking, as early adolescent friendships have often been thought to have a unique intensity (Berndt, 1982; see also Berndt, this volume). The creation of friendships in such a changing psychosocial context is a formidable developmental task in itself (Hirsch & Renders, 1986). Moreover, supports provided by peers can enable adolescents to cope with stressors in multiple spheres of life (Hirsch & Reischl, 1985). Consistent with these ideas, recent studies of adolescents have found the quality of peer ties to be related to psychological well-being (Cauce, 1986; Greenberg, Siegel, & Leitch, 1983; Hirsch & Rapkin, 1987). There is also growing evidence that positive peer ties can facilitate adjustment to junior high school (Fenzel & Blyth, 1986; Simmons, Carlton-Ford, & Blyth, 1986; Berndt, this volume).

School, in turn, may well play an important role in the ecology of early adolescent friendships. But this role may exacerbate rather than alleviate the stressors that early adolescents must confront. The junior high school (JHS)—the dominant school setting for most early adolescents—is not highly regarded in much of the literature on early adolescence. The JHS is frequently considered to have failed to provide a bridge between the more self-contained, protective environment of the elementary school and the departmentalized, more anonymous structure of high school. As Lipsitz (1977) declared: "The lack of fit between institution and client is more painfully obvious at this level than at any other in our public education system" (p. 92).

One of the complaints against the JHS is that it may decrease social support available for coping with the many demands of early adolescence. Nowadays, there typically is no intact peer group across classes. A student can be with one set of classmates during science and an entirely different set during social studies. This structure appears to set up *obstacles* to developing and maintaining friendships in the school setting, particularly given the influx of new classmates from different elementary schools. If JHS does have a negative effect on peer support, this is an important argument for redesigning schools. Indeed, an alternative structure already exists, at least in theory. The middle school emphasizes a school-within-school approach that, in part, provides for relatively more intact peer groups over the course of the school day and week (e.g., Alexander & George, 1981). Unfortunately, many middle schools do not actually implement the underlying educational model. The two types of schools often differ from each other in name only, making comparative evaluation a difficult enterprise. However, if the JHS were found not to have a negative effect on peer relations, this would lead us to doubt whether the two school models actually differ in this domain and thus undercut part of the rationale for middle schools.[1] Thus in addition to its theoretical importance, research addressing these issues bears on the ongoing policy debate on how best to organize schools for this age group.

Our aim in this chapter is to consider the linkage between school and peer ties in early adolescence. We begin by examining how the transition to junior high school affects peer friendships. We then explore the ecological relation of school and nonschool peer ties. In both sections, findings are reported from a cross-sectional sample of approximately 300 JHS

[1] We do not address other potentially important differences between the JHS and middle school that are less relevant to the concerns of this chapter. Furthermore, it should be clear that peer relationships are not the only outcome of interest to advocates of either model.

students. (A more complete description of the sample is reported in DuBois & Hirsch, 1987.)

OLD FRIENDS, NEW FRIENDS

Although the rationale for the alleged negative effect of JHS on peer ties has not been articulated in much detail, there are two principal hypotheses that presumably form the core of this position. Both center primarily on potential obstacles to peer ties presented by the lack of an intact peer group across classes. The first asserts that JHS will disrupt existing peer ties. An underlying premise is that some important friendship maintenance function is served by continuing to share classroom experiences side by side. The second hypothesis asserts that JHS will prevent early adolescents from forming new friendships. Presumably there is insufficient time to get to know others and "break the ice" in just one or two classes, a difficulty that may be compounded by the fact that the classes are typically not characterized by extensive peer interaction.

These hypotheses would lead us to expect a decline in the perceived quality of peer ties during the transition to junior high school. Some cross-sectional studies have found a decline in friendship ratings around seventh grade (LaGaipa, 1979; Sharbanay, Gershoni, & Hofman, 1981). In longitudinal research, Berndt and Hawkins (1985) found a decline in ratings of social self-esteem and a decline in the number of close friends, but an increase in intimacy and contact with friends by the end of seventh grade. Abramowitz and colleagues (1984) reported positive change from sixth to seventh grade.

These mixed findings may reflect several different factors that can affect friendships at this time. Developmentally, for example, there should be an increase in friendship domains such as self-disclosure. On the other hand, it is possible that JHS or the school transition per se might disrupt peer ties, leading to a decrease in support. Failure to differentiate such factors could lead to serious misunderstandings in theory, research, and practice.

As a first step toward untangling this issue, as part of a longitudinal study of the transition to JHS, we constructed a measure of peer social support that we did not believe would be subject to developmental effects (Hirsch & Rapkin, 1987). Items assessed both behavioral aspects of friendships (e.g., "I have a friend over to my house often") and evaluative components (e.g., "I feel that my friends really like me"). In order to check that the format of the measure would be sensitive to change over time, we included two additional items on the questionnaire that were expected to demonstrate developmental increases from sixth through seventh grade: engaging in intimate self-disclosure and involvement with the opposite sex. These two items, in fact, did significantly increase over time. However, on the measure of peer support itself, there was an increase in peer social support only for Black students of high academic competence. There was no significant change on this variable for other Black students or for White students regardless of gender or academic competence.

These initial results suggested that entering JHS does not lead to an overall disruption in peer support. With the present sample, we looked somewhat more directly at the hypothesized disruption of old friendships and difficulty in forming new friendships in JHS.

We found that most adolescents maintained close ties with several elementary school friends. More than half of the sample (58%) reported that they had stayed close friends with most of those individuals who had been their close friends in sixth grade. Approximately one-third (35%) indicated that they had not done so, and a small group (7%) reported having had no close friends in sixth grade. Similarly, Berndt (this volume) found that about half of the close friendships identified by students in sixth grade were still close friendships after entering JHS.

A comparable picture emerged when we inquired as to the current status of their relationship with the student who had been their best friend at the end of sixth grade. More than half of the sample reported that their sixth-grade best friend either was still their best friend (29%) or was still a close friend (28%). The next most common response was that they were still friends (21%). Only 14% reported that they hardly ever saw their sixth-grade best friend any more. (For an additional 9%, their best friend had moved out of town.) It is quite important to know the extent to which close, supportive ties are maintained, even if the individuals no longer consider themselves to be "best friends." Our findings suggest that most adolescents remain good friends with this person. Friendship stability also appears to play an important role in who becomes a new best friend in JHS. Among those students who no longer had the same best friend as they did when in sixth grade, 41% reported that their current best friend was someone who had been a close friend in elementary school. None of these findings are consistent with the hypothesis that JHS massively disrupts existing friendships. Moreover, since there appears to be considerable fluctuation in adolescent friendships to begin with (see Epstein, 1986, for a review), a significant portion of the friendship instability reflected in our findings may have had little or nothing to do with the transition to JHS.

Most students also were able to establish new, close friendships in JHS. More than half of the sample (59%) reported that they had gone to a different elementary school than most of their present close friends. An additional 10% reported that the majority of their present close school friends had been in their elementary school, but that they had not been close friends at that time. Despite the obstacles that JHS appears to set in their path, most adolescents appeared to succeed in making new close friendships.

Neither hypothesis concerning the effect of JHS on peer ties is supported by these data. We now consider some of the underlying processes by which JHS students may maintain old friendships and make new ones.

Several factors might account for how students are able to maintain old friendships. Given that close friendships had already been formed, they may be less dependent on school for maintaining their involvement. A variety of important nonschool activities may regularly occur, perhaps embedded in a peer network, which do not need school-based reinforcement to continue. Alternatively, it is possible that some shared classroom membership is important for maintaining friendships in early adolescence and that this happens often enough for several close friendships to be maintained. The fact that they continue to have class(es) together may arise out of happenstance or may result from common interests (e.g., German) or aptitude (e.g., math). For individuals who are already close friends, being in only one class together is probably sufficient to maintain the relationship (if this context is necessary at all). Finally, given that adolescents tend to have fairly dense, interconnected friendship networks, it is possible that being in a class with one member of the network can help to maintain ties with other members.

Similar processes may enable JHS students to meet and make new friends. It is likely that there will be several students who are in more than one class together, possibly for more than one semester. It could be (though we do not know) that it is from this specific pool of classmates that new friends are drawn. There are also some classes that tend to involve more direct interpersonal interaction among students (e.g., science lab, gym), which may foster friendship development.[2] Network factors may also come into play, as one acquaintance or friend can provide introduction to an entire peer group (Hirsch & Renders, 1986).

Thus although JHS appears to present structural obstacles to peer friendships, there also appear to be gaps in the structure. We have suggested several possible gaps; whether or not adolescents actually make use of them is a matter for empirical investigation.

We hypothesized that interaction with school friends outside of school may play an important role in the peer networks of early adolescents. This suggests the need for a broader ecological focus that takes into account interaction with friends that occurs both during and outside of the regular school day. An initial exploration of the school–nonschool ecology of peer ties is presented in the next section.

SCHOOL AND NONSCHOOL PEER TIES

Peer friendships can provide a wide variety of important social supports both in and outside of school. In school, peer support can enhance a sense of community and social integration. Peers also can provide useful support in dealing with academic tasks or other school requirements, can provide

[2] Epstein and Karweit (1983) discuss a variety of other school variables that may affect peer ties.

pleasant socializing interactions, can be a source of emotional support in the face of stressful experiences with teachers, and so on (cf. Asp & Garbarino, 1983). School-based peer support is thus of intrinsic importance.

Extending school ties with peers to nonschool settings should also be considered an important adaptive feature of adolescence. Interaction with peers outside of school, rather than just in school, makes peer support accessible in a wider variety of settings and is likely to foster stronger bonds that increase the value of supportive exchanges. For example, some adolescents may be more successful in developing closeness in their friendships outside of school where they are relatively free to pursue those activities that allow their most valued characteristics (e.g., skill at a particular craft) to become known to and appreciated by others. As mentioned previously, nonschool activity may also play an important role in maintaining friendship ties between students who are separated from one another during the school day. More generally, nonschool peer activities can help in negotiating new social identities and achieving increased independence from the family, two fundamental tasks of adolescence. Bronfenbrenner (1979) used the term *mesosystem* to refer to linkages between settings, such as school–nonschool, and emphasized the developmental significance of the individual's evolving understanding of and capacity to impact this ecology (see Tietjen, this volume, for a more detailed discussion of Bronfenbrenner's ecological model). Nevertheless, there is a paucity of research that examines the relation between school and nonschool peer ties in early adolescence.

In this context, we began by attempting to classify important types of activities and social settings that characterize peer relations during early adolescence. Students responded to a set of 20 items that tapped how frequently they engaged in a variety of activities with their best school friend. Activities were included that could occur only in school or only outside of school. Because of their importance to social support, we included other items that measured the extent of self-disclosure that could occur in either setting.

A principal components analysis of these items revealed four distinct components of activity (see DuBois & Hirsch, 1987, for details). As shown in Table 11.1, in-school and nonschool activities were neatly separated from each other and from self-disclosing conversations. The breakdown of nonschool activity into structured and unstructured kinds of contacts suggests the importance of ecological boundaries within nonschool settings. Structured nonschool activities (e.g., intramural sports) can serve as a first step beyond seeing a friend in the school setting only, with unstructured nonschool activity (e.g., home visits) following later. A differentiated perspective toward school and nonschool settings might help to uncover a hierarchy of setting boundaries that are typically crossed during the development of school friendships. We will have more to say about this later.

We next considered the frequency with which they engaged in out-of-school activities with school friends as opposed to friends who did not

TABLE 11.1. Means and Standard Deviations of Activities with Best School Friend

	M	SD
In-school		
Talk in class	3.5	1.1
Eat lunch together	3.3	1.2
Sports or games played during the regular school day	2.3	1.3
Talk between classes or before school starts	3.8	0.7
Structured nonschool		
After-school activities run by the school	2.0	1.2
Group activities not run by the school	2.2	1.2
Activities involving student's family	1.9	1.1
Shopping	2.2	1.1
Go to movies	2.3	1.0
Parties or dances	2.3	1.1
Unstructured nonschool		
Get together outside of the regular school day	3.2	1.0
"Hang out" together after school	2.9	1.2
Talk on telephone	3.3	1.0
Visit each other's houses	2.9	1.1
Play sports or games outside of the regular school day	2.6	1.3
Self-disclosing conversation		
Talk about the opposite sex	3.5	1.0
Talk about very private or personal concerns	3.0	1.2
Talk about a problem one of them is having	3.0	1.2
Talk about their friendship	2.5	1.3
Talk about personal matters concerning one of their families	2.8	1.2

Note: Four choices were available for each item: never/rarely (1); once a month (2); once a week (3); almost every day (4).

attend their school. For this sample, more than four-fifths reported seeing most of their school friends outside of school either almost daily (55%) or once a week (29%). In contrast, less than half of the students (46%) reported getting together at least once a week with neighborhood friends who did not attend their school. It is possible that more frequent contact with nonschool neighborhood friends might characterize samples in communities with more of a split between public and private schools, or where school boundaries bisect neighborhoods. Among this sample, nonetheless, it is clear that school friends are frequently seen outside of school.

It is also apparent that early adolescents place a premium on friendships with school friends that extend to nonschool settings. Almost four-fifths reported that it was true (41%) or mostly true (37%) that they felt closer to school friends with whom they spent a lot of time outside of school. A similar proportion (77%) indicated that they knew more about school friends whom they saw frequently outside of school.

Do school and nonschool interactions play different roles in the friendship development process? We asked students to select from among several circumstances the one in which they had met or become close with most of their school friends or their best school friend. Almost half of the students chose being in a class together as the circumstance in which they had met most of their school friends (see Table 11.2). A similar proportion indicated that this was how they had met their best school friend. There was also some indication of the importance of nonschool activity for meeting school friends. Almost one-third chose living in the same neighborhood (a nonschool circumstance) or hanging around with the same friends (a circumstance often, though not exclusively, tied to nonschool settings) as the reason they had met these friends.

TABLE 11.2. Percentage Breakdowns of Primary Circumstances for Developing Different Features of School Friendships

Circumstance	Most School Friends	Best School Friend
Meeting		
In a class together	47.6	47.3
In a school-run activity	1.6	1.1
In an activity run by someone other than the school	2.1	1.6
Hung around with same friend(s)	20.3	14.9
Lived in same neighborhood	9.1	15.4
Families knew each other	3.2	3.2
Other	16.0	16.5
Becoming Close		
During classes	28.9	25.3
During the regular school day, but outside of classes	13.9	8.4
In school-run activities	1.6	1.6
In activities run by someone other than the school	2.7	2.6
Dyadic meetings outside of school	26.2	38.9
With other friends outside of school	18.7	15.3
Other	8.0	7.9

Note: These data were obtained from seventh graders and ninth graders (approximately two-thirds of the entire sample). Figures are percentages and due to rounding may not add to 100.0 for an item.

Nonschool circumstances were more frequently chosen as the context for becoming close with school friends. An exclusively nonschool circumstance was chosen by almost half of the students for becoming close with most school friends and by more than half for becoming close with their best school friend. Dyadic and group meetings with friends outside of school were the most common choices, with dyadic meetings being particularly likely to be the context for becoming close with the best school friend. These findings may reflect a tendency for early adolescents to prefer or at least make better use of more structured environments, such as the school setting, for initiating friendships. Friendships once established may then become close most easily when school constraints are no longer present. This interpretation is consistent with the hierarchy of friendship settings that we discussed in connection with Table 11.1.

Although our findings suggest that nonschool activity with school friends is relatively common (see also Blyth, Hill, & Thiel, 1982), they also indicate that some children experienced considerable difficulty transforming in-school acquaintances to out-of-school friends. Hirsch (1985) presented a case study of an adolescent boy with low self-esteem that illustrates this latter situation. The boy reported several friends at school, but only limited contact with friends outside of school. Of his five school friends, he considered only the two he saw outside of school to be close friends. He spent the most nonschool time with his best friend; however, this amounted to only 3 hours weekly, focused almost entirely around playing sports, and took place almost always at the friend's initiative. His girlfriend was the only friend with whom he could talk about personal concerns, something he valued doing, but he never saw her outside of school nor expected to do so in the future. If engaging in nonschool activities with friends is important, then we need to understand why adolescents such as this boy are unable to do so or do so only with difficulty. As a first step in this direction, we constructed a 17-item scale that tapped the degree to which a variety of person and environmental factors inhibited nonschool contact with school friends.

A principal components analysis identified four components (see DuBois & Hirsch, 1987). The items loading on each of the components are presented in Table 11.3. The identification of a social skills component is consistent with the literature that emphasizes social skills deficits as a source of difficulty in adolescent peer relations (e.g., Adams, 1983; Argyle, 1985). Many of the social skills obstacles relate to skill and confidence in initiating nonschool contact with school friends. They seem related most closely to the component of social skills that Adams (1983) refers to as belief in the power of self-initiation. Friendships also provide opportunities to develop relationship skills (cf. Sullivan, 1953; Youniss, 1980), and benefits may accrue most readily when activity with friends occurs in situations more diverse and interpersonally intimate than those likely to be found in school. Thus some adolescents may miss out on an important opportunity to enhance their

TABLE 11.3. Means and Standard Deviations of Obstacles to Nonschool Activity with School Friends

	M	SD
Social skill problems		
I'm not sure what to ask them to do	1.8	0.9
I'm afraid they won't want to if I ask	1.7	0.8
I do not like to do the same things outside of school as they do	1.8	0.9
I'm not sure how to go about asking	1.6	0.8
I am not popular with their other friends	1.8	0.8
I don't know them well enough	1.6	0.8
There is never a good time to ask	1.7	0.7
They don't ask me to	2.0	1.0
I'm not good enough at the things they like to do outside of school	1.6	0.7
Competing activities		
I see enough of them during the regular school day	1.9	0.9
I have too many other things to do outside of school	2.3	1.0
I already do a lot of things with friends who do not go to this school	2.1	1.0
I already do a lot of things with my family	2.2	0.9
Home conflicts		
I live too far away from them	2.4	1.0
I would be embarrassed for them to come to my house	1.4	0.8
Moral concerns		
My parents do not allow me	1.7	1.0
I have different opinions than they do about drugs and alcohol	1.9	1.0

Note: Students were asked to report their degree of agreement that each obstacle was a reason why they sometimes ended up not getting together outside of school with school friends. Four choices were available for each item: strongly disagree (1); disagree (2); agree (3); strongly agree (4).

social competence via nonschool activity because they have actual or perceived social competence deficiencies to begin with.

The other three types of obstacles are related to features of the social or physical environment. They focus on home and parents (home conflicts; moral concerns), and on competition from other nonschool activities, such as interaction with family members or with peers not attending the same school (competing activities). The means for the items loading on these scales are generally larger than those for the social skills items.

The findings suggest the importance of situational obstacles to nonschool contact and their distinctiveness from the type of self-related obstacles represented by social skill problems. Particular types of friendships may be affected more by one type of obstacle than the other. For example, for best or close friends, the importance of social skills obstacles is likely to be diminished because of increased familiarity and closeness in the friendship. It also appears important to distinguish between types of situational obstacles. Some, such as those for the competing activities component, may most likely represent personal choices and alternative means for pursuing nonschool social contact, whereas others, such as those associated with the moral concerns or home conflicts components, may typically be indications of more problematic constraints.

Findings from this phase of our research are consistent with the hypothesized importance of nonschool activity. Most, though not all, JHS students appear able to transform in-school acquaintances to out-of-school friends, and nonschool activity is tied strongly to perceptions of familiarity and closeness with school friends. Indeed, whereas school is seen as the context for initiating friendships, nonschool activities are seen as the vehicle for turning those ties into close friendships. A variety of obstacles can make engaging in nonschool activity problematic, some of which are due to social skills problems, others of which are due to moral concerns, home-related conflicts, or competing activities.

It is important for future researchers to consider how school variables can affect the ease with which friendships are initiated in school, as well as the subsequent permeability of the school–nonschool boundary. Such research is important not only because it can increase our understanding of the ecology of adolescent friendships, but also because it can play a critical role in evaluating alternative educational practices.

One issue to be considered is the potential effect of structural or social climate differences among schools. For example, as mentioned earlier, the school-within-school approach of the middle school helps to provide for relatively more intact peer groups over the course of the school day and week. This practice should increase peer support within the school setting when the student has a good "fit" with classmates. (Sometimes students do not have a good fit; see Hirsch & Renders, 1986.) To this end, school curricula that include less traditional academic activities (e.g., crafts) or programs emphasizing common interests and concerns among students may also facilitate friendship formation by helping students to discover areas of fit between themselves and other members of the class. Finally, more cohesive classrooms should facilitate the formation of friendships within the school setting, independent of peer group intactness across classes (cf. Moos, 1979). These are all testable hypotheses.

One also can and should examine whether friendships formed in school proceed to develop beyond the school setting. Systematic variation in which friendships extend to nonschool settings may reflect important school variables, such as the kind and extent of classroom interaction. Hirsch (1985) suggested that nonschool contact among friends could be facilitated by curricula that encourage teachers (coaches, club leaders, etc.) to make assignments that involve students in out-of-school group activities. Indeed, the small minority of students who reported meeting or becoming close with school friends in school-run activities (see Table 11.2) suggests that schools can profitably play a more active role in facilitating nonschool friendship ties among students.

The role that school plays in the social support process may vary among subgroups of adolescents. The school factors discussed previously should be most salient to those adolescents with poor social skills; they may be most in need of and benefit most from school environments that foster peer friendships and the extension of these friendships to nonschool settings. Special attention should also be paid to adolescents under high levels of stress (e.g., parental discord, serious illness), as the stress-buffering hypothesis asserts that support is most health protective for that group (cf. Cohen & Wills, 1985).

We have focused on the extension of school-based peer ties to nonschool settings, and have found that such extension may promote familiarity and closeness among friends. It is worth noting that these benefits may affect the quality of peer ties in school as well as outside of school. For example, since nonschool contact provides friendship groups with an important base of shared experiences, students who do not see their friends outside of school may be more likely to feel left out or on the fringes of friendship groups that get together during school. This suggests the importance of paying attention to the possibility of reciprocal relationships between school and nonschool peer ties in future work.

CONCLUSION

Although there probably is not a global decline in well-being during early adolescence and the transition to JHS, there likely are subgroups of adolescents who do not do well at this time. Peer support may be one of the underlying processes that has an effect on adaptive outcomes at this age. School may play an important role in the peer support process, but the hypothesis that JHS has a substantial negative effect on the quality of peer ties is not well supported in the relatively few studies that have been conducted. Whether JHS is a more or less effective institution than middle school for promoting supportive peer friendships is another question and one for which there are even fewer data. As a step toward more differentiated conceptualization and research in this area, we have discussed the place of school in the ecology of early adolescent friendships. We have been especially concerned with the school–nonschool boundary.

Our own findings should be regarded as preliminary and exploratory. They clearly suggest the need for further research on school and nonschool settings and peer networks as contexts for meeting new friends, developing close friendships, and maintaining those friendships over time. The study of these factors in combination might prove especially valuable. For example, in a school that makes it difficult to meet new friends or to cross the school–nonschool boundary, early adolescents may rely more on friends from elementary school, with fewer new friends who did not attend the earlier school. By contrast, in a school that facilitates the development of new friendships and makes the school–nonschool boundary more permeable, friendships developed in the new school may dominate the peer network of early adolescents. These or other school differences could have significant effects on peer support and psychological well-being. On the other hand, these different patterns may each provide a reasonable balance of old and new friends for most students. This may especially prove to be the case if students progressively meet and develop new friendships through the course of their stay in the first type of school. Research on these issues is critical for increasing our understanding of the developmental ecology of adolescent friendships and for carefully designing supportive school environments for this important age group.

REFERENCES

Abramowitz, R., Petersen, A., & Schulenberg, J. (1984). Changes in self-image during early adolescence. In D. Offer, E. Ostrov, & K. Howard (Eds.), *Patterns of adolescent self-image* (pp. 19–28). San Francisco: Jossey-Bass.

Adams, G. (1983). Social competence during adolescence: Social sensitivity, locus of control, empathy, and peer popularity. *Journal of Youth & Adolescence, 12,* 203–211.

Alexander, W., & George, P. (1981). *The exemplary middle school.* New York: Holt, Rinehart, & Winston.

Argyle, M. (1985). Social behavior problems and social skills training in adolescence. In B. H. Schneider, K. H. Rubin, & J. E. Ledingham (Eds.), *Children's peer relations: Issues in assessment and intervention* (pp. 207–224). New York: Springer-Verlag.

Asp, E., & Garbarino, J. (1983). Social support networks and the schools. In J. Whittaker & J. Garbarino (Eds.), *Social support networks: Informal helping in the human services* (pp. 251–297). New York: Aldine.

Berndt, T. (1982). The features and effects of friendship in early adolescence. *Child Development, 53,* 1447–1460.

Berndt, T., & Hawkins, J. (1985). *The effects of friendships on students' adjustment after the transition to junior high school.* Paper presented at the meeting of the American Educational Research Association, Chicago.

Blyth, D., Hill, J., & Thiel, K. (1982). Early adolescents' significant others: Grade and gender differences in perceived relationships with familial and nonfamilial adults and young people. *Journal of Youth & Adolescence, 11,* 425–450.

Bronfenbrenner, U. (1979). *The ecology of human development.* Cambridge, MA: Harvard University Press.

Cauce, A. (1986). Social networks and social competence: Exploring the effects of early adolescent friendships. *American Journal of Community Psychology, 14,* 607–628.

Cohen, S., & Syme, L. (Eds.). (1985). *Social support and health.* New York: Academic.

Cohen, S., & Wills, T. (1985). Stress, social support, and the buffering hypothesis. *Psychological Bulletin, 98,* 310–357.

DuBois, D. L., & Hirsch, B. J. (1987). *School/nonschool friendship patterns and self-esteem in early adolescence.* Manuscript submitted for publication.

Epstein, J. L. (1986). Friendship selection: Developmental and environmental influences. In E. Mueller & C. R. Cooper (Eds.), *Process and outcome in peer relationships* (pp. 129–160). Orlando, FL: Academic.

Epstein, J. L., & Karweit, N. (Eds.). (1983). *Friends in school: Patterns of selection and influence in secondary schools.* New York: Academic.

Fenzel, L., & Blyth, D. (1986). Individual adjustment to school transitions: An exploration of the role of supportive peer relations. *Journal of Early Adolescence, 6,* 315–329.

Greenberg, M. T., Siegel, J. M., & Leitch, C. J. (1983). The nature and importance of attachment relationships to parents and peers during adolescence. *Journal of Youth & Adolescence, 12,* 373–386.

Hamburg, B. (1974). Early adolescence: A specific and stressful stage of the life cycle. In G. Coelho, D. Hamburg, & J. Adams (Eds.), *Coping and adaptation* (pp. 101–124). New York: Basic.

Hirsch, B. J. (1985). Adolescent coping and support across multiple social environments. *American Journal of Community Psychology, 13,* 381–392.

Hirsch, B. J., & Rapkin, B. D. (1987). The transition to junior high school: A longitudinal study of self-esteem, psychological symptomatology, school life, and social support. *Child Development, 58,* 1235–1243.

Hirsch, B. J., & Reischl, T. M. (1985). Social networks and developmental psychopathology: A comparison of adolescent children of a depressed, arthritic, or normal parent. *Journal of Abnormal Psychology, 94,* 272–281.

Hirsch, B. J., & Renders, R. (1986). The challenge of adolescent friendship: A study of Lisa and her friends. In S. Hobfoll (Ed.), *Stress, social support, and women* (pp. 17–27). Washington, DC: Hemisphere.

LaGaipa, J. (1979). A developmental study of the meaning of friendship in adolescence. *Journal of Adolescence, 2,* 201–213.

Lipsitz, J. (1977). *Growing up forgotten.* Lexington, MA: Heath.

Moos, R. H. (1979). *Evaluating educational environments.* San Francisco: Jossey-Bass.

Nottelmann, E. D. (1987). Competence and self-esteem during transition from childhood to adolescence. *Developmental Psychology, 23,* 441–450.

Sarason, I., & Sarason, B. (Eds.). (1985). *Social support: Theory, research and application.* The Hague: Martinus Nijhof.

Sharbanay, R., Gershoni, R., & Hofman, J. (1981). Girlfriend, boyfriend: Age and sex differences in intimate friendship. *Developmental Psychology, 17,* 800–808.

Simmons, R., Carlton-Ford, S., & Blyth, D. (1986). Predicting how a child will cope with the transition to junior high school. In R. Lerner & T. Foch (Eds.), *Biological-psychological interactions in early adolescence: A life-span perspective* (pp. 325–375). New York: Erlbaum.

Sroufe, L. A., & Rutter, M. (1984). The domain of developmental psychopathology. *Child Development, 55,* 17–29.

Sullivan, H. S. (1953). *The interpersonal theory of psychiatry.* New York: Norton.

Youniss, J. (1980). *Parents and peers in social development.* Chicago: University of Chicago Press.

PART 5

Implications of Supportive Involvements

CHAPTER 12

Social Support as a Protective Factor for Children in Stress

IRWIN N. SANDLER, PAUL MILLER, JEROME SHORT, AND SHARLENE A. WOLCHIK

INTRODUCTION

There is considerable evidence that stressful life experiences are a major contributor to the mental and physical health problems of children and youth (Garmezy, 1983; Rutter, 1983). However, some children seem to be relatively resilient, resisting the negative effects of life stressors, and understanding the sources of this resilience is an area of growing research interest (Cowen & Work, 1988). Several studies have reported that social support received by children is one important resource that protects them against the negative effects of life stressors (Garmezy, 1983; Sandler, Gersten, Reynolds, Kallgren, & Ramirez, in press; Werner & Smith, 1982). The question to be addressed in this chapter concerns the process by which this occurs; how children's social support reduces the negative effects that stressful situations have on their psychological adjustment.

The conceptual framework employed defines social support as a source of resilience to the extent that it positively affects intervening processes by which stressful situations lead to maladjustment in children and adolescents. In order to understand how support helps protect against the negative effects of stress, it is necessary to discuss the processes by which stress leads to maladjustment. Thus we will first discuss contrasting conceptualizations of the nature of stressful situations and of social support. Alternative models by which support may prevent, moderate, or counteract the negative effects of stressful situations are then discussed. While these models allow us to specify predictions about the effects of support on maladjustment, they do not address the processes by which these effects occur. Most of the research on the effects of social support has been guided by testing predictions from these models, and very little work has considered

This research was supported by NIMH grant MH39246-01 to establish a Prevention Research Center at Arizona State University.

the intervening processes. In contrast, the major focus of this chapter will be to consider three possible intervening processes: increasing self-esteem, increasing situationally appropriate control perceptions, and increasing the perceived security of social relations.

Conceptualization of Stressful Situations

Three important foci of current models of stressful situations can be identified: (1) the role of cognitive appraisals of the situations in leading to stressful effects; (2) the concept that stressful situations are an ongoing stream of person–environment transactions; and (3) the concept that stressors lead to strains in important role activities.

Lazarus and Folkman (1984) conceptualize stress as "a particular relationship between the person and the environment that is appraised by the person as taxing or exceeding his or her resources and endangering his or her well-being" (p. 19). According to this conceptualization, evaluations or appraisals of person–environment transactions are the critical mediators of stressful arousal. They conceptualize two kinds of appraisals. *Primary appraisal of stress* refers to whether the event involves some existing or threatened future harm or loss to the person; either physical harm, decrease in self-esteem, or loss of a valued personal relationship. Alternatively, an event could be seen as a challenge, with the expectation of future benefit. *Secondary appraisal* refers to evaluations of what can be done to manage the situation: What are the coping options? Can the individual apply them? Will they be successful? From this perspective, support may reduce the negative effects of stress by decreasing stressful appraisals.

The conceptualization of stressors as ongoing person–environment transactions has several implications. Felner, Farber, and Primavera (1980) proposed that major stressors consist of a series of smaller events that occur over time, each of which presents coping tasks for the individual. Illustratively, Sandler, Wolchik, Braver, and Fogas (1986) identified 62 events that occurred to children of divorce. In a cross-sectional study of two separate samples of children of divorce they found that these divorce-related changes were significantly correlated with children's psychological symptomatology. A second implication of the concept of transactional processes as developed by Lazarus and Launier (1978) is that the person and the environment are involved in a dynamic reciprocal interaction. Children under stress may actively seek out support, or the occurrence of stress may disrupt the social network, thus decreasing the opportunity to receive support. From this perspective support might be helpful by assisting coping with adaptive tasks, preventing the disruption of the social network, and by preventing the occurrence of the smaller stress events that often follow major stressors.

A third conceptualization of environmental stress is provided by Pearlin's concept of role strain. Pearlin (1983a) proposed that people organize their lives to a great extent around key social roles (e.g., friend, student, son, daughter), and that these role activities are invested with great importance. When people encounter difficulties in their role activities, it is a source of great concern to them; these role difficulties are significant sources of stress. Pearlin proposed further that the stressful impact of life events is derived not so much from the change they create in people's lives as from the strains brought about in performance of more enduring social roles. Pearlin described six types of role strain. Role strain may derive from the tasks inherent in the role, interpersonal conflict with others in the role set, conflict between multiple roles, being stuck or captive in an unwanted role, the loss of desired social roles, and the restructuring of existing role relationships. Since roles structure individuals' ongoing relationships within social systems, role strain tends to be a chronic, enduring source of stress. From this perspective, support may reduce the effects of stress by preventing or reducing subsequent role strain.

Conceptualization of Social Support

The construct of social support was developed in research on psychosocial processes involved in the epidemiology of physical and mental illnesses, and was meant to encompass the broad health-protective functions provided by social relations. Not surprisingly, defining the construct in a concise and distinctive way has been problematic throughout this research. Recently theoreticians have begun to conceptualize distinct aspects of support and have attempted to specify how these relate differentially to stress and psychological maladjustment (Barrera, 1986; Lin, 1986; Wheaton, 1985). Wolchik, Sandler, and Braver (1987) applied Barrera's (1986) concepts of social embeddedness, enacted support, and perceived quality of support to review the literature on the assessment and effects of social support for children and adolescents. Social embeddedness describes the linkages children have with others, including family, friends, and the larger community. It describes the structure of the linkages (number, density, etc.) but not the content of the transactions that occur between network members (Wellman, 1981).

Enacted support refers to the amount of helping transactions received, such as guidance, instrumental aid, recreation, positive feedback, and emotional support. *Perceived quality* refers to the child's evaluation of the support. Support can also include children's relationships with such critical others as parents and peers (e.g., Maccoby & Martin, 1983; Youniss, 1980). While some of the dimensions used to describe these relationships overlap with more traditional support dimensions (e.g., confiding, providing positive feedback), others may not (e.g., disciplining). Our conceptualization of support is driven by our interest in exploring how social relations impact on the processes by which stress leads to children's maladjustment. Therefore we included a broad array of social relationship variables as within the domain of support, so long as they could be shown to affect the process by which stress leads to child maladjustment.

Processes by Which Social Support Protects Against the Negative Effects of Stressful Situations

There is considerable evidence that support protects children from the negative effects of life stress on children's mental health. Research indicates that two sources of resilience for children exposed to severe stress are family support (e.g., warmth, guidance) and extrafamilial support from peers and adults (Cowen & Work, 1988; Garmezy, 1983; Werner & Smith, 1982). Despite examples given by these authors of the effects of support there has been relatively little discussion of the alternative ways by which support may be helpful for children in stressful situations.

This chapter identifies three intervening processes as central to understanding how support may be helpful to children under stress. Two intervening processes that have received the most attention in the support literature are esteem enhancement and assistance in coping with stress (Heller, Swindle, & Dusenbury, 1986; Thoits, 1986). We propose that coping assistance may have its effects by increasing perceptions of control over one's world so that two of our intervening variables are self-esteem and perceived control. Our third intervening process involves enhancing perceived security of social relations, and is derived from developmental theories of attachment (Ainsworth, 1982; Bowlby, 1980) and social support literature. The hypothesis here is that the perception of meaningful social ties per se is health protective (e.g., Henderson, Byrne, & Duncan-Jones, 1981).

A final orienting point is that several different models of how support and stress may affect these processes can by hypothesized (Barrera, 1986; Wheaton, 1985). Critical alternative paths within these models are systematically presented in Figure 12.1. In path A (preventive path), support prevents the occurrence of stressful events. For example, following a parental divorce a supportive family network may prevent the occurrence of stressors related to financial troubles, "bad-mouthing" of the parents, or the loss of the relationship between the noncustodial parent and the child. In path B (moderating path), support reduces the negative effects of stress on the variables leading to psychological maladjustment. For example, perceived support may increase the secondary appraisal that the individual has the resources to cope with stressful events. Furthermore, the receipt of supportive transactions such as advice, emotional support, and so on may enhance the effectiveness of children's coping with stress. Path C (counteracting path) shows that support may be unrelated to stress but may directly strengthen the variables leading to adjustment, thus counteracting the negative effects of stress. As will be discussed, support may increase self-esteem, perceived control, or perceived security of social ties. Path F specifies three possible effects of stress on support. Stress may lead to increased social support if the network becomes mobilized to provide the resources necessary to meet the coping demands of the situation. On the

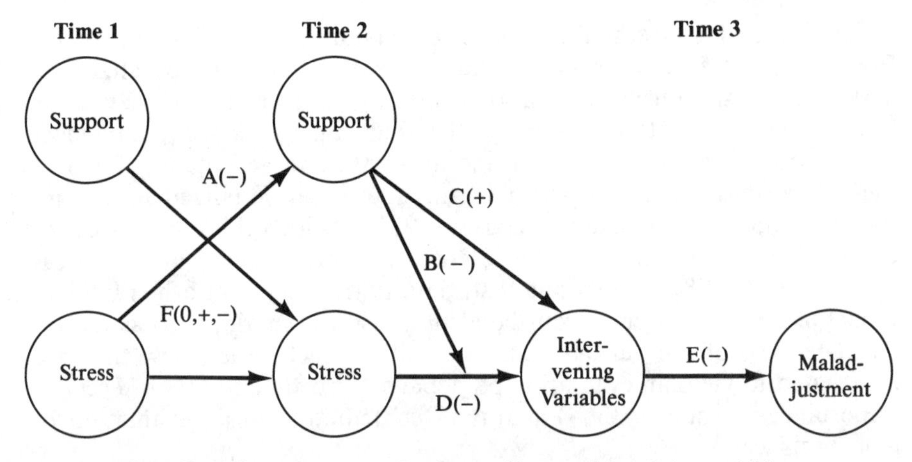

A - Preventing effect of support
B - Moderating effect of support
C - Counteracting effect of support
D - Stress effects on intervening variables
E - Intervening variable effects on maladjustment
F - Stress effects on support

Figure 12.1. Possible effects of support on the process by which stress leads to maladjustment.

other hand, stress may lead to a deterioration of the social network and this deterioration may be responsible for the negative effects of stress on adjustment. For example, parental divorce may lead to a worsening of children's relations with their parents and extended family, and this may be responsible for increased problems on variables (e.g., self-esteem, perceived control, security of social relations) affecting psychological symptomatology. Finally, support may be unaffected by the stress event and may have an independent effect on adjustment.

This chapter will now address the three hypothesized intervening processes through which stress and support may affect psychological adjustment of children. For each intervening process, we will first discuss the salient definitional and developmental issues. Then we will discuss theory and evidence that the effects of stress on symptomatology in children may involve each of these processes. Finally, we will discuss theory and evidence that support may reduce the effects of stress on each intervening process by preventing the stress (path A), reducing its effect (path B), or counteracting its effect (path C).

SOCIAL SUPPORT AND SELF-ESTEEM

Conceptual and Developmental Issues

A fundamental issue in the development of self-esteem concerns whether it is conceptualized as a global or a differentiated construct. Harter (1983) reviews several conceptualizations (Coopersmith, 1967; Epstein, 1973; Rosenberg, 1979) and proposes that self-esteem be conceptualized as a superordinate construct, and that specific dimensions be viewed as lower-order constructs. She proposes that four dimensions seem to be most often used: competence, control, moral worth, and acceptance. Each of these lower-order constructs can in turn be dimensionalized into more specific domains. For example, Harter (1982) has identified three areas of children's self-evaluation of competence: cognitive, social, and physical skills. Harter (1986) points out that, despite the appeal of a hierarchical model of self-esteem, numerous conceptual issues remain, such as the interrelatedness of the various subdomains with each other, how they are aggregated to yield an evaluation of global self-worth, and the differential importance of each of the domains in contributing to an evaluation of global self-worth.

Developmentally, children's self-evaluations are affected by their cognitive capacities and consequently change profoundly over the life course. Self-description progresses developmentally from a focus on concrete observable characteristics to a more conceptual trait system to a focus on psychological processes such as thoughts and attitudes (Harter, 1983; Montemayer & Eisen, 1977; Rosenberg, 1986). Developmental changes in children's ability to make social comparisons, to differentiate important self-attributions, and to make stable cross-situational self-judgments have important implications for the development of self-esteem (Dweck & Elliot, 1983; Harter, 1986; Ruble & Rholes, 1981). Harter (1986) proposes that, because the concept of "personness" as a generalization about the self is not firmly established until age 8, younger children cannot make global judgments of general self-worth. Developmental changes in the social ecology of children's role involvement also affect their developing self-esteem. Children judge their performance as a family member, member of a peer network, student, athlete, and in other roles.

Using the formulations of James and Cooley, Harter (1987) discusses two sources of self-esteem: evaluation of competence in activities of importance and perception of others' evaluations of the self. She tested this model in samples of children in grades three through six and grades six through eight to assess whether the determinants of global self-esteem changed during this developmental span. Self-perceived competence was assessed as self-ratings of success in five domains in relation to evaluations of the importance of success in each of these domains. A discrepancy between competence and the importance of the domain was used as one predictor of global self-worth.

Perceived evaluation of self-worth by four different types of significant others (parents, classmates, friends, teachers) was used as the measure of perceived acceptance. She found that perceived competence and perceived acceptance both contributed strongly and equally to global self-evaluation. Furthermore, the effects are additive, and no interaction of these two sources of self-worth was found. When she disaggregated the contribution of different domains of competence on global self-worth, she found that the domains of physical appearance and social acceptance were the strongest predictors. As Harter (1988) points out in a later paper, physical appearance and social acceptance may not be conceptualized as competence. Thus the overall role of competence in determining global self-worth of children may be less important than social acceptance. Furthermore, she found that acceptance by parents and acceptance by classmates were the most important contributors to self-worth in both age groups.

Rosenberg (1979) points out that there are developmental changes in the significance given to the perceived evaluation of the self by different significant others. The young child is primarily affected by the perceived evaluations of adult authority figures, whereas older children are increasingly concerned with the evaluations of peers, and in adolescence particular selected peers (best friends) are more important sources of self-evaluation. While the results are not entirely consistent (i.e., important gender differences were found), several studies have found that particular dimensions of parenting related to higher levels of self-esteem (Coopersmith, 1967; Maccoby & Martin, 1983; Wylie, 1979). For example, Coopersmith (1967) found that authoritarian parenting was related to lower self-esteem in boys 10 to 12 years old. In contrast, the parents of boys of higher self-esteem provide more (1) acceptance, affection, and interest, (2) consistency in rule enforcement, (3) noncoercive discipline, and (4) democratic attitudes toward considering the child's impact on family decisions.

This cursory overview highlights the fact that fundamental issues concerning the conceptualization and development of self-esteem are still being worked out. These issues have important implications for how self-esteem may intervene between stress and support in affecting the development of symptomatology. For example, from this brief review it is apparent that the effects of different sources of support (e.g., parents or peers) on self-esteem may differ for children at different developmental stages, and that global self-esteem should not be thought of as a mediator of stress process for children younger than age 8.

Self-Esteem and the Processes Intervening Between Stress and Psychological Maladjustment

There are two aspects of the process by which self-esteem affects the impact of stress on symptomatology. First is the process by which stress may lead to a decrease in self-esteem, and second is the process by which decreased self-esteem may lead to increased maladjustment. Theoretically (Kaplan, 1983,1984), stress may lead to a decrease in self-esteem either by directly threatening self-esteem or by disrupting esteem-supporting role relations and competence-enhancing experiences. Stressful life experiences may directly threaten self-esteem by their self-devaluing implications. They may reflect the individual's inability to attain valued states, meet felt obligations, or most generally avoid disvalued circumstances. For example, events such as failures in valued activities (e.g., academics, athletics, etc.) may directly indicate the lack of some valued state (e.g., being a good student or a good athlete). Alternatively, events may lead to a chain of experiences involving the loss of esteem-enhancing social relations or of opportunities to attain role competence. For example, parental divorce may precipitate a chain of events involving the loss of contact with the noncustodial parent, loss of friends, decreased success in school, and so on.

There is mixed empirical evidence about whether stressful experiences lead to decreased self-esteem of children and adolescents. Several researchers have found lower self-esteem in children and adolescents who have experienced such varied stressors as parental alcoholism (Roosa, Sandler, Beals, & Short, 1988) transition from elementary to junior high school (Simmons, Rosenberg, & Rosenberg, 1973), and parental divorce (Parish & Taylor, 1979). In one of the few prospective longitudinal studies, Cohen, Burt, and Bjorck (1987) reported that life stress events predicted lower self-esteem in a sample of adolescents when prior levels of esteem and stress were statistically controlled. As noted earlier, the effects of stress on self-esteem have not been unequivocally demonstrated. Some researchers have found no effects of school transitions on self-esteem: (Berndt & Hawkins, 1985; Hirsch & Rapkin, 1987), and others have found no effects of having an alcoholic parent on children's self-esteem (Clair & Genest, 1986). These inconsistent findings across studies may be due to a variety of factors that need further investigation, such as the effects of age, specific types of stressors, or specific domains of self-esteem.

Our model would predict that these stressors would impact on self-esteem in part through their effect on experiences of social acceptance and opportunities to develop competence in valued areas. To illustrate that stressful events often affect these proximal conditions we will focus on studies of children who have experienced parental divorce or parental death. There is abundant evidence that parental divorce is followed by negative changes in children's relationships with important people in their social networks (Sandler, Wolchik, & Braver, 1985). For example, Hetherington, Cox, and Cox (1981) found that in the 2 years following divorce mothers of preschool children were less affectionate, more inconsistent in their discipline, made fewer maturity demands, and gave more commands. While less is known about the quality of children's relationships with the noncustodial parent (usually the father), there is considerable evidence that the frequency of their interactions often decreases drastically. Fulton (1979), for example, found that at 2 years after the divorce only 20% of fathers maintained regular visits with their children while approximately 30% had ceased their visitation. There is less information about the effects of divorce on children's other relationships. Hetherington and colleagues (1981) reported that teachers develop more negative interactions with preschool children of divorce in reaction to their post-divorce acting-out behavior. There is also evidence that children of divorce develop more negative interaction patterns with their peers (Hetherington et al., 1981).

There is much more limited empirical research on bereaved children as compared with children of divorce. In one of the few studies in this area, Birtchnell (1980) found a history of disrupted parenting for women who experienced an early maternal death. Fifty percent had more than one mother replacement figure, and only 25% reported living continuously with their father and having a good relationship with him until they reached adulthood. In our own research, we found that bereaved children between the ages of 8 and 15 reported a marginally lower feeling of parental acceptance than did demographically comparable children from intact families (Sandler, Gersten, Reynolds, Kallgren & Ramirez, in press).

Evidence that stressful events decrease opportunities to develop role competence in valued areas is somewhat more sparse. Van Eerdewegh, Bieri, Parrilla, and Clayton (1982) in a study on a community sample found that bereaved children were reported as experiencing more school adjustment problems at 1 month and at 13 months after the parental death as compared to a demographically comparable nonbereaved group. Guidubaldi, Cleminshaw, Perry, and McLaughlin (1983), for example, in a nationwide study, found that children of divorce had more problems in school as evidenced by lower standardized achievement tests and poorer grades. Guidubaldi and colleagues (1983) also found that children of divorce experienced greater peer rejection, which in turn might reflect on their perceptions of their social skills. Felner, Stolberg, and Cowen (1975) found that bereaved children were described as having more problems of shyness and social withdrawal, problems that might reflect poorer social acceptance.

Several theories propose that decreased self-esteem leads to psychological maladjustment as evidenced by either negative affective states (Harter, 1986), depression (Abramson, Seligman, & Teasdale, 1978), or deviant behavior (Kaplan, 1983). Kaplan (1983,1984), for example, proposes that people are motivated to maximize the experience of positive self-attitudes and minimize the experience of negative self-attitudes. Experiences that lead to negative self-attitudes produce dysphoric affect, and groups that are associated with those experiences become associated with the negative affect. Consequently the individual loses motivation to conform to the norms and values of those groups and is motivated to find alternate, deviant, values and behavior patterns that become a source of self-esteem. Kaplan, Robbins, and Martin (1983) found some support for the model that lower self-esteem leads to higher maladjustment in a prospective longitudinal study that followed 1633 adolescents from seventh grade until 10 years later. They found that self-derogation by the seventh-grade students was related to higher psychological distress 10 years later. They also found that self-derogation at seventh-grade level moderated the negative effects of life stress on children's psychological distress 10 years later.

Social Support and Self-Esteem for Children Under Stress

Three mechanisms are proposed whereby social support may protect self-esteem for children under stress: preventing the occurrence of esteem-threatening events; moderating (reducing) the negative effects of stress events on self-esteem; and counteracting the effects of negative events by increasing esteem-enhancing experiences.

It is not difficult to envision how a supportive network may prevent the occurrence of esteem-threatening events. A supportive network may prevent the loss of support-enhancing social ties in the face of disruptive events. For example, after the death of a parent a strong and supportive network may maintain the family structure and prevent the child from being placed outside the nuclear family. Brown, Harris, and Bifulco (1986), in a retrospective longitudinal study of women who had experienced the death of a parent early in childhood, found that poor caretaking (e.g., being placed outside the home, rejecting parenting) was related to their vulnerability to becoming depressed as adults. Eloquent case studies of bereaved families describe how strong and determined surviving parents maintained cohesive, organized families following the death of their spouse. In a 10-year prospective longitudinal study of a community sample of children, Kaplan and colleagues (1983) found some evidence for a stress-preventive effect of support. They found that the absence of support (i.e., felt rejection) from family and peers as reported by seventh graders predicted the occurrence of stressful events over the following 10 years. A supportive network may also provide resources to prevent children's decreased involvement or failure in competence-enhancing activities. For example, supportive parents or extended network may provide the guidance or instrumental assistance to maintain children's successful involvement in school, social activities, or other valued activities.

Social support may reduce (moderate) the stressful effects of negative events by promoting esteem-maintaining appraisals of the events. Harter (1986) has described four cognitive strategies by which children maintain their self-esteem in the face of esteem-threatening, stressful experiences: downward social comparison; discounting; inflating one's perceived competence; and beneffectance. *Social comparison* refers to the process of evaluating the self by comparing one's attributes to those of relevant others. Harter reported that when learning-disabled or retarded students compared themselves to similar others their self-esteem was higher than when they compared themselves to regular students. *Discounting* refers to the process of decreasing the perceived importance of areas of low competence to maintain self-esteem. In support of this process, Harter reported that for children with high self-esteem the importance of areas of low competence was lower than for areas of high competence. This was not the case for children with low self-esteem. A third mechanism of esteem maintenance is slightly to inflate one's perceived competence. Harter reported that children with low self-esteem did not inflate their perceived competence (as compared with teacher ratings) in low-competent domains while high-self-esteem children did. The fourth mechanism discussed by Harter, beneffectance, is the tendency to see oneself as more responsible for one's successes than failures. Harter found evidence that children with high but not low self-esteem do this by the later elementary school years. While there has not been research on how the social network affects use of these strategies, we hypothesize that significant others can increase use of these strategies by such processes as modeling, direct instruction, or reinforcement.

Finally, support may counteract the negative effects of stress by directly increasing self-esteem. Belle and Longfellow (1984), for example, found a positive relationship between confiding in mother and self-esteem in a sample of preadolescent children between the ages of 5 and 12. They also found that the absence of a confiding relationship with anyone (i.e., mother, father, sibling, or friend) was related to lower self-esteem of children. Clair and Genest (1986) found that family cohesion was related to higher self-esteem for a sample of children of alcoholic parents. Short, Sandler, and Roosa (1988) developed a measure to assess the degree to which adolescents perceived people in their support network as enhancing or threatening their self-esteem. Adolescents were asked to name people who provided some form of social support in the past 4 weeks. They were then asked to rate the degree to which they perceived the supporters as either enhancing or threatening their self-esteem. Esteem enhancement was defined as the effect of the relationship to elicit positive self-cognitions and esteem threat as relationship effects that elicit negative self-cognitions. They found that, after controlling for demographic variables and the effects of social support network variables, esteem-enhancing relationships were related to higher self-esteem while esteem-threatening relationships were related to lower self-esteem, higher anxiety, and higher depression. These results indicate that supportive relationships may either increase or decrease self-esteem, a point also made by Hirsch and Reischl (1985). This is an important point that needs further investigation. Literature on recipient reaction to aid indicates some possible mechanisms for this: Support may threaten self-esteem if it is given in a way that implies inferiority, inadequacy, or dependency on the part of the recipient (Fisher, Nadler, & Whitcher-Alagna, 1982).

A supportive network may directly increase self-esteem by continuing esteem-building relationships, replacing or compensating for lost sources of esteem. For example, a warm and consistent relationship with the custodial parent following a major stress is consistently found to relate to better adjustment (Fogas, 1986; Guidubaldi, Cleminshaw, Perry, Nastasi & Lightel, 1983; Hess & Camara, 1979; Hetherington et al., 1981). A positive relationship between the child and the noncustodial parent also relates to better adjustment of children (Hess & Camara, 1979; Kurdek & Berg, 1983), with the positive quality of this relationship rather than the amount of time being the critical variable. Guidubaldi and colleagues (1983) found that children's positive relationships with other adult caretakers also predicted better adjustment. There is only indirect evidence that support may maintain esteem for children in stress by compensating for lost sources of esteem. Hetherington and colleagues (1981) reported that a good relationship with the custodial parent was significantly related to positive adjustment for children of divorce, even when there was a poor relationship with the noncustodial parent. Children in many stressful situations, such as school transitions and family restructuring, are exposed to new sources of support (e.g., friendships, nonparental caregiver, step-family members) that may compensate for the social losses they experience. These new sources may be particularly salient for children experiencing family transitions when single parents remarry or extended family become more involved in children's lives.

SOCIAL SUPPORT AND THE SECURITY OF SOCIAL RELATIONS

Conceptual and Developmental Issues

Cobb (1976) has provided one of the classic definitions of social support as "information leading the subject to believe that he/she is cared for and loved . . . esteemed and valued . . . that he/she belongs to a network of communication and mutual obligation" (p. 300). This definition emphasizes the importance of knowledge of belonging to a secure social network as a central component of social support. Evidence that close social ties (i.e., confidants) buffer the negative effect of stress is consistently found in the adult literature (Cohen & Wills, 1985). This evidence is usually interpreted as indicating the importance of the functions provided by these social ties such as self-esteem enhancement, or emotional support. However, another mechanism may be the very awareness of the secure presence of close social ties. In this section we will present a theoretical rationale for the stress-reducing role of secure social ties and review empirical evidence to support the importance of this mechanism. Several theoretical constructs share the common element of emphasizing the importance of secure social relations for children's psychological well-being. While these constructs diverge in many fundamental ways, they are similar in emphasizing the intrinsic importance of social relations and of the perceived security of those relations—that they can be counted on to persist over time.

The most extensive discussion of the nature and significance of secure social relations has been developed in attachment theory (Bowlby, 1980; Bretherton, 1985; Sroufe & Waters, 1977). Bowlby conceptualizes attachment as a goal-connected control system. The goal of this system is to maintain proximity to an attachment figure so that the child would move closer in times of danger or stress but would be free to move farther away and explore the environment in the absence of stress. The attachment behavior system is seen as biologically functional in maintaining protection from danger. Psychologically the goal is to maintain a subjective sense of *felt security* (Bretherton, 1985; Sroufe & Waters, 1977). When danger is perceived, felt security is decreased and contact with the attachment figure is sought. When no danger is perceived, felt security is high and the child can move away from the attachment figure. While most attachment research concerns interactions between mothers and infants, attachment relationships are also believed to be formed between infants and fathers, siblings, and adult caretakers (Lerner & Ryff, 1978; Rutter, 1981).

Lerner and Ryff (1978) discuss attachment as a life span concept. They point out that, while the behavioral indicators of an attachment relationship change across the life span, there may be continuity in the functions served by these behaviors. For example, while proximity seeking may occur by physical approach behaviors in the infant, in the older child proximity seeking may occur by looking and vocalizing. Weiss (1982) identifies three central characteristics of attachment relationships and discusses whether relationships having these characteristics continue across the life span. The central characteristics are proximity seeking in times of threat, security in the presence of attachment figure, and protest at attempts to threaten access to attachment figure. Weiss proposes that such relationships are maintained across the life span, although in a somewhat modified form. Attachmentlike relationships are formed with peers during adolescence and are relinquished with the parents. Attachment relationships are formed only with people of central emotional importance, and other relationships cannot compensate for the loss experienced by separation from the attachment figure.

Boyce (1985) proposes that the common factor behind the health-protective effects of social support is that they promote a sense of the stability of central elements of life experience. He views humans as having a basic human need for a sense of stability and permanence. Although Boyce proposes several sources of this sense of stability, he focuses primarily on family routines that provide a sense of consistency as well as affirmation of the continuity and permanence of family relations. More generally, support may provide protection from the negative effects of stressful situations by augmenting the sense of stability that is threatened or decreased by the occurrence of stressful events. In a similar vein, Wolin and Bennett (1984) discuss the concept of family rituals. Family rituals are "patterned, symbolic, rule-governed activities . . . within which family members assume roles that they repetitively re-enact over time" (Bennett, Wolin, Reiss, & Teitelbaum, 1987, p. 122). Rituals include the regular way the family carries out its daily activities such as meals, and the way it marks holidays and special occasions. Rituals have symbolic significance in that they signify the family's collective identity and continuity.

Secure Social Relations and the Processes Intervening Between Stress and Psychological Maladjustment

The most severe sources of stress for children often involve a threat to the continuation of important social ties. For example, Coddington (1972) had 243 mental health professionals rate the amount of change and readjustment that would be required for life events that might occur to children and adolescents. He found that for elementary school children and junior high school students more than half of the 10 most stressful events involved a disruption in a close social relationship, events such as parental divorce or separation or death being among the most stressful.

From a transactional perspective on stress, one can further analyze the more specific experiences that occur over the course of these events to identify those that are most stressful. As noted earlier, Sandler, Wolchik, Braver, and Fogas (1986) developed a 62-item event scale to assess the specific stressors for parental divorce. Many of these events can be seen as threatening the security of the child's ties to one or the other parent (e.g., parents saying bad things about each other to the child, decreased time spent with mom or dad, relatives saying bad things about parents).

Parental divorce can also be looked at from the perspective of the child's understanding of the experience. Kurdek and Berg (in press) assessed six beliefs that are thought to be problematic for children of divorce; peer ridicule; paternal blame; maternal blame; self-blame; fear of abandonment; and hope for reunification. Of these, fear of abandonment involves a fear of losing contact with both parents and is most relevant to our concern with security of social ties. Kurdek and Berg found that the fear of abandonment score was the only one of the six belief measures that correlated significantly with children's self-rated anxiety ($r\ (38) = .54$, $p < .001$) in a middle-class sample of children of divorce. Similarly, Ramirez, Sandler, and Wolchik (1988) found that children's fear of abandonment was related to higher levels of symptomatology for a sample of inner-city children of divorce. This study is notable because the correlations were high in magnitude (range of $r = .30$ to $.50$, median $r = .43$) and because the fear of abandonment score was the only one of four divorce-related beliefs to predict both parent and child reports of symptomatology of the child. Thus this relation is independent of any unique reporter effects.

A similar picture of the critical role of the security of important social relations can be seen in the literature on the effects of parental death on children. Again, the effects of this event can best be understood by considering it to be a process of experiences that occur over time and by unraveling the critical stressful components of this experience. Sandler, Gersten, Reynolds, Kallgren and Ramirez (in press) have reviewed the empirical literature on these stressful processes and have found that the most critical ones involved continued threat to the stability of the primary caretaking unit of the family. Illustratively, Brown and colleagues (1986), in a retrospective study of women who had lost a parent during childhood, found that "lack of care" by the surviving parental figure was the most critical link to the children's vulnerability to depression in adulthood. By lack of care they meant either prolonged separation from the home or rejecting or neglecting parenting.

Rosenberg and McCullough (1981) utilized data from four large-scale surveys to study the relationship between adolescents' perception that they mattered to their parents and indices of their mental health. That they mattered to their parents was assessed by items concerning their belief that they were important to their parents, that their parents were interested in them and concerned about them, that their opinions counted, and that they were wanted. This is seen as linked to secure parental relations in that it indicates the child's belief that the relationship is important to the parents and thus will be maintained by them. Across all four samples, they found that mattering to parents was correlated with higher self-esteem and lower psychological symptomatology of the adolescents. Furthermore, they distinguish between mattering to parents and parental positive attitudes to the adolescents. They found that the relation between mattering to parents and adolescent self-esteem was independent of the degree to which the adolescents believed that their parents thought well of them. Furthermore, they investigated whether the effects of mattering to parents on adolescents' mental health (e.g., depression, worries, anxiety, etc.) could be accounted for by self-esteem. They found that, even when controlling for the effects of self-esteem, mattering to parents was still related to better adolescent mental health.

Social Support and the Security of Social Relations for Children Under Stress

Social support may increase the security of social relations for children under stress in one of three ways: by preventing the occurrence of disruptions that decrease the security of social relations; by moderating the negative effects of stress events on security of social relations; and by counteracting the negative effects of stress events on security of social relations.

Although stressful events often disrupt significant social relations, some social networks are able to maintain children's beliefs that they are a secure part of a continuing and caring social unit. One obvious way that this might happen is if there is continuity of relationships despite the threatened disruption. For example, continuity of children's relationships with both parents following parental divorce is likely to increase their sense of security of these relations. Another mechanism might be the maintenance of selected patterns of behavior or rituals, which represent the continuation of the family unit. Wolin and colleagues (1980) studied the intergenerational transmission of alcoholism as a function of the disruption or maintenance of family rituals by the drinking of the alcoholic parent. They found that, in those families where family rituals were maintained, there was a lower probability of the children manifesting alcoholism problems. These effects could not be accounted for by the severity or duration of the parent's alcoholism. Similarly, in a later study, Bennet, Wolin, Reiss, and Teitelbaum (1987) found that the maintenance of the family dinner ritual despite the drinking of the alcoholic parent predicted lower alcoholism rates in the children.

A second illustration of the prevention of disrupted social relations during times of stress is Felner, Ginter, and Primavera's (1982) experimental change of the school social environment for adolescents making the transition to junior high school. They hypothesized that the instability and flux of the social environment of the high school contributed to the stress of the transition experience. They developed a change in the structure of the high school to minimize this instability, particularly in regard to the students' relations with other students and teachers. They restructured the role of the homeroom teacher to include many of the guidance and administrative duties usually carried out by other school personnel. They also restructured the peer network so that students were assigned to their core academic classes with the same group of peers. Thus by changes in the school social structure, they created an environment in which relations with teachers and friends were more stable and well organized. They found that students who experienced this more stable environment, as compared with matched controls, achieved better grades, had fewer absences and less of a decrease in self-esteem, and perceived the high school environment more positively. While several mechanisms may be responsible for these effects, one reasonable possibility is that the stability of the critical social relations provided a sense of security that they could be accessed when needed.

Several studies provide evidence that secure social relations moderate the negative effects of stress on children and adolescents. Research has demonstrated that 2-year-old children can be reliably assessed as to the security of their attachment to their parent and that more securely attached children are more readily comforted by proximity to their parent during times of stress (Ainsworth, Blehar, Waters, & Wall, 1978). Indeed the ability to be comforted in times of stress is a salient component of the concept of attachment (Bretherton, 1985). Armsden and Greenberg (1988) assessed security of attachment to parents and peers among late adolescents, using self-reports of high trust and communication and low alienation. They found that there was a stronger effect of stressful life events on psychological symptomatology for those classified as insecurely attached to their parents than for those classified as securely attached. Boyce (1981) postulated that the presence of regular family routines created the sense of permanence and stability that underlies the stress-protective effects of social support. He found some evidence for this in a sample of preschool children, where the presence of family routines reduced the negative effects of life events on children's respiratory illness.

Evidence for the stress-counteracting effect of supportive relations as decreasing psychological symptomatology is illustrated in several studies we have done focusing on the stability of interactions with these relations. Stability is a central component of the concept of security of social ties. A child may feel secure not simply because he or she has positive interactions with significant social figures, but because he or she believes these interaction are stable. In our recent research, children were asked to report on positive events (which primarily refer to positive interactions with significant others) that occurred to them during the prior 3 months. If an event occurred, they were asked whether it happened more than usual, less than usual, or about the same as usual. Three different event scores were derived to indicate the occurrence of increased, decreased, and stable positive events. In one study (Sandler, Gersten, Reynolds, Kallgren & Ramirez, in press) the relationship between positive events and psychological maladjustment was studied using a sample of recently bereaved children. As can be seen in Table 12.1 stable positive events were related to lower levels of maladjustment, decreased positive events were related to higher maladjustment, and increased positive events were uncorrelated with maladjustment. In this same study, the effects of stable positive events on symptomatology were examined as one of three mediators of the effects of parental death. Path analysis of the date indicates that stable positive events were directly related to lower psychological symptomatology, counteracting the positive relation between negative life stress and symptomatology.

TABLE 12.1. Correlations of Stable and Unstable Positive Events with Symptomatology for Bereaved Children (N = 92)

	Increased Positive Events	Decreased Postive Events	Stable Positive Events
Depression	.27[2]	.24[1]	−.40[2]
Anxiety	−.00	.23[1]	−.03
Conduct disorder	.05	.16	−.33[2]

[1] = $p < .05$
[2] = $p < .01$

Note: All measures of symptomatology are derived from a revised version of a structured diagnostic interview schedule, the CAS (Hodges, Kline, Stern, Cytryn & McKnew, 1982). Internal consistency reliability of these measures are adequate; depression $\alpha = .79$, anxiety $\alpha = .78$, conduct disorder $\alpha = .70$.

SOCIAL SUPPORT AND PERCEPTIONS OF CONTROL

Conceptual and Developmental Issues

The thesis of this section is that children's realistic belief in their ability to control the outcomes of stressful events affects the degree of stress they experience and their subsequent psychological adjustment. Weisz (1986) has suggested that control generally refers to "the capacity to cause an event consistent with one's intentions" (p. 22), and that it consists of two major components. The first component involves the ability to detect the degree of control or contingency of the outcome itself. The second component consists of the person's competence or skills relevant to producing the desired outcome. The concept of control is a complex one in that researchers have distinguished between individuals' perceived versus actual control beliefs, control beliefs regarding past versus future or expected outcomes, and internally versus externally based control beliefs.

Individuals' perceived control over aversive events has been studied extensively (e.g., Lefcourt, 1976; Nowicki & Duke, 1983), while relatively little attention has been paid to the concept of actual control. Recently, however, there has been increased interest in the relation between actual and perceived control through the study of errors in perceptions of control over event outcomes, and the implications these errors have for people's well-being (e.g., Fincham & Cain, 1986; Skinner, 1985; Weisz, 1986). While it has been assumed that accuracy of one's perceptions of actual control is associated with developmental maturity, recent evidence suggests that some overestimation of one's control over events is characteristic of both healthy adults and children (Fincham & Cain, 1986).

Recent theoretical formulations regarding control beliefs have integrated concepts from attribution, locus of control, and learned helplessness research. Attribution research typically focuses on factors associated with people's explanations of the causes of events that have occurred (e.g., their performance on a task). Locus of control and learned helplessness theory is concerned with determination of individuals' expectations of control over events. In current research on factors affecting individuals' perceptions of their ability to control events, their attributions about control over past and future events have been studied in terms of internal versus external control beliefs. Thus an individual may attribute the outcome of a past or future event to an internal or external cause, and the nature of the cause of the event may be attributed to a stable (e.g., ability) or unstable (e.g., effort) personal characteristic. The particular attributions used appear to have important consequences for individuals' subsequent motivation in the face of failure and other stressful events (e.g., Dweck & Elliot, 1973).

Weisz's (1986) definition of control presumes several cognitive skills. Children must be able to identify and distinguish contingent from noncontingent events and the characteristics associated with each. Further, children must understand the concepts of causality and intention and distinguish between them when judging the contingency of an event. For example, Weisz (1986) reports that preschool children believe that effort, age, and ability all can affect the outcome of chance events (e.g., drawing different playing cards), whereas children from 6 to 10 years discount age or ability but still believe effort can influence such events, which even carries over, although to a lesser extent, into adolescence.

A second developmental issue affecting children's control beliefs concerns their understanding that events are contingent upon certain competencies but not others (Weisz, 1986). Nicholls (1978) has proposed that children's accurate assessment of their competence is a function of their understanding of several skills with known developmental properties, namely, seriation, perspective taking, and the ability to see the contingency between events that are not temporally related. Nicholls and Miller (1984) report that children go through several levels in understanding the concepts of luck and task difficulty, and in estimating their ability to control event outcomes. At the preschool level, children equate ability with the tasks they have mastered. Between 5 and 8 years of age, children begin to differentiate between task difficulty and ability and understand that more ability is required to perform more difficult tasks. They understand less well, however, how ability and task difficulty are coordinated to produce actual outcomes. After 8, task difficulty and ability are increasingly differentiated, and children begin making estimations of their competence using social comparison processes. Fincham and Cain (1986), for example, show that, even in the face of failure on a task, preschool children's expectations for future success appear unaffected. After 6 years of age, however, changes in expectations of one's ability to succeed after failure on tasks begin to appear. In sum, children's cognitive skills may strongly affect their capacity to process information relevant to judging the contingent properties of events, to estimate their ability to control the outcomes of events, and to distinguish between their intentions and the actual skills required to control event outcomes.

Control Beliefs and the Processes Intervening Between Stress and Symptomatology

Two issues will be addressed here: (1) How might stress affect children's control beliefs? (2) How might children's control beliefs affect psychological symptomatology for children under stress? Children's control beliefs may be affected by stress events either directly or through the effects of stress on their social environments. Stress may directly affect children's belief in their ability to control the outcomes of events in a number of ways. First, the stress event itself may be a noncontingent, aversive event. In this situation, children would learn that there is no coping response they can perform that can prevent the event from happening. For example, a child may have to undergo a series of painful medical treatments, or may have a chronic disability that produces psychological or physical stress. Exposure to stress over time without the ability to counteract it would thus reinforce the belief that the individual has little control over his or her environment. For example, Newcomb and Harlow (1986) found that the occurrence of life stress events related to external control perceptions in a sample of adolescents.

The development of external control beliefs when exposed to aversive events also depends to a large degree on the attributions children make about their failure to control events (Abramson, Seligman, & Teasdale, 1978). According to the reformulated model of learned helplessness, people can attribute the failure to control events to personal factors (i.e., a lack of competence to produce the effective response) or to universal factors (i.e., no response produces the outcome). Personal attributions for failure are more likely to lead to external control beliefs, particularly if such attributions are generalized across time and situations.

Stress may also affect children's control beliefs indirectly through its effects on their relationships with significant others. Following Skinner (1985), parents who provide social environments that are contingently responsive to children promote their children's development of internal control beliefs. Further, Crandall and Crandall (1983) report that parental warmth, praise, and positive child-rearing practices are associated with children's perceptions of internal control. Should stress affect the parents' ability to provide a warm and contingently responsive interpersonal and social environment, however, children will have fewer opportunities to develop these beliefs. Moreover, if the stressful events detract from parents' typical ways of responding, children's expectations for what they can control based on past experience will be threatened, and thus diminish their perceptions of control. For example, Hetherington and colleagues (1981) report that mothers of preschool children become less affectionate and more inconsistent in their discipline practices following divorce. Thus their children experience less positive social interactions and more noncontingent events in their relationships with their mother, which would be expected to diminish their sense of control.

Considerable research has focused on the effects of control beliefs on symptomatology for people under stress. Cohen, Evans, Stokols, and Krantz (1986) review several different facets of control that have been discussed as reducing the negative effects of stress: behavioral control; cognitive control; and retrospective control.

In behavioral control, the person's responses influence the actual stressful situation. For example, Gunnar (1980a, 1980b) reported that in 12-month-olds the ability to control the onset of a frightening toy reduces fear of that toy. Gunnar indicated, however, that it is only when behavioral control is associated with the termination of the stressful experience that it leads to decreased stress. When the attempts at behavioral control are not associated with a decrease in the stress stimulus, it leads to more negative effects of stress. Janoff, Bulman, and Brickman (1980) refer to attempts to control uncontrollable situations as the pathology of high expectations. They propose that healthy adaptation requires the ability to discriminate situations one can change by one's behavior and situations that cannot be changed.

The term *cognitive control* refers to how people, by changing how they think, may reduce the stressful impact of an aversive environment that they cannot actually change. Rothbaum, Weisz, and Snyder (1982) refer to this as secondary control and point to four ways of accomplishing it. One can attempt to predict future aversive events so as to avoid disappointment. One can ally oneself with chance (e.g., by saying that one is lucky) or with powerful others (e.g., by identifying with them) so as to share in their power. Finally, one can attempt better to understand negative events so as to derive meaning from them and accept them. In the clinical literature, Wallerstein (1983) describes several of children's coping tasks in adapting to the divorce of their parents so as to indicate that positive adaptation involves coming to understand the divorce in a way that minimizes blame of self and parents.

The term *retrospective control* refers to people's attributions about the cause of an event after the event has occurred (Thompson, 1981). Cohen and colleagues (1986) proposed that people need to understand the world as being orderly and meaningful and that perceiving the cause of events helps maintain an understanding of the order of things. Children's attributions about the cause of negative events have been studied in research on the development of learned helplessness. This research, however, indicates that the causal attributions about the outcome of the event determine whether they lead to more or less stress. The reformulated model of learned helplessness, for example, proposes that when the cause of negative events is attributed to internal, stable, and global factors the result is likely to be depression (Abramson and colleagues, 1978), while attribution to effort might lead to less stress.

It is clear from this brief review that control does not invariably reduce the negative effects of stress. Behavioral control that is not followed by feedback that the control response has been effective results in increased stress. Similarly, attributions to global stable internal causes for negative events lead to the expectation of a lack of future control and thus result in more negative stress effects. Cohen and colleagues (1986) reviewed the theoretical processes that mediate the effects of control and identified four potential processes: increasing perceptions of self-efficacy; improving the choice of coping strategies that match the realistic controllability of events in the environment; providing a sense of the predictability of onset or safety from stressors; and providing a stable (more accurate) estimation of the maximum aversiveness that will be experienced in a situation.

Social Support and Children's Control Beliefs Under Stress

Social support can increase or help maintain the sense of control for children under stress by three mechanisms: preventing the occurrence of control-threatening events; moderating (reducing) the negative effects of stress on control beliefs; and counteracting the negative effects of stress by enhancing control beliefs.

The support network may prevent the occurrence of control-threatening events by maintaining a predictable social environment for the child in the face of potential disruptions. From a transactional perspective a major stressor such as parental divorce can precipitate a series of unpredictable, negative events that might be beyond the child's control. For example, in our own research on the events that follow parental divorce, 11 of the 18 negative events were rated as beyond the control of the child by a panel of expert ratings (Sandler, Wolchik, & Braver, in press). The support network may prevent the occurrence of events that for the child are uncontrollable. For example, following parental divorce many of these events derive from conflict between the parents, behaviors of the extended family, or behaviors of the custodial or noncustodial parent over which the child has little or no control (e.g., noncustodial parent missing visits). Changes in the social network that might affect the quality of the relationship between network members (e.g., decreased hostility between parents) might prevent the occurrence of control-threatening negative events. Also, assistance provided by the extended network may reduce the parents' level of stress, and thus prevent the child's experience of uncontrollable negative events such as seeing the parents in distress.

Social support may moderate the effects of stress on the development of maladaptive control beliefs by helping children make realistic assessments of their ability to control stressful events and by affirming their adaptive control beliefs. In this regard, parental attributional processes have been related to their children's attributions regarding control over events. Seligman and Peterson (1986) report that elementary school children's attributional style for bad events was significantly related to their mothers' attributional style for bad events. Similarly, Fincham and Cain (1986) report that parents' attributions of children's failure to the parents' own lack of effort were *negatively* related to the children's own effort attributions for their failures. They suggested that children learned to make external attributions for their failure (i.e., failure was due to parents' lack of effort) by the direct instruction provided by the parents' attributional statements that undermined the children's own attributions about their effort and ability.

Other researchers have shown that children's expectations for control can be acquired through interactions with adults other than their parents. Dweck (1975) experimentally demonstrated that teachers' attributions increased children's internal control attributions for failure experiences (i.e., to an internal locus focused on effort rather than their lack of ability) in a sample of specially selected "helpless" children. The results showed that these children could be directly instructed to attribute failure to lack of effort and that these learned attributions decreased their tendencies to give up after experiencing failure.

Theoretically, we would expect social support to contribute directly to children's perception of control and efficacy over stressful events and thereby counteract their negative effects. Bandura (1982) proposed that efficacy judgments are derived from several principal sources of information: perceptions of one's own successful coping (called enactive attainments); vicarious experiences; verbal persuasion; and physiological state. Vicarious experiences and verbal persuasion are principally social in nature. Vicarious experiences involve children's observing similar others performing the task (or tasks) effectively, or learning about effective strategies of control, as well as the general notion that outcomes are predictable by virtue of watching efficacious models over time. Children also may be verbally persuaded to believe that they have the capability to affect desired changes in their environment through a variety of social influence techniques. This is particularly true when such persuasion leads to persistence that is rewarded with successful outcome, thus enhancing perceptions of self-efficacy.

Finally, parents can create environmental conditions that enhance the development of internal control beliefs independent of the effects of stress. These positive control beliefs then may counteract the control-threatening effects of stress. Skinner (1985) proposed that parents who are responsive to their children's behavior model contingency by demonstrating that the child's actions affect parental behavior and can produce positive outcomes in the environment. She indicated further that parental consistency, warmth, support, and encouragement of children's active engagement in the environment promote their development of an understanding of control and a sense of competence in producing outcomes (see also Arend, Gore, & Sroufe, 1979; Bakeman & Brown, 1980; Lerner & Lerner, 1983).

CONCLUDING OBSERVATIONS

This chapter proposed three intervening processes (increasing self-esteem, increasing appropriate control perceptions, and increasing security of social relations) by which support may affect the psychological adjustment of children under stress. Furthermore, it described alternative paths by which support might affect these processes: preventive, moderating, and counteracting. In addition, developmental issues relevant to each intervening process were briefly described. The purpose of the chapter was to point to directions for future research in the belief that such research needs to be based on testing theoretically based models of the processes by which support affects children's adaptation to stress. In that vein several concluding comments are in order.

First, we think that it is important to focus on the intervening processes by which support affects children's adjustment rather than simply to study the relations (direct or interactive) between support and maladjustment. Studying the intervening processes should improve our theoretical understanding of how and under what conditions support may protect children from the negative effects of stress as well as seemingly analogous conditions where support has a negative effect on adjustment (e.g., Hirsch & Reischl, 1985). While we have treated the three intervening processes separately in this chapter, it is clear that they are not orthogonal to each other. In various theories they have been linked to each other causally (e.g., lower self-esteem results from a belief in personal helplessness; Abramson et al., 1978) or as components of each other (e.g., control as a component of self-esteem; Harter, 1986). Research is needed to assess the relations between these variables in terms of their conceptual overlap, causal interrelations, and joint effects as they act as intervening variables in the relations among stress, support, and maladjustment.

Second, there is a need to obtain a better understanding of how different social support constructs affect each of the intervening processes. In our review, it is apparent that some aspects of support lead to improvement in multiple intervening variables. For example, Belle and Longfellow (1984) found that children's confiding in their parents related to higher self-esteem, more internal control, and less loneliness. Similarly, a support network that maintains significant social ties in the face of threatened disruption may prevent decreased self-esteem, increased perceptions that the world is uncontrollable, and a loss of the perceived security that derives from being embedded in a stable social network. On the other hand, other facets of support may have a more specialized effect. For example, family rituals may primarily affect security of social relations. Also, some putatively supportive relations may have a negative effect on intervening variables such as self-esteem (e.g., Hirsch & Reischl, 1985; Short et al., 1988). Finally, as shown in Wolchik, Beals, and Sandler's chapter in this volume, the different support constructs need to be thought of as dynamically related to one another. Thus, for example, helping a mother to cope with her situation also improves the support functions she is able to provide to her children.

Third, a developmental perspective in these processes needs to be emphasized, as reviewed previously. Children's cognitive advances from early childhood through adolescence dramatically affect how they personally experience, understand, and are affected by these intervening processes. Thus unilateral applications of theory or interventions employing these variables, irrespective of children's developmental status, would, in our view, be misguided. For example, the structure and content of children's self-esteem change markedly from childhood to adolescence, as do the social sources of influence on their esteem. Thus for example the prevention of self-esteem threat for adolescents as compared to younger children is more likely to involve maintenance of their esteem-supporting peer relations.

Finally, the preventive, moderating, and counteracting effects need to be seen as part of a process that continues over time. These effects are complex in that the process involves mutual influences between the constructs. For example, a strong support network may prevent the occurrence of events; however, stress events may also act to disrupt the supportive network. These effects need to be studied using longitudinal designs in which alternative models are specified and tested (Lin, 1986; Wheaton, 1985).

As we assess the adequacy and shortcomings of these models to account for the observed relationships in our data, we will enhance our understanding of the effects of support as a protective factor for children in stress.

REFERENCES

Abramson, L., Seligman, M., & Teasdale, J. (1978). Learned helplessness in humans: Critique and reformulation. *Journal of Abnormal Psychology, 87,* 49–74.

Ainsworth, M. D. S. (1982). Attachment: Retrospect and prospect. In C. M. Parkes & J. S. Hinde (Eds.), *The place of attachment in human behavior* (p. 331). New York: Basic.

Ainsworth, M. D. S., Blehar, M. C., Waters, E., & Wall, S. (1978). *Patterns of attachment.* Hillsdale, NJ: Erlbaum.

Arend, R., Gore, F., & Sroufe, L. A. (1979). Continuity of individual adaptation from infancy to kindergarten: A predictive study of ego-resiliency and curiosity in preschoolers. *Child Development, 50,* 950–959.

Armsden, G. A., & Greenberg, M. T. (1988). *The inventory of parent and peer attachment: Individual differences and their relationship to psychological well-being in adolescence.* Manuscript submitted for publication.

Bakeman, R., & Brown, J. V. (1980). Early interaction: Consequences for social and mental development at three years. *Child Development, 57,* 437–447.

Bandura, A. (1982). Self efficacy mechanism in human agency. *American Psychologist, 37,* 122–147.

Barrera, M., Jr. (1986). Distinctions between social support concepts, measures, and models. *American Journal of Community Psychology, 14,* 413–445.

Belle, D., & Longfellow, C. (1984). *Confiding as a coping strategy.* Unpublished manuscript, Boston University.

Bennet, L. A., Wolin, S. J., Reiss, D., & Teitelbaum, M. A. (1987). Couples at risk for transmission of alcoholism: Protective influences. *Family Process, 26,* 111–129.

Berndt, T. J., & Hawkins, J. A. (1985, August). Friendships as social supports for children during school transitions. In *Social and developmental perspectives on the functions of friendship.* Symposium conducted at the meeting of the American Psychological Association, Washington, DC.

Birtchnell, J. (1980). Women whose mothers died in childhood: An outcome study. *Psychological Medicine, 10,* 699–713.

Bowlby, J. (1980). *Attachment and loss: Vol. III. Loss.* New York: Basic.

Boyce, W. T. (1981). Interaction between social variables in stress research. *Journal of Health & Social Behavior, 22,* 194–195.

Boyce, W. T. (1985). Social support, family relations and children. In S. Cohen & L. Syme (Eds.), *Social support and health* (pp. 151–172). New York: Academic.

Bretherton, I. (1985). Attachment theory: Retrospect and prospect. In I. Bretherton & E. Walters (Eds.), Growing points of attachment theory and research. *Monographs of the Society for Research in Child Development, 50,* (1-2, Serial No. 209).

Brown, G. W., Harris, T. O., & Bifulco, A. (1986). Long-term effects of early loss of a parent. In M. Rutter, C. E. Izard, & P. B. Read (Eds.), *Depression in young people: Developmental and clinical perspectives* (pp. 251–297). New York: Guilford.

Clair, D., & Genest, M. (1986). Variables associated with the adjustment of offspring of alcoholic fathers. *Journal of Studies in Alcohol, 48,* 345–355.

Cobb, S. (1976). Social support as a moderator of life stress. *Psychosomatic Medicine, 38,* 300–314.

Coddington, R. D. (1972). The significance of life events as etiologic factors in the diseases of children: I. A survey of professionals. *Journal of Psychosomatic Research, 16,* 7–18.

Cohen, D., Brurt, C. E., & Bjorck, J. P. (1987). Life stress and adjustment: Effects of life events experienced by young adolescents and their parents. *Developmental Psychology, 23,* 583–592.

Cohen, S., Evans, G. W., Stokols, D., & Krantz, D. S. (1986). *Behavior, health and environmental stress.* New York: Plenum.

Cohen, S., & Wills, T. A. (1985). Stress, social support, and the buffering hypothesis. *Psychological Bulletin, 98,* 310–357.

Coopersmith, S. (1967). *The antecedents of self-esteem.* San Francisco: Freeman.

Cowen, E. L., & Work, W. C. (1988). *Resilient children, psychological and primary prevention.*

Crandall, V. C., & Crandall, B. W. (1983). Maternal and childhood behaviors as antecedents of internal–external control perceptions in young adulthood. In H. M. Lefcourt (Ed.), *Research with the locus of control construct* (Vol. 2, pp. 58–97). New York: Academic.

Dweck, C. S. (1975). The role of expectations and attributions in the alleviation of learned helplessness. *Journal of Personality and Social Psychology, 31,* 674–685.

Dweck, C. S., & Elliott, E. S. (1983). Achievement motivation. In P. H. Mussen (Gen. Ed.) & E. M. Hetherington (Vol. Ed.), *Handbook of child psychology: Vol. IV. Socialization, personality, and social development* (4th ed.). New York: Wiley.

Epstein, S. (1973). The self-concept revisited or a theory of a theory. *American Psychologist, 28,* 405–416.

Felner, R. D., Farber, S. S., & Primavera, J. (1980). Children of divorce, stressful life events and transitions: A framework for preventive efforts. In R. H. Price, R. F. Ketterer, B. C. Bader, & J. Monahan (Eds.), *Prevention in mental health: Research, policy and practice.* Beverly Hills: Sage.

Felner, R. D., Ginter, M., & Primavera, J. (1982). Primary prevention during school transitions: Social support and environmental structure. *American Journal of Community Psychology, 10,* 277–290.

Felner, R., Stolberg, A., & Cowen, E. L. (1975). Crisis events and school mental health referal patterns of young children. *Journal of Consulting & Clinical Psychology, 43,* 305–310.

Fincham, F. D., & Cain, K. M. (1986). Learned helplessness in humans: A developmental analysis. *Developmental Review, 6,* 301–333.

Fisher, J. D., Nadler, A., & Whitcher-Alagna, N. (1982). Recipient reactions to aid. *Psychological Bulletin, 91,* 27–54.

Fogas, B. S. (1986). *Parenting behavior as a moderator of stress for children after divorce.* Unpublished master's thesis, Arizona State University.

Fulton, J. A. (1979). Parental reports of children's post-divorce adjustment. *Journal of Social Issues, 35,* 126–139.

Garmezy, N. (1983). Stressors of childhood. In N. Garmezy & M. Rutter (Eds.). *Stress, coping, and development in children* (pp. 43–85). New York: McGraw-Hill.

Guidubaldi, J., Cleminshaw, H., Perry, J. D., & McLaughlin, C. S. (1983). The impact of parental divorce on children: Report of the nationwide NASP study. *School Psychology Review, 12,* 300–323.

Guidubaldi, J., Cleminshaw, H., Perry, J. D., Nastasi, B. K., & Lightel, J. (1986). The role of selected family environment factors in children's post-divorce adjustment. *Family Relations, 35,* 141–151.

Gunnar, M. R. (1980a). Contingent stimulation: A review of its role in early development. In S. Levine & H. Ursin (Eds.), *Coping and health.* New York: Plenum.

Gunnar, M. R. (1980b). Control, warning signals, and distress in infancy. *Developmental Psychology, 16,* 281–289.

Harter, S. (1982). The Perceived Competence Scale for Children. *Child Development, 53,* 87–97.

Harter, S. (1983). The development of the self-system. In M. Hetherington (Ed.), *Handbook of child psychology: Social and personality development* (Vol. 4). NEw York: Wiley.

Harter, S. (1986). Processes underlying the construct, maintenance and enhancement of the self-concept in children. In J. Suls & A. Greenwald (Eds.), *Psychological perspectives on the self* (Vol. 3). Hillsdale, NJ: Erlbaum.

Harter, S. (1987). The determinants and mediational role of global self-worth in children. In N. Eisenberg (Ed.), *Contemporary topics in developmental psychology.* New York. Wiley.

Harter, S. (1988). Causes, correlates and the functional role of global self-worth: A life-span perspective. In J. Kolligian & R. Sternberg (Eds.), *Perceptions of competence and incompetence across the life-span.* New Haven, CT: Yale University Press.

Heller, K., Swindle, R. W., & Dusenbury, L. (1986). Component social support processes: Comments and integration. *Journal of Consulting & Clinical Psychology, 54,* (4), 466–470.

Henderson, S., Byrne, D. G., & Duncan-Jones, P. (1981). *Neurosis and the social environment.* Sydney, Australia: Academic.

Hess, R. D., & Camara, K. A. (1979). Post-divorce family relations as mediating factors in the consequences of divorce for children. *Journal of Social Issues, 35,* 79–96.

Hetherington, E. M., Cox, M., & Cox, R. (1981). Effects of divorce on parents and children. In M. Lamb (Ed.), *Nontraditional families* (pp. 233–288). Hillsdale, NJ: Erlbaum.

Hirsch, B. J., & Rapkin, B. D. (1987). The transition to junior high school: A longitudinal study of self-esteem, psychological symptomatology, school life, and social support. *Child Development, 58,* 1235–1243.

Hirsch, B. J., & Reischl, T. (1985). Social networks and developmental psychopathology: A comparison of adolescent children of a depressed, arthritic, or normal parent. *Journal of Abnormal Psychology, 94*(3), 272–281.

Janoff-Bulman, R., & Brickman, P. (1980). Expectations and what people learn from failure. In N. T. Feather (Ed.), *Expectancy, incentive and action.* Hillsdale, NJ: Erlbaum.

Kaplan, H. B. (1983). Psychological distress in sociological context: Toward a general theory of psychosocial stress. In H. B. Kaplan (Ed.), *Psychosocial stress: Trends in theory and research.* New York: Academic.

Kaplan, H. B. (1984). Self-attitudes and deviant responses: Toward the validation of a general theory of deviant behavior. In S. Mednick, M. Halway, & K. Finello (Eds.), *Handbook of longitudinal research: Vol. 2. Teenage and adult cohorts.* New York: Praeger.

Kaplan, H. B., Martin, S. S., & Robbins, C. (1982). Application of a general theory of deviant behavior: Self-derogation and adolescent drug use. *Journal of Health & Social Behavior, 23,* 274–294.

Kaplan, H. B., Robbins, C., & Martin, S. S. (1983). Antecedents of psychological distress in young adults: Self-rejection, deprivation of social support, and life events. *Journal of Health & Social Behavior, 24,* 230–244.

Kurdek, L. A., & Berg, B. (1983). Correlates of children's adjustment to their parents' divorce. In L. A. Kurdek (Ed.), *Children and divorce* (pp. 47–61). San Francisco: Jossey-Bass.

Kurdek, L. A., & Berg, B. (in press). The children's belief about parental divorce scale: Psychometric characteristics and concurrent validity. *Journal of Consulting & Clinical Psychology.*

Lazarus, R. S., & Folkman, S. (1984). *Stress, appraisal, and coping.* New York: Springer.

Lazarus, R. S., & Launier, R. (1978). Stress-related transactions between person and environment. In L. A. Pervin & M. Lewis (Eds.), *Perspectives in interactional psychology* (pp. 287–327). New York: Plenum.

Lefcourt, H. M. (1976). *Locus of control: Current trends in theory and research.* Hillsdale, NJ: Erlbaum.

Lerner, J. V., & Lerner, R. M. (1983). Temperament and adaptation across life: Theoretical and empirical issues. In P. B. Baltes & O. G. Brim, Jr. (Eds.), *Life-span development and behaviors* (Vol. 5, pp. 197–231). New York: Academic.

Lerner, R. M., & Ryff, C. D. (1978). Implementation of the lifespan view of human development. The sample case of attachment. In P. B. Baltes (Ed.), *Lifespan development and behavior* (Vol. 1, pp. 1–43). New York: Academic.

Lin, N. (1986). Modeling the effects of social support. In N. Lin, A. Dean, & W. Ensel (Eds.), *Social support, life events, and depression* (pp. 173–209). Orlando, Florida: Academic.

Maccoby, E., & Martin, J. (1983). Socialization in the context of the family: Parent–child interaction. In P. H. Mussen (Gen. Ed.) & E. M. Hetherington (Vol. Ed.), *Handbook of child psychology: Vol. IV. Socialization, personality and social development* (4th ed., pp. 1–101). New York: Wiley.

Melamed, B. G., & Bush, J. P. (1986). Parent–child influences during medical procedures. In S. M. Auerbach & A. L. Stolberg (Eds.), *Crisis intervention with children and families* (pp.123–143). New York: Hemisphere.

Montemayer, R., & Eisen, M. (1977). The development of self-conceptions from childhood to adolescence. *Developmental Psychology, 13,* 314–319.

Newcomb, M. D., & Harlow, L. L. (1986). Life events and substance abuse among adolescents: Mediating effects of perceived loss of control and meaninglessness in life. *Journal of Personality & Social Psychology, 51,* 564–577.

Nicholls, J. G. (1978). Development of the concepts of effort and ability, perception of academic attainment and the understanding that difficult tasks require more ability. *Child Development, 49,* 800–814.

Nicholls, J. G., & Miller, A. T. (1984). Development and its discontents: The differentiation of the concept of ability. In J. G. Nicholls (Ed.), *The development of achievement motivation.* Greenwich: JAI.

Nowicki, S., Jr., & Duke, M. P. (1983). The Nowicki-Strickland Life-Span Locus of Control Scales: Construct validation. In H. M. Lefcourt (Ed.), *Research with the locus of control construct* (Vol. 2, pp. 13–43). New York: Academic.

Parish T. S., & Taylor, J. C. (1979). The impact of divorce and subsequent father absence on children's and adolescents' self-concepts. *Journal of Youth & Adolescence, 8,* 427–432.

Pearlin, (1983a). Interpersonal role strain as a precursor of psychological distress and associated conditions: An evaluation and synthesis of the literature. In H. B. Kaplan (Ed.), *Psychosocial stress: Trends in theory and research.* New York: Academic.

Pearlin, L. I. (1983b). Role strains and personal stress. In H. B. Kaplan (Ed.), *Psychosocial stress* (pp. 3–32). New York: Academic.

Ramirez, R., Sandler, I. N., & Wolchik, S. (1988). *Children's attitudes about divorce: Its relationship to divorce-related life events and children's adjustment in an inner-city sample of children of divorce.* Unpublished manuscript.

Roosa, M. W., Sandler, I. N., Beals, J., & Short, J. L. (1988). Risk status of adolescent problem-drinking parents. *American Journal of Community Psychology, 16,* 225–239.

Rosenberg, M. (1979). *Conceiving the self.* New York: Basic.

Rosenberg, M. (1986). Self-concept from middle childhood through adolescence. In J. Suls & A. G. Greenwald (Eds.), *Psychological perspectives on the self* (Vol. 3). Hillsdale, NJ: Erlbaum.

Rosenberg, M., & McCullough, B. C. (1981). Mattering: Inferred significance and mental health among adolescents. *Research in Community & Mental Health, 2,* 163–182.

Rothbaum, F., Weisz, J. R., & Snyder, S. S. (1982). Changing the world and changing the self: A two process model of perceived control. *Journal of Personality & Social Psychology, 42,* 5–37.

Ruble, D. N., & Rholes, W. S. (1981). The development of children's perceptions and attributions about their social world. In J. H. Harvey, W. Ickes, & R. Kidd (Eds.), *New directions in attribution research* (Vol. 3). Hillsdale, NJ: Erlbaum.

Rutter, M. (1981). *Maternal deprivation reassessed* (2nd ed.). Harmondsworth, England: Penguin.

Rutter, M. (1983). Stress, coping and development: Some issues and some questions. In N. Garmezy & M. Rutter (Eds.), *Stress, coping, and development in children* (pp. 1–43). New York: McGraw-Hill.

Sandler, I. N., Gersten, J. C., Reynolds, K., Kallgren, C., & Ramirez, R. (in press). Using theory and data to plan support interventions: Design of a program for bereaved children. In B. Gottlieb (Ed.), *Marshalling social support: Formats, processes and effects.* Beverly Hills: Sage.

Sandler, I. N., Wolchik, S., & Braver, S. (1985). Social support and children of divorce. In I. G. Sarason & B. R. Sarason (Eds), *Social support: Theory, research and applications* (pp. 371–391). Dordrecht: Martinus Nijhoff.

Sandler, I. N., Wolchik, S. A., & Braver, S. L. (in press). The stressors of children's post-divorce environments. In S. A. Wolchik & P. Karoly (Eds.), *Children of divorce: Empirical perspectives in adjustment.* New York: Gardner.

Sandler, I. N., Wolchik, S. A., Braver, S. L., & Fogas, B. S. (1986). Significant events of children of divorce: Toward the assessment of risky situations. In S. M. Auerbach & A. L. Stolberg (Eds.), *Crisis intervention with children and families* (pp. 65–81) New York: Hemisphere.

Seligman, M. E. P., & Peterson, C. (1986). A learned helplessness perspective on childhood depression Theory and research. In M. Rutter, C. E. Izard, & P. B. Read (Eds.), *Depression in young people* (pp. 223–251). New York: Guilford.

Short, J. L., Sandler, I. N., & Roosa, M. W. (1988). *Adolescents' perceptions of social support: Esteem enhancement and esteem threat.* Unpublished manuscript, Arizona State University.

Simmons, R. G., Rosenberg, F., & Rosenberg, M. (1973). Disturbance in the self-image at adolescence. *American Sociological Review, 38,* 553–568.

Skinner, E. A. (1985). Action, control judgements, and the structure of control experience. *Psychological Review, 92,* 39–58.

Sroufe, L. A., & Waters, E. (1977). Attachment as an organizational construct. *Child Development, 48,* 1184–1199.

Tesser, A., & Campbell, J. (1983). Self-definition and self-evaluation maintenance. In J. Suls & A. G. Greenwald (Eds.), *Psychological perspectives on the self* (Vol. 2). Hillsdale, NJ: Erlbaum.

Thoits, P. A. (1986). Social support as coping assistance. *Journal of Consulting & Clinical Psychology, 54,* 416–423.

Thompson, S. C. (1981). A complex answer to a simple question: Will it hurt if I can control it? *Psychological Bulletin, 90,* 89–101.

Van Eerdewegh, M. M., Bieri, M., Parrilla, R. H., & Clayton, P. J. (1982). The bereaved child. *British Journal of Psychiatry, 140,* 23–29.

Wallerstein, J. S. (1983). Children of divorce: Stress and developmental tasks. In N. Garmezy & M. Rutter (Eds.), *Stress, coping and development in children* (pp. 265–303). New York: McGraw-Hill.

Weiss, R. S. (1982). Attachment in adult life. In C. M. Parkes & J. Stevenson-Hinde (Eds.), *The place of attachment in human behavior* (pp. 171–185). New York: Basic.

Weisz, J. R. (1986). Understanding the developing of control. In M. Perlmutter (Ed.), Cognitive perspectives on children's Social and Behavioral Development. *The Minnesota Symposia on Child Psychology, 18.* Hillsdale, NJ: Erlbaum.

Wellman, B. (1981). Applying network analysis to the study of support. In B. Gottlieb (Ed.), *Social networks and social support* (pp. 171–201). Beverly Hills: Sage.

Werner, E. E., & Smith, R. S. (1982). *Vulnerable but invincible: A longitudinal study of resilient children and youth.* New York: McGraw-Hill.

Wheaton, B. (1985). Models for the stress-buffering function of coping resources. *Journal of Health & Social Behavior, 26,* 352–364.

Wolchik, S. A., Sandler, I. N., & Braver, S. L. (1987). Social support: Its assessment and relation to children's adjustment. In N. Eisenberg (Ed.), *Contemporary topics in developmental psychology* (pp. 319–350). New York: Wiley.

Wolchik, S. A., Sandler, I. N., Braver, S. L., & Fogas, B. S. (1986). Events of parental divorce: Stressfulness ratings by children, parents and clinicians. *American Journal of Community Psychology, 14,* 59–75.

Wolin, S. J., & Bennett, L. A. (1984). Family rituals. *Family Process, 23,* 401–420.

Wolin, S. J., Bennett, L. A., Noonan, D. L., & Teitelbaum, M. A. (1980). Disrupted family rituals: A factor in the intergenerational transmission of alcoholism. *Journal of Studies on Alcohol, 41,* 199–214.

Wylie, R. (1979). *The self-concept: Vol. 2. Theory and research on selected topics.* Lincoln, NE: University of Nebraska Press.

Youniss, J. (1980). *Parents and peers in social development: A Sullivan-Piaget perspective.* Chicago: University of Chicago Press.

CHAPTER 13

Obtaining Support from Friends During Childhood and Adolescence

THOMAS J. BERNDT

A sixth-grade girl in one elementary school was asked how she felt about moving to junior high school for her seventh-grade year. She replied, "I'm nervous. We're going to have all new teachers, and I know I'm going to get lost. I will know people there but I'll still be nervous my first day. I'll be the little seventh grader, the newcomer to the school." She went on to describe other things that troubled her about moving to the new school, saying, "I'm scared about the kids that I'm not going to know that are coming from other [elementary] schools. Mary [her best friend] isn't going to my school; I'll be all by myself. I sort of want to be by myself, but I'm nervous starting out in a new school without a best friend right there with me."

By contrast, one sixth-grade boy in the same elementary school replied to the initial question about the move to junior high by saying, "I think I really want to go, since I've been in this school since kindergarten and I want to change, and a lot of my friends will also be going to [the school]." When asked what else he liked about moving to junior high, he said, "for the change, to meet new friends," and "for the extracurricular activities." When asked what he didn't like about moving, he said, "I'll be leaving some of my old friends who are in fifth grade, and because it's a new school it will be awhile until I learn my way around it. There will be new teachers that I don't know, and I'm not sure what they will be like."

The two sets of comments suggest that elementary school children view the transition to junior high as less threatening when they expect their friends to move to the new school with them. In more general terms, the comments suggest that children assume their friends will support them when they face such potentially stressful events as a school transition. That is, children perceive close friendships as supportive relationships that can reduce the stress associated with life events.

The preparation of this paper was supported in part by grants from the William T. Grant Foundation and the Spencer Foundation. Their support is gratefully acknowledged.

Previous research with adults suggests that children's perceptions may be quite accurate. Adults who have close and supportive relationships do cope more successfully with stressful events than adults who do not (see Cohen & Wills, 1985). To determine whether friendships have the same benefits for children and adolescents, three questions must be answered.

First, are the features of friendships in childhood and adolescence comparable to the features of supportive relationships among adults? Second, do friendships that children perceive as supportive actually contribute to their social adjustment when they are under stress? In other words, is the support that children obtain from their friends clearly beneficial? Third, what accounts for the variations among children in the support that they obtain from friends? The two children's comments about the junior high transition suggest that factors in the social environment (e.g., adults' decisions about which junior high school a child will attend) have the greatest impact on the availability of friends' support. Drawing this conclusion would be unwise, however, because the fate of children's friendships probably depends to some extent on the personality and social skills of the children themselves. Consequently, both environmental and personal factors must be considered in explaining the variations in the amount of support that children obtain from their friends.

My goal in this chapter is to examine the three major questions about supportive friendships. Evidence on the support that children and adolescents obtain from friends is still rather limited, so I rely heavily on research and reviews that focused on adults' relationships (Cohen & Syme, 1985a; Cohen & Wills, 1985; Sarason & Sarason, 1985). Nevertheless, I discuss research on children's and adolescents' friendships when relevant data are available. In particular, I present illustrative data from a recently completed longitudinal study of the transition to junior high (Berndt & Hawkins, 1987). The two sixth graders whose comments were quoted earlier were in the sample for the longitudinal study. After I consider the three questions about friends' support, I discuss the implications of current theories and research for interventions designed to enhance the amount of effective support that children and adolescents are able to obtain from their friends.

FEATURES OF FRIENDSHIP AND TYPES OF SOCIAL SUPPORT

Are children's friendships comparable to the supportive relationships of adults? Two separate literatures must be brought together to answer this question. The features of children's friendships have been investigated in a large number of studies by asking children about their conceptions of friendship or their impressions of their own friendships (see Berndt, 1986a; Hartup, 1983). The characteristics of supportive relationships among adults have also been investigated in many studies (see Cohen &

Syme, 1985a; Sarason & Sarason, 1985), usually by asking people whether they have a confidant with whom they can talk about their problems or by having people respond to standard questions about the types of support that they obtain from friends and family.

Nevertheless, the foundations for the two types of research are somewhat different. In the first studies of children's friendship conceptions, researchers asked children open-ended questions like "How can you tell that someone is your best friend?" The researchers then grouped the children's responses into categories that were generated largely empirically. That is, researchers tried to devise categories that captured the most important similarities and differences in children's own answers (see Berndt, 1986a). By contrast, researchers studying adults' relationships typically took ideas about the nature of social support from theoretical writings (e.g., Cobb, 1976) and then devised questions, items, or scales based on those ideas. Thus the formulation of measures was more theoretically driven in the work on social support than in that on children's friendships.

Despite the differences in approach and the almost complete independence of the two research areas, the resulting descriptions of children's friendships and of supportive relationships in adulthood are substantially the same. The parallels between the features of children's friendships and the types of social support received by adults are illustrated in the following discussion of four major types of support (cf. Cohen & Wills, 1985). At the same time, information on developmental changes in the features of friendships is reviewed. Sullivan (1953) hypothesized that friendships become more supportive relationships between middle childhood and early adolescence. As indicated in the following review, the findings in recent research are largely consistent with Sullivan's hypothesis.

Esteem Support

The term *esteem support* refers to statements or actions that convince people of their own worth or value. One item reflecting esteem support is "I have someone who takes pride in my accomplishments" (Cohen, Mermelstein, Kamarck, & Hoberman, 1985). This type of support has also been called *emotional support* (e.g., Thoits, 1985), because its aim is to make people feel better about themselves or their life situation. The corresponding feature of friendship was labeled *self-esteem enhancement* by Berndt and Perry (1986). To assess this feature, they used questions such as "If you did a good job on something, would [friend's name] tell you that you did?"

Sullivan (1953) emphasized the ability of friends to enhance one another's self-esteem when he wrote about the critical elements of adolescent friendships. Sullivan assumed that the degree to which friends enhance one another's self-esteem increases between childhood and adolescence. Unfortunately, the items for self-esteem enhancement in Berndt and Perry's research were part of a scale that also included items for liking or attachment.

Mean scores on the full scale did not change significantly between second and eighth grade. Other researchers have used measures for friendship features that overlap with esteem support (e.g., Bigelow & La Gaipa, 1980; Furman & Buhrmester, 1985), but either they examined children at only one age or they found developmental changes that were not consistent across studies. Consequently, whether esteem support is more characteristic of friendships in adolescence than in middle childhood remains to be determined.

Informational Support

The term *informational support* refers to advice or guidance that is helpful in coping with problems. One item for assessing informational support is "When I need suggestions for how to deal with a personal problem I know there is someone I can turn to" (Cohen et al., 1985). The corresponding feature of friendship has been called *intimacy* by most researchers, although Sharabany, Gershoni, and Hofman (1981) used the label *frankness and spontaneity.* One question that measures the presence of informational support or intimacy in children's friendships is "If you had a problem at home or at school, would you tell [friend's name] about it?" (Berndt & Perry, 1986).

Sullivan (1953) stated that the intimacy of friendships increases dramatically between middle childhood and adolescence. In fact, he regarded the emergence of intimate self-disclosure between friends as the hallmark of the change in friendships between childhood and adolescence. Sullivan's hypothesis has been fully confirmed in subsequent empirical research. All studies of developmental changes in conceptions of friendships and impressions of actual friendships have found significant increases in references to intimacy with increasing age (Berndt, 1982, 1986a). Moreover, children below the fifth or sixth grade rarely describe their friendships as involving intimate self-disclosure (see, e.g., Selman, 1981). The appearance of intimacy as an important feature of friendship in early adolescence is perhaps the strongest evidence for the hypothesis that friendships become more supportive relationships during adolescence.

Instrumental Support

Instrumental or *tangible support* refers to the provision of resources or services that are necessary for solving practical problems. One item that assesses this type of support is "If I got stranded 10 miles out of town, there is someone I could call to come get me" (Cohen et al., 1985). The corresponding feature of friendship has been labeled *prosocial behavior* (Berndt & Perry, 1986), *taking and imposing* (Sharabany et al., 1981), and *sharing or helping* (Bigelow & La Gaipa, 1980; Furman & Bierman, 1984). One question on instrumental support from friends is "Would [friend's name] share some lunch with you or loan you some money if you needed it?" (Berndt & Perry, 1986).

Sullivan (1953) assumed that friends become especially sensitive to each other's needs and desires during adolescence. This change might be expected to lead to increases in comments about friends' instrumental support. The available data are inconsistent, however. Increases with age in comments about friends' generosity and helpfulness were found in some studies but not others (see Berndt, 1986a).

Youniss (1980) argued that distinctive of adolescents' friendships is the motivation to help friends in need so that situations do not arise in which one friend has something that the other lacks. That is, Youniss (1980) assumed that adolescents are especially concerned about maintaining a state of equality between themselves and their friends. Berndt (1986b) conducted a series of studies of friends' actual behavior that yielded data compatible with Youniss's hypothesis. In these studies, elementary school children were likely to share less with close friends than with other classmates when they found themselves in situations where they might lose a contest by sharing liberally. In the same situations, adolescents in junior high shared more with close friends than with other classmates. Additional data suggested an age change in motives for behavior, with adolescents showing a stronger preference than younger children for equal sharing rather than competition with friends. These data reveal a second way in which adolescents' friendships appear to be more supportive than those of younger children. The data are particularly convincing because they derive not only from children's and adolescents' reports on their friendships but also from their actual interactions with friends.

Companionship Support

Often, the simple opportunity to share activities with another person, or to have a companion, is supportive. This type of support is also called *belonging*. One pertinent item is "There are several different people with whom I enjoy spending time" (Cohen et al., 1985). The corresponding feature of friendship has been given various labels, including *play* (Bigelow & La Gaipa, 1980), *association* (Furman & Bierman, 1984), *contact* (Berndt & Hawkins, 1987), *common activities* (Sharabany et al., 1981), and *interaction frequency* (Berndt, Hawkins, & Hoyle, 1986). One item for play or association that closely matches those used in scales for adults is "Do you ever spend your free time with [friend's name]?" (Berndt & Perry, 1986).

Neither Sullivan (1953) nor other theorists have written specifically about the amount of companionship support or the frequency of interaction between friends at different ages. Moreover, current data are inconsistent. Observational studies suggest an increase in interactions with *peers,* that is, close friends and acquaintances, between childhood and adolescence (Ellis, Rogoff, & Cromer, 1981). With interview measures of interaction frequency, however, age changes are sometimes found (Berndt & Hawkins, 1987) but sometimes absent (Berndt & Perry, 1986; Sharabany et al., 1981). Current evidence can be summarized conservatively as indicating that companionship is an important part of friendship during childhood and adolescence. Whether companionship becomes more critical to friendships in adolescence is uncertain.

Other Features or Types of Support

The four types of support emphasized by Cohen and Wills (1985) do not include all of the features of friendships identified in previous research. For example, children also refer directly to their liking or affection for friends (e.g., Furman & Bierman, 1984). Children also talk about the faithfulness of friends. In particular, they say that they value friends who pick them as partners for activities and never leave them for someone else (Berndt, 1986a).

Moreover, there are types of support that match the features of friendship not tied directly to the four major support types. For example, Furman and Buhrmester (1985) included scales for affection (or liking) and reliable alliance (or faithfulness) in their Network of Relationships Inventory. The inventory included scales for 10 types of social provisions (cf. Weiss, 1974) that people obtain from close personal relationships. Each type of social provision could be viewed as a distinct type of social support.

The proliferation of friendship features and support types can be restrained, however, by empirical data. Strong correlations are typically found between measures of different friendship features. Berndt and Perry (1986) reported that measures for five positive features of friendship loaded on a single factor that accounted for 65% of the variance in scores. Cohen and colleagues (1985) reported strong correlations among his subscales for different types of social support. In several studies (e.g., Cohen, Sherrod, & Clark, 1986), he used a total score across all subscales as the primary measure of social support. Similarly, Sternberg and Grajek (1984) reported a strong first factor for interpersonal communication, sharing, and support in their analyses of scales for love and liking in various personal relationships.

Of course, there are differences in the types of support that are usually provided by different types of close relationships. Furman and Buhrmester (1985) found that fifth and sixth graders judged companionship as greater between friends than between children and parents. Conversely, reliable alliance was judged as greater between children and parents than between friends (see also Furman, this volume). Similarly, Sternberg (1986) has discussed differences in the qualities of love toward parents, children, spouses, and friends. When dealing with a single type of relationship, however, such as same-sex friendship in childhood and adolescence, distinctions between various positive features or various forms of support may not be necessary or useful. A single measure that assesses the major positive features of a friendship may be most suitable in research.

On the other hand, relationships are not defined completely by their supportive aspects. Even close relationships involve greater or lesser degrees of conflict. Braiker and Kelley (1979) reported that married couples' judgments about the amount of conflict in their relationship were uncorrelated with their judgments about their affection for each other. Berndt and Perry (1986) found that a measure of conflicts in children's friendships loaded on a separate factor from the measures of positive friendship features. Berndt and Hawkins (1987) reported that composite scores for the positive features and the negative features of close friendships were not significantly correlated. Similarly, Rook (1984) found that measures of the support that adults obtain from individuals in their social networks were not correlated with measures of the problems that they had with individuals in their networks. The results of these studies strongly suggest that the effects of friendships or other social relationships on individuals' adjustment can be fully understood only when both the supportive aspects and the problematic aspects of these relationships are considered simultaneously.

Summary

Ample evidence from previous research confirms that the features of close friendships in childhood and adolescence are comparable to the types of support that adults derive from their social relationships. Friendships do not appear to be equally supportive at all ages, however. As Sullivan (1953) assumed, friendships are marked by greater intimacy and friends show greater sensitivity to each other's needs and desires during adolescence than during middle childhood. That is, adolescents obtain more informational support and more instrumental support from friends than younger children do. The current evidence regarding age changes in other types of support is limited and inconsistent.

Nevertheless, there are good reasons for assuming that adolescents' friendships are generally more supportive than those of younger children. Research with children, adolescents, and adults has shown that measures of various types of social support are often strongly correlated. That is, supportive relationships provide many different types of support. Adolescents are likely, therefore, not only to obtain informational and instrumental support from their intimate and mutually sensitive friendships, but also to obtain esteem support, companionship, and several more specific types of support from friends.

Neither friendship nor any other type of relationship could be accurately portrayed, however, without some attention to its negative features. Children and adolescents also report conflicts and competition with friends. To judge fully the contributions of friendships to behavior or adjustment, both their supportive aspects and their problematic aspects must be examined.

WHEN ARE SUPPORTIVE FRIENDSHIPS BENEFICIAL?

Do supportive friendships ever contribute to the adjustment of children and adolescents? The answer to this question may seem obvious, so obvious that the question itself is illogical. If friendships never had a positive influence on children's and adolescents' adjustment, how could we describe them as supportive? The question makes more sense, however, when restated in ways that match the hypotheses tested in previous research (see Cohen & Syme, 1985b; Sarason & Sarason, 1985). Two different hypotheses have been tested most often. The first hypothesis is that individuals who have a greater number of close relationships, for example, more close friends, show greater psychological and physical health and cope more successfully with stressful life events. This hypothesis implies that friendships are inherently supportive relationships and thus individuals with more friends necessarily receive more social support.

The second hypothesis is that individuals who perceive their friendships as more supportive show better health and more successful coping. This hypothesis implies that individuals' perceptions of the support that they can obtain from friends are more critical for adjustment than the sheer number of friends that they have. Indeed, several theorists have argued that perceptions of available support may reduce the harmful effects of stress even when individuals do not ask for or receive any specific type of support during interactions with friends. Perceptions of support may buffer stress, for example, simply by increasing people's confidence that they have or can obtain the resources that they will need to cope with a stressor (Cohen & Wills, 1985). For this and other reasons, measures of perceived support have frequently been used in research on the effects of supportive relationships.

In research with adults (Cohen & Wills, 1985), both the number of close relationships a person has and the person's perceptions of the support provided by their relationships appear to influence the person's health and adjustment. Nevertheless, perceptions of support are often viewed as more direct mediators of reactions to stress than the sheer size of a person's social network (Heller & Swindle, 1983).

The comparable issue regarding children's friendships has rarely been examined. That is, few researchers have assessed both the number of friends that children name and the children's perceptions of the support that those friends offer. In the study of the junior high transition (Berndt & Hawkins, 1987), however, measures of the number of friends named by a child and the features of these friendships were both obtained. The measure for number of friends was negatively correlated with a measure for positive features of friendship. That is, children who named more friends described their friendships as having fewer positive features.

The measure for positive features was a mean score for up to three close friends. Thus its negative correlation with the number of friends named may simply illustrate that children who named many friends mentioned both their closest friends and other friends with whom they did not have a close relationship. Consequently, their mean scores were lower than those for students who named only their closest friendships. The negative correlation should not be dismissed as completely artifactual, however, because it demonstrates that not all friendships are perceived as equally supportive.

Moreover, the number of friends that children named was seldom related to the measures of adjustment in the transition study. In contrast, children's reports on the features of their friendships were consistently related to adjustment, as shown more specifically later in the chapter. Therefore, the following discussion of the contributions of supportive friendships focuses on children's perceptions of their friends' support rather than the number of friends that they have. The general hypothesis is that supportive friendships can contribute positively to adjustment, but certain conditions must be met before they do. Thus the discussion centers on the question: When are friendships that are perceived as supportive actually beneficial for children and adolescents?

When the Friendship Is Not Ended by a Stressor

The prevailing view in the literature on social support is that friendships and other supportive relationships can reduce negative reactions to a stressor if they themselves survive the stressor. If the stressor involves the loss of social support, people's ability to cope is seriously impaired. For example, many studies have shown that loss of a spouse through bereavement is among the most severe stressors that people encounter in their lives. Current research also suggests that the unavailability of the support provided by the spouse is a major contributor to the mental and physical problems that are experienced by individuals who have been recently widowed (Stroebe & Stroebe, 1983). The research on bereavement is just one basis for the general conclusion that the loss of social supports through death, relocation, or other causes is a primary source of life stress for adults (Dohrenwend & Shrout, 1985).

Not surprisingly, children also view the loss of social support and, specifically, the loss of supportive friendships as stressful. The children's remarks at the beginning of this chapter and other data (e.g., Field, 1984) indicate that children are upset by the prospect of losing old friends when they move to a new school. Moreover, their concern is justified. In the school transition study (Berndt & Hawkins, 1987), only about half of the close friendships identified in the spring of sixth grade were still close friendships in the fall of seventh grade. Only about half of the close friendships identified in the fall of seventh grade were still close friendships in the following spring. Although comparable data for groups of sixth graders who did not move to a new school are unavailable, the results demonstrate that the entire first year of junior high is a period of considerable fluctuation in friendships.

The more critical question, of course, is whether children who lose old friends after the junior high transition adjust less successfully to their new school. Correlational data from the transition study imply that the answer is "yes." Children with more stable friendships between the spring of sixth grade and the fall of seventh grade were more popular and were judged by their peers as more sociable and less aggressive during the first semester of junior high. Conversely, children who made more new friendships immediately after the transition were judged by peers as less sociable and more aggressive; they were rated by teachers as engaging in more misconduct.

The transition data do more than suggest the advantages of stable friendships at times of environmental change. They also suggest that forming new friendships immediately after entry into a new school is not necessarily a sign of successful adaptation. Rather, the rapid formation of new friendships may illustrate children's inability to maintain their old friendships. In addition, rapid friendship formation may be facilitated by patterns of aggressive and disruptive behavior that give children high visibility but do not make them generally attractive to classmates or teachers.

One other implication of the findings on friendship stability and adjustment is of considerable theoretical significance. Several writers have argued that friendships have a pervasive influence on social and personality development (Sullivan, 1953; Youniss, 1980). Friendships may, for example, contribute to increases in self-esteem and identity. These hypotheses can be assimilated fairly readily to other ideas about the importance of social relationships for the development of attributes and skills that make people invulnerable to life stress or, at least, resilient when confronted with stressful situations (Garmezy & Rutter, 1983).

If supportive friendships had this kind of inoculating or strengthening effect, then adjustment after the transition to junior high would be affected less by the stability of elementary school friendships than by the supportiveness of those prior friendships. Yet no measure of elementary school friendships contributed significantly to the prediction of adaptation after the transition to junior high. That is, the support provided by sixth-grade friendships had no apparent effect on the changes in adjustment between elementary school and junior high school. Children seemed to benefit only when their friendships were stable despite the changes in schools.

Research with adults also suggests that supportive relationships reduce the harmful effects of stress only when they are maintained during the period of stress (Cohen & Wills, 1985). Some writers might argue that significant relationships early in life have more lasting effects, but confirming evidence may be difficult to obtain. Even relationships with parents during the first year of life may not build the kind of resilience discussed in the developmental literature. Security of attachment to parents may be related to later behavior and personality, for example, only when there is stability in the parent–child relationship (Lamb, Thompson, Gardner, & Charnov, 1985).

The proposition that relationships with parents, friends, or other adults and peers do not contribute to the molding of lasting patterns of thinking and action is difficult to accept, although there are proponents of similar hypotheses (cf. Mischel, 1968; Mischel & Peake, 1982). More directly relevant to this chapter, however, are the related propositions that most individuals benefit from stable relationships and that few individuals can bear the loss of close relationships without some ill effects. Children and adolescents, in particular, appear to benefit from stability in their friendships when other facets of their environments are in flux.

When the Support Obtained from Friends Matches the Stressor

Cohen and Wills (1985) argued strongly that supportive relationships have the greatest influence on psychological and physical health when they offer the specific type of support needed to deal with a particular stressor. For example, when a child needs help with homework, a friend who answers questions about the assignment (i.e., provides instrumental support) may render more effective support than a friend who simply tries to make the child feel more confident about his or her abilities (i.e., provides esteem support).

This hypothesis about the need for a match between stressors and supports is intuitively plausible, but current evidence for it is indirect. One problem, mentioned earlier, is that types of support are difficult to distinguish because measures of various support types tend to correlate highly. A second problem is that the type of support likely to be most helpful in any specific situation is difficult to decide a priori. Many writers assume, for example, that the informational support provided by a confidant is especially useful in coping with events that leave people feeling upset or depressed. In a recent study, however, Cutrona (1986) found that college undergraduates reported their strongest depressive feelings on days when they spent the most time confiding with friends. Cutrona's data were correlational, and she suggested that students may feel the greatest need to confide in friends on days when they have experienced the most severe stressors.

Cutrona's interpretation of her results is similar to that used by Cohen and Wills (1985) to explain occasional positive correlations between social support and psychological problems. That is, individuals receiving more support sometimes show poorer psychological adjustment than those receiving less support. According to Cohen and Wills (1985), these positive correlations may reflect the provision of support to those in need, rather than the ineffectiveness of social support in reducing stress.

Yet other authors have been more willing to accept the conclusion that talking with friends about worries and concerns may not always be beneficial. Hobfoll (1985) suggested that Israeli women whose husbands were mobilized for war sometimes spent much of their time talking with each other about their fears, and so impaired their own adjustment. Mechanic (1983) offered the general hypothesis that frequent introspection about one's own feelings is rarely healthy and often contributes to an increase in reported symptoms. Mechanic further argued that friendships are beneficial in adolescence precisely because they do not foster this kind of introspection. Instead, he argued, they involve adolescents in exciting activities and so distract them from attention to themselves.

Few studies of friendships in childhood and adolescence were designed to test specific hypotheses about the support types most helpful in coping with specific stressors. The transition study of Berndt and Hawkins (1987) was no exception. Nevertheless, the results suggest both the major sources of stress associated with a school transition and the primary means by which friendships alleviate this stress.

Based on a long period of participant observation in schools, Davies (1982) proposed that school transitions are stressful primarily because they place children in a new social world, a world consisting mostly of other children who initially are strangers to them. Obviously, the children quoted at the beginning of this chapter agreed with Davies's proposition. Systematic coding of the statements by children in the transition study confirmed that the changes in peer groups that coincided with the move to junior high school were a source of considerable concern.

According to Davies (1982), children feel more secure when they enter a new school along with at least one close friend. Thus friendships help children feel less anxious and less apprehensive when in a new setting (see also Bronfenbrenner, 1979; Hartup, 1983). Anxiety about the new setting decreases in a matter of days, but complete adaptation does not occur so quickly. Throughout the first semester and even the second semester in the new school, peer groups, reputations, and the hierarchy of popularity or sociometric status are realigned (Berndt & Hawkins, 1987). Seventh graders are likely to view this process of realignment as quite stressful, because their ultimate position in the peer group has major implications for their social life and their self-concepts (Hymel & Franke, 1985).

Berndt and Hawkins (1987) found that friendships had an important influence on the ultimate position that children reached in the peer group of junior high. As mentioned earlier, elementary school friendships did not affect adjustment in the fall of seventh grade, but children who had more supportive friendships in the fall increased in popularity between the fall and the following spring. Similarly, the children with more supportive friendships in the fall acquired an increasingly positive reputation with peers and more positive attitudes toward their classmates by the spring. Berndt and Hawkins explained these findings in terms of a widening circle of friendship. Children who had supportive friends in the fall of the year gradually developed good relationships with many of their classmates. A few supportive friendships were thus the focus of a circle that widened as the year progressed.

Although the evidence for the hypothesis about a widening circle of friendship is indirect, the hypothesis itself is intuitively plausible. If entering a new school is stressful mainly because it brings changes in the composition and the structure of the peer group, then the most valuable kind of support promotes assimilation into the new peer group and facilitates the attainment of a satisfying social position. Close friendships provide this kind of support for children and adolescents, just as involvement in a variety of role relationships contributes to the social integration of adults (Cohen & Wills, 1985). Thus the findings of the transition study are consistent with current ideas about how supports can match the needs created by specific stressors. The findings are particularly significant because they illustrate more clearly than in most previous studies how supportive friendships can enhance social adjustment in a particular setting.

When Children Are Able to Obtain Their Friends' Support

A third condition for effective support is that individuals must access or take advantage of the support that is available to them. Accessing support resources is frequently described as an active, purposeful process. Writers refer, for example, to seeking support (Heller & Swindle, 1983) or to the mobilization of supports (Hobfoll, 1985). The underlying assumption is that individuals who do not actively seek support will have a reduced capability for coping with stress (see Heller & Swindle, 1983). Moreover, if coping with stress depends partly on individuals' support seeking, their success in seeking support can be treated as one indicator of their coping skill (Gore, 1981). Conversely, an inability to get effective support from close relationships can be viewed as an indicator of limited coping skill.

Taking a different perspective, Thoits (1985) and Pearlin (1985) have proposed that social support is usually obtained as an automatic and even unintentional by-product of participation in close relationships. Close relationships normally give people a sense of belonging and security that enhances psychological well-being. Close relationships also involve frequent conversations that often include statements of mutual respect and approbation. Such statements in turn contribute to positive self-evaluations. These and other benefits of close relationships do not depend on people consciously trying to help one another cope with life's difficulties. Rather, the benefits come naturally from having relationships with other people.

In principle, the distinction between the two perspectives on social support could be examined in research on supportive interactions. Partly for this reason, reviewers of the literature on social support have called for investigations of supportive transactions (Kessler, Price, & Wortman, 1985) or the processes that account for the beneficial effects of social support (Cohen & Wills, 1985). To date, few researchers have responded to the call, probably because an investigation of supportive interactions in natural settings is easier said than done. Moreover, the results are sometimes hard to interpret, as

Cutrona's (1986) data on the relation of depression to emotional confiding among college students illustrate.

An alternative strategy for exploring the two perspectives on social support is to consider the determinants of individual differences in social support. The individual differences in children's perceptions of their friends' support, for example, may be attributed to personal causes, environmental causes, or some combination of both. If obtaining support from friends depends on individuals' seeking or mobilizing their support resources, then children who report greater support should also have greater coping skill. Their coping skill might be measured directly or estimated with measures of personality and adjustment (cf. Jones, 1985).

If, on the other hand, obtaining support from friends depends primarily on having close friendships, then the determinants of friends' support should correspond to the factors influencing the formation and maintenance of friendships. Friendships are likely to be influenced not only by children's personalities or social adjustment, but also by their social environment (see Hartup, 1983).

In summary, questions about when children are able to obtain their friends' support are difficult to answer because the processes of accessing and receiving support are poorly understood and rarely investigated directly. These questions may be easier to answer if they are rephrased so that they refer to the determinants of support obtained from friends. These determinants are likely to include personal factors or characteristics of an individual child as well as environmental factors or characteristics of the settings and contexts for children's interactions.

PERSONAL AND ENVIRONMENTAL DETERMINANTS OF FRIENDS' SUPPORT

An analysis of the determinants of friends' support should also begin to answer the third major question in this chapter: What accounts for the variations among children in the support that they obtain from friends? Before addressing this question directly, a close look at the evidence on the comparable question about adults' relationships is useful.

Influences on Adults' Social Support

Few writers have attempted to explain the individual differences in adults' access to supportive relationships. Many research reports contain no comments about the possible causes of individual differences in social support. Researchers often imply that variations in social support are due to largely random factors or, in colloquial terms, to good or bad luck. People who suffer the loss of their spouse through bereavement may be considered as unfortunate, or victims of bad luck. People who have a spouse with whom they can openly talk about their personal feelings and problems may be seen as fortunate, or beneficiaries of good luck.

An alternative view is that the environmental determinants of variations in social support are not entirely random, although they may still reflect circumstances not under a person's control. Research has shown, for example, that social relationships among adults show different patterns in different types of neighborhoods (Fischer, 1982; Gottlieb, 1981). These differences have been a subject of sociological research for nearly a century, going back to Durkheim's (1897/1951) classical studies of suicide.

On the whole, researchers have been more willing to accept the possibility of environmental determinants of social support than to explore the possibility that variations in support are due to personal characteristics of individuals. As indicated earlier, the guiding hypothesis for most of the research is that supportive relationships buffer or reduce the harmful effects of life stress. Yet if the personal characteristics of individuals are responsible for variations in social support, the causal role of support in buffering stress is called into question. Individuals who appear to be less well adjusted may lack supportive relationships not because the lack of social support is harmful, but because access to supportive relationships is a symptom of adjustment. Thus social support and adjustment are overlapping or confounded constructs.

The confounding of social support and adjustment may be aggravated by the common practice of assessing both social support and adjustment with self-report measures. Individuals may be asked first about the degree to which they can rely on other people for various types of support, and then about whether they feel depressed, angry, or have other symptoms of emotional turmoil. People who take a negative view of their own psychological states are likely to have a negative view of their social worlds as well (cf. Dohrenwend & Shrout, 1985).

A few investigators have attempted to reduce the potential confounding of measures by conducting longitudinal studies in which measures of social support at one time are related to measures of adjustment at a later time. Even if these relations are significant, however, other problems of interpretation arise. When prior measures of adjustment are obtained, they often correlate not only with subsequent adjustment but also with social support (Cohen et al., 1986). Indeed, this pattern of correlations is assumed when social support is seen as one facet of coping skill and coping skill is seen as one facet of adjustment (Gore, 1981). That is, social support may mediate the relation between initial adjustment and adjustment after exposure to a stressor without making an independent contribution to later adjustment.

Recently, researchers who recognized the problems and ambiguities in past research began to examine directly the personal determinants of individual differences in social support. They have consistently found strong relations between social support measures and measures of personality, social skill, and adjustment (e.g., Cohen et al., 1986; Jones, 1985; Sarason et al., 1985). In response, other investigators have presented evidence from longitudinal studies that confirms the relation of social support to indicators of adjustment prior to exposure to stress but shows as well an independent effect of support on later adjustment (Brown & Bifulco, 1985). These findings demonstrate that individual differences in access to social support are not due entirely to personal factors; environmental factors, whether random or systematic, also play a role. Subsequent adjustment, in turn, is influenced jointly by personal factors reflected in prior adjustment and by variations in social support.

Influences on Children's Support from Friends

Few researchers trained in developmental psychology would be surprised by the recent controversies over the explanation of variations in adults' access to supportive relationships. For years, developmental psychologists have debated comparable questions about the respective roles of heredity and environment (or nature and nurture) in psychological development. Nor would most developmental psychologists be surprised by the current turns of the debate, because the conventional wisdom is now that most aspects of psychological development are influenced jointly by heredity and environment. Current controversies center on more specific questions such as how much any specific attribute is influenced by heredity and how much by environment, or how heredity and environment jointly influence behavior and personality at different points in development (see, e.g., Scarr & McCartney, 1983).

The corresponding questions about the variations in the support that children obtain from friends concern the extent to which these variations are influenced by personal causes as opposed to environmental causes, and the extent to which the relative influence of personal and environmental causes changes with age. Of course, just as in the research with adults there is the further question of how much variations in friends' support, by themselves, affect coping ability and adjustment to stress. Indeed, if no attention were paid to the consequences of the variations in support, the preceding questions would lose much of their theoretical and practical significance.

Unfortunately, there is too little information about friends' support, or the effects of friendships in general, to furnish definitive answers to these questions (see Berndt, 1982; Hartup, 1983). Given the scarcity of data, the best strategy may be simply to illustrate the major issues, problems, and possibilities. Three sets of findings from the school transition study (Berndt & Hawkins, 1987) can serve as useful illustrations.

First, the stability of children's friendships across the interval of the school transition was related, as mentioned earlier, to several indicators of social adjustment during the first semester of junior high. For example, children with more stable friendships were more popular and were judged by their junior high classmates as more sociable than children with less stable friendships. These correlations could be used as evidence for the conclusion that stable friendships provide various types of support that contribute to a successful adaptation to junior high school. This conclusion would be premature, however, or at least overstated. The measures of adjustment that were related to friendship stability in the first semester of junior high were also related to friendship stability during the spring of sixth grade, even before the school transition. Moreover, individual differences in these measures of adjustment were themselves moderately stable over time.

The entire set of correlations implies that friendship stability was less an independent contributor to adjustment after the junior high transition than a symptom of lasting variations in adjustment. Better-adjusted students, that is, those higher in popularity and sociability, were better able to maintain their friendships despite the school transition. Because these aspects of adjustment were themselves stable, any claim that friendship stability was an independent contributor to adjustment after the transition is unwarranted.

A second set of findings from the transition study suggests that support from friends is sometimes a consequence of children's adjustment rather than a cause or a symptom. Children who described their elementary school friendships as more supportive did not show greater increases in their adjustment (or smaller declines in their adjustment) after the transition to junior high. Moreover, in the fall of seventh grade children's reports on the support that they obtained from friends were not significantly related to any measures of social or academic adjustment, regardless of whether those measures were derived from self-reports, classmates' ratings, or teachers' ratings and official records. In short, there was no evidence that supportive friendships in the sixth grade contributed to adjustment immediately after the transition. There was no evidence that supportive friendships during the first term of seventh grade had any influence on adjustment to the new school at that time. By contrast, there were relations of students' adjustment in elementary school to changes in friends' support after the school transition. Students who had more positive attitudes about their relationships with classmates developed more supportive friendships between the spring of sixth grade and the fall of seventh grade. Conversely, students who were judged by their elementary school classmates as more aggressive were likely to show a net decrease in support obtained from friends between the spring of sixth grade and the fall of seventh grade. These correlations indicate that children's personal characteristics affected their ability to form supportive friendships in the new junior high school. In other words, although the change in the school environment had some effect on all of the children's friendships, children's own characteristics affected the ease with which they formed or maintained supportive friendships in the novel environment.

A third set of findings from the transition study demonstrated that supportive friendships are valuable to children in a new school environment.

These findings were mentioned earlier, but they bear repetition because they illustrate the type of evidence that unambiguously establishes an independent influence of supportive friendships on children's adjustment. Children who had more supportive friendships in the fall of seventh grade showed increases in their popularity and in positive attitudes toward classmates between the fall and the following spring. Because friends' support was related to changes in adjustment, not merely individual differences in adjustment at a later time, the impact of supportive friendships was not confounded with continuity in adjustment itself. Moreover, the findings are particularly convincing because they are consistent with the intuitively plausible hypothesis of a gradually widening circle of friendships. As children get to know each other in a new school, those children who have close friendships will often get acquainted with friends of friends and so develop a positive reputation in the class as a whole.

Three sets of findings from a single study obviously do not provide an adequate base for conclusions about the determinants of variations in the support that children obtain from their friends. Yet the findings can be seen as starting points for a research agenda. The data illustrate that variations in friends' support are not purely random and cannot be treated as if they were determined entirely by environmental causes. Children's own characteristics partly determine how supportive their friendships are. These characteristics may themselves be influenced by experiences in previous social relationships, for example, in the family (Hartup, 1983), or by genetic factors (Scarr & Kidd, 1983). The current findings from research with children and adults indicate most clearly that social support can no longer be conceived solely as an exogenous or independent variable in research. Rather, researchers must attempt to specify its position in a large network of variables that causally influence and are influenced by one another.

CONCLUSIONS AND IMPLICATIONS

Previous research has shown that children expect to receive multiple types of support from friends. In their conversations with friends, they assume that they will be treated with respect and told that they are a person of value. They expect to be able to talk about their problems with friends, to discuss their feelings openly, and to receive helpful advice and comfort. When they are in need, they count on their friends for help. When they want a companion for activities, they assume that their friends will be eager to join them. In these and other ways, children view their friendships as supportive relationships.

Adolescents perceive their friendships as more supportive than younger children do. Younger children are more likely than adolescents to compete with friends rather than to try for equality under all circumstances

(Berndt, 1986b). Younger children are less likely than adolescents to disclose their thoughts and feelings to their friends. In other respects, however, young children's friendships appear to be as supportive as those of adolescents (Berndt & Perry, 1986; Hartup, 1983).

Many theorists have claimed that friendships have beneficial effects on the adjustment and development of children and adolescents (e.g., Sullivan, 1953; Youniss, 1980), but the evidence for these claims is scarce. A large and growing literature with adults can be used to identify the conditions in which friendships during childhood and adolescence might be expected to have positive effects on behavior and adjustment. Friendships are most likely to have positive effects when they themselves are stable. Friendships that are disrupted by a school transition, for example, are not likely to have any lasting effect on adjustment after the transition.

Friendships are most likely to have positive effects when they provide the type of support needed in a specific situation. When children need help in adjusting to a new social situation, for example, friends who provide companionship and advice can be a significant source of support. By contrast, when children need to turn their attention away from their problems, friends who encourage them to dwell on their worries and concerns may actually be harmful.

Friends cannot be effective supporters unless children are able to obtain their support when in need, but the processes by which children obtain support from friends are not well understood. Even in research with adults, the processes by which support is accessed and received are mostly a matter of conjecture. Some writers suggest that obtaining support is an active process of soliciting help or mobilizing support resources. Other writers suggest that obtaining support is a natural, unintentional by-product of participation in social relationships.

The issue of how children obtain support from their friends raises additional questions about the determinants of variations in friends' support. Some writers have implied that variations in social support are due largely to random or environmental causes. This position undoubtedly contains a kernel of truth. The transition to junior high, for example, leads to changes in friendship that would be unlikely to occur if children stayed in the same school with the same set of classmates. Yet recent studies have established that the characteristics of individuals also affect their ability and motivation to form supportive relationships. For example, children who have more positive attitudes toward their classmates in elementary school are more successful in forming supportive friendships after they move to junior high school. Children who are more popular and less aggressive are more likely to maintain their elementary school friendships after moving to junior high. The joint influence of personal and environmental factors on variations in friends' support is analogous to the joint influence of heredity and environment as determinants of psychological development.

Current conceptions of the roles of heredity and environment in psychological development merit closer scrutiny by researchers interested in social support, because the personal characteristics that affect how much support a child or adolescent obtains from friends may be genetically determined to some degree. Moreover, through various forms of gene–environment correlation (Scarr & McCartney, 1983), a child's genotype may influence the formation and maintenance of their friendships. Children genetically predisposed toward sociability and extraversion, for example, seem likely to have more stable friendships.

Scarr and McCartney (1983) further hypothesized that adolescents are more likely than young children to attempt to create their own environments, and so to produce a gene–environment correlation by their own activity. This hypothesis has intriguing implications for an understanding of developmental changes in friends' support. Adolescents may, for example, seek friends who can provide particular forms of support and ask for those forms of support from friends. Young children, by contrast, may simply accept the friendships and the types of support from friends that come to them without deliberate action on their part. This hypothesis about developmental changes in the processes by which support is obtained from friends is interesting in its own right. Its interest is increased when placed in the context of a broader theory of psychological development.

Finally, the current findings have implications for interventions designed to increase the beneficial impact of friends' support on children's adjustment. First, interventions that reduce or minimize the disruption of children's friendships are desirable. Children benefit from stability in their relationships. Although some writers have argued for the benefits of changing friends or "playing the field" (Bigelow & La Gaipa, 1980), the existing data on friendships are inconsistent with this position. Second, because variations in friends' support depend partly on children's personal characteristics, interventions that focus solely on changes in the social environment are shortsighted. Some children who do not have supportive friendships may need not only a supportive environment, but also training in the skills that are necessary for forming and maintaining friendships. Third, although current theories do not clearly identify the skills needed for obtaining support from friends, both the basic skills needed for participating in social relationships and the more specialized skills needed for seeking particular types of support from friends may be important.

Joint attention to the personal and environmental influences on children's ability to obtain support from friends may be the touchstone for successful interventions. Because of the importance of social skills for forming friendships and obtaining friends' support, successful interventions are likely to build social skills rather than ignoring or attempting to bypass them. Environments are not always supportive, and children will adapt most successfully if they can form supportive friendships in a wide range of environments. Yet no child is so resilient that he or she can thrive in a completely unsupportive environment. Therefore, environmental change may be an essential element of a successful intervention. Changes in environments should be designed to increase children's chances of obtaining the type of support from friends that they need to cope with the stressors in their lives.

REFERENCES

Berndt, T. J. (1982). The features and effects of friendships in early adolescence. *Child Development, 53,* 1447–1460.

Berndt, T. J. (1986a). Children's comments about their friendships. In M. Perlmutter (Ed.), *Cognitive perspectives on children's social and behavioral development* (pp. 189–212). Hillsdale, NJ: Erlbaum.

Berndt, T. J. (1986b). Sharing between friends: Contexts and consequences. In E. C. Mueller & C. R. Cooper (Eds.), *Process and outcome in peer relationships* (pp. 105–127). New York: Academic.

Berndt, T. J., & Hawkins, J. A. (1987). *The contribution of supportive friendships to adjustment after the transition to junior high school.* Unpublished manuscript, Purdue University.

Berndt, T. J., Hawkins, J. A., & Hoyle, S. G. (1986). Changes in friendship during a school year: Effects on children's and adolescents' impressions of friendship and sharing with friends. *Child Development, 57,* 1284–1297.

Berndt, T. J., & Perry, T. B. (1986). Children's perceptions of friendships as supportive relationships. *Developmental Psychology, 22,* 640–648.

Bigelow, B. J., & La Gaipa, J. J. (1980). The development of friendship values and choice. In H. C. Foot, A. J. Chapman, & J. R. Smith (Eds.), *Friendship and social relations in children* (pp. 15–44). New York: Wiley.

Braiker, H. B., & Kelley, H. H. (1979). Conflict in the development of close relationships. In R. L. Burgess & T. L. Huston (Eds.), *Social exchange in developing relationships* (pp. 135–168). New York: Academic.

Bronfenbrenner, U. (1979). *The ecology of human development.* Cambridge, MA: Harvard University Press.

Brown, G. W., & Bifulco, A. (1985). Social support, life events, and depression. In I. G. Sarason & B. R. Sarason (Eds.), *Social support: Theory, research, and applications* (pp. 349–370). Dordrecht, the Netherlands: Martinus Nijhoff.

Cobb, S. (1976). Social support as a moderator of life stress. *Psychosomatic Medicine, 38,* 300–314.

Cohen, S., Mermelstein, R. J., Kamarck, T., & Hoberman, H. M. (1985). Measuring the functional components of social support. In I. G. Sarason & B. R. Sarason (Eds.), *Social support: Theory, research, and applications* (pp. 73–94). Dordrecht, the Netherlands: Martinus Nijhoff.

Cohen, S., Sherrod, D. R., & Clark, M. S. (1986). Social skills and the stress-protective role of social support. *Journal of Personality & Social Psychology, 50,* 963–973.

Cohen, S., & Syme, S. L. (Eds.). (1985a). *Social support and health.* New York: Academic.

Cohen, S., & Syme, S. L. (1985b). Issues in the study and application of social support. In S. Cohen & S. L. Syme (Eds.), *Social support and health* (pp. 3–22). New York: Academic.

Cohen, S., & Wills, T. A. (1985). Stress, social support, and the buffering hypothesis. *Psychological Bulletin, 98,* 310–357.

Cutrona, C. E. (1986). Behavioral manifestations of social support: A microanalytic investigation. *Journal of Personality & Social Psychology, 51,* 201–208.

Davies, B. (1982). *Life in the classroom and playground.* London: Routledge & Kegan Paul.

Dohrenwend, B. P., & Shrout, P. E. (1985). "Hassles" in the conceptualization and measurement of life stress variables. *American Psychologist, 40,* 780–785.

Durkheim, E. (1951). *Suicide* (J. A. Spaulding & G. Simpson, Trans.). New York: Free Press. (Original work published 1897)

Ellis, S., Rogoff, B., & Cromer, C. C. (1981). Age segregation in children's social interactions. *Developmental Psychology, 17,* 399–407.

Field, T. (1984). Separation stress of young children transferring to new schools. *Developmental Psychology, 20,* 786–792.

Fischer, C. S. (1982). *To dwell among friends.* Chicago: University of Chicago Press.

Furman, W., & Bierman, K. L. (1984). Children's conceptions of friendship: A multidimensional study of developmental changes. *Developmental Psychology, 20,* 925–931.

Furman, W., & Buhrmester, D. (1985). Children's perceptions of the personal relationships in their social networks. *Developmental Psychology, 21,* 1016–1024.

Garmezy, N., & Rutter, M. (Eds.). (1983). *Stress, coping, and development in children.* New York: McGraw-Hill.

Gore, S. (1981). Stress-buffering functions of social support: An appraisal and clarification of research methods. In B. S. Dohrenwend & B. P. Dohrenwend (Eds.), *Stressful life events and their contexts* (pp. 202–222). New York: Prodist.

Gore, S. (1985). Social support and styles of coping with stress. In S. Cohen & S. L. Syme (Eds.), *Social support and health* (pp. 263–278). New York: Academic.

Gottlieb, B. H. (Ed.). (1981). *Social networks and social supports.* Beverly Hills: Sage.

Hartup, W. W. (1983). Peer relations. In E. M. Hetherington (Ed.), *Handbook of child psychology* (Vol. 4, pp. 103–196). New York: Wiley.

Heller, K., & Swindle, R. W. (1983). Social networks, perceived social support, and coping with stress. In R. D. Felner, L. A. Jason, J. N. Moritsugu, & S. S. Farber (Eds.), *Preventive psychology* (pp. 87–103). New York: Pergamon.

Hobfoll, S. E. (1985). Limitations of social support in the stress process. In I. G. Sarason & B. R. Sarason (Eds.), *Social support: Theory, research, and applications* (pp. 391–414). Dordrecht, the Netherlands: Martinus Nijhoff.

Hymel, S., & Franke, S. (1985). Children's peer relations: Assessing self-perceptions. In B. H. Schneider, K. H. Rubin, & J. E. Ledingham (Eds.), *Children's peer relations: Issues in assessment and intervention* (pp. 75–91). New York: Springer-Verlag.

Jones, W. H. (1985). The psychology of loneliness: Some personality issues in the study of social support. In I. G. Sarason & B. R. Sarason (Eds.), *Social support: Theory, research, and applications* (pp. 225–241). Dordrecht, the Netherlands: Martinus Nijhoff.

Kessler, R. C., Price, R. H., & Wortman, C. B. (1985). Social factors in psychopathology: Stress, social support, and coping processes. *Annual Review of Psychology, 36,* 531–572.

Lamb, M. E., Thompson, R. A., Gardner, W., & Charnov, E. L. (1985). *Infant-mother attachment.* Hillsdale, NJ: Erlbaum.

Mechanic, D. (1983). Adolescent health and illness behavior: Review of the literature and a new hypothesis for the study of stress. *Journal of Human Stress, 9* (2), 4–13.

Mischel, W. (1968). *Personality and assessment.* New York: Wiley.

Mischel, W., & Peake, P. K. (1982). Beyond deja vu in the search for cross-situational consistency. *Psychological Review, 89,* 730–755.

Pearlin, L. E. (1985). Social structure and processes of social support. In S. Cohen & S. L. Syme (Eds.), *Social support and health* (pp. 43–60). New York: Academic.

Rook, K. S. (1984). The negative side of social interaction: Impact on psychological well-being. *Journal of Personality & Social Psychology, 46,* 1097–1108.

Sarason, B. R., Sarason, I. G., Hacker, T. A., & Basham, R. B. (1985). Concomitants of social support: Social skills, physical attractiveness, and gender. *Journal of Personality & Social Psychology, 49,* 469–480.

Sarason, I. G., & Sarason, B. R. (Eds.). (1985). *Social support: Theory, research, and applications.* Dordrecht, the Netherlands: Martinus Nijhoff.

Sarason, I. G., Sarason, B. R., & Shearin, E. N. (1986). Social support as an individual difference variable: Its stability, origins, and relational aspects. *Journal of Personality & Social Psychology, 50,* 845–855.

Scarr, S., & Kidd, K. K. (1983). Developmental behavior genetics. In M. M. Haith & J. J. Campos (Vol. Eds.) & P. H. Mussen (Series Ed.), *Handbook of child psychology: Vol 2. Infancy and developmental psychobiology* (pp. 345–434). New York: Wiley.

Scarr, S., & McCartney, K. (1983). How people make their own environments: A theory of genotype environment effects. *Child Development, 54,* 424–435.

Selman, R. L. (1981). The child as a friendship philosopher: A case study in the growth of interpersonal understanding. In S. R. Asher & J. M. Gottman (Eds.), *The development of children's friendships* (pp. 242–272). Cambridge, England: Cambridge University Press.

Sharabany, R., Gershoni, R., & Hofman, J. E. (1981). Girlfriend, boyfriend: Age and sex differences in intimate friendships. *Developmental Psychology, 17,* 800–808.

Sternberg, R. J. (1986). A triangular theory of love. *Psychological Review, 93,* 119–135.

Sternberg, R. J., & Grajek, S. (1984). The nature of love. *Journal of Personality & Social Psychology, 47,* 312–329.

Stroebe, M. S., & Stroebe, W. (1983). Who suffers more? Sex differences in health risks of the widowed. *Psychological Bulletin, 93,* 279–301.

Sullivan, H. S. (1953). *The interpersonal theory of psychiatry.* New York: Norton.

Thoits, P. A. (1985). Social support and psychological well-being: Theoretical possibilities. In I. G. Sarason & B. R. Sarason (Eds.), *Social support: Theory, research, and applications* (pp. 51–72). Dordrecht, the Netherlands: Martinus Nijhoff.

Weiss, R. S. (1974). The provisions of social relationships. In Z. Rubin (Ed.), *Doing unto others.* Englewood Cliffs, NJ: Prentice-Hall.

Youniss, J. (1980). *Parents and peers in social development.* Chicago: University of Chicago Press.

CHAPTER 14

The Need for Support in Relation to the Need for Autonomy

BRENDA K. BRYANT

The aim of this chapter is to examine the importance of considering the child's need for social support in relation to the need for experiences of autonomy. This will be done in two ways. First, there will be a theoretical and empirical consideration of human development from infancy through old age in which the dual need for support and autonomy is presented as a basic requirement for human development and a phenomenon that varies in coordination with developmental constraints and opportunities. The second part of the chapter will focus on middle childhood. Here the issue of the need for social support and autonomy will focus on operationalizing this dual requirement in terms that will be useful to individuals making everyday decisions pertaining to the caretaking arrangements of school-age children. Of particular theoretical and practical importance is how to provide experiences of adult supervision and support along with experiences of autonomy that are relevant to the developmental requirements of middle childhood in the United States. The degree to which independent responsibility must be accompanied by adult supervision and support for optimal social–emotional development during middle childhood will be explored based on findings from an ongoing study of middle childhood. Maternal employment status and family size will be considered in relation to the school-age child's need for both support and autonomy.

I wish to thank Cindy Litman and Pat Worley for their assistance in data analyses. Appreciation to Larry Harper and Emmy Werner is also extended for their "middle of the hall" conferences with me about matter appearing in this chapter. Debbie Belle and Randy Lennon provided valuable feedback on an early draft of this chapter. Portions of this chapter were presented at the 1987 biennial meetings of the Society for Research in Child Development, Baltimore, Maryland. The funding for the data analyses was provided by the Kellogg Public Policy Research and Dissemination Program and the USDA Agriculture Experiment Station Research Program.

NEED FOR SOCIAL SUPPORT AND AUTONOMY THROUGHOUT THE LIFE SPAN

Americans have had a long-standing love affair with the idea of individualism and autonomy, and this romance has at times resulted in a struggle with and ambivalence about the meaning or value of relatedness to others. Although cooperation is an inherent requirement in most work and home lives, we Americans as a group maintain a suspicion and ambivalence about overtly valuing cooperative endeavors (Johnson & Johnson, 1975). This suspicion about cooperation, the Johnsons argue, is based on the mythical ideal of the value of independence and fear of losing individuality in cooperative activities. Our love of the idea of individualism and individual competition parlayed against a suspicion of cooperation is keenly illustrated by a predominantly individualistic and competitively structured American schooling system, so structured despite an extensive body of research documenting that cooperative learning groups more than competitive or individualistic learning environments enhance complex problem solving, social cohesion, and person well-being (Johnson & Johnson, 1975).

Historically, Alexis de Tocqueville (1969) is probably the best known social critic of the American obsession with individualism. More recently, Bellah, Madsen, Sullivan, Swidler, and Tipton (1985) have argued that Americans have become dangerously engaged with the ideal of individualism and personal autonomy, dangerously in that we have lost or are losing a meaningful sense of connectedness to others, and without a clear involvement in a meaningful social network, individuality and life itself lose meaning. American heroes such as the cowboy (e.g., the Lone Ranger) or the more modern loner detective (e.g., Sam Spade, Serpico, Rockford), they argue, have in common that they save individuals and communities without fully belonging to society. They are outsiders, if you will, never successful by standard norms of successful career, family man, or community leader. Rather, they stand on the edge of a community and do good for others without ever fitting in themselves. As with our folk heroes, norms for mental health and well-being traditionally emphasize autonomous functioning (Jahoda, 1958).

Our traditional notions of the overwhelming value of autonomous functioning are beginning to be tempered by our recognition of the need for social support, as is so well documented in this book. Similarly, recent formulations concerning the definition of mental health increasingly articulate the need for connectedness to others, at least in the form of the need to care about others and be open to new people (Jourard & Landsman, 1980). When we do get around to acknowledging the need for support, we do so without figuring in the relatively simultaneous and ongoing need for autonomy as well. As Toqueville down to the authors of *Habits of the Heart* caution us, however, on the individual as well as on the societal level of analysis, we need to pay attention to the dual need for social support and meaningful connection *and* independence and autonomy. I will argue in this chapter that it is useful to conceptualize support for human development to include both experiences of relatedness to others and experiences of autonomy from others. This is a more comprehensive view of support than those that traditionally focus solely on the need for relatedness to others.

Erikson's (1950, 1964) theory of psychosocial development well illustrates the position that humans have a vital need for both social support and autonomy throughout the life cycle. Although Erikson's position is often erroneously characterized as a summary list of achievements (i.e., first being trusting, then becoming autonomous, followed by initiating, being industrious, being committed to an identity, etc.; see Franz & White, 1985), Erikson more accurately at each stage proposes that issues of connection to others and autonomy from others are simultaneously at play. Thus trust needs to develop along with mistrust for healthy development to occur. At every one of Erikson's proposed stages of development are the vital resolution and constant work of achieving and maintaining a healthy balance between social connectedness and separateness. It is a developmental proposition in that the form of this duality changes with both developmental and cultural dictates. Let me emphasize that Erikson does *not* propose a list of achievements beginning with trust, followed by autonomy, then initiative, industry, and so forth. Rather, Erikson proposes that it is necessary to acquire a sense of trust along with a sense of mistrust, a sense of autonomy along with a sense of shame and doubt, a sense of initiative along with a sense of guilt, and so on. While trust requires social connectedness, mistrust requires some detachment from others; while autonomy requires some independence from others, shame and doubt brought about in part by parental sanctions or limits of the child's autonomous functioning and parental responses to a child's experiences of failure firmly plant these issues in a social context. At each stage of development the need for some sort of mastery to keep us independent from others is to be balanced by a kind of mastery to keep us connected with others. Thus support can be viewed as helping to establish both aspects of psychosocial development, the side that forges connection to others and the side that provides necessary detachment from others.

The model of psychosocial development presented more recently by Wertheim (1978) is congruent with Erikson's. She argues that optimal adaptation throughout the life span is based on a balance between the need for autonomy and the need for social and physical support, a balance that changes in form and degree with development. Similarly, Kegan (1982) in his work on the development of self also suggests that social connectedness is part and parcel of the human experience and so the development of self-identity is not simply one of individuation or separation from others but rather involves the reconstruction of the relationship between self and others. This reconstruction is a lifelong process. The nature of autonomy and social connectedness as well as the relationship or balance between autonomy and social embeddedness changes over time (i.e., develops). Again autonomy and social embeddedness are inextricably intertwined.

NEED FOR AUTONOMY AND CONNECTION ACROSS THE LIFE CYCLE

Although the research literature on stress and support has by and large ignored the importance of a balance of the experience of social support and autonomy, other available empirical research supports the importance of considering both autonomy from and relatedness to others as supportive of social–emotional functioning. Since researchers have not been directly interested in the dual requirement of support for social connection and support for autonomous functioning, my review of the literature was not based on a tight, systematic definition of support for autonomy. Rather I looked for examples where both social connection and social autonomy were considered empirically throughout the life cycle. Autonomy is recognized in two forms: (1) independence from another and (2) personal power in a relationship. This latter view is particularly relevant to the idea of providing support for autonomous functioning within the context of adult–child relations.

Interactional synchrony marks the infant's first demonstration of social responsiveness, albeit connectedness (Bower, 1979). Indeed, based on a current review of infant research, it is thought today that babies not only need to experience feeding and cuddling, which are clear forms of social support, but also must experience the benefits of self-motivation (Scarr, Weinberg, & Levine, 1986). I am arguing that this self-motivation reflects the need for some autonomous functioning. Pediatric researchers in the field of infant development such as Brazelton (1982) also argue that development during infancy requires not only the need for attention from the "mothering" one (i.e., social support) but also the need to allow the child some autonomy, if you will, in dictating the degree to which an interaction grows longer and more or less intense. Infants who experience this duality of respect for their own need for regulation and social support from the mothering person demonstrate greater communicative engagement with the mother as well as enhanced self-regulation (Brazelton, 1982). Similarly, Schaffer, Collis, and Parsons (1977) in their study of infants and toddlers note that it is the children rather than the mothers who generally set the pace of vocal exchanges, with children generally initiating new bouts of vocal exchanges. For this to occur means that mothers are highly watchful (i.e., supportive) of their children's gestures. Bruner (1977) also outlines the mutuality (child responsiveness to mothers' cues and vice versa) of the parent–infant relationship from a surprisingly early age (e.g., 4 months) whereby joint selective attention between an infant and caretaker is assured—under the control either of the caretaker or of the child. In other words, even in infancy American children experience social support and autonomy in the parent–child relationship. It is useful to view the infant as both autonomous and socially connected within a social relationship.

Burton White's (1978) work on development from infancy to early childhood also provides empirical support for the importance of adults providing social support along with support for relatively autonomous exploration. Regular confinement to a small room, a crib, a jumpseat, or a playpen was related to less advanced development later on, particularly less expression of curiosity. Opportunity for relatively unrestricted exploration during infancy, an early form of autonomy, was juxtaposed with the reported usefulness of having a caretaker not merely physically near the child but readily available and interested in matters of importance to the child (White, 1978). More specifically, a high amount of "procuring the service of another" (p. 151), meaning that the mother (in most cases) was socially responsive to the child's bidding, was related to overall competence, with the overall competence ranking produced by taking the average of the social and nonsocial competence ranking for each subject and ranking it with those of all the other children in the study. Baumrind's (1967) classic work with preschool children speaks to the value of fixing the child within close bounds of the parents while also infusing the child with the basis for autonomy. Her authoritative parenting strategy is one in which parents demonstrate considerable warmth (i.e., social support) and discipline (i.e., the adult takes a stand separate from that of the child) that includes providing rationales so children can understand that the limit is being set independent of the parents' mood or impulse and also have the basis for socially responsible thinking and action on their own. Children of these authoritative parents were found likely to be independent (i.e., assertive, self-reliant, achievement oriented), socially involved, and responsible (i.e., friendly and cooperative). Finally, Werner and Smith (1982) also report that resilient children, even in the early years of childhood, appear to balance a strong social orientation and social competence with a great deal of autonomy and independence.

Autonomy vis-á-vis experiences of aloneness has been found relevant to later social interchanges during middle childhood. In particular, it has been documented that being in the nonchosen continual presence of others does not support satisfying social interaction, whereas experiences with chosen aloneness (i.e., experiences of autonomy) can promote satisfying social interaction at a later time (Wolfe, 1978). Experiences of satisfying autonomy and social relations appear crucially interrelated. In other research of prosocial functioning during middle childhood, the concept of responsive mothering furthers the portrait of the dual value of maternal social support and respect for the child's autonomy (see Bryant & Crockenberg, 1980). Responsive mothering was coded when the mother provided help, attention, and/or approval in direct response to her child's bid for a response. Responsive mothering was related to infrequent antisocial and frequent prosocial interaction between her children. In contrast, maternal help, attention, and approval not asked for did not respect the child's unspoken request for continued autonomy in a challenging task and were unrelated to prosocial behavior between siblings. Further discussion of middle childhood follows in the second part of this chapter.

During adolescence, issues of independence and autonomy have traditionally been recognized as important. The need for parental support and involvement in adolescents' lives has often been overlooked. I would argue that adolescence is often problematic not so much because of adolescents' need for autonomy as because of their ambivalence and awkward expressions of need of support. Across studies, Hamburg (1974) reports that parental interest, guidelines, and social support, particularly of the parent of the same sex, are linked to the young adolescent most successfully negotiating the developmental tasks associated with the challenges posed by the biological changes of puberty, the challenges posed by the entry into the new social system called junior high school, and the challenges posed by entering a new role status of "teen." Elder (1980) too found, according to adolescents' self-reports, that parent–child relations were an important component of smooth functioning in adolescence. His research, however, directly links parental social support with parental support of the adolescents' autonomous decision making. In particular, adolescents who enjoyed social support from their parents as reflected in enjoyed joint activities between themselves and their parents were also allowed more autonomy in making a myriad of decisions. In addition, these youth tended to choose friends whose values were like those of their parents; thus peer relations did not develop in opposition to parent–child relations. Again, we see that providing children as well as adolescents with social support *and* autonomy goes hand in hand with satisfying social–emotional functioning.

During adulthood, issues of social support and autonomy in the workplace have been identified as related to home stress and overall sense of well-being for the adults and their children (Galinsky, 1986). More specifically, with respect to social autonomy, when people feel they are able to solve problems as they occur in the workplace and have the authority to do so, they are more likely to be satisfied at work and at home and enjoy an overall sense of well-being (Pearlin & Schooler, 1978; Piotrkowski & Crits-Cristoph, 1982; Renshaw, 1976). Similarly, having measurable control over both the timing and content of tasks at work is related to lowered stress (Mason & Espinoza, 1983). With respect to social support in the workplace, relations with both one's supervisor and one's co-workers are related to stress and well-being at work and at home. For example, Fernandez (1985) found the level of stress at home was related to having a supervisor who was not supportive about employees' child-care needs. Similarly, Piotrkowski (1985) reported that conflict among co-workers predicted lower psychological and physical health of workers up to 1½ years later. A sense of autonomy and support from supervisors and co-workers, then, are both needed for optimal functioning during adulthood, both as an individual and as a parent.

Commitment (i.e., social connectedness over time) and freedom (i.e., autonomy) remain important themes of healthy functioning not only in young and middle adulthood, but in late adulthood as well (Santrock, 1985). This is seen in the study of persons in their seventies in which rewards from personal activity as well as from close friendships were found related to life satisfaction (Flanagan, 1981).

IMPLICATIONS FOR DEVELOPMENTAL RESEARCH

To understand the roles that both social support and autonomy play in social–emotional as well as cognitive functioning, studies need to consider the concepts of social support and autonomy and their balance as forces impinging on the functioning and development of humans. It seems unnecessarily narrow to study the role of social support without also considering the useful role of some aspects of autonomy when studying children's response to stressful life events, as has been the rule. How we define social support and autonomy needs considerable work as well. Normative and cultural perspectives on these matters are called for. Finally, a developmental perspective need not disregard the individual variation that might be warranted in describing social support and autonomy needs among groups of children. This will be considered in the more in-depth analysis of children in middle childhood that follows.

AN ILLUSTRATION OF RELATIVE NEED FOR SUPPORT AND AUTONOMY IN MIDDLE CHILDHOOD

Consider that as the child develops the complexity of his or her life ordinarily increases: The child does more, with more people, in more places (Garbarino & Gilliam, 1980). Furthermore, as people move through different stages of the life cycle, they continually establish new sets of social relationships, which, at least in part, serve to define particular stages in the life cycle (Blyth, 1982). Relationships and involvements in activities that are developmentally appropriate in the lives of young children, for example, are thought to lose their meaning and appropriateness for teenagers (Polansky, Chalmers, Buttenwieser, & Williams, 1981). With respect to middle childhood, the 10-year-old is seen as influencing many adults (not just parents) and other children (not simply siblings) in many settings (not simply in the home), and having many ways of communicating (not simply cries, eye contact, and smiles) (Garbarino & Gilliam, 1980). School-age children, in comparison to infants, have been viewed in particular as having extended areas of activities (e.g., crossing the street, going to school, visiting friends) because of their greater freedom of movement (Lewin, 1951). The 10-year-old is viewed as significantly more limited, though, than the adolescent (Garbarino & Gilliam, 1980). With respect to self-care or latchkey issues, there are some who strongly argue that it is middle childhood (ages 6 to 13) that warrants concern as to self-care status after school (Rodman, Pratto, & Nelson, 1988) since children in adolescence are quite capable of self-care as well as providing and being paid to provide care for those younger than themselves. Just when children are old enough and competent enough to care for themselves and others without direct adult supervision is a troublesome question, especially for employed parents of school-age children.

The recent California Senate Office of Research (1983) report *Who's Watching Our Children? The Latchkey Child Phenomenon* documents quite clearly the increased relevance of the working status of women to children. "During the past two decades, vast numbers of women of all socioeconomic levels have joined the work force. In 1940, mothers working outside their homes were the exception rather than the rule: Only 9% of mothers were in the labor force . . . By 1979, more than half (nearly 17 million) of all mothers with children under age 18 nationwide and 1,728,360 such mothers in California were in the labor force working outside their homes. Some predict that this proportion will reach two out of every three by 1990." (p. 2) This trend has contributed to the growing number of school-age children needing child care. While we have been studying and working on defining what quality child-care programs should look like for infants and preschool children, we are not ready to delineate the kind of after-school care needed for these older children. The need, then, to coordinate family with out-of-home care is critical to many school-age children. This part of the chapter addresses developmental considerations that might serve as guidelines for developing after-school or self-care child-care programs.

Some researchers have argued that working mothers are withdrawing important sources of support from their children, which conspires to isolate children from the rest of society (Bronfenbrenner, 1972; Long & Long, 1983). Others note that not a small minority of latchkey children are not isolated at home alone but rather are "hanging out" with peers or going to a friend's unsupervised home (Steinberg, 1986, 1988). It has been argued that mothers who are not employed outside the home link themselves and their children to the neighborhood and its sources of support more closely and extensively than do working mothers (Fischer et al., 1977). Overall, there is the concern for the growing phenomenon of the school-age "latchkey" child whose social environment is unrestricted by direct, continuous adult support and supervision during the early after-school hours (Garbarino & Gilliam, 1980). Thus consideration of the modern societal trend whereby mothers are leaving the home setting for a paid work setting demands a responsive look at developmentally satisfying networks of support needed for healthy social and emotional development under current conditions of a family's work life.

The questionable need for direct adult supervision during middle childhood embodies the developmental requirements of support and autonomy. The extent of support and autonomy in the neighborhood was assessed in relation to the working status of the children's mothers and the children's social–emotional functioning. Social support was viewed as both casual and intimate relations with others in the peer, parent, and grandparent generation as well as participation in formally structured organizations and activities such as 4-H clubs and team sports in which adult supervision is direct and focused. Support for autonomy focused on independence from direct *adult* supervision and leadership by way of getting off by themselves, participating in formally sponsored unstructured opportunities for activities such as those provided by parks, schoolyards, and libraries, and playing in informal settings with peers such as playing over at other children's homes, in neighborhood forts, or in other child-derived clubs. This perspective on autonomous functioning revolves around independence from adult supervision, and, as such, it is ecologically confounded by ongoing experiences with peers during this time. Even children's reports of getting away by themselves often include going to a bedroom shared with a sibling. While it is classic to argue that during middle childhood children become more peer oriented (see Furman's chapter in this volume), recent research has indicated that 7-year-olds in comparison to 10-year-olds find more peers to be among the most important individuals in their lives (Bryant, 1985). Relations with adults appear extremely important to children in middle childhood despite the changing nature of their peer relations.

Data generated by children 7 and 10 will now be presented to look more closely at the need for varying forms of support *and* autonomy by children in middle childhood. Factors of maternal employment status and family size in relation to children's need for both support and autonomy will now be explored.

Illustrative Study

One hundred sixty-eight children (72 children 7 years old and 96 children 10 years old) participated in this project, with equal numbers of boys and girls represented. Fifty-nine mothers were not employed outside the home, 72 worked part-time, and 37 worked full-time. The sample was restricted to English-speaking families and to families living in nonmetropolitan and rural areas in northern California near Sacramento.

Although the sample included equal numbers of boys and girls, equal numbers of small (two-child) and large (three or more children) families, and equal numbers of older brothers and sisters (2 to 3 years older than the target child), the working status of the mother was not balanced. Table 14.1 presents the breakdown of the working status of the mother according to the developmental and family-context factors of sex of child, sex of older sibling, family size, and age of the child.

Children interviewed in this study were growing up in relatively secure and low-stress conditions in modern American society. The children in this study had continuous contact with both parents and at least one older sibling. At the time of the children's births, the parents were young adults, presumably ready for the demands of parenting (not "high-risk" teenage parents). All but one father was employed at the time of the study, and 65% of

TABLE 14.1. Mother's Employment Status in Sample

Developmental and Family-Context Factors	Unemployed	Part-Time	Full-Time	Number
	Sex of target child			
Male	26	40	18	84
Female	33	32	19	84
	Sex of sibling			
Brother	32	36	16	84
Sister	27	36	21	84
	Family size			
Small	21	40	23	84
Large	38	32	14	84
	Age of target child			
7-year-olds	29	28	15	72
10-year-olds	30	44	22	96

the mothers were employed. No child was living in poverty conditions, and each child benefited from some degree of advantageous conditions afforded in American society by some minimal socioeconomic status, comfortable housing conditions, and majority ethnic status. Finally, although there are some community differences, these children were living in what have traditionally been considered ideal, stable, small towns or rural conditions with parents having easy access to local community resources as well as the riches of major metropolitan centers (Campbell, 1981) (see Bryant, 1985, for a more detailed description of this sample). Given this "low stressed" sample, the results focus on the need for relative support and autonomy during middle childhood in the "best of situations."

Mothers were employed in a variety of jobs available in the selected nonmetropolitan and rural northern California area studied. Table 14.2 presents the actual types and range of employment situations held by the mothers participating in this study. Children and their families in this study resided in one of six counties, with the majority (87%) living in one county. In this dominant county eight towns were represented with populations ranging in size from 40 to 36,000. The county seat of this county, Community CS, contributed the most subjects and represented 44% of the sample. A university town, Community U, contributed another 39% of the sample. The remaining 17% predominantly represented a more rural setting, Community R, surrounding these two larger towns. All three settings support agricultural concerns of a northern California agricultural center. Community U is a university community with a major college of agriculture and environmental sciences and cooperative outreach program. Community CS is a

TABLE 14.2. Types of Maternal Employment

Part-Time	Full-Time
Hostess, fast-food chain	Accounting clerk, administrative assistant
Clerical	School bus driver
Day care, baby-sitting	Office manager
Teacher's aide	Production scheduling-secretary
Bank employee	Teacher, principal
Weighmaster	Mid-management
Nursing	Bookkeeper
Rural route trucking (substitute)	Secretary (legal, insurance)
Cake decorating, crafts, needlework	Education specialist
Substitute teacher	Grocery store checker
Own and husband's business	Centrifugal operator
Library assistant	Nurse
Education specialist	Real estate agent
Teacher, junior college, adult education	Real estate property manager
Physical and vision therapist	Mental health counselor
Housekeeping	Escrow officer
Fruit packing, cannery lab	Own retail store
Home decorating	Professor
Florist	Assistant to optometrist
Organist	Store clerk
Tax counselor	
Attorney	
Accountant	
Office and apartment manager	

central agricultural and marketing center (e.g., processing plants, major transportation center) and historically provides support services (e.g., hospitals) to the central valley agricultural community. The more rural areas surrounding these two towns provide "country homes" for professionals working in the larger towns as well as others more directly involved in agricultural development and marketing. Finally, people in all three communities have easy access (i.e., less than 2 hours by car) to two major urban areas (i.e., the state capital and San Francisco).

Data collection began with taking children on Bryant's (1985) Neighborhood Walk followed by an assessment of social–emotional functioning. Two sets of indices were derived from this interview schedule: (1) interpersonal sources of support (grandparent, parent, and peer involvements); and (2) environmental sources of support (places to get off to by self; formally sponsored organizations—structured activities such as 4-H club; formally sponsored organizations—unstructured activities such as community park; informal, unsponsored meeting places such as friend's home or informal children's neighborhood fort). Indices of social–emotional functioning analyzed for this report include: (1) empathy (Bryant, 1982); (2) social perspective taking (Rothenberg, 1970); (3) locus of control (Nowicki & Duke, 1974; Nowicki & Strickland, 1973); attitudes about

(4) cooperative; (5) competitive; and (6) individualistic classroom conditions (Ahlgren, Christensen, & Lum, 1977); and (7) acceptance of individual differences (Bryant, 1982). As point of reference, attitudes toward cooperation have consistently related to a broad range of positive attitudes toward schooling at all grade levels (Johnson & Ahlgren, 1976), whereas competitiveness changed its pattern of correlates, showing relationships to several positive attitudes only in high school but showing no such relationships during the elementary school years (Johnson & Ahlgren, 1976), and individualism has been linked to mental health problems (Johnson & Norem-Hebeisen, 1977; Norem-Hebeisen & Johnson, 1981) (see Bryant, 1985, for details of these measures, including information regarding reliability and validity).

Data analyses involved MANOVAS and hierarchical regressions that took into account the following factors: age of child; sex of child; working status of the mother (unemployed, part-time employed, and full-time employed); and family size. In addition father's education level and occupation were used as an index of socioeconomic status according to Hollingshead (1965) schemata and were used as covariates throughout all analyses.

Did It Matter Whether Mothers Worked Full-Time or Part-Time?

Although research on the effects of maternal employment has not typically differentiated full-time from part-time employment, it seemed questionable that this lumping made sense with respect to the impact of maternal employment on child functioning. The answer became clear. It would greatly confound the results of data analyses if we were to use a dichotomous coding scheme of working versus unemployed mothers. It was important to distinguish part-time from full-time working mothers and these from the unemployed. These distinctions were relevant for differentiating the extent and nature of children's out-of-school experiences and for the relation between out-of-school experiences and social–emotional functioning.

More specific findings include the following:

1. Age of the child interacted with mother's employment status to predict how much children knew and interacted with peers, $F(2, 143) = 4.05$, $p < .05$>. Whereas 10-year-olds with mothers who worked full-time tended to know and interact with more peers than did their peers whose mothers were unemployed or employed part-time, the opposite was true of their 7-year-old counterparts. Among the 7-year-olds, those whose mothers worked full-time tended to know and interact with fewer peers.
2. Mother's employment status interacted with the sex of the child and the family size to predict the extent of the child's involvement with informal, unsponsored (loosely or not at all supervised) meeting places such as play at friends' homes and play in neighborhood forts,

$F(2, 143) = 5.35$, $p < .01$. When mothers didn't work, boys from small families got a lot more exposure to peers in informal settings than did boys in large families. This finding highlights the relevance of family-context factors that interact with mother's working status to affect the child's experience.

3. The working status of mothers affected not only the extent of involvement with peers in informal, unsponsored meeting places; for the 10-year-olds, these experiences differentially predicted social perspective-taking skill, $F(1, 112) = 6.69$, $p < .05$. Among the 10-year-olds, children of working mothers showed a negative relationship between amount of informal peer involvement and social perspective taking whereas there was a positive association for these experiences among 10-year-old children whose mothers were not employed. Thus among the 10-year-old children with moms presumably at home in fairly constant direct supervision of their children, social functioning was "benefited" by having some "free" time off with their peer friends. On the other hand, 10-year-olds who lacked steady supervision from their moms did not "benefit" but "suffered" from increased "free" time off with their peers.
4. This last interpretation is supported by the next finding involving participation in formal organizations with structured activities such as scouts, sports teams, and the like (i.e., considerable adult supervision). Specifically, involvement with formal organizations interacted with maternal employment status to predict social perspective taking $F(8, 104) = 2.33$, $p < .05$. While the children with unemployed mothers showed a negative relationship between participation in formally sponsored organizations and social perspective-taking skill, $F(1, 38) = 4.54$, $p < .05$, children with mothers employed part-time and full-time had a positive association between these factors (see Fig. 14.1). This set of relationships was especially true for 10-year-olds.
5. Another set of findings indicates that this differential response to adult-structured, organized activities is a fairly reliable phenomenon. Mother's employment status interacted with age and involvement in formal organizations with structured activities to predict attitudes toward individualism, $F(1, 112) = 8.46$, $p < .01$, with individualism being more consistently and positively related to mental health problems than attitudes toward competition or cooperation (Johnson & Norem-Hebeisen, 1977; Norem-Hebeisen & Johnson, 1981). Children who participated in these adult-structured organizations were less likely to be individualistic if their mothers worked full-time and they were 10 years old. So 10-year-olds in particular, if they participated in adult-supervised organizations with structured activities and if their mothers were employed full-time, were both less individualistic and better skilled in social perspective taking.

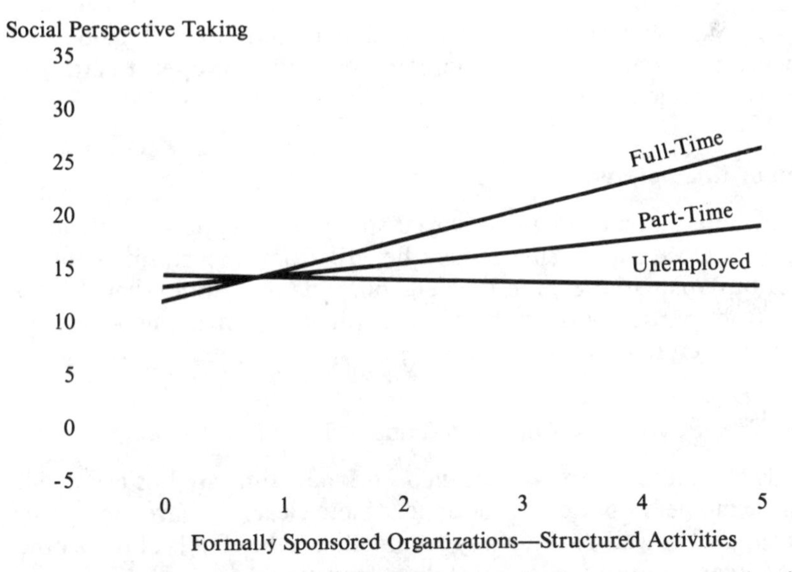

Figure 14.1. Participation in formally sponsored organizations with structured activities according to mother's employment to predict social perspective taking.

6. Knowing and interacting with peers (i.e., casual peer relations in the neighborhood) predicted greater individualistic attitudes among children whose mothers worked full-time, both for small families, $F(1, 12) = 7.13$, $p < .05$, and for large families, $F(1, 27) = 4.26$, $p < .05$. A clearly positive relationship held between knowing and interacting with peers and attitudes toward individualism among children whose mothers worked full-time.
7. Finally, among children whose mothers worked full-time, knowing and interacting with the grandparent generation was associated with less competitive attitudes, $F(1, 122) = 4.01$, $p > .05$. Again, supplementary involvement with adults appears beneficial for children whose mothers work full-time.

Taken together, these findings have differential implications for children whose mothers work full-time, work part-time, or are unemployed.

Children Whose Mothers Work Full-Time

Results, then, indicate that supplementary adult supervision involving the parent as well as grandparent generation appears beneficial for children whose mothers work full-time. These findings are especially true for the 10-year-olds who may be more likely than the 7-year-olds to be free of adult supervision in the home and neighborhood. Similarly, consistent with the findings of Steinberg (1986), greater "roaming" and casual relationships with peers among children whose mothers work full-time appear detrimental to social–emotional functioning.

Children of Unemployed Mothers

Children whose mothers are unemployed and, therefore, presumably home for relatively close supervision indeed benefit from opportunities for casual relationships with peers in the neighborhood and do not benefit, but "suffer," from participation in highly structured organizations with close adult supervision (e.g., see Fig. 14.1).

Children Whose Mothers Work Part-Time

The needs of children with mothers who work part-time are less clear; children whose mothers work part-time appear more clearly to have the balance of adult support as well as autonomy that mediates the effects of these other supports (organizations; casual peer relationships).

Summary Pertaining to Maternal Employment

Overall, supplementary adult supervision involving the parent as well as grandparent generation appears beneficial for children whose mothers work full-time. These findings are especially true for 10-year-olds who appear more likely to be freer of adult supervision in the home neighborhood. Greater "roaming" and casual relationships with peers do not appear beneficial to children whose mothers work full-time. In contrast, children whose mothers are unemployed and, therefore, presumably home for relatively close supervision indeed "benefit" from opportunities for casual relationships with peers in the neighborhood and do not benefit but "suffer" from highly structured organizations with close adult supervision. The needs of children with mothers who work part-time are less clear, but these children appear more clearly to have the balance of adult support as well as autonomy so as to make these other supports (organizations; casual peer relationships) have less dramatic effects.

Family Size

Concerns voiced in behalf of children of employed mothers have been similar to those expressed in behalf of children from large families as compared to small families. It has been observed by several researchers that families implicated in child neglect and/or abuse are likely to have more children than those in comparison groups (Giovannoni & Billingsley, 1970; Polansky et al., 1981; Wolock & Horowitz, 1979; Young, 1964). The fact of having many children has the potential to increase frustrations for parents when they are trying to deal with the complexities of meeting the needs of individual children (Kidwell, 1981). In addition, having lots of children, especially young children, has been related to maternal depression and "minimal" parenting style (Belle, 1982; personal communication, July, 1987). Indeed, children from large families may have greater need of supportive figures to supplement the support they can garner from parents who are more often overloaded by needs of others than do children from small families. Earlier and previously reported analyses from the present sample, in fact, revealed that supplemental involvement with the adult generations, both parent and grandparent, appears useful to children in large families but not useful to children in small families (Bryant, 1985). What appear more critically useful to children in small families are opportunities for independence from the nuclear family, to get off by themselves away from their families, alone or with others in informal settings away from home. It appears that experiencing privacy, autonomy, and independence from one's nuclear family, especially the adult generation of the nuclear family, is associated with enhanced social–emotional functioning among children in small families.

Conclusions

What appears to be the optimal level of support for children in California in middle childhood seems to be influenced by the size of their nuclear family and by the working status of their mothers. The findings are consistent with the view that children in middle childhood need a sense of autonomy from adults as well as clear support and supervision from them and that this balance is particularly salient by age 10. As we design programs for children, we need to begin to be aware of how children's needs in these areas are being met in the family and to recognize that some children will need clear adult support whereas others need increased autonomy from adults and greater access to peers. Similarly, parents who are full-time homemakers are advised to be aware of the likely relevance to school-age children of some "free" time with peers in situations relatively free of adult supervision. The working status of mothers and the child's family size provide two such clues to the child's need in this area. Program planning can take into account needs for structure and adult (parent and grandparent generation) contact or supervision as well as needs for unstructured opportunities with peers. This seems particularly crucial for planners of after-school programs since current research is indicating the ineffectiveness of such programs and the apparent enrollment of the more troubled children in these programs (Vandell, 1987). The present research does not inform us as to how children coming from these differing family contexts "request" or "elicit" adult support or autonomy from adults to participate with peers. This will be crucial to determine if we are to provide a healthy balance of social support and support for autonomous functioning.

Research is needed to understand how to "read" children on this matter. This is important because we know from the work of Condry and Simon (1974) and Elder (1980) that children without supportive parental relationships are more peer than adult oriented. Thus strong peer interest does not necessarily reflect a lack of need of adult support. Research is also needed to generate a taxonomy of meaningful experiences of autonomy and social connectedness throughout the life span and to provide normative data regarding the likelihood of a range of these autonomy and social connectedness experiences. The present research has suggested that opportunities to engage with peers with little direct adult supervision provide one form of autonomy from adults while participation in organized activities with direct adult supervision is an example of adult support that is developmentally relevant to some children in middle childhood. The present illustration did generate findings conceptually consistent with the proposal that a balance of experiences with social support *and* autonomy is crucial for healthy social–emotional functioning. Continued focus on this duality of experiences is urged of others interested in examining the role of support in human development.

REFERENCES

Ahlgren, A., Christensen, D. J., & Lum, K. (1977). *Minnesota school affect assessment.* Minneapolis: University of Minnesota.

Baumrind, D. (1967). Child care practices anteceding three patterns of preschool behavior. *Genetic Psychology Monographs, 75,* 43–88.

Bellah, R. N., Madsen, R., Sullivan, W. M., Swidler, A., & Tipton, S. M. (1985). *Habits of the heart: Individualism and commitment in American life.* Berkeley: University of California Press.

Belle, D. (1982). The stress of caring: Women as providers of social support. In L. Goldberger & B. Breznitz (Eds.), *Handbook of stress: Theoretical and clinical aspects.* New York: Free Press.

Blyth, D. A. (1982). Mapping the social world of adolescents: Issues, techniques and problems. In F. Serafica (Ed.), *Social-cognitive development in context* (pp. 240–272). New York: Guilford.

Bower, T. G. (1979). *Human development.* San Francisco: Freeman.

Brazelton, T. B. (1982). Joint regulation of neonate–parent behavior. In E. Z. Tronick (Ed.), *Social interchange in infancy: Affect, cognition, and communication* (pp. 7–22). Baltimore: University Park Press.

Bronfenbrenner, U. (1972). *Two worlds of childhood: U. S. and U.S.S.R.* New York: Russell Sage.

Bruner, J. (1977). Early social interaction and language acquisition. In H. R. Schaffer (Ed.), *Studies in mother–infant interaction* (pp. 271–290). New York: Academic.

Bryant, B. (1982). An index of empathy for children and adolescents. *Child Development, 53,* 413–425.

Bryant, B. (1985). The Neighborhood Walk: Sources of support in middle childhood. *Monograph of the Society for Research in Child Development, 50*(3, Serial No. 210).

Bryant, B., & Crockenberg, S. (1980). Correlates and dimensions of prosocial behavior: Female siblings with their mothers. *Child Development, 51,* 529–544.

California Senate Office of Research. (1983). *Who's watching our children? The latchkey child phenomenon.* Sacramento, CA: The Office.

Campbell, A. (1981). *The sense of well-being in America.* New York: McGraw-Hill.

Condry, J., & Simon, M. (1974). Characteristics of peer- and adult-oriented children. *Journal of Marriage & the Family, 36,* 543–554.

Elder, G. (1980). *Family structure and socialization.* New York: Arno.

Erikson, E. H. (1950). *Childhood and society.* New York: Norton.

Erikson, E. H. (1964). *Insight and responsibility: Lectures on the ethical implications of psychoanalytic insight.* New York: Norton.

Fernandez, J. (1985). *Child care and corporate productivity: Resolving family/work conflict.* New York: Lexington Books, Heath.

Fischer, C. S., Jackson, R. M., Stueve, C. A., Gerson, K., Jones, L. M., & Baldassari, M. (1977). *Networks and places: Social relations in the urban setting.* New York: Free Press.

Flanagan, J. (1981, August). *Some characteristics of 70-year-old workers.* Paper presented at the meeting of the American Psychological Association, Los Angeles.

Franz, C. E., & White, K. M. (1985). Individuation and attachment in personality development: Extending Erikson's theory. *Journal of Personality, 53,* 224–256.

Galinsky, E. (1986). Family life and corporate policies. In M. W. Yogman & T. B. Brazelton (Eds.), *In support of families* (pp. 109–145). Cambridge, MA: Harvard University Press.

Garbarino, J., & Gilliam, G. (1980). *Understanding abusive families.* Lexington, MA: Lexington Books.

Giovannoni, J. M., & Billingsley, A. (1970). Child neglect among the poor: A study of parental adequacy in families of three ethnic groups. *Child Welfare, 49,* 196–204.

Hamburg, B. A. (1974). Early adolescence: A specific and stressful stage of the life cycle. In G. V. Coelho, D. A. Hamburg, & J. E. Adams (Eds.), *Coping and adaptation* (pp. 101–126). New York: Basic.

Hollingshead, A. (1965). *Two factor index of social position.* New Haven, CT: Yale Station.

Jahoda, M. (1958). *Current concepts of positive mental health: A report to the staff director, Jack R. Ewalt.* New York: Basic Books.

Johnson, D. W., & Ahlgren, A. (1976). Effects of cooperative versus individualized instruction on student prosocial behavior, attitudes toward learning, and achievement. *Journal of Educational Psychology, 68,* 446–452.

Johnson, D. W., & Johnson, R. T. (1975). *Learning together and alone: Cooperation, competition, and individualization.* Englewood Cliffs, NJ: Prentice-Hall.

Johnson, D. W., & Norem-Hebeisen, A. A. (1977). Attitudes toward interdependence among persons and psychological health. *Psychological Reports, 109,* 253–261.

Jourard, S. M., & Landsman, T. (1980). *Healthy personality: An approach from the viewpoint of humanistic psychology* (4th ed.). New York: Macmillan.

Kegan, R. (1982). *The evolving self: Problem and process in human development.* Cambridge, MA: Harvard University Press.

Kidwell, J. S. (1981). Number of siblings, sibling spacing, sex, and birth order: Their effects on perceived parent–adolescent relationships. *Journal of Marriage & the Family, 43*(2), 315–332.

Lewin, K. (1951). *Field theory in social science: Selected theoretical papers.* New York: Harper.

Long, L., & Long, T. (1983). *The handbook for latchkey children and their parents.* New York: Arbor House.

Mason, T., & Espinoza, R. (1983). *Executive summary of the final report: Working parents project.* Washington, DC: National Institute of Education. Cited in Galinsky (1986), Family life and corporate policies. In M. W. Yogman & T. B. Brazelton (Eds.), *In support of families.* Cambridge, MA: Harvard University Press.

Norem-Hebeisen, A. A., & Johnson, D. W. (1981). The relationship between cooperative, competitive, and individualistic attitudes and differentiated aspects of self-esteem. *Journal of Personality, 49,* 415–426.

Nowicki, S., & Duke, M. (1974). A preschool and primary internal–external control scale. *Developmental Psychology, 10*(16), 874–880.

Nowicki, S., & Strickland, B. (1973). A Locus of Control Scale for Children. *Journal of Consulting & Clinical Psychology, 40,* 148–154.

Pearlin, L. I., & Schooler, C. (1978). The structure of coping. *Journal of Health & Social Behavior, 19*(3), 2–21.

Piotrkowski, C. S. (1985). *Research Interest Group Presentation.* New York: Bank Street College. Cited in Galinsky (1986), Family life and corporate policies. In M. W. Yogman & T. B. Brazelton (Eds.), *In support of families.* Cambridge, MA: Harvard University Press.

Piotrkowski, C. S., & Crits-Christoph, P. (1982). Women's jobs and family adjustment. In J. Aldous (Ed.), *Two paychecks: Life in dual-earner families* (pp. 105–127). Beverly Hills: Sage.

Polansky, N. A., Chalmers, M. A., Buttenwieser, E. W., & Williams, D. P. (1981). *Damaged parents: An anatomy of child neglect.* Chicago: University of Chicago Press.

Renshaw, J. (1976). An exploration of the dynamics of the overlapping worlds of work and family. *Family Process, 15*(1), 143–165.

Rodman, H., Pratto, D. J., & Nelson, R. S. (1988). Toward a definition of self-care children: A commentary on Steinberg (1986). *Developmental Psychology,* 24(2), 292–294.

Rothenberg, B. (1970). Children's social sensitivity and the relationship to interpersonal competence, intrapersonal comfort and intellectual level. *Developmental Psychology, 2*(3), 335–350.

Santrock, J. W. (1985). *Adults development and aging.* Dubuque: Wm. C. Brown.

Scarr, S., Weinberg, R. A., & Levine, A. (1986). *Understanding development.* New York: Harcourt Brace Jovanovich.

Schaffer, H. R., Collis, G. M., & Parsons, G. (1977). Vocal interchange and visual regard in verbal and pre-verbal children. In H. R. Schaffer (Ed.), *Studies in mother–infant interaction* (pp. 291–324). New York: Academic.

Steinberg, L. (1986). Latchkey children and susceptibility to peer pressure: An ecological analysis. *Developmental Psychology, 22*(4), 441–439.

Steinberg, L. (1988). Simple solutions to a complex problem: A response to Rodman, Pratto, and Nelson (1988). *Developmental Psychology, 24*(2), 295–296.

Tocqueville, A. de (1969). *Democracy in America* (J. P. Mayer, Ed.; G. G. Lawrence, Trans.). New York: Doubleday Anchor.

Vandell, D. (1987, April). *What to do with the kids after school: Comparisons of children in different forms of after school care.* Paper presented at the biennial meeting of the Society for Research in Child Development, Baltimore.

Werner, E. E., & Smith, R. S. (1982). *Vulnerable, but invincible: A longitudinal study of resilient children and youth.* New York: McGraw-Hill.

Wertheim, E. S. (1978). Developmental genesis of human vulnerability: Conceptual re-evaluation. In E. J. Anthony, C. Koupernik, & C. Chiland (Eds.), *The child in his family: Vol. 4. Vulnerable children* (pp. 17–36). New York: Wiley.

White, B. L. (1978). *Experience and environment: Major influences on the development of the young child* (Vol. 2). Englewood Cliffs, NJ: Prentice-Hall.

Wolfe, M. (1978). Childhood and privacy. In I. Altman & J. R. Wohlwill (Eds.), *Children and the environment* (pp. 175–222). New York: Plenum.

Wolock, I., & Horowitz, B. (1979). Child maltreatment and material deprivation among AFDC-recipient families. *Social Service Review, 53,* 175–194.

Young, L. (1964). *Wednesday's children: A study of child neglect and abuse.* New York: McGraw-Hill.

Author Index

Subject Index

(continued from front)

Handbook of Research Methods in Clinical Psychology *edited by Philip C. Kendall and James N. Butcher*

A Social Psychology of Developing Adults *by Thomas O. Blank*

Women in the Middle Years: Current Knowledge and Directions for Research and Policy *edited by Janet Zollinger Giele*

Loneliness: A Sourcebook of Current Theory, Research and Therapy *edited by Letitia Anne Peplau and Daniel Perlman*

Hyperactivity: Current Issues, Research, and Theory (Second Edition) *by Dorothea M. Ross and Sheila A. Ross*

Review of Human Development *edited by Tiffany M. Field, Aletha Huston, Herbert C. Quay, Lillian Troll, and Gordon E. Finley*

Agoraphobia: Multiple Perspectives on Theory and Treatment *edited by Dianne L. Chambless and Alan J. Goldstein*

The Rorschach: A Comprehensive System. Volume III: Assessment of Children and Adolescents *by John E. Exner, Jr. and Irving B. Weiner*

Handbook of Play Therapy *edited by Charles E. Schaefer and Kevin J. O'Connor*

Adolescent Sexuality in a Changing American Society: Social and Psychological Perspectives for the Human Service Professions (Second Edition) *by Catherine S. Chilman*

Failures in Behavior Therapy *edited by Edna B. Foa and Paul M.G. Emmelkamp*

The Psychological Assessment of Children (Second Edition) *by James O. Palmer*

Imagery: Current Theory, Research, and Application *edited by Aneés A. Sheikh*

Handbook of Clinical Child Psychology *edited by C. Eugene Walker and Michael C. Roberts*

The Measurement of Psychotherapy Outcome *edited by Michael J. Lambert, Edwin R. Christensen, and Steven S. DeJulio*

Clinical Methods in Psychology (Second Edition) *edited by Irving B. Weiner*

Excuses: Masquerades in Search of Grace *by C.R. Snyder, Raymond L. Higgins and Rita J. Stucky*

Diagnostic Understanding and Treatment Planning: The Elusive Connection *edited by Fred Shectman and William B. Smith*

Bender Gestalt Screening for Brain Dysfunction *by Patricia Lacks*

Adult Psychopathology and Diagnosis *edited by Samuel M. Turner and Michel Hersen*

Personality and the Behavioral Disorders (Second Edition) *edited by Norman S. Endler and J. McVicker Hunt*

Ecological Approaches to Clinical and Community Psychology *edited by William A. O'Connor and Bernard Lubin*

Rational-Emotive Therapy with Children and Adolescents: Theory, Treatment Strategies, Preventative Methods *by Michael E. Bernard and Marie R. Joyce*

The Unconscious Reconsidered *edited by Kenneth S. Bowers and Donald Meichenbaum*

Prevention of Problems in Childhood: Psychological Research and Application *edited by Michael C. Roberts and Lizette Peterson*

Resolving Resistances in Psychotherapy *by Herbert S. Strean*

Handbook of Social Skills Training and Research *edited by Luciano L'Abate and Michael A. Milan*

Institutional Settings in Children's Lives *by Leanne G. Rivlin and Maxine Wolfe*

Treating the Alcoholic: A Developmental Model of Recovery *by Stephanie Brown*

Resolving Marital Conflicts: A Psychodynamic Perspective *by Herbert S. Strean*

Paradoxical Strategies in Psychotherapy: A Comprehensive Overview and Guidebook *by Leon F. Seltzer*

Pharmacological and Behavioral Treatment: An Integrative Approach *edited by Michel Hersen*